# 999 AMAZING
# ANIMAL
# FACTS

This edition is published by Armadillo,
an imprint of Anness Publishing Ltd,
Blaby Road, Wigston, Leicestershire LE18 4SE;
info@anness.com

www.annesspublishing.com

Anness Publishing has a new picture agency outlet
for images for publishing, promotions or advertising.
Please visit our website www.practicalpictures.com for
more information.

Publisher: Joanna Lorenz
Editorial Directors: Judith Simons; Helen Sudell
Managing Editors: Gilly Cameron Cooper; Linda Fraser;
  Sue Grabham
Compendium Editor: Lucy Doncaster
Project Editors: Nicky Barber, Simon Beecroft; Rebecca
  Clunes; Jennifer Davidson; Sarah Eason; Rasha Elsaeed;
  Leon Gray; Peter Harrison; Charlotte Hurdman; Nicole
  Pearson; Laura Seber; Linda Sonntag; Dawn Titmus;
  Sarah Uttridge; Joy Wotton
Editorial Reader: Rosanna Fairhead
Text by: Michael Bright; John Farndon; Jen Green; Tom
  Jackson; Robin Kerrod; Rhonda Klevansky; Mark O'Shea;
  Barbara Taylor

Consultants: Michael Chinery; Dr Sarah A. Corbet;
  Dr Nigel Dunstone; Ian K. Fergusson; Mathew Frith;
  Dr Richard A. Griffiths; Rachel Hevesi; Andy and Nadine
  Highfield; Jemima Parry Jones, M.B.E.; Dr Adrian Lister;
  John Michaels; Ian Redmond; Dr Douglas Richardson
Designers: Aztec Design; Vivienne Gordon; Jill Mumford;
  Mirjana Nociar; Linda Penny; Caroline Reeves; Ann
  Samuel; Traffika Publishing Ltd; Simon Wilder; Sarah
  Williams; Rita Wuthrich
Picture Researchers: Su Alexander; Adrian Bentley;
  Caroline Brooke-Johnson; Veneta Bullen; Gwen Campbell;
  Liz Heasman; Kay Rowley; Cathy Stastny; Elizabeth Walsh;
  Wendy Wilders

Photographer: John Freeman; Kim Taylor
Illustrators: Julian Baker; Peter Bull; Vanessa Card; Stuart
  Carter; A Durante (Milan Illustrations Agency); John Francis;
  Martin Knowledon; Stuart Lafford; Linden Artists; Rob
  Sheffield; Sarah Smith; David Webb
Maps: Anthony Duke
Production Manager: Steve Lang

A CIP catalogue record is available from the British Library.

Previously published as *Fascinating Animal Facts*

PUBLISHER'S NOTE
*Although the advice and information in this book are believed to be
accurate and true at the time of going to press, neither the authors nor
the publisher can accept any legal responsibility or liability for any
errors or omissions that may have been made nor for any inaccuracies
nor for any loss, harm or injury that comes about from following
instructions or advice in this book.*

Manufacturer: Anness Publishing Ltd, Blaby Road, Wigston,
Leicestershire LE18 4SE, England
For Product Tracking go to:
www.annesspublishing.com/tracking
Batch: 3594-22260-1127

# 999 AMAZING
# ANIMAL
# FACTS

Featuring whales, elephants, bears, wolves, monkeys, turtles, snakes, birds, bees, ants and many, many more

•

More than 1950 images – stunning illustrations and pictures by top wildlife photographers, including close–up and habitat shots

KLEVANSKY • GREEN • BRIGHT • JACKSON • TAYLOR • KERROD • O'SHEA • FARNDON

ARMADILLO

# Contents

INTRODUCTION  6

**Big Cats  8**
What is a Cat? • The Big Cats • Bones and Teeth
• Muscles and Claws • Sight and Sound • Touching,
Tasting and Smelling • Spots and Stripes
• Communication • Hunting Prey • Killing Prey
• Living Together • Big Cat Relatives

**Wolves  34**
What is a Wolf? • The Wolf Family • Body
Shapes • Body Parts • Fur Coats • Sight and
Sound • Smell, Touch and Taste • Focus on a
Wolf Pack • Home Territory • A Meaty Diet
• Relatives and Namesakes

**Wild Horses  58**
Saved from Extinction • Shapes and Sizes • Coats
and Grooming • Built for Speed • Body Power
• Intelligence and Senses • Eating for Energy
• Social Life • Communication • World View
• Early Ancestors

**Bears and Pandas  82**
The Bear Facts • Family Groups • Size of a Bear
• Bones and Teeth • Strong Muscles • Warm
Fur • Using Brain and Senses • Finding Food
• Winter Hibernation • Where Bears are Found
• Finding the Way • Ancient Bears

**Monkeys  108**
Prosimians – The First Primates • Monkeys
Take Over • Outward Appearances • Inner
Power • Sensing the Surroundings • On
the Move • Brainpower • Diets for Living
• Territorial Rights • Living Together
• Communication • Changing Habitats

**Great Apes  134**
What is a Great Ape? • Ape Shapes and Sizes
• Bodies and Bones • Hairy Apes • Hands
and Feet • Smart Apes • Living in a Group
• Communication • Defence • Ape Habitats
• Ape Ancestors

**Elephants  158**
What is an Elephant? • African or Asian? • Big
Bones • Tusks • Body Parts • Elephant Senses
• Trunks • Feeding • Living Together • Elephant
Habitats • Elephant Migrations • Ancestors

**Whales and Dolphins  184**
Whale Order • Whales Large and Small
• Whale Bones • Whale Bodies • Staying Alive
• Whale Brain and Senses • Feeding Habits
• Sounds and Songs • Swimming • Social Life
• Where Whales are Found • Migration

**Sharks  210**
What is a Shark? • The Eight Families • Shapes
and Sizes • Light and Strong • Tough Teeth
• Shark Bodies • Brain and Senses • Feeding •
Filter Feeders • Stay in Line • Look in any Ocean

**Turtles and Tortoises  234**
What are Turtles and Tortoises? • Familiar Faces
• Strange Species • The Turtle Shell • How the
Body Works • Temperature Check • Plodders
and Swimmers • Eyes, Ears and
Noses • What Chelonians Eat • Focus
on Sea Turtles • Ancient Chelonians

## Crocodiles 258

What is a Crocodilian? • Croc or Gator?
• Large and Small • Scaly Skin • Bodies and
Bones • Jaws and Teeth • Temperature Check
• Crocodilian Senses • Food and Hunting
• Communication • On the Defensive •
Ancient Crocodiles

## Lizards 284

Top Reptiles • Hard Tongues • Bone and
Cartilage • Skin and Scales • Getting Around
• Sensing the Surroundings • Body Temperature
• Defence Methods • Colour and Camouflage
• Where in the World? • Lizard Relatives

## Snakes 308

Snake Life • Snake Families • Shapes and Sizes
• How Snakes Work • Scaly Skin • Focus on
New Skin • Snakes on the Move • Snake Senses
• Food and Hunting • Stranglers and Poisoners
• Where Snakes Live

## Penguins 332

What Makes Penguins Special? • How the Body
Works • Fantastic Feathers • Different Colours
and Crests • Flightless Wonders • Waddle, Hop,
Slide and Jump • Eyes, Ears and Noses • Food
and Feeding • Warming Up, Cooling Down
• Penguin Talk • Where Penguins Live
• Prehistoric Penguins

## Birds of Prey 358

What is a Bird of Prey? • Orders and Families
• Shapes and Sizes • How the Body Works
• The Senses • Wings and Flight • Focus on
Hawk Flight • Bill and Talons • The Hunted
• Building Nests and Laying Eggs • On the Move

## Tropical Birds 382

What are Tropical Birds? • Rainforest Birds
• Grassland Birds • Wetland Birds • Sight and
Sound • Built for Flight • How they Fly • On
the Ground • Foot and Mouth • Wings and
Feathers • Migration

## Ants, Bees, Wasps and Termites 406

What are Social Insects? • Body Parts • On the
Wing • Lively Legs • Amazing Senses • How
Insects Eat • How Social Insects Communicate
• The Search for Food • Insect Enemies • Social
Insect Habitats • How Insects Evolved

## Butterflies and Moths 430

Winged Beauties • Superfamilies • How
Butterflies Look • How Moths Look • Scaly
Wings • Focus on Flight • Senses • Focus on
Metamorphosis • Nectar and Food • Around
the World • Migration

## Beetles and Bugs 454

Nature's Success Story • Body Parts • On the
Move • Focus on Beetles in Flight • Senses
• Plant-eaters and Pests • Scavengers and Hunters
• Natural Disguises • The Life Cycle of Beetles
• The Life Cycle of Bugs • Homes and Habitats

## Spiders 478

Introducing Spiders • Spider Families • Shapes
and Sizes • How Spiders Work • On the Move
• Spider Eyes • Spinning Silk • Catching Food
• Moulting • Spiders Everywhere

## GLOSSARY 500
## ACKNOWLEDGEMENTS 506
## INDEX 508

# Introduction

Over millions of years, animals have had to adapt to their environments in order to survive in an often harsh and unpredictable world. The Earth's diverse ecology has given rise to many weird and wonderful adaptations, from fur, fins, feathers and claws to wings, stings, gills and trunks. This intriguing compendium of fascinating facts takes a detailed look at the biology, ecology and behavioural traits of 20 different animal groups, from big cats, wolves and horses to sharks, snakes and insects.

Each animal has its own way of finding and catching food, depending on the habitat in which it lives and its unique physiology. Sharp eyes, sensitive noses and acute hearing are all useful, but some animals have evolved with other, more specialized, senses and skeletons. Snakes, for example, can follow their prey by flicking their tongues to detect tiny particles of scent in the air. The cheetah has long shoulder bones, wide nostrils and specially adapted paws that enable it to reach speeds of up to 70mph/115kph, making it the fastest land animal in the world.

### PENGUIN

Penguins are warm-blooded, and must keep their blood temperature at a constant 38°C/100°F. To help them to maintain this temperature they have dense overlapping feathers and a layer of fat, or blubber, beneath the skin.

### PEACOCK

Colourful displays, scents and sounds all help animals to find mates. The peacock is famous for the huge fan of brightly coloured iridescent feathers that he displays to the female.

### CHAMELEON

Many animals avoid being attacked by using camouflage to blend in with their surroundings so that their enemies cannot spot them. Chameleons and some spiders can change their colours to match different backgrounds.

Defence against attack is a crucial aspect of every animal's life, and they adopt various means by which to protect themselves. Bees, wasps, snakes and many ants use stings and poisonous bites to deter would-be predators, while many other animals use camouflage to avoid being spotted in the first place. Insects are particularly good at this and can make themselves look just like twigs and dead leaves. Butterflies sometimes use their body shape or markings to confuse predators, so that they mistake the tail-end for the head. Predators also use camouflage both to hide from their enemies and to stalk prey. The tiger's stripes, for example, help it to hide in the long grass while it inches closer to its victim, and the leopard's spots disguise it among the trees and bushes.

Social interaction, cooperation and communication play a vital role in the lives of many species. Apes, wolves, lions, ants and bees, to name but a few, live in highly evolved and complex communities. Other animals, such as some sharks, most big cats and all bears, however, spend the vast majority of their adult lives alone, coming together only to mate. Species also interact with each other, both on a territorial level and as an inevitable aspect of the hierarchy of food chains and the endless interplay between the hunter and the hunted.

**WOLF**

The fiercely territorial grey wolf scent-marks boundaries and makes its presence known to other wolf packs by howling. Rival packs may answer these calls with those of their own. A wolf that has been driven from or has left the pack is called a lone wolf.

**LEOPARD**

Young leopards stay with their mother for about two years, learning how to hunt and fend for themselves. After this they go off alone to establish their own territories, which they defend ferociously against other leopards. They are excellent climbers and spend much of their time in trees where they sleep through the hot days, lie in silent ambush, and can safely store their kill beyond the reach of scavengers such as lions, hyenas and vultures. The leopard's strongly contrasting markings break up the outline of its body and help it to blend into the forest, concealing it from both potential enemies and victims.

**HONEY BEE**

Worker honey bees unload their cargo of precious nectar into special larder cells. This is then used to make honey, which enables them to survive the long, cold winter months when other worker bees and wasps die.

# BIG CATS

The big cats form one of the two groups which make up the cat (Felidae) family, and they include the tiger, lion, leopard, snow leopard and jaguar. These awesome hunters have fine fur, sharp claws, lethal teeth, acute senses and powerful agile bodies which make them experts at running, climbing, swimming and jumping.

*Author*: Rhonda Klevansky
*Consultant*: Dr Nigel Dunstone

# What is a Cat?

Cats are native to every continent except Australia and Antarctica. All cats are mammals with fine fur that is often beautifully marked. They are skilled hunters and killers with strong agile bodies, acute senses and sharp teeth and claws. Cats are stealthy and intelligent animals, and many are solitary and very mysterious. Although cats vary in size from the domestic (house) cat to the huge Siberian tiger, they all belong to the same family, the Felidae. This means that both wild and domestic cats look alike and behave in very similar ways. In all, there are 38 different species of cat.

▲ LONG TAIL
A cat's long tail helps it balance as it runs. Cats also use their tails to signal their feelings to other cats.

All cats have a short, rounded head.

Whiskers help a cat feel its surroundings.

The body of a cat is muscular and supple, with a broad, powerful chest.

▲ BIG BITE
As this tiger yawns, it reveals its sharp teeth and strong jaws that can give a lethal bite. Cats use their long, curved canine teeth for killing prey.

▲ BIG CATS
Cats are very specialized meat-eaters. They are the perfect carnivore, with excellent hearing and eyesight. Their curved, razor-sharp claws, used for catching and holding prey, are retractable. This means they can be pulled into the paws to protect them when running. The hair covering a cat's paws and pads helps it move silently.

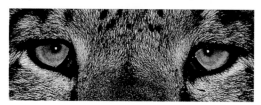

## ▲ NIGHT SIGHT

The pupils (dark centres) of cats' eyes close to a slit or a small circle during the day to keep out the glare. At night they open up to let in as much light as possible. This enables a cat to see at night as well as during the day.

**The Lion and the Saint**
*St Jerome was a Christian scholar who lived from about AD331 to 420. According to legend, he found an injured lion in the desert with a thorn in its paw. Instead of attacking him, the lion befriended the saint when he removed the thorn. St Jerome is often shown with a lion sitting at his feet.*

Very soft fur is kept clean by regular grooming with the tongue and paws.

A long tail helps the cat balance when it runs and leaps on prey.

Did you know? Some Arctic cultures believe that cats represent the spirits of the dead.

Cats walk on their toes, not on the whole foot.

Large ears draw in sounds.

### CATS' EARS ▶

A cat's ears are set high on its head. This gives a keen hunter the best possible chance of picking up sounds. The ears have a rounded shape, which enables them to pick up sounds from many directions. Cats can also rotate their ears to face the source of a sound.

# The Big Cats

Scientists classify (arrange) the members of the cat family into related groups. The two main groups are small cats (the domestic cat and many wild cats) and big cats (the tiger, lion, leopard, snow leopard and jaguar). The clouded leopard and the cheetah are each grouped separately, but many people regard them as big cats. Big cats differ from small cats not only because of their size. Big cats can roar, but small cats can only purr. Small cats have a special bone, called the hyoid, at the base of the tongue which enables them to breathe and purr at the same time. Big cats have elastic cartilage instead and can only purr when they breathe out. The puma is, in fact, a very large small cat. It is discussed here because of its size.

▲ **LION**
The lion is the only social cat and lives in a family group called a pride. Adult male lions, unlike other big cats, have a long, thick mane of hair. Female lions do not have a mane.

▲ **PUMA**
The puma is also called the cougar or mountain lion. Although it is about the same size as a leopard, a puma is considered a small cat because it can purr. Pumas live in North and South America.

◀ **CHEETAH**
The tall cheetah is built like a slim athlete and is able to chase prey at great speed. Cheetahs are different from other cats in that they have retractable claws, but no sheaths to cover them. It was once thought that the cheetah was related to the dog, but scientists now think that its closest cousin is the puma.

## ▲ SNOW LEOPARD

The snow leopard is a different species from the true leopard. This rare cat has a very thick coat to keep it warm in the high mountains of Central Asia. It has a very long tail, which helps it to balance as it leaps from rock to rock in its mountainous surroundings.

## ▲ LEOPARD

The leopard is built for bursts of speed and for climbing trees. Heavier than a cheetah, this cat is not as large and bulky as a tiger or a lion. Its spotted coat helps to hide the cat as it hunts in wooded grassland. Black leopards are called panthers. They are the same species, but their spots are hidden.

## ▼JAGUAR

The jaguar is sometimes confused with the leopard, but it is stockier and not as agile. It lives throughout South America in forested habitats, where it needs strength to climb rather than speed to run.

## ▲ TIGER

The most powerful and largest of all the big cats is the tiger, which reaches an average length of over 2m/6$\frac{1}{2}$ft and weighs about 225kg/500lb. The biggest tigers live in the snowy forests of Siberia in Russia. A few tigers also live in tropical forest reserves and swamps in Asia.

Did you know? Although lions are called the King of the Jungle, they do not live there.

# Bones and Teeth

The skeleton of a cat gives it its shape and has 230 bones (a human has about 206). Its short and round skull is joined to the spine (backbone), which supports the body. Vertebrae (the bones of the spine) protect the spinal cord, which is the main nerve cable in the body. The ribs are joined to the spine, forming a cage that protects the cat's heart and lungs. Cats' teeth are designed for tearing and chewing meat. Wild cats must be careful not to damage their teeth, because with broken teeth they would quickly die from starvation.

spine

The number of bones in the tail varies according to the species. Tigers have from 23 to 26, but cheetahs have 28.

The big, flexible rib cage has 13 ribs.

The bones of a cat's powerful hind legs are longer than the front leg bones.

### ▲ THE FRAME

The powerfully built skeleton of a tiger is similar to all cats' skeletons. Cats have short necks with seven compressed vertebrae. These help to streamline and balance the cat so that it can achieve greater speeds. All cats have slightly different shoulder bones. A cheetah has long shoulder bones to which sprinting muscles are attached. However, a leopard has short shoulder bones and thicker, tree-climbing muscles.

### ◀ CANINES AND CARNASSIALS

A tiger reveals its fearsome teeth. Its long, curved canines are adapted to fit between the neck bones of its prey to break the spinal cord. Like all carnivores, cats have strong back teeth, called carnassials. These do most of the cutting by tearing off pieces of meat.

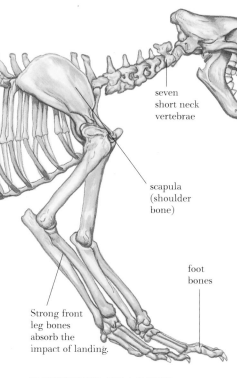

seven short neck vertebrae

scapula (shoulder bone)

foot bones

Strong front leg bones absorb the impact of landing.

**LANDING FEET** ▶

As it falls, this cat twists its supple, flexible spine to make sure its feet will be in the right place for landing. Cats almost always land on their feet when they fall. This helps them to avoid injury as they leap on prey or jump from a tree.

### ▼ CHEWING ON A BONE

Ravenous lions feast on the carcass of their latest kill. Cats' jaws are hinged so that their jaw bones can move only up and down, not from side to side. Because of this, cats eat on one side of the mouth at a time and often tilt their heads when they eat.

### ▼ CAT SKULL

Like all cats' skulls, this tiger's skull has a high crown at the back, giving a lot of space for its strong neck muscles. Big eye sockets allow it to see well at the sides as well as at the front. Its short jaws can open wide to deliver a powerful bite.

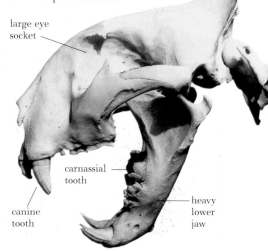

large eye socket

carnassial tooth

canine tooth

heavy lower jaw

# Muscles and Claws

Both inside and out, cats are designed to be skilled hunters and killers. Thick back and shoulder muscles help them to be excellent jumpers and climbers. Sharp, curved claws that grow from all of their digits (toes) are their weapons. One of the digits on a cat's front foot is called the dew claw. This is held off the ground to keep it sharp and ready to hold prey. Cats are warm-blooded, which means that their bodies stay at the same temperature no matter how hot or cold the weather is. The fur on their skin keeps them warm when conditions are cold. When it is hot, cats cool down by sweating through their noses and paw pads.

**Heracles and the Nemean Lion**
*The mythical Greek hero Heracles was the son of the god Zeus and was tremendously strong. As a young man he committed a terrible crime. Part of his punishment was to kill the Nemean lion. The lion had impenetrable skin and could not be killed with arrows or spears. Heracles chased the lion into a cave and strangled it with his hands. He wore its skin as a shield and its head as a helmet.*

## ▼ KNOCKOUT CLAWS

Cheetahs have well-developed dew claws that stick out from their front legs. They use these claws to knock down prey before grabbing its throat or muzzle to strangle it. Other cats use their dew claws to grip while climbing or to hold on to prey. Cats have five claws, including the dew claw, on their front paws. On their back paws, they have only four claws.

*Did you know? Cats cannot digest sugar so they prefer not to eat sweet things.*

dew claw

dew claw

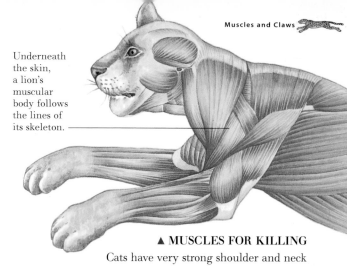

Underneath the skin, a lion's muscular body follows the lines of its skeleton.

## ▲ TIGER CLAW

This is the extended claw of a tiger. Cats' claws are made of keratin, just like human fingernails. They need to be kept sharp all of the time.

## ▲ MUSCLES FOR KILLING

Cats have very strong shoulder and neck muscles for attacking prey. The muscles also absorb some of the impact when the cat pounces.

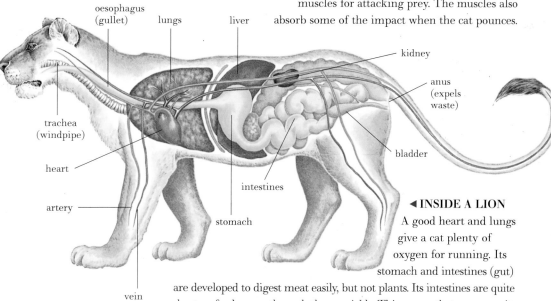

oesophagus (gullet)  lungs  liver  kidney

anus (expels waste)

trachea (windpipe)

heart

artery

intestines

stomach

bladder

vein

## ◄ INSIDE A LION

A good heart and lungs give a cat plenty of oxygen for running. Its stomach and intestines (gut) are developed to digest meat easily, but not plants. Its intestines are quite short, so food passes through them quickly. This means that as soon as it needs more food, a cat is light enough to run and pounce. However, once a lion has had a big meal, it does not need to eat again for several days.

## CLAW PROTECTION ►

Cats retract (pull back) their claws into fleshy sheaths to protect them. This prevents them from getting blunt or damaged. Only cheetahs do not have sheaths.

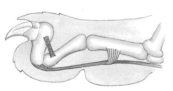

The sheathed claw is protected by a fleshy covering.

flexed muscle

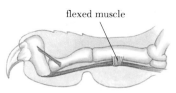

The claw is unsheathed when a muscle tightens.

# Sight and Sound

To hunt well and not be seen or heard by prey or enemies, cats use their senses of sight, sound and touch. Cats' eyesight is excellent. Their eyes are adapted for night vision, but they can also see well during the day. Cats' eyes are big compared to the size of their heads. They have good binocular vision, which allows them to judge accurately how far away objects are. At night, cats see in black and white. They can see colours in the day, but not as well as humans can. Cats have very good hearing, which is much better than a human's. They can hear small animals rustling through the grass or even moving around in their burrows underground.

▲ CAUGHT IN BRIGHT LIGHT
Cats' eyes are very sensitive to light. During the day in bright light, the pupils of the eyes close right down, letting in only as much light as is needed to see well. A domestic cat's pupils close down to slits, while most big cats' pupils close to tiny circles.

◄ GLOWING EYES
Behind the retinas (light sensitive areas) in this leopard's eyes is a reflecting layer called the tapetum lucidum. This helps to absorb extra light in the dark. When light shines into the eyes at night, the reflectors glow.

Did you know? A cat's pupils open wide when it is frightened and close up when it is angry.

**PREY IN SIGHT ▶**
As it stalks through the long grass, a lion must pounce at just the right moment if it is to catch its prey. Binocular vision helps the cat to judge when to strike. Because its eyes are set slightly apart at the front of the head, their field of view overlaps. This enables a cat to judge the position of its prey exactly.

**▲ ROUND-EYED**
This puma's rounded pupils have closed down in daylight. In dim light, the pupils will expand to let in as much light as possible.

Large earflaps concentrate sound waves deep into each ear.

**SHARP EARS ▶**
Cats' ears are designed for them to hear very well. This Siberian lynx lives in snowy forests where the sound is often muffled. It has specially shaped, big ears to catch as much sound as possible.

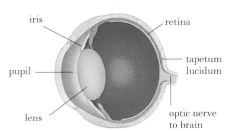

iris

retina

pupil

tapetum lucidum

lens

optic nerve to brain

**▲ INSIDE THE EYE**
The lens focuses light rays to produce a sharp image on the retina. Impulses from the retina are carried to the brain by the optic nerve. Cats have a membrane that can be pulled over the surface of the eye to keep out dirt and dust.

# Touching, Tasting and Smelling

Like all animals, cats feel things with nerves in their skin, but they have another important touching tool – whiskers. These long, stiff hairs on the face have very sensitive nerve endings at their roots. Some whiskers are for protection. Anything brushing against the whiskers above a cat's eyes will make it blink. Cats use smell and taste to communicate with each other. A cat's tongue is a useful tool, and its nose is very sensitive. Thin, curled bones in the nose carry scents inward to smell receptors. Unlike most animals, cats have special places on the roofs of their mouths to distinguish scents, especially of other cats.

**▲ TONGUE TOOL**

A leopard curls the tip of its tongue like a spoon to lap up water. After several laps it will drink the water in one gulp. As well as drinking, the tongue is used for tasting, scraping meat off a carcass and grooming.

**◄ ROUGH TONGUE**

A tiger's bright pink tongue has a very rough surface. Cats' tongues are covered with small spikes called papillae. The papillae point backward and are used by the cat, together with its teeth, to scrape meat off bones. Around the edge and at the back of the tongue are taste buds. Cats cannot taste sweet things and can actively recognize pure water.

The tiger raises its head and grimaces to taste the air.

Cats twitch their tails from side to side as they concentrate. When angry, the tail lashes up and down.

## WHO PASSED BY? ▶

By tasting the air, a tiger uses his Jacobson's organ (the special scent centre on the roof of the mouth) to detect the scent left by another tiger. To get as much of the scent as he can, he wrinkles his nose, curls his lips upward, bares his teeth, and lifts his head. This action is known as flehmen. Males use it especially to locate females ready to mate.

Did you know? Hairballs coughed up by lions are worn as talismans in some parts of Africa.

## ▲ CATS' WHISKERS

This snow leopard's face is surrounded by sensitive whiskers. Cats use their whiskers to judge how far away objects are. The most important whiskers are on the sides of the face. These help a cat to feel its way in the dark or when it is walking through tall grass.

## ▼ COAT CARE

The long, rough tongue of a lion makes a very good comb. It removes loose hairs and combs the fur flat and straight. Cats wipe their faces, coats and paws clean. They need to keep well groomed and spend a lot of time looking after their fur. Hair swallowed by grooming is spat out as hairballs.

# Spots and Stripes

A cat's fur coat protects its skin and keeps it warm. The coat's colours and patterns help to camouflage (hide) the cat as it hunts prey. Wild cats' coats have two layers – an undercoat of short soft fur and an outercoat of tougher, longer hairs, called guard hairs. Together these two layers insulate the cat from extreme cold or extreme heat. Some guard hairs are sensitive and help a cat to feel its way. Cats have loose skin, making it difficult for an attacker to get a good grip and helping to prevent injury. The colours and patterns of a wild cat's coat depend on where it lives.

▲ TIGER IN THE GRASS
The stripes of a tiger's coat are the perfect camouflage for an animal that needs to prowl around in long grass. The colours and patterns help to make the cat almost invisible as it stalks its prey. These markings are also very effective in a leafy jungle, where the dappled light makes stripes of light and shade.

Did you know? Domestic cats have a wider range of colours and markings than wild cats.

◄ KING OF THE HILL
King cheetahs were once thought to be different from other cheetahs. They have longer fur, darker colours and spots on their backs that join up to form stripes. Even so, they are the same species. All cheetahs have distinctive tear stripes running from the corners of their eyes down beside their muzzles.

## ▲ FRATERNAL TWINS

Many big cats of the same species come in variations of colour, depending on where they live. These two leopard cubs are twins, but one has a much darker, blackish coat. Black leopards are called panthers. (Black jaguars and even pumas are sometimes called panthers.) Some leopards live deep in the shadows of the forest, where darker colouring allows them to hide more easily. Panthers are most common in Asia.

## ▼ SPOT THE DIFFERENCE

Spots, stripes or blotches break up the outline of a cat's body. This helps it to blend in with the shadows made by the leaves of bushes and trees, or the lines of tall grass. In the dappled light of a forest or in the long grass of the savannah, cats are very well hidden indeed.

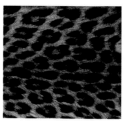

A leopard's spots are actually small rosettes.

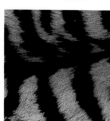

The tiger has distinctive black stripes.

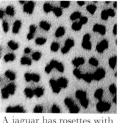

A jaguar has rosettes with a central spot of colour.

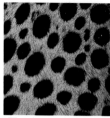

The cheetah has many spots and no rosettes.

## ◄ WHITE FOR SNOW

A snow leopard has a shaggy, off-white coat with darker spots. This colouring helps the snow leopard to stay well hidden in the rocky, mountainous terrain where it lives. It moves around early in the morning or in the late afternoon, blending with its habitat as it looks for prey.

A snow leopard's pale, thick coat has dark irregular spots and streaks. This helps it to hide between the rocks and snow.

# Communication

All big cats communicate with one another. They tell each other how old they are, whether they are male or female, what mood they are in and where they live. Cats communicate by signals such as smells, scratches and sounds. The smells come from urine and from scent glands. Cats have scent glands on the head and chin, between their toes and at the base of the tails. Every time they rub against something, they transfer their special smell. Cats make many different sounds. Scientists know that cats speak to each other, but still do not understand much about their language. Cats also communicate using body language. They use their ears to signal their mood and twitch their tails to show that they are excited or agitated.

**▲ A MIGHTY ROAR**

The lion's roar is the loudest sound cats make. It is loud enough for all of the "neighbourhood" lions to hear. Lions roar after sunset, following a kill and when they have finished eating. Lions make at least nine different sounds. They also grunt to each other as they move around.

**HISSING LEOPARD ▶**

An angry leopard hisses at an enemy. Cats hiss and spit when they feel threatened, or when they are fighting an enemy. The position of a cat's ears also signals its intentions. When a cat is about to attack, it flattens its ears back against its neck.

## ▲ EAR SIGNALS

Many wild cats, such as this tiger, have white markings on the back of their ears. They turn their ears to show the markings to an enemy when they are angry.

## ▲ MARKS FOR SHOW

Cats like to scratch things to clean their claws and stretch their limbs. At the same time, they leave a scented mark for others to both see and smell. When this lioness scratches, she leaves her own personal scent from the glands between her toes on the scratch marks.

Did you know? When they are close together, lions chirrup, meow and yowl to each other.

## ▲ CAT SPRAY

A king cheetah marks its territory by spraying urine at points along its trails. Scent marks left by a male tell other males to stay away. The scent left by a female will tell a male passing through her range if she is ready to mate.

## BABY TALK ▶

Mothers talk to their cubs often. The sounds are quiet so that enemies do not hear. The softest and safest sound of all is purring.

# Hunting Prey

All cats, big and small, are carnivores – they eat meat. Their bodies are not designed to digest plants. Big cats must hunt down and kill their own food. However, most big cats are only too happy to eat someone else's meal and steal kills from other animals whenever they can. Cheetahs are an exception and eat only animals they have killed themselves. To catch and kill their food, big cats must hunt. Some, like cheetahs, patrol their territories, looking for prey. Others, such as jaguars, hide in wait and then ambush their victims. Many cats, such as leopards, do both.

### King Solomon

*Solomon ruled Israel in the 900s BC and was reputed to be a very wise ruler. His throne was carved with lions because of his admiration for these big cats, which killed only out of necessity. In law, if a man was said to have fallen into a lion's den, it was not proof of his death.*

**◄ THE MAIN COURSE**
A big lion can kill large, powerful animals like this buffalo. A big cat usually attacks from behind, or from the side. If the prey is too big to grab right away, the cat will knock it off balance, hold on to it and bite into its neck.

**CHOOSING A MEAL►**
A herd of antelope and zebra grazes while keeping watch on a lioness crouched in the grass. She lies as close to the ground as possible, waiting to pounce. Finally, when focused on a victim, she will bring her hind legs back into position and dart forward.

## ▲ WARTHOG SPECIAL

Four cheetahs surround an injured warthog. The mother cheetah is teaching her three cubs hunting techniques. The cheetah on the right is trying a left paw sideswipe, while another tries using its dew claw. Cheetahs love to eat warthogs but also catch antelope and smaller animals such as hares.

## ▲ CAT AND MOUSE

A recently killed capybara (a large rodent) makes a tasty meal for a jaguar. Jaguars often catch their food, such as fish and turtles, in water. On land they hunt armadillos, deer, opossums, skunks, snakes, squirrels, tortoises and monkeys.

Did you know? Cheetahs will only chase prey if it runs. If it stops, so does the cheetah.

## SLOW FOOD ▶

If a lion has not been able to hunt successfully for a while, it will eat small creatures such as this tortoise. Lions usually hunt big animals such as antelope, wildebeest, warthogs, giraffes, buffalo, bush pigs and baboons. They work together in a group to hunt large prey.

# Killing Prey

The way a big cat kills its prey depends on the size of the cat and the size of its meal. If the prey is small with a bite-size neck, it will be killed with a bite through the spinal cord. If the prey has a bite-size head, the cat will use its powerful jaws to crush the back of its skull. Large prey is killed by biting its throat and suffocating it. Lions often hunt together and use a combined effort to kill large prey. One lion may grab the prey's throat to suffocate it, while other lions attack from behind.

*Did you know? Lions try to flip porcupines on to their backs to avoid the sharp spines.*

▼ **OLD AGE**

When big cats get old or injured, it is very difficult for them to hunt. They will eventually die from starvation. This lion from the Kalahari Desert in South Africa is old and thin. It has been weakened by hunger.

◀ **FAIR GAME**

A warthog is a small, delicious meal for a cheetah. The bigger the cat, the bigger its prey. A cheetah is quite a light cat, so to kill an animal the cheetah first knocks it over, then bites the prey's neck to suffocate it.

▲ **A DEADLY EMBRACE**

A lioness immobilizes a struggling wildebeest by biting its windpipe and suffocating it to death. Lions are very strong animals. A lion weighing 148–247kg/ 330–550lb can kill a buffalo more than twice its weight. Female lions do most of the hunting for their pride.

## ◀ SECRET STASH

A cheetah carries off its prey, a young gazelle, to a safe place. Once it has killed, a cheetah will check the area to make sure it is secure before feeding. It drags the carcass to a covered spot in the bushes. Here it can eat its meal hidden from enemies. Cheetahs are often driven off and robbed of their kills by hyenas and jackals or even other big cats.

## A SOLID MEAL ▶

These cheetahs will devour as much of this antelope as they can. Big cats lie on the ground and hold their food with their forepaws when they eat. When they have satisfied their hunger, cheetahs cover up or hide the carcass with grass, leaves, or whatever is available, in order to save it for later.

## LIONS' FEAST ▶

A pride of lions gathers around their kill, a zebra. They eat quickly before any scavenging hyenas and vultures can steal the meat. Each lion has its place in the pride. Even if they are very hungry, they must wait until it is their turn to eat. Usually the dominant male lion eats first.

# Living Together

Most big cats live alone. They hunt alone, and the females bring up their cubs alone. Big cats come together only when they want to mate. They are solitary because of the prey that they hunt. There is usually not enough prey in one area for a large group of big cats to live on. Lions are the exception. They live in family groups called prides. (Male cheetahs also sometimes live in groups with up to four members.) All wild cats have territories (home ranges). These territories are a series of trails that link together a cat's hunting area, its drinking places, its lookout positions, and the den where it brings up its young. Females have smaller home ranges than males. Males that have more than one mate have territories that overlap with two or more female home ranges.

Did you know? Big cats' territories range from a few sq km/miles to over 1,600km/1,000 sq miles.

▲ BRINGING UP BABY
Female snow leopards bring up their cubs on their own. They have up to five cubs, which stay with their mother for at least a year. Although snow leopards are loners, they are not unsociable. They like to live near each other, and they let other snow leopards cross their territories.

◄ THE LOOKOUT
A puma keeps watch over its territory from a hill. Pumas are solitary and deliberately avoid each other except during courtship and mating. The first male puma to arrive in an area claims it as his territory. He chases out any other male that tries to live there.

## ▲ A PRIDE OF LIONS

The lions in a pride drink together, hunt together, eat together and play together. A pride is usually made up of related females and their young. Prides usually try not to meet up with other prides. To tell others to keep out of its territory, the pride leaves scent markings on the edge of its range.

### Daniel and the Lions' Den
*A story in the Bible tells how Daniel was taken prisoner by Nebuchadnezzer, king of Babylon. When Daniel correctly interpreted the king's dreams, he became a favourite of the king. His enemies became jealous of his position and had him thrown into a lions' den, a common punishment for prisoners at the time. But instead of eating Daniel, the lions befriended him. They were tamed by his great faith in God.*

## ▲ FAMILY GROUPS

A cheetah mother sits between her two cubs. The cubs will stay with her until they are about 18 months old. The female then lives a solitary life. Males, however, live in small groups and defend a territory. They only leave their range if there is a drought or if food is very scarce.

## ▲ WELL GROOMED

Cats that live together groom each other. They do this to be friendly, to keep clean and also to spread their scent on each other, so that they smell the same. This helps them to recognize each other and identify strangers.

*31*

# Big Cat Relatives

Fossil remains show that the ancestors of today's cats first roamed the earth 65 million years ago. They were small animals called miacids. Scientists think that the miacids may be the forerunners of all carnivorous mammals on Earth today. About 35 million years ago the first cat-like carnivores appeared. Many of these early cats were large and dangerous creatures that have become extinct (died out). The best known are the sabre-toothed cats, which, unlike modern cats, used their canines for stabbing rather than biting. Fossil records of cats very similar to modern cats date back about 10 million years. Today, there are 37 species of wild cat, big and small, and over 300 breeds of domestic cat.

**▲ ANCIENT ANCESTOR**
Miacids are thought to have been the first true carnivorous mammals. They first lived about 65 million years ago, around the same time that the dinosaurs died out. They are the first animals to have carnassial teeth – the strong back teeth used for shearing meat.

*Did you know? The bones of sabre-toothed cats were found under Trafalgar Square, London.*

**◄ SABRE-TOOTH**
This skeleton of a sabre-toothed cat called Smilodon is 15,000 years old. It was about the size of a present-day lion and lived in North America. Smilodon was a ferocious predator and hacked down mammoth and bison with its huge teeth.

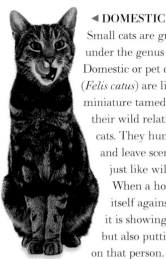

### ◄ DOMESTIC CATS

Small cats are grouped under the genus *Felis*. Domestic or pet cats (*Felis catus*) are like miniature tamed versions of their wild relatives, the big cats. They hunt, groom and leave scent marks just like wild cats.

When a house cat rubs itself against a human, it is showing affection but also putting its smell on that person.

*Classification Chart*

| | |
|---|---|
| Kingdom | **Animalia** (all animals) |
| Phylum | **Chordata** (animals with backbones) |
| Class | **Mammalia** (animals with hair on their bodies that feed their young with milk) |
| Order | **Carnivora** (mammals that eat meat) |
| Family | **Felidae** (all cats) |
| Genus | *Panthera* (big cats) |
| Species | *leo* (lion) |

### ▲ CAT NAMES

Scientists classify every cat within the animal kingdom and give it a Latin name. This chart shows how the lion is classified.

### SERVAL ►

The serval (*Felis serval*) is a spotted, fleet-footed wild cat. It lives near water in southern and central Africa. Although it has long legs like a cheetah, it belongs to a different group and purrs like a domestic cat.

### CARACAL ►

The caracal's (*Felis caracal*) most startling feature is the long tufts on its ears. These may help it to locate prey. The caracal is related to both the leopard and the lynx. It lives in grasslands, open woodland and scrub in Africa and parts of Asia.

### BOBCAT ►

The bobcat (*Felis rufus*) is related to the lynx (*Felis lynx*). Both have short tails and live in many sorts of habitats, but prefer the rocks and shrubby plants of mountain slopes. The bobcat is only found in northern North America where it is able to survive the harsh winter conditions.

# WOLVES

Wolves are a member of the canid family, which contains over 37 species, including jackals, coyotes and domesticated dogs. They are highly intelligent pack animals and have an advanced system of communication and complex social interactions. They are found in most climates, although they have been hunted almost to extinction.

*Author*: Jen Green
*Consultant*: Douglas Richardson
Zoological Director, Rome Zoo

# What is a Wolf?

large, triangular ears, usually held pricked (erect)

powerful shoulders and supple body

Wolves are the wild members of the dog family, canids, with gleaming yellow eyes and lean, muscular bodies. The 37 different species of canids include wolves, jackals, coyotes, foxes, and wild and domestic dogs. Canids are native to every continent except Australia and Antarctica. All of them share a keen sense of smell and hearing, and are carnivores (meat-eaters). Wolves and wild dogs hunt live prey, which they kill with their sharp teeth. However, many canids also eat vegetable matter and even insects. They are among the most intelligent of all animals. Some, such as wolves, are social in habit and live together in groups.

**BODY FEATURES ▶**
The wolf is the largest wild dog. It has a strong, well-muscled body covered with dense, shaggy fur, a long, bushy tail and strong legs made for running.
Its muzzle (nose and jaws) is long and well developed, and its ears are pricked up. Male and female wolves look very similar, although females are generally the smaller of the two.

**▲ PRODUCING YOUNG**
A female wolf suckles (feeds) her cubs. All canids are mammals and feed their young on milk. Females produce a litter of cubs, or pups, once a year. Most are born in an underground den.

**◄ KEEN SENSES**

The jackal, like all dogs, has very keen senses. Its nose can detect faint scents, and its large ears pick up the slightest sound. Smell and hearing are mainly used for hunting. Many canids also have good vision.

*The Big, Bad Wolf*

*Fairy tales often depict wolves as wicked, dangerous animals. In the tale of "The Three Little Pigs", the big, bad wolf terrorizes three small pigs. Eventually he is outwitted by the smartest pig, who builds a brick house that the wolf cannot blow down, and all the pigs are safe.*

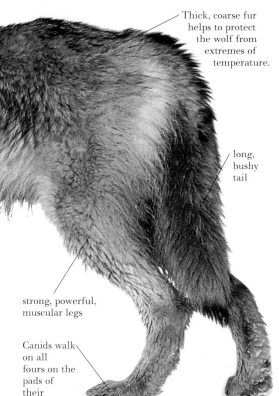

Thick, coarse fur helps to protect the wolf from extremes of temperature.

long, bushy tail

strong, powerful, muscular legs

Canids walk on all fours on the pads of their toes.

**▲ LIVING IN PACKS**

Wolves and a few other wild dogs live in groups called packs of about 8–20. Each pack has a hierarchy (social order) and is led by the strongest male and female.

**EXPERT HUNTERS ▶**

A wolf bares its teeth in a snarl to defend its kill. Wolves and other canids feed mainly on meat but eat plants too, particularly when they are hungry.

# The Wolf Family

Wolves were once common throughout the northern hemisphere, right across North America, Europe and Asia. In the past, people hunted them mercilessly. In many areas, they died out altogether. Across the north, wolves from various regions may look quite different, but they all belong to one species, *Canis lupus*. However, there are many subspecies (different types). Two of the main types are the grey wolf, also known as the timber wolf, and the Arctic, or tundra wolf. Many other subspecies are named after the area or habitat they come from, such as Mexican and steppe wolves. The same type of wolf may be known by different names in different areas. For example, the Arctic wolf is the same as the tundra wolf. The wolf's closest relatives are the coyote, the jackal, the dingo and the domestic dog.

▲ **NEARLY EXTINCT**
The red wolf (*Canis rufus*) is found only in the south eastern U.S.A. It was once widespread, but became extinct in the wild. Today's red wolves stem from captive-bred wolves. They have longer legs and larger ears than the grey wolf and are named after the reddish fur on their heads, ears and legs. The grey wolf is thought to be a hybrid (cross) between the coyote and the wolf.

▼ **MOUNTAIN HOME**
The Simien wolf is found only in the Simien Mountains of Ethiopia, East Africa. It is about the same size as a coyote (90cm/3ft long) and has a reddish-brown coat, with pale fur on its belly and throat. The Simien wolf was once thought to be a kind of jackal. Now scientists have found out that it is a small wolf.

Did you know? Wolves kill prey animals as small as mice, as large as bison and

**Simien wolf**
(*Canis simensis*)

**dingo**
*(Canis familiaris)*

### ◄ DOG WITHOUT A BARK

The dingo lives in Australia and South-east Asia. It is now wild, but its ancestors were descended from tame dogs that Aboriginal people brought to the region from Asia more than 8,000 years ago. Dingoes are found mainly in dry areas such as the dusty Australian interior. They live in small families and sometimes join other dingo families to hunt.

### JACKAL ►

Jackals are found on the grassy plains and in the woodlands of Africa, south-eastern Europe and southern Asia. They live in pairs and stay with the same mate for life. There are three species of jackal – side-striped and black-backed jackals (found only in Africa), and golden jackals.

**black-backed jackal**
*(Canis mesomelas)*

### ▲ COYOTE

The coyote (*Canis latrans*) is found in North and Central America. It lives mainly on prairies (grassy plains) and in open woodlands and is also known as the prairie or brush wolf. Full-grown coyotes are half the size of grey wolves. They live alone, or in pairs and small family groups.

**miniature poodle**
*(Canis familiaris)*

### ◄ DOMESTIC DOG

You may not have seen a wolf in the wild, but you will know one of its relatives, for all domestic dogs are descended from the wolf. Dogs were the first animals to be tamed by people over 12,000 years ago. Now there are over 400 breeds of dog, including the miniature poodle.

*39*

# Body Shapes

Like all mammals, wolves and dogs are vertebrates (animals with backbones). The backbone protects the spinal cord, the main nerve of the body. The bones in the skeleton support the body and give it a distinct shape. The skeletons of wolves and dogs are different from other mammals. They have long skulls with large teeth, longish necks, and long, strong leg bones. Narrow collar bones help to make them slim and streamlined for speed over the ground, while their joints at the shoulders and hips pivot freely, giving them great agility. Wolves, foxes and wild dogs also generally have long tails. Many have a well-defined tail shape that can help to identify the animal at a distance.

backbone (spine)

tail bones

toe bones

Elastic ligaments and tendons connect the bones together.

## ▲ TALL AND GRACEFUL

The maned wolf has longer leg bones than a true wolf. It uses them to hunt in the tall grass of its homeland. Its leg bones are weaker than a wolf's, so it often lacks the power and strength to run down swift-moving prey. It has a short tail.

## ▲ BUILT FOR POUNCING

A fox's skeleton looks small and delicate compared to a wolf's. The leg bones are shorter in relation to its body size. Foxes spend much of their lives crouching and slinking through the undergrowth rather than running down prey.

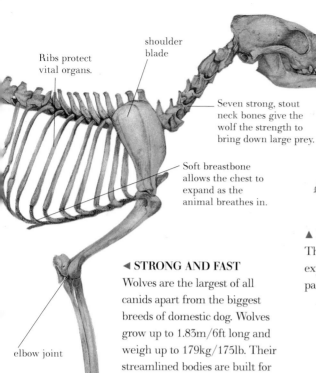

skull

shoulder blade

Ribs protect vital organs.

Seven strong, stout neck bones give the wolf the strength to bring down large prey.

Soft breastbone allows the chest to expand as the animal breathes in.

elbow joint

### ◀ STRONG AND FAST

Wolves are the largest of all canids apart from the biggest breeds of domestic dog. Wolves grow up to 1.83m/6ft long and weigh up to 179kg/175lb. Their streamlined bodies are built for fast running. Strong leg bones make the wolf a tireless hunter.

### ▲ EXPRESSIVE TAIL

The wolf holds its tail in different positions to express its feelings and show its position in the pack. Its bushy tail grows up to 45cm/1¹/₂ft long.

*Strong like the Wolf*

*Native Americans admired the strength, courage and intelligence of wolves and wild dogs. Plains tribes such as the Blackfoot and the Mandan formed warrior-bands called Dog Societies to honour the loyalty shown by wild dogs to other dogs in their pack. This Hidatsa shaman (medicine man) is dressed for the Dog Dance. Dances were performed in celebration and for good luck.*

### ▲ BALANCING BRUSH

The red fox's tail, known as a brush, is long and bushy. It grows up to 45cm/1¹/₂ft long and helps to balance the animal when running and jumping.

### ▲ TAIL TALK

The African hunting dog's tail is short compared to most canids, measuring about 30–45cm/ 1–1¹/₄ft long. Its white tip stands out clearly and is used to signal to other pack members.

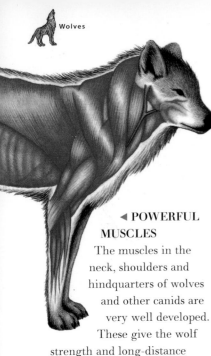

# Body Parts

Muscular, fast-running wolves and wild dogs are built for chasing prey in open country. Thick muscles and long, strong legs enable them to run fast over great distances. The long skull helps the wolf to seize prey on the run. The wolf has a large stomach that can digest meat quickly and hold a big meal after a successful hunt. Wolves, however, can also go without food for more than a week if prey is scarce. Teeth are a wolf's main weapon, used for biting enemies, catching prey and tearing food. Small incisors (front teeth) strip flesh off bones. Long fangs (canines) grab and hold prey. Towards the back, jagged carnassial teeth close together like shears to chew meat into small pieces, while large molars can crush bones.

◀ **POWERFUL MUSCLES**
The muscles in the neck, shoulders and hindquarters of wolves and other canids are very well developed. These give the wolf strength and long-distance stamina as well as speed. Muscle-power alone is not enough, however, to catch prey. Wolves also need to use their cunning and stealth if the hunt is to succeed.

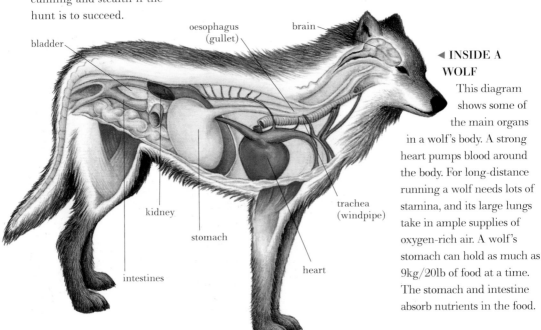

bladder

oesophagus (gullet)

brain

kidney

stomach

intestines

trachea (windpipe)

heart

◀ **INSIDE A WOLF**
This diagram shows some of the main organs in a wolf's body. A strong heart pumps blood around the body. For long-distance running a wolf needs lots of stamina, and its large lungs take in ample supplies of oxygen-rich air. A wolf's stomach can hold as much as 9kg/20lb of food at a time. The stomach and intestine absorb nutrients in the food.

## ▼ WOLF'S SKULL

A wolf's head has a broad crown and a tapering muzzle. The bones of the skull are strong and heavy. They form a tough case that protects the animal's brain, eyes, ears and nose. The jaws have powerful muscles that can exert great pressure as the wolf sinks its teeth into its prey.

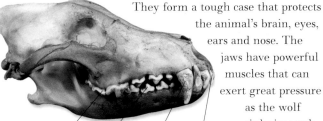

molar  carnassial  canine  incisor

## ▼ BAT-EARED FOX SKULL

The bat-eared fox has a delicate, tapering muzzle. Its jaws are weaker than a wolf's and suited to dealing with smaller prey, such as insects. This fox has 46–50 teeth, which is more than any other canid. Extra molars at the back of the animal's mouth enable it to crunch insects, such as beetles, which have a tough outer casing on their bodies.

molar  carnassial  canine  incisor

## ▲ TIME FOR BED

A wolf shows its full set of meat-eating teeth as it yawns. Wolves and most other canids have 42 teeth. In wolves, the four large, dagger-like canines at the front of the mouth can grow up to 5cm/2in long.

## COOLING DOWN ▶

Like all mammals, the wolf is warm-blooded. This means its body temperature remains constant whatever the weather, so it is always ready to spring into action. Wolves do not have sweat glands all over their bodies as humans do, so in hot weather they cannot sweat to cool down. When the wolf gets too hot, it opens its mouth and pants with its large tongue lolling out. Moisture evaporates from the nose, mouth and tongue to cool the animal down.

# Fur Coats

black-backed jackal
(*Canis mesomelas*)

Wolves and other members of the dog family have thick fur coats. This dense layer of hair helps to protect the animal's body from injury and keeps it warm in cold weather. Wolves and other canids that live in cold places have extra-thick fur. Dingoes, jackals and wild dogs that live in warm countries close to the Equator have sparser fur. The fur is made up of two layers. Short dense underfur helps to keep the animal warm. Long guard hairs on top have natural oils that repel snow and rain to keep the underfur dry. A wild dog's fur coat is usually black, white or tan, or a mixture of these colours. Markings and patterns on the fur act as camouflage to disguise these animals, so they can sneak up unseen on their prey.

## ▲ JACKAL COLOURS

The three species of jackal can be distinguished by their different markings. As its name suggests, the black-backed jackal has a dark patch on its back as well as brown flanks and a pale belly. The golden jackal is sandy brown all over. The side-striped jackal is so named because of the light and dark stripes that run along its sides.

## ◄ WAITING FOR SPRING

Two raccoon dogs shelter under a bush waiting for the snow to melt. They already have their summer coats of grey with pale and dark patches. This will help to camouflage them among the summer grasses and vegetation. In autumn, they will moult (shed) these coats and grow a pure-white coat, ready for the winter snow.

### ◄ MANES AND RUFFS

The maned wolf gets its name from the ruff of long hairs on its neck. This may be dark or reddish brown in colour. Wolves also have a ruff of longer hairs that they raise when threatened to make themselves look larger.

### ▲ HANDSOME CAMOUFLAGE

African hunting dogs have beautiful markings, with tan and dark grey patches on their bodies, and paler, mottled fur on their heads and legs. The patterns work to break up the outline of their bodies as they hunt in the dappled light of the bush.

**Arctic wolf**
*(Canis lupus tundrarum)*

### ▲ WARM COAT

The Arctic wolf has very thick fur to keep it warm in icy temperatures. Its winter coat is pure white so that it blends in with the snow. In spring, the thick fur drops out, and the wolf grows a thinner coat for summer. This coat is usually darker to match the earth without its covering of snow.

**grey wolf**
*(Canis lupus)*

### VARYING COLOURS ►

Grey wolves vary greatly in colour, from pale silver to buff, sandy, red-brown or almost black. Even very dark wolves usually have some pale fur, often a white patch on the chest.

# Sight and Sound

Wolves have excellent hearing. They can hear the sound of a snapping twig up to 3km/2 miles away and are alert to the smallest noise that might give away the presence of potential prey. Wolves hear a wider range of sounds than humans. They can hear ultrasounds (very high-pitched noise) that are too high for human ears to catch. This means they can track down mice and other rodents in the dark. Sight is less important than hearing for hunting. Wolves are good at spotting movement, even at a great distance, but find it harder to see objects that keep still. Canids that hunt at night rely on sound and smell rather than sight. African hunting dogs and dholes, however, hunt by day, often in open country, and have keener sight.

**▲ PRICKED EARS**

Wolves cock (turn) their ears in different directions to pinpoint distant sounds. Even a tiny noise betrays the hiding place of a victim.

**Coyote**
*(Canis latrans)*

**▲ LISTENING IN**

An African hunting dog's large, rounded ears work like satellite dishes to gather sound. Keen hearing is vital in the hunt and allows pack members to keep in touch in the undergrowth.

**HOWLING HELLO ▶**

Coyotes and other wild dogs keep in touch with distant members of their group by howling. The coyote call is actually a series of yelps that ends in a long wail.

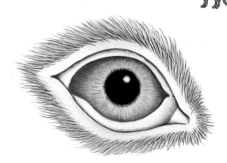

### ◄ BARKING MAD

Some domestic dogs, such as this German shepherd, have been bred to bark loudly to warn their owners of approaching strangers. Wolves also bark if they meet an intruder near the den, but more quietly and less aggressively.

### ▲ A THIRD EYELID

Wolves' eyes have a third eyelid, called a nictitating (blinking) membrane. This membrane is inside their upper and lower eyelids, and sweeps over the surface of the eye when the wolf blinks. It protects the eye from dust and dirt that might damage it otherwise.

### ◄ GLOWING EYES

Wolves have round, yellow eyes. In dark conditions, a layer at the back of the eye, called the *tapetum lucidum*, intensifies what little light there is. This allows a wolf to see at night. The layer also reflects light, making the wolf's eyes glow in the dark if a strong light is shone into them.

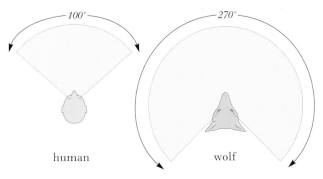

*100°*    *270°*

human        wolf

### ◄ WOLF VISION

Wide-set eyes in the front of its face give a wolf a very wide field of vision. As the view from each eye overlaps, binocular vision (using both eyes at the same time) allows a wolf to focus at close range and pounce on its prey.

# Smell, Touch and Taste

Of all the senses, smell is the most important for wolves and wild dogs. These animals are constantly surrounded by different scents, and their keen sense of smell can distinguish them all. They follow the scent trails left behind by other animals in their quest for food, and they can pick up even faint whiffs of scent on the wind. This helps them to figure out the direction of distant prey. Canids that hunt in packs use scent to identify and communicate with other pack members. They also communicate by sight and touch. Like other mammals, wolves and wild dogs have taste buds on their tongues to taste their food. They eat foods they find the tastiest first. The tongue is also used to lap up water.

▲ **TRACKING PREY**
Nose to the ground, a wolf follows a scent trail in the snow. From the scent, a wolf can tell what type of animal left it, whether it is well or ill, how far away it is, and whether another wolf is following the trail.

▶ **ON THE SCENT**
Bloodhounds were specially bred as tracking dogs. They have a very acute sense of smell and can follow a scent that is several days old. They keep their noses very close to the ground. Their drooping ears help to channel scent into the nose.

▲ **PLEASED TO MEET YOU**
When two wolves meet they sniff the glands at the base of the tail. Pack members all have a familiar scent. Scent is also used to signal mood, such as contentment or fear, or if a female is ready to breed.

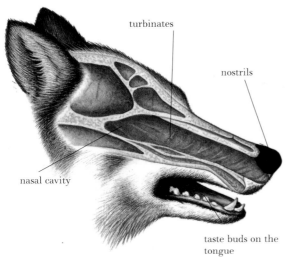

turbinates

nostrils

nasal cavity

taste buds on the tongue

## ▲ INSIDE THE SNOUT

Inside a wolf's snout is a large nasal cavity used for smelling. Scent particles pass over tubes of very thin bone in the roof of the nasal cavity. These tubes, called turbinates, are connected to a nerve network that sends signals to the brain.

## ▲ TOUCHY-FEELY

Wolves use touch to bond with each other. They rub bodies, lick one another, and thrust their noses into each other's fur when they meet. Pack members play-fight by wrestling with locked jaws, or chasing each other.

## ▼ SENSITIVE NOSE

The wolf's leathery outer nose is set right at the end of its snout. Two nostrils draw air laden with scents into the nasal cavity. The wolf may flare its nostrils to take in extra air. The animal may lick its nose before scenting, because a damp nose helps its sense of smell. Long, sensitive whiskers on either side of the snout are used for touching things at close range.

## ▲ WELL GROOMED

A wolf nibbles at the tufts of hair between its paw pads. It is removing ice that might cut and damage the paw. Wolves groom (clean) their fur to keep it in good condition. Licking and running fur through the teeth helps to remove dirt and dislodge fleas.

# Focus on

A wolf pack has a strict social order, and each member knows its place. The senior male and female, known as the alpha male and female, are the only animals to breed. The alpha male takes the lead in hunting, defends the pack members from enemies, and keeps the other animals in their place. In most packs, a second pair of wolves, called the beta male and female, come next in the ranking order. The other pack members are usually the offspring of the alpha pair, aged up to three years old.

**LEADER OF THE PACK**
An alpha male wolf greets a junior pack member. Wolves use different body positions and facial expressions to show rank. The leader stands upright with his tail held high. The junior has his ears laid back and his tail tucked between his legs.

**IT'S A PUSHOVER**
A junior wolf rolls over on its back in a gesture of submission to a more dominant pack member. A junior wolf can also pacify a stronger animal by imitating cub behaviour, such as begging for food.

**SHOWING WHO IS BOSS**
A wolf crouches down to an alpha male. The young wolf whines as it cowers, as if to say, "You're the boss." The pack leader's confident stance makes him look as large as possible.

# a Wolf Pack

### "I GIVE UP"
A male grey wolf lays its ears back and sticks its tongue out. Taken together, these two gestures signal submission. A wolf with its tongue out, but its ears pricked, is sending a different message, showing it feels hostile and rebellious.

### REJECTED BY THE PACK
Old, wounded or sickly wolves are often turned out of the pack to become lone wolves. Although pack members may be affectionate with each other, there is no room for sentiment. Young wolves may also leave to start their own packs. Lone wolves without the protection of a pack are much more vulnerable to attack and must be more cautious.

### SCARY SNARL
A grey wolf bares its canine teeth in a snarl of aggression. Studies have shown that wolves use up to 20 different facial expressions. Junior wolves use snarling expressions to challenge the authority of their leaders. The alpha male may respond with an even more ferocious snarl. If it does so, the junior wolf is faced with a choice. It must back down, or risk being punished with a nip.

**▲ KEEP TO THE TRAIL**

A pack of wolves runs along a snowy trail in single file. Each wolf treads in the tracks of the one in front. This saves a lot of energy that would be wasted if each animal broke a separate trail through the deep snow. Wolves use well-worn paths inside their territories. These connect meeting places with lookout points and good ambush sites.

# Home Territory

Territories are areas that animals use for finding food or for breeding. An animal will defend its territory against others that might present competition. Wolf packs use their territories as hunting grounds and also as safe places to raise their cubs. Wolf territories vary in size, depending on how much food is available to feed the pack. Small territories cover about 168 sq km/65 sq miles. Large territories may be 10 or even 100 times this size. At the heart of the territory is the rendezvous, a meeting place where the wolves gather. This place also acts as a nursery where older cubs are left to play. The borders of the territory are patrolled by the pack on a regular basis, and are marked with urine. Strong-smelling urine sprayed at marker sites lasts several days, while howling also serves as a long-distance warning. The pack will defend its territory fiercely if a rival pack tries to enter.

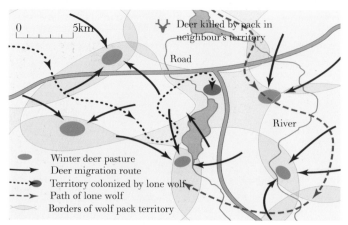

0    5km

Deer killed by pack in neighbour's territory

Road

River

● Winter deer pasture
→ Deer migration route
·····▶ Territory colonized by lone wolf
---▶ Path of lone wolf
◁▷ Borders of wolf pack territory

**◀ NEIGHBOURING TERRITORIES**

Several wolf territories may lie close to each other. Where food is plentiful, for example where deer breed, territories may overlap (see diagram). Rivers, towns and roads form natural boundaries. There may be a neutral 0.8km/¹/₂-mile-wide no-go area between territories. If food becomes scarce, however, wolves will enter this zone.

## ▲ SCENT SIGNAL

A wolf smells a rock that another pack member has marked with urine. The scent lingers for several days after the animal has moved on. A wolf smelling this signal can tell how many animals have passed this way and whether they belong to its pack. Wolves from a rival pack will mark the other side of the rock to reinforce territory boundaries.

## ▲ BORDER DISPUTE

A wolf snarls at a wolf from another pack on the boundary between their territories. When food is scarce, packs are more likely to trespass or raid each other's territory. In times of plenty, scent signals keep trespassers out, so border disputes are rare.

## ◄ SCENT-MARKING

A dhole marks the edge of its territory by spraying urine on a patch of grass. Some canids, such as African hunting dogs and foxes, leave piles of droppings too. In a wolf pack, it is usually the alpha male that marks the boundaries.

## KEEP-OUT CALL ►

Three wolves raise their heads in a group howl. Each animal howls a slightly different note, making an eerie harmony. The sound carries over a long distance – 10km/6 miles or more. If it reaches a rival pack, the other wolves may howl back. Howling is also used to rally the pack, for example, before a hunt.

53

# A Meaty Diet

Wolves and their relatives are carnivores (meat-eaters). They kill prey for fresh meat but also eat carrion (dead animals). When no meat is available, wolves eat plants, such as fruit and berries, and also grass to aid digestion. Large herd animals such as musk oxen, moose, deer and caribou are the favourite targets of the wolf pack. All canids target other kinds of prey if a particular creature becomes scarce. For example, they hunt a wide range of smaller animals, including birds, rabbits, mice and beavers.

Wolves swim well and chase fish, frogs and crabs, but still spend much of their lives with empty bellies. When food is scarce, they sometimes approach towns and villages, where they riffle through rubbish or kill domestic sheep, goats, cattle and horses.

**▲ NOT-SO-FUSSY FEEDERS**
Raccoon dogs of eastern Asia are omnivores – they eat all kinds of different foods, including rodents, fruit and acorns. They are strong swimmers and catch frogs, fish and water beetles in streams and rivers. They also scavenge carrion and scraps from people's rubbish bins (trash cans).

**▼ COYOTE PREY**
Three coyotes tear at the carcass of a moose. Coyotes usually hunt small prey, such as mice, but sometimes they band together to go after larger creatures, such as moose. Teams of coyotes also gang up on other predators and steal their kills.

### ◄ FAST FOOD

A pack of dholes works quickly to eat the deer carcass. Each one eats fast to get its share. A hungry dhole can eat up to 4.5kg/10lb of meat in an hour. Mammals form a large part of a dhole's diet, but if meat is scarce, a dhole will also eat berries, lizards and insects.

### ▲ MEAT AND FRUIT-EATER

A maned wolf lopes off in search of prey. Without a pack to help it hunt, it looks for easy prey, including armadillos and small rodents, such as agoutis and pacas. It also feeds on birds, reptiles, frogs and insects, fruit and sugar cane.

### ▲ BEACH SQUABBLE

Two black-backed jackals squabble over the carcass of a seal pup. Jackals eat almost anything – fruit, frogs, reptiles and a wide range of mammals, from gazelles to mice. Jackals also scavenge kills from other hunters.

### STORING FOOD ►

A wolf looks for a suitable spot in the snow to bury a freshly caught rabbit. After a pack has killed a large beast, or when a lone hunter has eaten its fill, it hides the remains of its food. Then, when food is scarce, the wolf can return to the hidden cache and retrieve its kill.

**grey wolf**
*(Canis lupus)*

Did you know? All canids are quick feeders, but dholes in particular consume their food at a great rate.

# Relatives and Namesakes

Wolves, foxes, and other members of the dog family have taken millions of years to evolve (develop). Scientists can trace their history through bones and other fossils preserved in the Earth from ancient times. Somewhere around 65 million years ago, a family of tree-dwelling mammals called miacids developed. These carnivorous mammals tore the flesh from their prey using jagged carnassial teeth similar to those of modern dogs and wolves. Later, around 30 million years ago, one branch of the miacid family evolved into fast-running, mongoose-like creatures called cynodictis. In turn, cynodictis and relatives such as hesperocyon developed into the first distinctively wolf-like creatures. From such ancestors, modern canids evolved around 300,000 years ago.

**▲ ANCIENT ANCESTOR**
Hesperocyon is the prehistoric ancestor of wolves and other carnivores. Like wolves, it had a long, dog-like snout and sharp carnassial teeth. Over millions of years, hesperocyons had evolved from earlier tree-dwelling creatures, called miacids. These creatures gradually evolved strong legs and feet to make them fast runners.

**◄ DIRE WOLVES**
The long-extinct dire wolf is an ancient relative of the modern wolf. Remains of these prehistoric creatures have been found in fossil pits in California. Dire wolves lived on Earth about two million years ago. They were fierce predators, much bigger than today's wolves, that preyed on large camelids (camels) and American rhinos (both now extinct), and (the now rare) bison.

## ◄ WOLF-DOG HYBRID

A wolf-dog skirts farmland in Italy. This animal is the offspring of a grey wolf and a German shepherd dog. Coy-wolves, red wolves and coy-dogs are other hybrids that resulted from interbreeding between coyotes, wolves and domestic dogs. These animals may resemble domestic dogs, but they cannot usually be tamed.

## TASMANIAN WOLVES ►

Tasmanian wolf
(*Thylacinus cynocephalus*)

This engraving of the 1800s shows two thylacines, or Tasmanian wolves. As the name suggests, these creatures lived on the island of Tasmania, off Australia. With their long snouts and strong legs, thylacines looked a lot like wild dogs and barked like dogs, too. However, they were marsupials, a group of mammals that carries its young in pouches. They preyed upon kangaroos and wallabies, but when they started to take sheep, farmers hunted them to extinction.

Did you know? Dogs have been domesticated for at least 12,000 years.

## ▲ SCAVENGERS AT WORK

Hyenas gather at a Kenyan water hole to finish off a buffalo killed by lions. Hyenas look like African hunting dogs but are from the Hyaenidae family. They can crunch through the toughest bones with their powerful jaws and strong, sharp teeth.

## ▲ DESCENDED FROM ONE ANCESTOR

All domestic dogs are descended from the wolf. Human and dog came together thousands of years ago for mutual benefit. By Roman times, around 500BC, many of the breeds we know today had already developed.

# WILD HORSES

Domestic and wild horses, asses and
zebras are all members of the equid
family. These versatile herbivores were
once wild, until they were tamed
and trained by humans 6,000 years
ago. Although many equids are
now domesticated, there are still
a large number of wild species
roaming the world.

*Author*: Michael Bright
*Consultant*: Dr Nigel Dunstone
Durham University

# Saved from Extinction

Wild horses once ranged throughout the world. Climate change reduced their numbers until they almost became extinct. However, about 6,000 years ago, horses were tamed by people. Through breeding, many shapes and sizes of horse developed to serve different human needs. Horses became essential to human society, and as a result, they are found all over the world again.

Domestic and wild horses are a single species (*Equus caballus*). They belong to a larger family called equids. Asses and zebras are also equids, and are closely related to horses. The three groups evolved different characteristics that enabled them to survive in particular habitats. Wild horses lived on the open steppes of Central Asia and zebras on the grasslands of southern Africa. Asses flourished in hot desert lands.

long neck for grazing on the ground

large eyes, ears and nostrils for detecting predators

prominent mane of coarser hair on the back of the neck

coat of tightly packed, weatherproof hair

powerful legs – where a horse's main strength lies – particularly in the hind limbs

◄ **ZEBRA STRIPES**
All three species of zebra – the plains (*Equus burchelli*), mountain (*E. zebra*) and Grevy's (*E. grevyi*) – live in Africa. Each zebra has a unique pattern of stripes so others in the herd can recognize it.

▲ **FREE FERAL HORSES**
Mustangs are "feral" horses that roam in parts of North America. Feral describes horses that are descended from domestic animals that were turned loose or escaped and have reverted to the wild.

## ▼ HORSE HIGHLIGHTS

Przewalski's horse (*Equus ferus przewalskii*) from Mongolia is the last true species of wild horse. It has a large head and a squat body, but its general shape is shared by all equids. Although extinct in the wild, it survived in captivity and has been returned to the wild in nature reserves.

long tail, useful for swatting flies

## ► DESERT ASSES

The Persian onager (*Equus hemionus*) is a type of Asian wild ass that lives in Iran. It is very rare. The typical ass-shape is more compact than that of a horse. There are two other ass species, the kiang (*E. kiang*) which lives in Tibet and the African wild ass (*E. asinus*). All asses live in desert regions.

## ► ROAMING FREE

These horses are "semi-wild". Although they are owned by people, the horses are turned loose for most of the year and are left to range freely over a wide area.

### A Symbol of Purity

Ancient myths tell of beautiful, pure white horses with a single, magical horn. These gentle and shy creatures of fairy tales and legends came to be known as unicorns. The unicorn's first recorded appearance is on Assyrian stonework of 3,400 years ago. This may have been inspired by an animal described by early travellers from the East – the Indian rhinoceros! The unicorn resurfaced in the writings of the ancient Greeks, and in medieval myths. Traditionally, it is depicted with a spiral tusk like that of a narwhal (a type of whale), a lion's tail and cloven feet like a goat's.

# Shapes and Sizes

Equids take their place in the animal world as medium-size plant-eaters. Their heads and necks are long to suit a grazing lifestyle. Their bodies range in shape from the stocky zebras, with their broad heads and short legs, to the slender-headed, long-limbed Arab breed of domestic horse. Truly wild horses and zebras stand 1–1.22m/ 3–4ft tall at the shoulder. Domestic horses vary greatly in size because they have been bred for particular purposes. A shire horse, bred for heavy farm work, can stand up to 1.5m/5ft tall. They weigh around 1 tonne/ton, and can pull up to 50 tonnes/tons in weight. New miniature horse breeds may be the size of a large dog. Fully grown mares (female horses) – both domestic and wild – are usually about 10 per cent smaller than stallions (male horses).

▲ SCOTTISH MINIATURE

Shetland ponies are one of the smallest breeds of horse and very hardy. They have stocky bodies and short legs and range in height from 60cm to 1m/2 to 3ft. The ponies have lived semi-wild on the storm-lashed Shetland Isles off the Scottish coast for 2,000 years. Their diet is heather, rough grass and seaweed. In the 1800s, many were put to work in coal mines because they are small but remarkably strong.

▼ GERMAN GIANT

The Schwarzwälder Kaltblut, or Black Forest heavy horse, is a robust working horse standing up to 1.6m/5¼ft at the shoulder. It was bred to pull ploughs and wagons before tractors and trucks appeared. It is also tough and can withstand the harsh conditions in mountain regions. Today, the Schwarzwälder is rare, but it can be found pulling sleighs at ski resorts.

◄ **COWBOY CARRIER**

Criollo horses were bred from *baguales*, the feral horses of the Pampas grasslands in Argentina. These, in turn, were descended from Spanish horses that escaped from or were abandoned by explorers in the 1500s. Strong, agile and medium-size at about 1.5m/5ft, they make ideal mounts for cowboys and polo players.

**AFRICAN ANCESTOR ►**

The Nubian subspecies of the African wild ass stands up to 1.45m/4¾ft tall at the shoulder. It is thought to be the ancestor of the domestic donkey. Fully grown donkeys can be from 1m/3ft tall up to the size of a horse, depending on the breed.

▼ **BORN IN THE USA**

American mustangs are medium-size with a strong build, like the Spanish horses they are descended from. Their feet have evolved a special adaptation called a mule foot. The sole is concave, like that of a mule, to avoid getting bruised on rocky terrain.

▲ **LINK TO THE PAST**

Grevy's zebra is the largest wild equid. It may weigh nearly twice as much as a plains zebra. With its narrow stripes, large head, slender build and long legs, it is thought to resemble the common ancestor of all equids.

# Coats and Grooming

Horses have coats of tightly packed hairs that provide protection against the weather. Wild horses and asses are usually coloured grey or brown above and white below, blending in with the plains and deserts where they live. Many have a dark stripe running the length of their spine. Some, such as the African ass, have stripes on their legs, while zebras have stripes all over.

Wild equids have an erect mane of coarse hair. Its function is unclear, but it may provide some protection against biting insects and the weather. The tail is certainly used as a fly swatter. Horses have long tails of loose hair, while asses and zebras have tails ending with tufts of hair.

**▲ KEEPING WARM**

The length of a horse's hair varies according to where it lives. Horses that live in cold climates, such as this Dartmoor pony, have long hair and a thick mane. Horses often shed their heavy winter coats in spring. Equids in hot countries, such as the wild ass and zebra, have short hair all year around.

**▲ SCRATCH AN ITCH**

All horses and asses must go into great contortions to scratch some of the more inaccessible parts of their bodies. This khur, a type of ass from north-west India, uses its hind leg to scratch its neck.

**▲ SOCIAL GROOMING**

All equids groom each other, picking off fleas and ticks. Grooming keeps the coat in good condition by removing loose hair and dead skin. It also strengthens relationships.

**◄ IT'S A ROLL OVER**
Wallowing in grass, dust and dry or damp sand is one way horses keep their coats in good condition. It also helps remove dandruff and reduce external parasites such as blood-sucking ticks. Unlike cattle, all equids can roll over completely.

**▲ GROOMING NIBBLE**
A Camargue horse grooms its legs by nibbling its skin with its teeth. Just above the knee, on the inside of each leg, all equids have a wart-like, hairless callus. These are known as chestnuts. Their function is unknown.

**HELPING HAND ►**
Equids scratch the parts they cannot reach with teeth or hooves by rubbing against trees and rocks. There is often a line at popular scratching posts. Who goes first depends on social rank in the herd.

# Built for Speed

Equids are designed to be able to flee from predators. Their skeletons are lightweight, strong and geared for maximum speed with minimum energy. A horse's upper leg bones, for example, are fused into a single, strong bone, while in humans, their equivalents are two separate bones. The joints are less flexible than those of a human. Instead, they are strong in an up-and-down direction to support and protect powerful tendons and muscles. A horse's skeleton is designed to absorb the weight and impact of its body as it moves over the ground.

**▲ RESTING ON AUTOMATIC**

When equids are standing at rest, the patella (kneecap) slots into a groove in the femur (leg bone). This locks their back legs into an energy-saving position, just like our knees. Another mechanism keeps the horse's head from dropping to the ground. A ligament in the neck acts like a piece of elastic, returning the head to an upright resting position when the horse is not grazing.

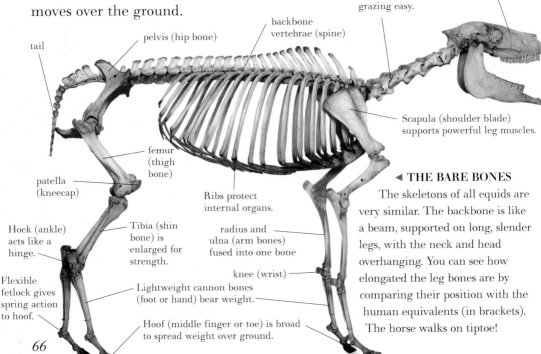

Long neck vertebrae make grazing easy.

long, narrow skull

backbone vertebrae (spine)

tail

pelvis (hip bone)

Scapula (shoulder blade) supports powerful leg muscles.

femur (thigh bone)

patella (kneecap)

Ribs protect internal organs.

**◀ THE BARE BONES**

The skeletons of all equids are very similar. The backbone is like a beam, supported on long, slender legs, with the neck and head overhanging. You can see how elongated the leg bones are by comparing their position with the human equivalents (in brackets). The horse walks on tiptoe!

Hock (ankle) acts like a hinge.

Tibia (shin bone) is enlarged for strength.

radius and ulna (arm bones) fused into one bone

knee (wrist)

Flexible fetlock gives spring action to hoof.

Lightweight cannon bones (foot or hand) bear weight.

Hoof (middle finger or toe) is broad to spread weight over ground.

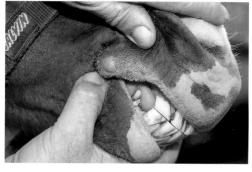

## ◀ SPACE FOR CHEWING

The long and narrow skull provides space for the big molar teeth, and enables the eye sockets to fit in behind them. This means that when the horse chews, there is no pressure on the eye. The large eye sockets provide enough space for the horse to have all-around vision.

## ▼ FIGHTING TEETH

Can you see the small tushes (or tusker) teeth, just behind the big incisors? They are used in fights between stallions. Females have very small tushes teeth or none at all.

### Pegasus

*Greek mythology tells the story of a winged horse called Pegasus. He appeared from the blood of the evil Medusa when she was beheaded. Pegasus was ridden by the hero Bellerophon. Together they defeated the fire-breathing monster, the Chimera. Bellerophon tried to ride Pegasus to heaven, but the gods were angry and he was thrown off and killed. Pegasus became a constellation in the night sky.*

## ▶ TEETH FOR THE JOB

Mares have 36–40 teeth, and stallions have 44 teeth. A horse's teeth are specially adapted for its diet. Chisel-shaped incisors at the front snip through grass. Molars at the side of the mouth grind down the grass before it is swallowed. The degree of wear on teeth is sometimes used to calculate a horse's age. This can be misleading, as some foods wear down the teeth more than others do.

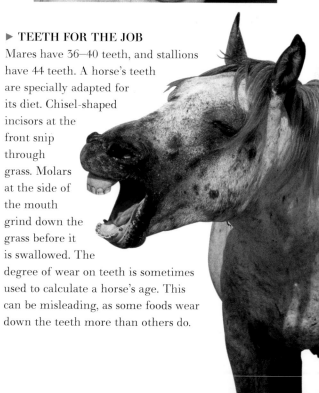

# Body Power

The horse is one of the fastest long-distance runners in the animal world. Its digestive system processes large quantities of food in order to extract sufficient energy. The digestive system is in two parts. The food is partly digested in the stomach, then moves quickly through to the hindgut (the cecum, the large colon and the small colon). Here, bacteria break down the cell walls of the plants. The nutrients are released, and special cells lining the gut are ready to absorb them.

Equids also have a big heart and large lungs. This allows them to run quickly and over a long distance. The bigger the heart, the faster the horse.

Elastic tendons are another speciality. Together with the joints and ligaments, they stretch and give like elastic to conserve energy and cushion impact on the ground when the horse is on the move.

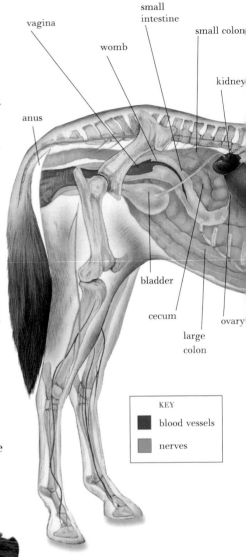

small intestine
vagina
womb
small colon
kidney
anus
bladder
cecum
ovary
large colon

KEY
■ blood vessels
■ nerves

◀ **FLEXIBLE LIPS**
The horse's mobile, sensitive lips are described as prehensile (able to grasp). They are used to select and pick food. When a horse wants to use its power of smell to full effect, it curls its lips back.

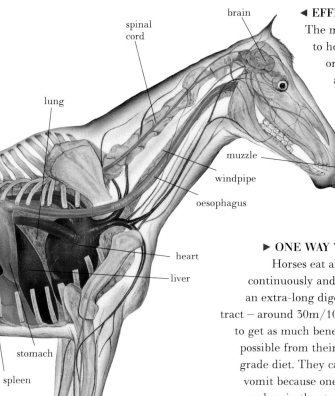

brain

spinal
cord

lung

muzzle

windpipe

oesophagus

heart

liver

stomach

spleen

### ◀ EFFICIENT BODYWORKS

The main body of the horse is big enough to house the powerful muscles and large organs that the animal needs for speed and endurance. The large heart, for example, pumps at 30–40 beats per minute when resting – about half the rate of a human's. This can rise to a top rate of 240 – nearly twice the rate of a human's – when working hard. This means that blood circulates around the body very efficiently.

### ▶ ONE WAY TRIP

Horses eat almost continuously and have an extra-long digestive tract – around 30m/100ft – to get as much benefit as possible from their low-grade diet. They cannot vomit because one-way valves in the stomach prevent food from being regurgitated. Eating something poisonous could, therefore, be fatal.

### ▶ MUSCLE POWER

Large masses of muscle enable horses to move quickly over long distances and to use their limbs in the most efficient way. Cheek muscles are extra-powerful too, to grind down tough food.

# Intelligence and Senses

The horse has a relatively large brain that interprets information from its well-developed senses. As a result, equids have excellent memories, a brilliant sense of direction and an extraordinary ability to sense mood and danger. The senses work together in other ways too. Eyes are set well back on each side of the skull, giving almost all-around vision. But there is a blind spot directly behind the head. To cover this, the horse swivels its ears right around, and switches over to its sense of hearing. Only when horses look straight ahead do both eyes operate together to give binocular vision. Then, it can see three-dimensional images and judge distances. This enables them to jump obstacles with great accuracy.

## ▲ CHECK IT OUT

A stallion uses its excellent sense of smell to check out deposits of dung and urine from another herd. He will find out how recently the other herd passed by, if it contains a mare in heat and if the herd is led by a stallion.

## GATHERING SMELLS ▶

Curling back the lips is a horse's reaction to unfamiliar smells, known as the flehmen reaction. This is also used to identify females who are in a receptive sexual state. With its acute sense of smell, a horse can be alerted to predators and detect subtle changes in food quality.

## ▲ THE TASTE TEST

Little is known about a horse's sense of taste, although it is likely to be fairly sensitive. This can be seen from the way it grazes, pushing aside some plants to reach others. Taste may also be involved when horses groom each other.

**▲ CLEVER HORSE**

Memory is important for survival. Remembering where water or food can be found and which plants are good to eat may be a matter of life or death for a wild horse. Horses do well in intelligence and memory tests. In one test, horses were taught to recognize patterns. When they were tested a year later they could remember almost all of them, a score far better than most humans could do.

**▼ SHARP EYES**

A horse can see objects clearly at short and long distances at the same time because they register on different areas of the eye. This is useful for keeping watch for predators while grazing. (Human eyes have variable focus that automatically adjusts to distances.) A horse can see better than a cat or a dog during daylight, and its night-time vision is also very good.

**◄ ALERT EARS**

All equids have ears that behave somewhat like radar dishes. They can turn in the direction of a sound quite independently of each other, while the rest of the body remains still. The rotating action is operated by no fewer than 16 muscles. This, together with the large size of the outer ear, means that a horse's sense of hearing is far more acute than a human's.

# Eating for Energy

Wild horses graze for about 16 hours a day, from early in the morning until around midnight. In hot countries, asses and zebras graze from dawn until late morning, rest during the hottest part of the day, and then graze again until late afternoon. All equids are vegetarian and have adapted to making the most of low-grade food, mainly grass.

The nutrients in grass are difficult for an animal's body to extract. Equids solve the problem by having an extra-long digestive system, and by pushing as much food as they can through their bodies. The food converts to energy in as short a time as possible. Horses nibble vegetation with their front incisor teeth, then grind it down with their molars before swallowing. It's a virtually nonstop cycle of eating, digesting and producing waste. Equids can survive on food of a poorer quality than cattle can.

▲ CHEW WELL!
A slow, deliberate style of eating ensures that food is thoroughly ground down. Cows have an extra stomach to help break food down, but horses have only one. This means that equids must chew slowly and wash the food down with plenty of saliva to aid digestion.

◄ HARD TIMES
Cold weather has made the ground hard, and snow covers the scant winter vegetation. These horses must paw at the ground to uncover the grass and dig up roots. They may even eat tree bark. Weak horses may not survive a hard winter.

**STRESS IN THE STABLE ▶**

When domestic horses are brought into stables, they are fed well but often only three times a day. This is very different from a horse's natural feeding pattern, which is continuous and varied grazing. Bored stabled horses sometimes develop "vices", such as crib-chewing, tongue swallowing and rug-chewing. Although a horse may be given nutritious fodder, it is denied its natural behaviour.

**◀ SURVIVAL IN DRY LAND**

Grevy's zebras live in dry thornbush country. If water is scarce, they migrate to the highlands. However, if water and grazing remain available, they stay and survive on grasses, or even bushes, that are too tough for other herbivores to eat. They dig water holes — and defend them fiercely.

**▲ ALTERNATIVE FOODS**

A semi-wild horse from the New Forest, England, uses its flexible lips to pick some gorse flowers. Horses often choose more interesting foods than grass when they are available. They push out unwanted bits with their tongue.

**▲ WATERHOLE**

Wild horses drink daily, although they can go without water for long periods of time. Most animals only drink fresh water. Wild asses, Grevy's and mountain zebras can tolerate brackish (stale, salty) water. This gives them a better chance of surviving droughts than fellow grazers, such as antelope.

# Social Life

All equids are herd animals. Horses, plains and mountain zebras form what is described as a "stable" herd. Each member of the herd knows everyone else. The groups are strictly structured, with each animal knowing its place. There is a single stallion with a harem of mares and their foals. Stable herds do not identify with a particular territory.

Wild asses and Grevy's zebras have a loose, or "unstable", herd structure. They live in dry habitats where individual dominant males defend territories that contain water and food. Females live in unstable groups, usually with related animals or with those of the same social status. They enter the territories of resident males to feed and drink, and so join their herds temporarily.

▲ **LEARNING BEHAVIOUR**
A foal learns its first lessons in survival from its mother. In a process called imprinting, foals bond to the animal they see most often, which is usually their mother, within a few days of being born. They later learn from watching other members of the herd.

▶ **BACHELOR BOYS**
Mustang colts have banded together in a bachelor group. At two to three years, they are old enough to form a threat to the reigning stallion, and have been driven from their herd. Lone stallions find survival difficult away from the herd.

### ▲ FERAL ORDER

This group of mustangs consists of a dominant stallion, six mares and a foal. The foal will have the same social status as its mother until it grows up. A filly (young female) may remain with the same herd, or she may be attracted elsewhere, or kidnapped by a rival stallion to join his herd.

### ◄ SOCIAL RISE

Each member of a herd of plains zebras has its position in the pecking order. Recently recruited mares are the least important. However, as they gain experience over time, they can climb the social ladder.

### ► FEMALE POWER

Like all semi-wild horses, these Icelandic ponies form a stable herd. It is usually the dominant mare who decides where to graze and when to move. The stallion keeps the group together and prevents mares from leaving the herd.

### ◄ SEASONAL CHANGE

Khurs live in the desert in small groups for most of the year. During the wet season there is more food, and khurs gather in larger groups of up to 50. They mate at this time of year.

# Communication

Because horses are social animals that live in herds, they need to communicate with each other. They have a wide range of expressive behaviour, ranging from sounds and smells to a complex body language.

Animals recognize each other by their appearance and smell, and certain sounds are common to all equids. The short whinny is a warning call, while the long version is a sign of contentment. Contact and territorial calls vary with each species. Horses whinny, asses bray, Grevy's zebras "bell" (so called because the sound is said to resemble a deep bell), mountain zebras whistle, and plains zebras bark. Horses, asses and zebras recognize and react to the calls of all other species of equids but do not respond to the calls of cattle or antelope.

▲ ON YOUR GUARD!
This horse has flattened its ears back in a threatening posture. It is showing its dominance without resorting to a fight. Ears flattened to the side may also indicate boredom or tiredness.

▲ BABY TALK
Young horses show respect to their elders by holding their ears to the side, displaying their teeth and making chewing movements. This is not a sign that the foal might bite but is rather like preparing for a mutual grooming session. It's a way of saying "I'm friendly."

▲ TAKING NOTE
Horses are alert to the signals of others in their herd. If one horse is curious about something, its ears will prick forward, and the rest of the herd will take an interest.

## ◄ MUTUAL GROOMING

Horses, like all other equids, will nibble a favourite partner, grooming those places they cannot reach for themselves. The amount of time two horses spend grooming each other shows how friendly they are. Grooming helps to keep a herd together, and it occurs even when coats are in perfect condition.

## ► FRIENDLY GREETING

When members of a herd meet up, they welcome each other with a series of greeting rituals. They may stretch heads, touch and sniff noses, push each other and then part. Good friends may lay their heads on each other's backs.

## ◄ WILD AT HEART

Mares often develop personal bonds with other horses in the herd. For domestic horses, this is usually with close relatives, such as sisters or adult daughters. In feral horses, these bonds are more likely to develop between unrelated mares. In all herds, the bonds are less strong in groups led by a stallion, because he becomes the mares' centre of attention.

# World View

Zebras and asses live in both temperate and dry, tropical regions. They roam over open landscapes such as the savannahs (grasslands) of Africa and the rocky plains and dry scrubland of Asia. Their range in these areas is limited by the extent of human settlement in their habitats.

Zebras are only found in Africa, south of the Sahara Desert. There are isolated populations of wild asses in eastern Africa, the Middle East and India.

Feral horses occur in many parts of the world, wherever they have been released by or have escaped from people. Semi-wild herds are allowed to run free in many European countries, where large tracts of open country are left unfenced.

NORTH AMERICA

1   8

2

3

SOUTH AMERICA

4

◀ **AUSTRALIA**
Brumbies are found in a wide range of habitats throughout Australia. They run wild over dry plains, wetlands, grasslands and in the mountains. Australia has the largest number of feral horses in the world.

▼ **SOUTH AMERICA**
These feral horses live on the Falkland Islands, near Argentina. They were taken there by the French in 1764. Their home is one of bleak moorland, sand-dunes and rocks.

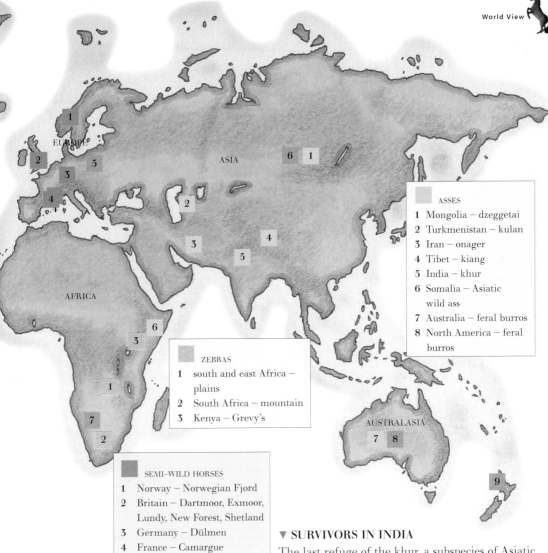

**ASES**

1 Mongolia – dzeggetai
2 Turkmenistan – kulan
3 Iran – onager
4 Tibet – kiang
5 India – khur
6 Somalia – Asiatic
wild ass
7 Australia – feral burros
8 North America – feral
burros

**ZEBRAS**

1 south and east Africa –
plains
2 South Africa – mountain
3 Kenya – Grevy's

**SEMI-WILD HORSES**

1 Norway – Norwegian Fjord
2 Britain – Dartmoor, Exmoor,
Lundy, New Forest, Shetland
3 Germany – Dülmen
4 France – Camargue

**FERAL HORSES**

1 Western North America – mustang
2 Sable Island, Canada – Sable Island
3 Assateague Island, USA – Assateague,
Chincoteague
4 Argentina – Criollo
5 Poland – tarpan
6 Mongolia – Przewalski
7 Namibia – Namib Desert
8 Australia – brumby
9 New Zealand – Kaimanawa

## ▼ SURVIVORS IN INDIA

The last refuge of the khur, a subspecies of Asiatic
wild ass, is an area of bleak desert called the Rann
of Kachchh. It lies in Gujarat, in the north-west
corner of India, near the border with Pakistan.

# Early Ancestors

The earliest horselike creatures were the size of a fox. They appeared on Earth about 54 million years ago. There was not much change in the equine body for the next 20 million years. Legs became longer, though, making flight from predators and long-distance travel easier.

Then, grassland vegetation evolved. Earlier species had lived in forests and browsed on woody plants and trees. The new food supply triggered many different horselike species to evolve. The ones that survived best in the open grasslands were those with the longest legs and biggest bodies. Less than two million years ago, the one species that was to survive as the modern horse evolved. It is called *Equus* (from which we get the word equestrian).

Early horses had digits like human fingers and toes. To help the horse run faster, these gradually reduced to the single digit of the hoof.

▲ **ECHOES OF THE PAST**
Przewalski's horse is similar in appearance to the original *Equus* species. The body is short and stocky, the head is large and there is a dark strip along the spine.

▼ **EVOLUTION AND SURVIVAL**
Biologists often use the development of the horse to teach evolution because there are so many prehistoric horse fossils. Many different branches of horse evolved from around 20 million years ago (mya), but only *Equus*, the ancestor of the modern horse, survived. *Equus* died out in the Americas because of climatic changes at the end of the Ice Age. Its domestication by humans in Asia saved it from extinction.

*Hyracotherium*
54 mya

*Mesohippus*
30 mya

*Merychippus*
20 mya

*Equus*
2 mya

▶ **FLAT-FOOTED ANCESTOR**

One of the earliest fossil horses is *Hyracotherium* or *Eohippus*. It was no bigger than a dog and was a general plant eater. It had four digits on its front foot and three on the hind foot, and ran on the flat of its feet rather than on its toes.

◀ **BROWSING EXPERT**

*Mesohippus* appeared 38–25 mya. Its forefoot had three digits, and it was bigger than *Hyracotherium*. The chewing surface of its teeth increased so that it could browse more efficiently on the shoots and leaves of trees and shrubs.

**VICTIM OF SUCCESS** ▶

The three-toed horse, *Anchitherium*, was one of many horselike creatures that evolved 25–5 mya. It invaded Eurasia from North America but became extinct and had no descendants. It may have become very well adapted to a particular environment. When that environment disappeared, due to climatic change, *Anchitherium* died out.

◀ **GRASSLAND INHABITANT**

The great expansion of savannah grassland around 20 mya in North America gave rise to horses such as *Merychippus*. The browsers were still around, but new species evolved that were specially adapted to grassland vegetation and open country. Their legs and stride became longer, and their backs strengthened, so that they could flee from danger.

# BEARS
# AND
# PANDAS

There are eight living species of bear
and they live in both warm and cold
climates all over the world, from Arctic
tundra and mountain slopes to scrub
desert and tropical forest. Most
bears are meat-eaters, although
with the exception of the
polar bear they will eat almost
anything they can find.

*Author*: Michael Bright
*Consultant*: Dr Douglas Richardson
Zoological Director, Rome Zoo

# The Bear Facts

Bears may look large, cuddly and appealing, but in reality they are enormously powerful animals. Bears are mammals with bodies covered in thick fur. They are heavily built with short tails and large claws. Most bears are omnivores (eating both animals and plants), and enjoy a mixed diet with the occasional meat snack. The exceptions are the polar bear, which feasts on the blubber (fat) of seals, and the giant panda, which eats only bamboo. There are eight living species of bear: the brown bear, American black bear, Asiatic black bear, polar bear, sun bear, sloth bear, spectacled bear, and the giant panda. They live in both cold and tropical regions of the world. Bears are solitary, and many of them are unpredictable, which makes them potentially dangerous to people.

**WINNIE-THE-POOH**
*The teddy bear Winnie-the-Pooh was created by A.A. Milne. Like real bears, he loved honey. Teddy bears became popular as toys in the early 1900s. The President of the United States, Theodore Roosevelt, refused to shoot a bear cub on a hunting trip. Toy bears went on sale soon after, and were known as "teddy's bears."*

**BEAR FACE**
The brown bear shares the huge dog-like head and face of all bears. Bears have prominent noses, but relatively small eyes and ears. This is because they rely mostly on their sense of smell to help them find food.

**BIG FLAT FEET**
A polar bear's feet are broad, flat and furry. The five long, curved claws cannot be retracted (pulled back). One swipe could kill a seal instantly.

Thick fur covers a heavily built body.

A bear's main strength is in its massive shoulders and front legs.

Its broad, flat feet have long claws.

## ◄ POINTS OF A BEAR

The brown bear is called the grizzly bear in North America. Fully grown brown bears weigh nearly half a tonne/ ton. They fear no animals other than humans. They can chase prey at high speeds, but they seldom do as they feed mainly on plants.

A bear has a large head, with small eyes and erect, rounded ears.

The long, prominent, dog-like snout dominates the face.

## ▲ GIANT PANDA

China's giant panda, with its distinctive black and white coat, is a very unusual bear. Unlike most other bears, which will eat anything, pandas feed almost exclusively on the bamboo plant.

## ◄ ARCTIC NOMAD

Most bears lead a solitary life. The polar bear wanders alone across the Arctic sea ice. It will not usually tolerate other bears. The exceptions are bears that congregate at rubbish (garbage) dumps, or mothers with cubs, as shown here.

85

**▲ SLOTH BEAR**

Very little is known about the origins of the Indian sloth bear (*Melursus ursinus*). Few fossils (remains preserved in stone) have been found for this species of tropical bear. Sloth bears are thought to have evolved during an ice age that started about 1.6 million years ago.

# Family Groups

The eight species of living bears belong to the family Ursidae. They all have the same general appearance, but in different parts of the world, each is adapted to a particular lifestyle. Bears in tropical places tend to be small and spend more time in the trees. Those in northern lands are larger and live mostly on the ground. To help them study bears, scientists divide the eight living species into three smaller groups, or subfamilies. The giant panda and spectacled bear are the sole survivors of two ancient subfamilies, the Ailuropodinae and Tremarctinae. The rest of the bears are grouped together in a third subfamily, the Ursinae. A bear's Latin name reveals how that particular species is grouped.

**◀ BROWN BEAR**

Brown bears (*Ursus arctos*) first appeared in China about 500,000 years ago. From there they migrated right across the Northern Hemisphere into North America and Europe.

**▲ POLAR BEAR**

The polar bear (*Ursus maritimus*) is the most recent bear to have evolved. Its closest relative is the brown bear. In zoos, polar bears and brown bears are sometimes interbred.

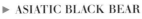

**▲ GIANT PANDA**

The giant panda (*Ailuropoda melanoleuca*) is the sole survivor of the earliest group of bears, the Ailuropodinae. It first appeared around 10 million years ago. Fossils of giant pandas have been found throughout China.

**▶ ASIATIC BLACK BEAR**

The Asiatic black bear evolved from the same ancestor as most other species of bear, *Ursus minimus*. It is found mainly in the hilly areas of southern Russia, Japan and southern Asia. This bear is in danger of extinction in some areas, because it is still hunted for food and medicine.

**▼ SUN BEAR**

The sun bear (*Helarctos malayanus*) is another tropical bear about which very little is known. It too probably evolved during the last Ice Age. Today, sun bears are under threat from pressures such as farming. The bears tear out the hearts of oil palms, which ruins the crop.

**▼ SPECTACLED BEAR**

The spectacled bear (*Tremarctos ornatus*) evolved about 2 million years ago. It is the last remaining member of a group of primitive short-faced bears (Tremarctinae) that were found mainly in the Americas.

sloth bear
(*Melursus
ursinus*)

# Size of a Bear

The two largest bears in the world are
the polar bear and the brown bears of Kodiak
Island, Alaska. Kodiak bears grow up to
2.7m/9ft long and can weigh 439kg/975lb,
while polar bears have a maximum length of
3m/10ft and weigh as much as 644kg/1,430lb.
Brown bears in Europe and Asia are smaller
than grizzlies (American brown bears). The
largest is the Kamchatka brown bear of
eastern Russia. A full-size adult grizzly weighs
as much as a bison, and even the smallest is
bigger than a wolf. The smallest bear is the
sun bear at 1.4m/4½ft long and 65kg/143lb.
In between are American and Asiatic black
bears (both 1.7m/5½ft long and up to 119kg/
264lb), the spectacled bear (2m/7ft long,
up to 198kg/440lb) and the sloth bear
(1.8m/6ft long, up to 114kg/253lb).

## ▲ SLOTH BEAR

Long curved claws, a mobile snout and
long fur are the distinguishing features
of the sloth bear. It lives in India
and Sri Lanka and feeds mainly
on insects called termites
and on fruit.

American
black bear
(*Ursus
americanus*)

## ▼ SPECTACLED BEAR

The South American spectacled bear
gets its name from the distinctive
markings on its face. It is the only
bear found in South America,
and is a good climber.

spectacled bear
(*Tremarctos ornatus*)

## ▲ AMERICAN BLACK BEAR

There are ten times as many black bears as
brown bears living in the forests of North
America. Black bears resemble small brown
bears, except that they lack a shoulder hump.

**Polar bear**
*(Ursus maritimus)*

### ◄ ICE GIANT

The male polar bear is a giant among
bears. It is bigger than pandas and brown
bears, but less robustly built, with a
longer head and neck. Female polar
bears are smaller, and each tends to
weigh less than half as much as a
grown adult male. Polar bears live in
the frozen lands of the Arctic. They
can swim in the icy sea, protected by
fur and layers of
thick fat.

**brown bear**
*(Ursus arctos)*

### ► BIG BROWN BEARS

The brown bear is the most common bear and
lives in Europe, Asia and North America. Its size
varies in different parts of the world. This is due
to diet and climate rather than any genetic
differences. For example, large Kodiak bears
catch a lot of protein-rich salmon.

### ▼ THE SUN BEAR

The sun bear is the smallest of all the bears.
It lives in the thick forests of South-east
Asia. Because it lives in a hot tropical
climate, the sun bear also has a short
coat. Its feet have naked soles and long,
curved claws, which can grip well
when climbing trees.

**Did you know?** The heaviest known Kodiak brown bears weigh up to 750kg /1650lb.

**sun bear**
*(Helarctos malayanus)*

89

# Bones and Teeth

Bears have a large and massive skull, a solidly built skeleton, relatively short and stocky limbs, a small tail and short feet. Each foot has five equal-size digits (toes), with strong, curved claws for digging and tearing. The claws cannot be retracted so are constantly worn down. In most bears' jaws, the carnassial teeth (large meat-shearing teeth) common to all carnivores are reduced or even missing. Instead, bears have broad flat molars for crushing plant food. Only the polar bear has flesh-slicing carnassials to deal with its animal prey. The sloth bear is also unusual because it lacks the inner pair of upper incisors (front teeth). This helps it suck up insects from their nests.

▲ A MIGHTY ROAR
As this bear roars, it bares its large canine teeth. However, on average only 20 per cent of a brown bear's diet is made up of animal flesh. Instead, bears rely on their large molars to crush their vegetable food.

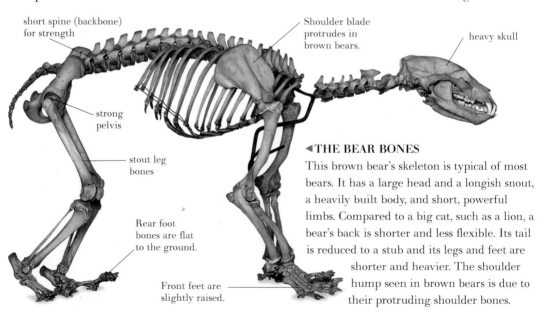

short spine (backbone) for strength

Shoulder blade protrudes in brown bears.

heavy skull

strong pelvis

stout leg bones

Rear foot bones are flat to the ground.

Front feet are slightly raised.

◀ THE BEAR BONES
This brown bear's skeleton is typical of most bears. It has a large head and a longish snout, a heavily built body, and short, powerful limbs. Compared to a big cat, such as a lion, a bear's back is shorter and less flexible. Its tail is reduced to a stub and its legs and feet are shorter and heavier. The shoulder hump seen in brown bears is due to their protruding shoulder bones.

90

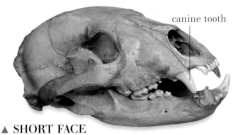

canine tooth

carnassial tooth

## ▲ SHORT FACE

This brown bear's skull is shorter and more robust than that of the polar bear. North American brown bears tend to have larger skulls than bears in other parts of the world.

## ▲ LONG FACE

This polar bear's skull is longer and more slender than that of other bears. Like other carnivores, it has prominent, dagger-like canine teeth and meat-slicing carnassials at the back.

## ▲ PRIMITIVE BEAR

The spectacled bear is grouped separately from other bears. Apart from the giant panda, it is the most primitive bear. Its short muzzle and the unique arrangement of teeth in its jaw give it a more rounded head shape than its fellow bears.

## ▲ GIANT PANDA

The giant panda has the most massive skull in relation to its size of all living bears. Its round face and head are the result of large jaw muscles needed to grind tough bamboo stems.

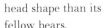

## ▶ SLENDER SWIMMING BEAR

The polar bear has a more elongated body than other bears. Its neck and skull are relatively long and slim. These are adaptations that help the bear to swim through water by streamlining its body. It also has lower shoulders, well-developed hindquarters and large, broad feet.

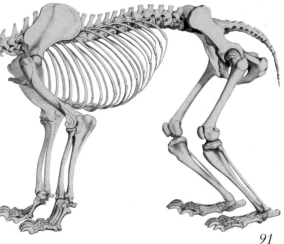

# Strong Muscles

Bears are the bullies of the animal kingdom. Their strength is mainly in the muscles of their legs and shoulders. Unlike cats and dogs, which run on their toes for speed, bears walk on the flat soles of their broad feet, just as humans do. What bears lack in speed they make up for in strength. Their powerful, mobile limbs can be put to good use digging, climbing, fishing and fighting. They will attack others of their own kind and defend themselves skilfully from enemies. In a fight, a bear can do considerable damage and survives by sheer brute force. Male bears are generally much larger than females of the same species.

▲ **CLAWS DOWN**

The sun bear has particularly large, curved claws for climbing trees. It spends most of the day sleeping or sunbathing in the branches. At night it strips off bark with its claws, looking for insects and honey in bees' nests.

◀ **PUTTING ON WEIGHT**

This grizzly bear is at peak size. Most bears change size as the seasons pass. They are large and well-fed in autumn, ready for their winter hibernation. When they emerge in spring, they are scrawny with sagging coats.

*BEOWULF*

*An Anglo-Saxon poem tells of the hero Beowulf (sometimes translated as 'bear-wolf'). He had the strength of a bear and had many heroic adventures. Here, Beowulf as an old man lies dying from the wounds inflicted on him by a fire-breathing dragon.*

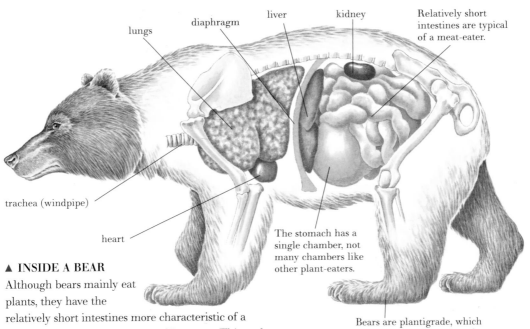

lungs
diaphragm
liver
kidney
Relatively short intestines are typical of a meat-eater.

trachea (windpipe)

heart

The stomach has a single chamber, not many chambers like other plant-eaters.

Bears are plantigrade, which means they walk on the soles of their feet.

## ▲ INSIDE A BEAR

Although bears mainly eat plants, they have the relatively short intestines more characteristic of a meat-eater, instead of a long gut like a cow. This makes it hard for them to digest their food. Strangely, the bamboo-eating giant panda has the shortest gut of all. Because of this, it can digest no more than 20 percent of what it eats, compared to 60 percent for a cow.

## ▲ SHORT BURSTS

Bears are not particularly agile and swift, but they can run fast over short distances. The brown bear can charge at 48kph/30mph (lions reach about 64kph/40mph) and does sometimes chase its food. A bear at full charge is a frightening sight and quickly scares away enemies.

## ▲ SWEET TOOTH

The sun bear's long, slender tongue is ideal for licking honey from bees' nests and for scooping up termites and other insects. Like all bears, it has mobile lips, a flexible snout and strong jaws.

93

# Warm Fur

All bears have thick fur all over their bodies, including the face. Ground-living bears even have fur between the pads of their feet, while the soles of tree-climbing bears are naked. A thick coat insulates well in the cold but can cause overheating in the summer, so many bears moult. Most bears' coats tend to be brown, black, cinnamon (reddish-brown), grey or white, and some have face and chest markings. The most strikingly marked bear is the giant panda. Its contrasting black and white pattern blends in with the shadowy bamboo of its mountain home. This is particularly so at dawn and dusk, the panda's most active times. In winter, against snow, black rocks and trees, the panda is almost invisible.

▲ **WHITE BEAR**
The Chinese call the giant panda *bei-shung* (white bear). It is considered to be basically white with black ears, eye patches, legs and shoulders. Sometimes the black areas have a chestnut-reddish tinge.

▲ **VELVET COAT**
The sun bear has relatively short fur, a little like velvet. It is generally black with a grey to orange muzzle and pale feet. Some bears have white or pale orange-yellow, crescent-shaped markings on the chest.

**BERSERKIR**
*Among the most feared of Viking warriors were berserkirs. They were named after the bear pelts or bear-skin shirts they wore. Berserkirs worked themselves up into a frenzy before battle. We still use the Norse word "berserk" to mean crazy or wild. This walrus ivory berserkir is part of a chess set from the island of Lewis off the west coast of Scotland. The berserkir is shown biting his shield and clasping his sword in the rage of battle.*

## ▲ BEAR FOOT

The broad, flat paw of a brown bear has thick fur on the upper surface and some between the toes, too. Ground-living bears, such as the brown bear, use their claws to hold on to a salmon or to catch and kill a young deer.

## ▼ SILVER TIP

The grizzly (American brown bear) gets its name from the way in which the long hairs of its shoulders and back are frosted with white. This gives the bear's coat a grizzled appearance. Brown bears, like the grizzly, are usually a dark brown colour, but they may also be any shade between light cream and black.

## ▲ FACIAL MARKINGS

The spectacled bear is generally dark brown or black. It has an unmistakable spectacle-like pattern of white or yellowish hairs around the eyes and across the nose. These markings may extend to the chest.

## ► LONG HAIR

The sloth bear has long, black shaggy fur. The longest hair is between the shoulders. The black fur can be tinged with brown or grey. There is a white, or yellow to chestnut-brown, patch in the shape of a U or Y on the bear's chest. Chest markings may act as a warning sign when the bear stands up.

# Using Brain and Senses

All bears are very intelligent. Size for size, they have larger brains than other carnivores, such as dogs and cats. They can remember sources of food and are very curious. Bears use their brains to find food or a mate, and to stay out of trouble. However, since they are mainly solitary plant-eaters they have little need to think of hunting tactics or ways of communication. They rely on smell (the part of their brains that detects scent is the largest of any carnivore), with small eyes and ears compared to their head size. Bears often appear short-sighted, although they have colour vision to recognize edible fruits and nuts. People can easily happen upon a bear and take it by surprise, prompting the startled animal to attack in self-defence.

**▼ SCENT MARKING**
An American black bear cub practises marking a tree by scratching. When it is older, the bear will leave a scent mark to indicate to other bears that the territory is occupied.

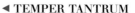

**◄ TEMPER TANTRUM**
A threatened bear puts on a fierce display. First it beats the ground or vegetation with its front feet. Then it stands up on its back legs to look larger. This is accompanied by a high-pitched snorting through open lips or a series of hoarse barks. The display of aggression finishes with snapping the jaws together.

## ▲ FOLLOW YOUR NOSE

A brown bear relies more on smell than sight. It often raises its head and sniffs the air to check out who or what is around. It can detect the faintest trace of a smell.

## ▼ GETTING TO KNOW YOU

Polar bear cubs rub against their mother to spread her scent over themselves. Smell allows a mother and cubs to recognize each other. They also communicate with sounds. Distressed cubs make low-pitched snores that develop into high whines.

### BRUNO THE BEAR

*Aesop's Fables are a set of tales written by the ancient Greek writer Aesop. One fable features Bruno the bear. He is shown as stupid and easily deceived. Bears were considered slow-witted because they sleep a lot. But Bruno was kind, unlike the cunning Reynard the fox. Bruno cared about others and forgave those who played pranks on him. Bruno was the forerunner of characters such as Winnie-the-Pooh.*

## ▲ SNOWY SCENT TRAIL

Even in the Arctic, polar bears can pick up the trails of other bears and follow them. There are few objects around for polar bears to use as scent posts, so trails may be marked by dribbling urine on the ground.

# Finding Food

Most bears eat whatever is available at different times of the year. They have binges and store fat in times of plenty, then fast when food is scarce. Brown bears are typical of most bears in that they eat an enormous variety of food, from grasses, herbs and berries to ants and other insects. They also catch salmon and rodents, and on rare occasions hunt down bigger game, such as caribou, seals and birds. Only polar bears eat almost entirely meat, especially young seals. In summer, however, as the ice melts and they are unable to hunt, polar bears supplement their diet with grasses and berries. All bears, even the bamboo-loving panda, also scavenge on the carcasses of prey left by other animals. They often rummage through rubbish bins (garbage cans) and rubbish (trash) left behind in campsites.

**GOLDILOCKS**
*The famous story of "Goldilocks and the Three Bears" was first told in 1837. In the story, the bears and their ability to organize themselves properly are used to make a strong moral point. In contrast, Goldilocks is shown as a foolish, unthinking girl.*

▶ **HUNTING DOWN A MEAL**
This American black bear has caught a white-tailed deer fawn. Both black and brown bears are successful hunters. They are able to ambush large animals and kill them by using their considerable bulk, strong paws and jaws. The size of the bear determines the size of its prey. Large brown bears may prey on moose, caribou, bison, musk oxen, seals and stranded whales. Black bears are smaller than brown bears and take smaller prey, such as deer fawns, lemmings and hares. Roots, fruit, seeds and nuts, however, form up to 80 percent of brown and black bears' diets.

## ▶ WALRUS CITY

Polar bears arrive on the northern coast of Russia each year to hunt walruses that have come there to breed. Enormous adult walruses shrug off attacks, but the young walrus pups are more vulnerable.

## ▲ BEACHCOMBING

Brown bears are attracted to beaches beside rivers and in estuaries. They overturn stones to feed on aquatic creatures, such as crabs and crayfish, that are hiding underneath.

## ▲ FRUIT LOVERS

An American black bear snacks on the ripe berries of a mountain ash tree. It carefully uses its incisors to strip the berries from their woody branch.

## ▲ INSECT EATERS

Two sloth bear cubs learn to dig up termites. The sloth bear uses its sickle-shaped claws to break open ant hills, bees' nests and termite mounds. Because it feeds mainly on termites, it has an ingenious way of collecting its insect food. First, it blows away the dust. Then it forms a suction tube with its mouth and tongue, through which it can vacuum up its food.

99

# Winter Hibernation

Black bears, brown bears and pregnant female polar bears hibernate. They do so because food is scarce, not because of the cold. Scientists argued for years whether bears truly hibernate or merely doze during the winter months. Now, according to recent research, the hibernation of bears is thought to be even more complete than that of small mammals. During hibernation, a brown bear's heart rate drops to about 35 beats per minute, half its normal rate. American black bears reduce their blood temperature by at least one degree. They do not eat or drink for up to four months. Bears survive only on the fat that they have stored during the summer. A bear might have lost up to 50 percent of its weight by the end of the winter.

▲ FAT BEARS

Before the winter hibernation a bear can become quite obese. Fat reserves make up over half this black bear's weight. It needs this bulk to make sure that it has enough fat on its body to survive the winter fast. In the weeks leading up to hibernation, a bear must consume large amounts of energy-rich foods, such as salmon.

Did you know?
Some hibernating bears sleep for 5½ months non-stop.

◀ HOME COMFORTS

A brown bear pulls in grass and leaves to cushion its winter den. American black bears and brown bears sleep in small, specially dug dens. These are usually found on the sunny, south-facing slopes of mountains.

## ▲ SCANDINAVIAN REFUGE

A hole dug by a brown bear serves as its winter den in this Swedish forest. Bears spend winter in much stranger places, such as under cabins occupied by people, under bridges or beside busy roads.

## ▲ READY FOR ACTION

If disturbed, a bear wakes easily from its winter sleep. Although it is dormant, a bear's body is ready for action. It is able to defend itself immediately against predators, such as a hungry wolf pack.

## ▲ SNOW HOUSE

Female polar bears leave the drifting floes in winter and head inland to excavate a nursery den. They dig deep down into the snow and ice, tunnelling about 4.5m/15ft into the ground. Here they will give birth to their cubs. In severe weather, a male polar bear rests by lying down and allowing himself to be covered by an insulating layer of snow.

## ▲ WINTER NURSERY

In the early winter, one bear enters a den, but three might emerge in spring. Female polar bears, like most bears, give birth (usually to twins) while hidden in their dens. The tiny cubs are born in the middle of winter, in December or January.

*101*

# Where Bears are Found

Bears are found in a variety of habitats, including the Arctic tundra, mountain slopes, scrub desert, temperate and tropical forests and tropical grasslands. Each species of bear, however, has its own preferred environment. The polar bear, for example, inhabits the lands and sea ice bordering the Arctic Ocean. It favours the shoreline areas where the ice breaks up and cracks appear, as this is where seals congregate. Most other bears are less specialized and have the uncanny ability to turn up wherever food is abundant. However, many of the wilderness areas where bears live are under threat. Habitat loss, as more land is cultivated for farmland and forests all over the world are cut down, is a major threat to many bears.

▲ IN THE BAMBOO FORESTS

The giant panda is restricted to areas of abundant bamboo forest. It was once much more widespread across eastern Asia, but it now survives in just three provinces of western China – Gansu, Shanxi and Sichuan.

▼ MOUNTAIN BEAR

The spectacled bear lives in South America. It lives high in the Andes Mountains of Peru, Ecuador, Venezuela and Colombia. It is found in forests, including rainforests, cloud forests and dry forests, as well as on steppes (grassland) and rocky outcrops.

▲ BROWN BEAR

The brown bear is the most widespread of all bears. It is found in Europe, the Middle East and across Russia and northern Asia to Japan. North American brown bears live in Alaska and the Canadian Rockies.

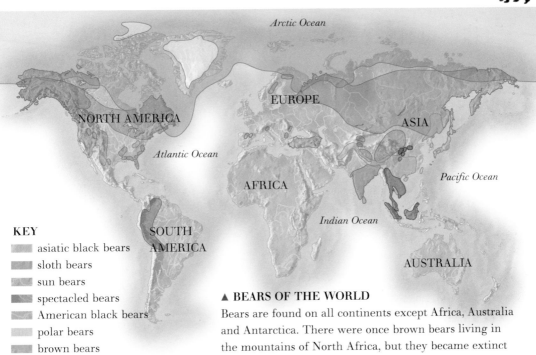

Arctic Ocean

EUROPE

NORTH AMERICA

ASIA

Atlantic Ocean

Pacific Ocean

AFRICA

Indian Ocean

SOUTH
AMERICA

AUSTRALIA

**KEY**
- asiatic black bears
- sloth bears
- sun bears
- spectacled bears
- American black bears
- polar bears
- brown bears
- giant pandas

## ▲ BEARS OF THE WORLD

Bears are found on all continents except Africa, Australia and Antarctica. There were once brown bears living in the mountains of North Africa, but they became extinct (died out) in the 1800s.

## ▲ ASIATIC BLACK BEAR

The Asiatic black bear lives in mountainous regions over a wide area of southern and eastern Asia. It is found in northern India, Pakistan, Japan and Taiwan.

## ▲ LIFE IN THE FOREST

The sloth bear (*above*) lives in dense, dry forests in India and Sri Lanka. The Malayan sun bear lives in similar lowland but tropical forests of South-east Asia. It is also thought to live in Yunnan in southern China, although no recent sightings have been reported.

103

# Finding the Way

Bears have an uncanny knack of finding their way home even in unfamiliar territory. How they do this is only just beginning to be understood. For long distances, they rely on an ability to detect the earth's magnetic field. This provides them with a magnetic map of their world and a compass to find their way around. When closer to home, they recognize familiar landmarks. In fact, bears have amazing memories, especially where food is involved. For example, a mother and her cubs are known to have trekked 39km/24 miles to a favourite oak tree to feast on acorns. Five years later, the same cubs (now adults) were reported to have been seen at the same tree.

**STARS IN THE SKY**
*The Great Bear constellation in the Northern Hemisphere is known to astronomers as Ursa Major. In Greek mythology, it was said to have been made in the shape of a she-bear and placed in the heavens by Zeus. The Great Bear is also worshipped in Hindu mythology as the power that keeps the heavens turning. The Inuit believe these stars represent a bear being continually chased by dogs.*

▲ **ARCTIC NOMADS**
Polar bears are capable of swimming long distances between ice floes at speeds of up to 10kph/6mph. They may travel thousands of miles across the frozen Arctic Ocean and the surrounding lands in search of prey.

▲ **PROBLEM BEAR**
A sedated polar bear is transported a safe distance out of town. Problem bears are often moved this way, but they unerringly find their way back.

## ◄ TO AND FROM THE FOREST

The polar bears of Hudson Bay, Canada, migrate to the forests in the summer and return to hunt on the sea ice in the winter. On their return journey, they often stop off at the town of Churchill. They gather at the rubbish (garbage) dump to feed, while they wait for ice to re-form.

### KEY

 Bears return to ice in winter

 Bears come ashore in June and July

 Bears walk north in autumn

## ▲ REGULAR ROUTES

Polar bears move quickly, even on shifting ice floes. A bear moving north, for example, against the southward-drifting ice in the Greenland Sea, can travel up to 80km/50 miles in a day.

## ▲ HAVING KNOWLEDGE

Male brown bears live in large home ranges covering several hundred square kilometers/miles. They must remember the locations of food and when it is available.

# Ancient Bears

There were bears living in the past that were much bigger than today's huge Kodiak and polar bears. The giant short-faced bear, weighing over 990kg/2,200lb, was twice the size of a Kodiak. It is the largest known carnivorous mammal ever to have lived on land. However, bears had much smaller beginnings. The first recognizable bear appeared about 20 million years ago. Called the dawn bear, it was about the size of a fox. Early bears split into three groups. The first group, the Ailuropodinae, followed a plant-based diet, and of these only the giant panda still survives. The second group, Tremarctinae, included many species of short-faced bears whose only living relative today is the spectacled bear. The third group, Ursinae, includes most of the bears we see today, as well as the now-extinct cave bears.

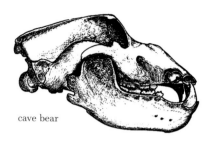

cave bear

brown bear

### ▲ BIG HEAD

The ancient cave bear (*Ursus spelaeus*) had a bigger skull than modern brown bears. Its high-domed skull anchored powerful chewing muscles. Enormous back teeth show that it mainly ate plants. It died out about 10,000 years ago.

### ◄ DAWN BEAR

Evolving from an animal that looked part dog, part bear and part raccoon, the dawn bear (*Ursavus elmensis*) was the ancestor of all known bears living today. Twenty million years ago, it probably spent most of its time hunting in the tree-tops. From studying its teeth, scientists think the dawn bear supplemented its diet of meat with plant material and insects.

## ▶ GIANT SHORT-FACED BEAR

The giant short-faced bear
(*Arctodus simus*) had much
longer legs than today's bears and
probably ran down its prey. In profile it
resembled a big cat. In its jaws were canine
teeth capable of delivering a killing bite and
back teeth for shearing meat. It probably hunted
ancient camels, bison and horses that once lived
on the plains of North America. The only living
descendant of the short-faced bear is the
spectacled bear (*Tremarctos ornatus*), the sole
species of bear to be found in South America.

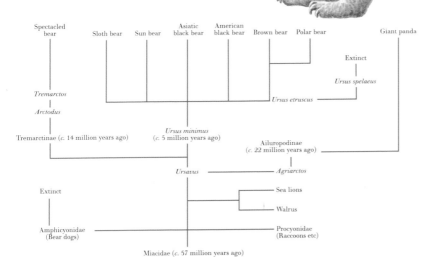

## ◀ FAMILY OF BEARS

This chart shows
how ancient bears
gave rise to modern
ones. The more
ancient bears are at
the bottom, and the
modern bears are
at the top.

## ◀ GREAT EUROPEAN CAVE BEAR

About 500,000 years ago, the cave
bear (*Ursus spelaeus*) evolved.
It was about the size of today's
Kodiak bears, with massive front legs,
broad paws with claws, and a huge
head and large muzzle. Large numbers
of bones found in caves throughout
Europe indicate that many died during
winter hibernation, probably because they
failed to put on enough fat to survive until spring.

107

# MONKEYS

Primates are human's closest relatives
and they have been around for 35
million years. These tree-loving
creatures have large brains, versatile tails
and opposing thumbs, which have
enabled them to develop a whole range
of acrobatic skills as well as complex
social lives and the ability to learn
and remember useful information.

*Author*: Tom Jackson
*Consultant*: Rachel Hevesi
The Monkey Sanctuary Trust

# Prosimians – The First Primates

The earliest primates roamed the world about 25 million years before monkeys evolved. They were the prosimians – which means "pre-monkeys". Amazingly, there are still many species of prosimians alive today, including aye-ayes, bush babies, lemurs, lorises and tarsiers.

The prosimians' hands mark them as primates. They have flexible fingers, and thumbs that work in opposite directions, making it possible for them to hold and pick things up.

Prosimians rely heavily on their sense of smell to communicate and to find food. The advanced primates – the monkeys and apes – use their sight more. In areas where monkeys and prosimians lived together and competed for the same food, the monkeys were more successful, and so prosimians had to develop specialized tactics to survive.

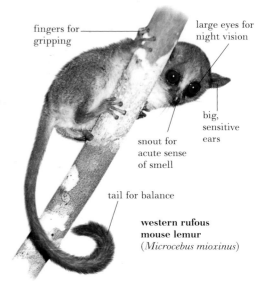

fingers for gripping

large eyes for night vision

big, sensitive ears

snout for acute sense of smell

tail for balance

**western rufous mouse lemur** (*Microcebus mioxinus*)

## ▲ TYPICAL PROSIMIAN

This lemur is the smallest primate of all. It weighs only 25g/1oz, about the same as a tablespoonful of sugar. Lemurs have characteristics common to all prosimians, but are a distinct group of their own. They live only on the island of Madagascar. Monkeys never crossed the sea to the island once it was cut off from Africa 100 million years ago, so prosimian lemurs survived and evolved into many different species.

**EXCLUSIVE OLD WORLDERS ▶**

Prosimians live only in parts of Asia and Africa. No species are found in the Americas or in Australia. Bush babies and lorises are found in central and southern Africa. Lemurs live off the east coast of Africa, on the island of Madagascar. The islands and peninsulas of South-east Asia are home to lorises and tarsiers.

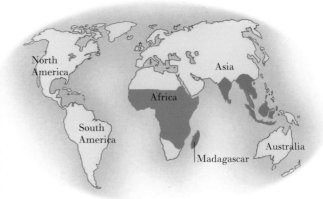

North America

Asia

Africa

South America

Madagascar

Australia

*110*

**◄ USING YOUR EYES**

Despite its goggle-eyed appearance, the tarsier from South-east Asia is more closely related to monkeys than to other prosimians. Most prosimians rely heavily on their sense of smell to communicate and find food. With the tarsier, however, eyesight has become more important. It can swivel its head 180 degrees in each direction to look over its back.

**▲ NIGHTWATCH**

After monkeys evolved some prosimians, such as bush babies and galagos, survived by becoming nocturnal and feeding during the night when the monkeys slept. Bush babies live in African forests, where they feed on fruit and insects. This South African galago is only about 15cm/6in long, but it can leap up to heights of 5m/15ft.

**SCENTED PATH ►**

Like other prosimians, the slow loris from South-east Asia stakes out its territory with scent. It rubs urine on its hands and feet so that it can imprint its smell in specific places. It also uses the smell to mark its path. The loris moves slowly to avoid attracting attention from predators in the forest. If something frightens it, the loris can easily return to the safety of its nest by following the scented path.

**Did you know?** Bush babies can grip tightly to a branch for hours without getting tired.

**◄ SOCIAL LEMURS**

Ring-tailed lemurs are almost as versatile as monkeys. They are agile climbers, and scamper like cats on the ground. They live in large groups, in which females do all the leading and fighting for dominance. Male ring-tailed lemurs fight only over females.

# Monkeys Take Over

In the fierce, overcrowded world of the ancient forests, monkeys had many advantages over prosimians. They had bigger brains and keener eyesight, which enabled them to adapt to different habitats and conditions.

Apes and monkeys evolved around 35 million years ago. At first, apes dominated the forests, but the versatile monkeys soon reigned supreme because they could access food all over the forest, from the top to the bottom. Because of this, monkeys are still generally built for life in the trees. Most species continue to inhabit warm, wet forests around the Equator, although some have adapted to life on the ground, in desert scrub, on mountains or even in bustling cities.

**▲ DOWN TO EARTH**

Unlike many monkey species, baboons do not live in trees. This is a typical olive baboon, which lives in grassland. Baboons are Old World monkeys, mostly from Africa. They live in large social groups that are among the most complicated and interesting of all monkey societies. All four baboon species are bigger than most monkeys.

**◄ OLD WORLDS AND NEW**

Monkeys evolved in Africa, and spread to the Americas and Asia. The monkey populations on each side of the ocean developed in different ways. Those that remained in Africa and Asia became known as the Old World monkeys. They evolved into many different species, but all have narrow noses and downward-pointing nostrils. The American, or New World, monkeys have wider noses with outward-facing nostrils.

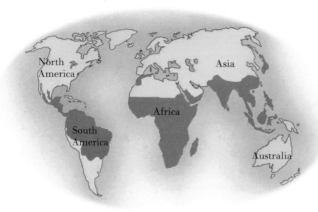

North America

Asia

Africa

South America

Australia

## ◀ NEW WORLD NOSE STYLE

Like all other monkeys that evolved in the New World, this cotton-top tamarin has a flat nose with outward-facing nostrils. New World monkeys live in the forests of Central and South America. Most of them have tails that, unlike those of Old World monkeys, can wrap around and grip on to things, and are used as an extra limb.

tail usually longer than body

forward-facing eyes

long, flexible spine

sitting pads – on Old World monkeys only

## WALKING FRAME ▶

This Old World monkey from India has many characteristics that are common to all monkeys. Long, slender limbs of about equal length make for easy walking on all fours. Tails are long and flexible – especially on New World monkeys. Hands and feet are designed for climbing, walking on the ground and holding leaves and fruits.

deep, flat chest

long, slender limbs with five-digit hands and feet

**hanuman langur**
(*Semnopithecus entellus*)

Did you know? Monkeys usually have ridged palms to help them grip on to trees.

## OLD WORLD PORTRAIT ▶

Look at the downward-pointing, closely spaced nostrils of this pig-tailed macaque. They are typical features of an Old World monkey. These monkeys are more closely related to the great apes such as gorillas and chimpanzees that also live in the Old World. The wide space between lip and nose is typical of many monkeys and apes but unlikely to be seen on prosimians.

113

# Outward Appearances

Monkeys and prosimians became experts in forest survival. As different species evolved, each adapting to a particular way of life, a great variety of shapes and sizes emerged. All, however, had the primate speciality of flexible hands and fingers. Thumbs work in the opposite direction to the fingers, so that the digits can close together and grasp. Long arms and legs are geared for climbing. In many species the arms and legs are of similar length – which means the animals can walk comfortably on all fours. In others, strong hind legs provide power for leaping. These primates can stand or sit on their haunches, leaving both hands free.

▲ UNDER THE THUMB
The pygmy marmoset from South America is small enough to fit on your hand. It is only about 30cm/12in from its head to the tip of its tail, and weighs about 100g/4oz – 500 times less than a mandrill.

▼ BIG AND BULKY
Male mandrills are the world's biggest monkeys. They weigh 50kg/110lb, about the same as a small adult human. Mandrills walk on all fours and have limbs of roughly the same length. They do not live in trees, so they don't need a tail.

▲ THE FIFTH LIMB
A black-handed spider monkey has a muscular tail that can wrap around a branch. A hairless stretch of ridged skin on the underside provides extra grip, like the ridges on the palm of a primate hand. Only New World monkeys have tails with this prehensile (grasping) power. The tails of prosimians and Old World monkeys simply help to balance them when they are leaping through the trees.

## ▲ HANDS ON

The long, flexible fingers of the tarsier are padded for extra grip when climbing. The tarsier is a prosimian from South-east Asia. Like almost all primates, it has fingernails. For animals that forage for plant food, fingernails are more useful than claws. They can be used for picking, peeling and gouging as well as for scratching and grooming.

## ▲ GETTING A GRIP

A young vervet makes the most of its hands and feet to climb. Its opposing thumbs curve in to help it grip. Balanced securely on two feet and one hand, the monkey has one hand free for eating. Monkey hands need to hold small items, so tend to be smaller and more flexible than their feet.

## ◄ PROBLEM HAIR AND SKIN

A rhesus macaque pulls ticks from her friend. The fur of monkeys is home to many tiny insects that suck the host's blood or make the skin flaky. Monkeys deal with the problem by grooming each other. Grooming is also an important way of making friends. Monkey skin darkens with age because of the effects of sunlight, so many monkeys avoid spending too much time in the sun.

## A HANDY FUR COAT ►

For a new-born chacma baboon, mother's fur is handy to cling on to. In the sun-baked savannahs, baboons do not need to keep warm, so the baby's fur will become coarse and sparse like its mother's. Fur also gives some necessary protection against the burning sun, and its grey-brown colour provides good camouflage on the African plains.

# Inner Power

In terms of brainpower, monkeys and other primates are often considered more "advanced" than other animals. Their bodies, however, are basically the same as most other mammals. Primates did not develop special physical features like animals that grew hooves or horns.

Small primate bodies are built for flexibility and agility, with hinged joints supported by long, elastic muscles to allow the maximum range of movement. Different species have body shapes adapted for whether they climb and leap through trees or move along the ground. Head shape and size depend on whether brainpower or the sense of smell or sight is the top priority. Digestive systems vary according to diet.

**▲ DENTAL PRACTICE**
Monkeys and prosimians have four types of teeth. There are incisors for cutting, canines for stabbing and ripping, and molars and premolars for grinding tough leaves and fruit into a mushy paste.

**▼ INTERNAL VIEW**
A monkey's bones and strong muscles protect the vital organs inside its body. Its facial muscles allow it to make expressions. Monkey legs are generally shorter in relation to the bodies than prosimian legs. This gives monkeys more precise climbing and reaching skills, especially in the treetops.

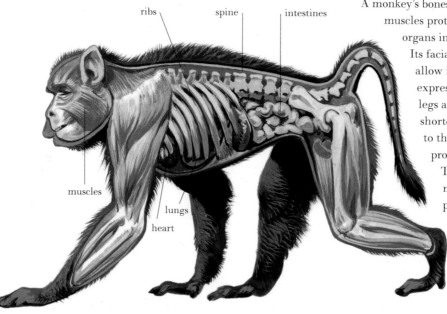

ribs          spine          intestines

muscles

lungs

heart

## ▼ BIG EYES

The tarsier has the biggest eyes of any animal in relation to its body size. There is not much room left in its skull for a brain, and each of the eyes is heavier than the brain. Prosimians lead simpler lives than monkeys and do not need big brains. Instead, they have an array of sharp senses – more sensitive than a monkey's – that help them to survive. As well as its huge eyes, this tarsier has large ears that prick up at the slightest sounds in the quiet of the night.

## ▲ A STRONG STOMACH

A baboon's digestive system can cope with raw meat as well as plant food. Although meat is nutritious, it can be harmful if it stays in the body too long. Meat-eaters have shorter guts than vegetarians, so that food passes through the body quickly. Most monkeys and prosimians eat mainly plants and have longer guts because leaves and other plant foods are hard to digest.

## INSIDE LOOK AT A LEMUR ▶

The skeleton of this prosimian, a ruffed lemur, is quite different from that of a monkey. It has a long, narrow head, which has less space for the brain, and its legs are very long compared to the length of its body. Their long legs help lemurs to leap great distances from tree to tree. Because their legs and feet are designed for climbing, they can also cling in a relaxed fashion to sheer, upright tree trunks.

# Sensing the Surroundings

Monkeys are usually active in the daytime, and they make the most of their excellent colour vision. Most prosimians are nocturnal, and they have eyes to help them see at night. The eyes of all primates are lined with a combination of cone cells and rod cells. Monkeys have many colour-sensitive cone cells. Prosimians have plenty of rod cells, designed to see in dim light. Their eyes glow in the dark like cats' eyes because they are backed by a mirror-like layer that reflects every bit of available light.

Sight is very important to monkeys, but prosimians rely much more on the senses of smell and hearing. The ears of prosimians are constantly on the alert. The slightest rustle in the dark could identify an insect snack or an approaching predator.

**▲ COLOUR SELECTION**

Thanks to its colour vision, an African vervet monkey can select its favourite flowers when they are at the peak of perfection. Many leaf-eating monkeys have eyes that are particularly sensitive to different shades of green. This means that they can easily identify the fresh green of tender young leaves that are good to eat.

**MIDNIGHT MONKEY ▶**

Douracouli monkeys are the only nocturnal monkeys. They live in South America where there are no prosimians to compete with. Like prosimians, their eyes are big, to catch maximum light. They are able to pick up detail but not colour.

**▲ EYES LIKE SAUCERS**

Unlike the eyes of many prosimians, tarsier's eyes have no reflective layer, but their size means they catch as much light as possible. Like monkeys, their eyes have a sensitive area called the fovea, which picks out very sharp detail.

## ▼ A KEEN SENSE OF SMELL

An emperor tamarin monkey marks its territory with scent. New World monkeys and prosimians have a smelling organ in the roof of their mouths that Old World monkeys do not have. They use their sense of smell to communicate with each other and to identify food that is good and ready to eat.

## ▼ MUFFLED SENSE OF HEARING

The furry ears of squirrel monkeys probably muffle sound. But although these and other monkeys use sound to communicate with each other, hearing is not as important for them as keen eyesight. Nocturnal primates, however, have highly sensitive, delicate-skinned ears.

## ▲ WET-NOSED SMELLING AIDS

Look at the shiny nose of this ruffed lemur. It is more like that of a cat or dog than a monkey. Most prosimians have this moist nostril and lip area, called the rhinarium. It gives them a better sense of smell. The nose has a layer of sensitive cells to detect chemicals in the air. The cells work better when they are wet.

119

# On the Move

Primates are the most versatile movers of the animal world. Many can walk and run, climb and swim. Small monkeys and the larger lemurs can leap between branches. This method is risky for larger animals, in case a branch breaks beneath their weight. Heavier primates play safe by walking along branches on all fours and avoiding jumping if possible.

When branches are bendy, climbers move with caution. They may use their weight to swing from one handhold to the next, but they do not let go of one handhold until the other is in place.

Tree-climbing monkeys have long fingers to curl around branches and help them to grip. Monkeys that live on the ground use their hands, as well as their feet, to propel themselves along the ground.

Did you know? A spider monkey's tail is so strong it can support the monkey's entire weight.

**spider monkey**
(*Ateles geoffroyanus*)

◄ **CLIMBING POWER**
New World monkeys rarely move at ground level. They swing from tree to tree, stop and whip their tail around a branch, let go with both hands and grab something to eat. Old World monkeys do not have a prehensile tail. Many have lost their tails altogether or have very short ones, which they use to help balance in the trees.

◄ **PADDED MITTS**
The palm of a sifaka lemur is just one of the features that makes it a star jumper. The wrinkles and flesh pads are like a baseball glove, giving extra holding power. Sifakas can push off with their long hind legs to leap up to 5m/ 15ft high. Their arms are short, making it impossible to walk on all fours. Instead, sifakas hop on both feet.

### ◄ BABOONS ON THE MOVE

A troop of baboons makes its way down a track in the African savannah. They are strong and tough because they have to walk long distances to find enough food to feed the troop. Baboons and other monkeys that walk on the ground, such as mandrills, geladas and macaques, put their weight on the fingertips and palms of their hands and feet. This is different from apes, such as gorillas and chimpanzees, which walk on their knuckles.

### LIGHT AS AIR ►

A pygmy marmoset can perch on the flimsiest of twigs. It has to be small, light and quick so that it can catch insects to eat. Marmosets scurry along branches, like squirrels, and for this reason are the only primates to have claws instead of nails. They are also able to sit up on their hind legs to free their hands for collecting food, as well as for feeding.

### ▲ SLENDER LORIS

Lorises from Sri Lanka and southern India are known for their slow, deliberate movements. They have long, thin arms and legs with very flexible ankles and wrists. A loris can wriggle its way through and get a grip on dense twigs and small branches. Due to its strange appearance, some people describe the animal as a banana on stilts.

121

# Brainpower

To survive in the complicated world of forest branches, monkeys developed intelligence. They have excellent hand-eye coordination to make the most of their grasping hands and forward-facing eyes. In the forest, monkeys move fast and make split-second decisions such as: "Will that branch hold my weight?" They can work out what the likely effect of their actions might be.

As they live in groups, monkeys have developed their brainpower so that they can negotiate with each other. Another skill for group living is a good memory, and monkeys are certainly good at remembering things. They rely on their memory to identify areas where they found last year's choicest food supplies.

### ▼ THE EVIDENCE FOR INTELLIGENCE

The skull of a sifaka (*below*) has little brain space, even though it is probably the most intelligent prosimian. The brain makes up less than half the length of the sifaka's skull. The front section – the nose – is long, which reflects the importance of the sifaka's sense of smell. The vervet monkey skull (*right*) is a different shape, with a much larger area behind its eye sockets for the brain.

### ◀ PROSIMIAN TEAM

Prosimians that are active in the day, such as these ring-tailed lemurs, are usually cleverer than nocturnal prosimians. Like monkeys, they live in groups and have to work together to control territory and find food.

**Monkey Dance**
*In Mexico, people dress up as monkeys for some traditional dances. The Mayans believed that when the world began, monkeys were types of humans. The monkeys fled to live high in trees because they were tired of being laughed at by other humans.*

## ▲ FINE JUDGMENT

Thanks to its large brain, this red colobus monkey can make death-defying leaps with absolute precision. Even on jumps of over 20m/65ft — the length of a tennis court — it can work out that the jump is possible and where to land safely. The monkey's sense of sight is also vital for gauging the distance between take-off and landing.

## ▲ LOOK AND LEARN

Toque macaques probably learned to raid rubbish bins (garbage cans) for food by watching humans. Their big brains give them the capacity to learn. This means that monkeys can adapt to new environments. Macaques have worked out how to survive in a greater variety of habitats than any other monkey.

## ▲ SOCIAL CONSCIENCE

The members of this troop of chacma baboons all know each other very well. Because they are intelligent, each baboon can remember how other baboons have behaved and reacted in the past. As a result some are good friends, while others are not so close. Some baboons are even enemies. A monkey's intelligence means that it can live in complicated societies like this.

## ▲ LIMITED NEEDS, SMALL BRAIN

Most prosimians do not need to move and think quickly. They do not have the stimulation of group living, so they do not need as big a brain as a monkey.

# Diets for Living

Very few small primates eat just one type of food. Most eat whatever is available through the seasons. Some species, such as mandrills and baboons, range over a wide territory to find enough food to feed the troop. Some become specialists, such as the leaf-eating colobus monkeys of Africa and Asia. They have sharp molar teeth to chop the leaves finely, and extra-big stomachs to extract as much goodness as possible from the tough fibres. Most monkeys eat a varied diet of fruit, nuts and insects, and a few eat eggs and small animals. In general, small monkeys eat more high-energy foods than larger monkeys because they burn up energy faster and need more efficient fuel.

▲ CLEAN FOOD

A Japanese macaque washes meat before eating it. It does not understand that unclean meat may make it ill, but knows that dirt spoils the taste. Once one monkey started to wash food, others in the group copied it. The habit will be passed on to their children. Other troops have not learned to do this.

▲ LAID-BACK EATERS

Red colobus monkeys usually eat leaves, although they also like flowers and fruits. Colobus monkeys do not need to look far for food, as leaves are plentiful. They spend a long time sitting still, digesting the leaves to make the most of the limited goodness in them.

▲ SAP EXTRACTION

A bare-faced tamarin licks the thick, sweet juice from a fruit. Tamarins and their marmoset cousins eat a lot of resin from trees, including liquid rubber. Marmosets have pointed bottom teeth with which they pierce the bark so that the liquid flows out.

## ▼ SAVING FOR LATER

A drill has filled its cheek pouches with chewed food. Some other Old World monkeys have this habit too. They do this when they are eating leaves so that chemicals in the monkeys' spit begin to break the leaves down. The monkey's stomach will be able to absorb the nutrients more easily from the resulting mush.

## ▲ BABOON ATTACK

A male olive baboon normally eats seeds, insects and grasses, but it will not refuse the carcass of a baby animal. This African antelope fell victim to a baboon troop. The monkeys edge toward a herd until a young, weak animal is isolated. Then they rip it to shreds.

## ▲ EAT UP YOUR PETALS

Flowers are a good supply of food, as this ring-tailed lemur is discovering. The pollen has a higher concentration of protein than any other part of the plant. Many insects are also attracted to flowers, and they are another good source of protein for monkeys and prosimians.

125

# Territorial Rights

Troops of monkeys spend their lives in one clearly defined area. They create mental maps of their territories, knowing exactly where seasonal food supplies are, for example. Monkeys and social prosimians, such as sifakas and ring-tailed lemurs, defend their territory from neighbouring bands. These group-living primates mark their territory with scent and fiercely defend it against rivals of the same species who may be looking for more space or better food.

Small nocturnal prosimians live solitary lives and do not worry when a neighbour crosses their patch. They are more likely to mate with it or even ignore it altogether.

A primate's territory varies in size according to how many other animals there are and depending on the food supply. A rainforest rich in food can support many animals in small territories. On the plains, animals need to range over a wide area to find enough food.

**▲ CALLING CARD**
The female leader of a troop of ring-tailed lemurs from Madagascar marks her territory with scent from a gland on her chest. In ring-tailed lemur society, it is the females who fight to defend territory. Male lemurs fight only over females.

**◄ FOREST RANGERS**
Squirrel monkeys live in large societies of up to 50 members. Groups move around a home range of 32sq km/12½sq miles, but territorial boundaries are blurred. One troop may merge with another without a hint of a fight. These bands of monkeys have no permanent troops or leaders. They roam through the South American forest looking for fruit and keeping track of each other with high-pitched calling.

**◄ ON THE MOVE**

Baboons live on the African savannah, where food supplies are spread out. They live in troops of up to 150 animals, which gives them the power to defend huge territories of 64sq km/25sq miles. The monkeys walk about 5km/3 miles daily to collect enough food for the troop. Most other monkeys move through only a few trees each day.

**UNITED WE STAND ►**

Langurs live in large troops that are controlled by a single male. They patrol big home ranges throughout India, but do not live in rainforests. The troop's leader is always wary of attack from rival males wishing to steal his females and land. The whole langur troop may become involved in a battle with neighbouring troops for control of territory.

**◄ KEEP OFF MY LAND**

A howler monkey gives a loud, roaring howl warning other troops to keep out of its territory. Both males and females make this noise, and fight off invaders. In the thick forest, sound is a more effective way to assert territorial rights than scent. Fiercely defensive species, such as howler and proboscis monkeys, are the noisiest monkeys of all. The males are the most aggressive, as they also fight for the right to mate with females.

127

# Living Together

All primates communicate in some way with other members of their species, and most of them live in social groups. Community living has advantages. There are more eyes to spot predators and several animals can work as a team to fight off attack or forage for food. As a community, they stand a better chance of survival if there is a problem with the food supply – during a drought, for instance. The leaders will feed themselves and their young first to make sure that they survive. Solitary animals may have a hard time finding a mate, but within a group, there is plenty of choice. When there are young to be cared for, a community can provide many willing helpers.

Nocturnal prosimians rely on being solitary and silent to avoid being noticed by predators. Among bush babies and lorises, even couples live independently of each other, but they occupy the same patch, and their paths often cross. Babies stay with their mothers until they are old enough to live alone.

▲ **TREE-SHARING**
Sifakas work together in groups of about seven adults to defend their territory. They are generally led by the females, and males may switch groups. These prosimians gather in the higher branches of the trees in western Madagascar. If danger threatens, they all begin to make a hiccuping groan.

**HAPPY COUPLE** ▶
In the jungles of South America, male and female sakis mate and usually live as a couple for a year. The female cares for the young. The father may not spend the day with his family, but he does return to them at night. If there is plenty of food, families mingle with each other, forming large, loosely knit groups.

## ◀ FEMALE RULE

A female is in charge of this troop of black tufted-ear marmosets. As with most other New World marmosets and tamarins, there may be several other females, but only the head female breeds. She mates with all the males to make sure her top-level genes are passed on. As none of the males knows who is the father, they all help rear and protect the young.

## EQUAL SOCIETY ▶

The relationship between a woolly monkey mother and her children can last for life. Woolly monkeys live in troops — there may be 20 to 50 of them in each group, with roughly equal numbers of males and females. Adult males often cooperate, and all of the males and females can mate with each other. Individual females care for their own young. Woolly monkey groups are bound by an intricate web of relationships between all members that is hard for outsiders to understand.

## ◀ MALE POWER

These female hamadryas baboons are just two in a harem of several females. One top male mates with all the females to make sure he fathers all the children. Males with no harem live in separate bachelor groups of two or three. They try to mate with a member of the harem when the leader is not looking. When the leader gets old, a few young males will team up to depose him. Once he has been chased away, the victors fight for control of the harem.

*129*

# Communication

Attracting attention in a noisy forest is a challenge. Groups of tree-living monkeys and prosimians lose sight of each other and keep in touch by calling. Nocturnal prosimians, however, need to keep a low profile, and so leave scent messages, which are easier to place accurately.

All prosimians and, to a lesser extent, monkeys send messages of ownership, aggression or sexual readiness with strong-smelling urine, or scent from special glands. Monkeys can also express their feelings with facial expressions and gestures, and some use their ability to see in colour. African guenons, for example, have brightly coloured patches on their bodies that can be seen by their companions when they are hurtling through the trees. Even fur and tails can be useful. Ring-tailed lemurs swish their tails menacingly at rivals and, at the same time, fan terrible smells over them.

▲ **DON'T HURT ME**
This toque macaque is showing by its posture and expression that it is not a threat. If an adult monkey wants to make friends, it may make a sound like a human baby gurgling. The other monkey will usually respond gently.

Did you know? Monkeys have more face muscles than prosimians and make more expressions.

**PERSONAL PERFUME ▶**
A black spider monkey smears a strong-smelling liquid on a branch. The liquid is produced by a gland on the monkey's chest. Its smell is unique to this monkey. When other monkeys smell it, they know that another of their kind has been there. If they meet the particular monkey that left the scent, they will recognize it.

### ◄ TELL-TAIL SIGNS

In complicated langur societies, high-ranking males hold their tails higher than lesser members of the group. Primates that live in complex social groups have a wider range of communication skills than solitary species. More information has to be passed around among a greater number of individuals.

### ▲ YOU SCRATCH MY BACK...

Grooming a fellow monkey not only gets rid of irritating fleas and ticks, but also forges a relationship. A lot of monkey communication is about preventing conflicts among group members. Forming strong personal bonds holds the troop together.

### ▲ BE CAREFUL

A mandrill has mobile face muscles to make different expressions. Here, he pulls back his gums and snarls. This makes him look very menacing to other males.

### ▲ I'M ANGRY

When a mandrill becomes angry, he opens his mouth in a wide yawn to show the size of his teeth, and roars. Another monkey will hesitate before confronting this male.

### LOOKING FIERCE ►

This marmoset is literally bristling for a fight. Its fur stands on end like an angry cat's to make it look much bigger. It may scare its rival into withdrawing. Marmosets look cute, but they squabble a lot among themselves.

# Changing Habitats

Nearly all monkeys and prosimians live in steamy rainforests, like their early ancestors. Many monkeys may never touch the ground. Some live right at the top of the tallest trees, leaping from branch to branch. Others live lower down, where branches are so thick that they form an almost solid platform. Species that live in the forest understorey are agile, both on the ground and in the trees.

Ground-based baboons and monkeys evolved later than the forest-dwellers. Sometimes, they live far from forests. There are fewer species and smaller social groups in open areas than in the forest, as food is more scarce.

## ▲ GROUND-BASED

Gelada baboons come from the open grasslands of the Ethiopian highlands in Africa. They are the only monkeys that eat mostly grass, and they live in groups for safety from predators. Like other ground-based monkeys, they have strong bodies for walking long distances in search of food.

Did you know? Some females don't eat in the dry season, living off the fat they store in their tails.

## EXTREME VERSATILITY ▶

A Tibetan macaque has a thick winter coat and must rest more than other monkeys to save energy for keeping warm. It gets very cold high in the mountains, and food is scarce. The macaques grow thick winter coats to trap heat. Macaques are among the most adaptable of monkeys. Different species have learned to survive farther north than any other monkey, in mountain forests and in cities.

*Monkey Gods*
*Black-faced langurs*
*are named after the*
*Hindu monkey*
*god, Hanuman.*
*According to legend,*
*Hanuman stole a*
*mango plant and faced punishment by fire. When*
*the fire was lit, the god tried to put it out. His face*
*and paws were burned in the process. According to*
*the story, this is why hanuman langurs have black*
*faces and paws. Although the monkeys are often pests*
*in modern India, they are considered sacred. On the*
*feast day of the god Hanuman, the monkeys are fed*
*offerings at Hindu temples.*

## ▲ LIFE IN THE FOREST

A baby squirrel monkey hitches a ride
on an adult. These monkeys are part of a
big troop on a fruit-hunting expedition
through the lower levels of the trees.
Because there is such a rich variety
of food all year round, large numbers
of monkeys live in the tropical forests.

## ◄ POISONOUS SNACK

The favourite food of the rare golden bamboo lemur is a
variety of giant bamboo that contains enough cyanide to
kill almost any other animal. These
lemurs eat only bamboo and live
only where they can find
it, in the forests of
south-eastern
Madagascar.

## ADAPT AND SURVIVE ►

De Brazza's guenons are excellent
swimmers and have carved out a niche
for themselves in dense, flooded
rainforests in Africa, often on islands.
Guenons are one of the most varied
monkey species. Most are tree-living,
but some, such as the vervet, have
adapted to life on the African plains.

133

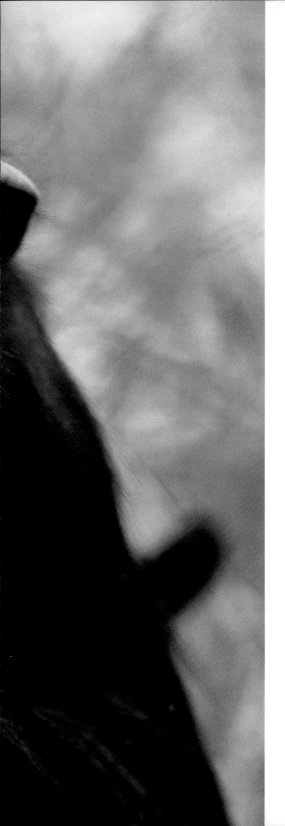

# GREAT APES

The first apes lived on Earth about
20 million years ago, and they are our
closest living relatives. There are four
main groups – chimpanzees, gorillas,
bonobos and orangutans. They are
extremely intelligent and are able
to solve problems, use tools, learn
languages and communicate both
with each other and us.

*Author*: Barbara Taylor
*Consultant*: Ian Redmond
Chairman, Ape Alliance

# What is a Great Ape?

The four great apes – the chimpanzee, bonobo, gorilla and orangutan – look similar to us because they are our closest animal relatives. Humans are sometimes called "the fifth great ape". The great apes are also closely related to the lesser apes, the gibbons. Nearly 99 percent of our genes are the same as those of a chimpanzee. In fact, chimpanzees are more closely related to humans than they are to gorillas. Like us, the other great apes are intelligent, use tools, solve problems and communicate. They can also learn a language, although their vocal cords cannot produce the right range of sounds to speak.

▼ **APE FEATURES**

Gorillas are the largest of the great apes. Typical ape features include long arms (longer than the ape's legs), flexible wrist joints, gripping thumbs and fingers, and no tail. Apes are clever, with big brains.

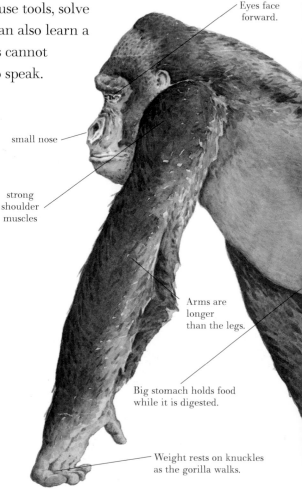

Eyes face forward.

small nose

strong shoulder muscles

Arms are longer than the legs.

Big stomach holds food while it is digested.

Weight rests on knuckles as the gorilla walks.

▲ **RED APE**

Red, shaggy orangutans are the largest tree-living animals in the world. Their name means "person-of-the-forest". Orangutans live on the islands of Borneo and Sumatra in South-east Asia.

**▲ STUDYING APES**

Much of what we know today about wild apes is based on the work of scientists such as Dr Dian Fossey, who spent many years carefully observing gorillas in the wild.

**GROUPS ►**

Family groups of between five and 40 gorillas live together in the misty rain forests and mountains of Central Africa. Each group is led by an adult male. He decides where the group will feed, sleep and travel.

Apes do not have a tail.

**King Kong**

*At the beginning of the 1930s, the film* King Kong *showed a giant gorilla as a dangerous monster. In the movie, a team of hunters capture Kong and take him to America. We now know that gorillas are peaceful animals, very different from the movie monster.*

**▼ APE FACES**

Have you ever watched a chimpanzee in a zoo and found that it has turned to watch you? Great apes are often as interested in watching us as we are in watching them.

Feet rest flat on the ground.

# Ape Shapes and Sizes

It is hard to believe that a tiny newborn gorilla, half the weight of most human babies, may grow up to be a heavyweight male that weighs almost 198kg/440lb. Gorillas are the largest of the four great apes, while chimpanzees and bonobos are the smallest – similar in size to a 12-year-old boy or girl. Male great apes are up to twice the size and weight of females. This helps them to frighten predators and rivals. Male and female gibbons, however, are the same size. They are much smaller than the great apes, and so are known as the lesser apes. Their small size allows them to live high in the trees all of the time. Large male gorillas are too heavy for a permanent treetop lifestyle, although they do climb trees for fruit and buds.

**▲ SMALL APE**
Male chimpanzees stand just under 1.5m/5ft tall and weigh up to 40kg/88lb. Females are a little shorter and lighter. Chimpanzees have muscular bodies and are strong for their size.

**orangutan**
*(Pongo pygmaeus)*

**◀ BIG FACE**
A fully grown male orangutan has fatty pads the size of dinner plates on his cheeks. They make him look bigger and help him to frighten off rival males.

**▲ SIZE DIFFERENCE**
Male gorillas are incredibly muscular, are twice the size of females and can stand about 2m/6ft tall. A female gorilla is shorter – about 1.5m/5ft – and weighs 90kg/198lb.

**bonobo or pygmy chimpanzee**
*(Pan paniscus)*

### ◀ A NEW SPECIES

Bonobos were formerly known as pygmy chimpanzees, but they were recognized as a separate species in 1929. Bonobos are about the same height as chimpanzees at the shoulder, but they have a more slender and leggy body. Bonobos also have smaller, rounder heads compared to chimpanzees. The hair on a bonobo's head usually looks like it has been parted in the middle.

Did you know? A big male orangutan is the weight of a heavyweight boxer.

### ▶ LESSER APE

The gibbons are the smallest and lightest of the apes. Most gibbons measure just over 60cm/24in in length and weigh less than 7kg/15lb. There are 11 species of gibbon in total. The heaviest species is the siamang — the males weigh up to 14kg/31lb.

**white-cheeked gibbon**
*(Hylobates concolor leucogenys)*

### Yeti and Bigfoot

*Some people believe that an apeman lives hidden in the high mountains of Asia and the wilderness areas of North America. It is called the Yeti or the Abominable Snowman in the Himalayas and Bigfoot or Sasquatch in North America.*

# Bodies and Bones

Characteristic features of great apes
are their long, strong arms and flexible
shoulders, which they use to clamber through
the trees at great speed. They do not have tails
to help them balance and grip the branches.
Instead of hooves or paws, apes have hands
and feet that can grasp branches and hold food
very well. On the ground, an ape's strong arms
and fingers take its weight as it walks on all
fours. Humans are different from the other
apes, because they have short arms and long
legs. Human arms are about 30 percent shorter
than human legs. Our bodies and bones are also
designed for walking upright, rather than for
swinging through the trees. All the apes have
a large head, with a big skull inside to protect
an intelligent brain.

◀ APE SKELETON
One of the notable
features of an ape
skeleton is the
large skull that
surrounds and
protects the big
brain. Apes also
have long,
strong finger
and toe bones
for gripping.
The arm
bones of
the orangutans,
gorillas and
chimpanzees are also
extended, making
their arms
longer than
their legs.

Did you know? Female orangutans weigh up to 36kg/80lb, but males can weigh over 90kg/200lb.

▼ THE BIG FIVE
The five great apes have similar bodies, although a human's body is
less hairy and muscular than the body of other great apes. The
main differences between ape bodies lie in
the shape of the skull and the length of the
arms and legs. Orangutans have extra long
arms to hang from branches, but
humans have long legs for
walking upright.

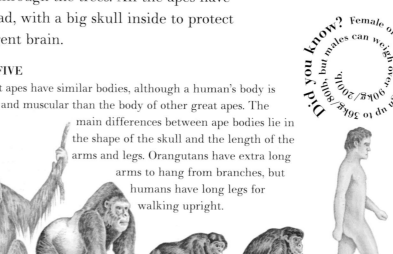

orangutan          gorilla          bonobo          chimpanzee          human

140

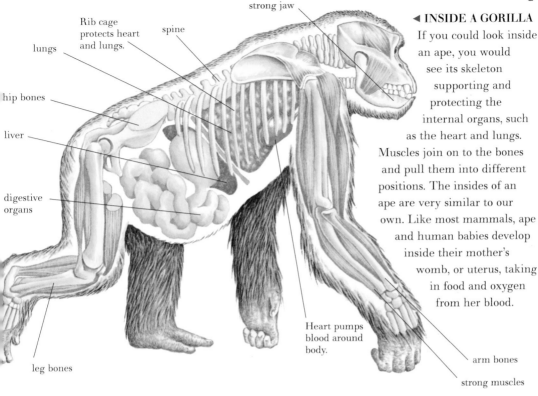

lungs

Rib cage protects heart and lungs.

spine

strong jaw

hip bones

liver

digestive organs

leg bones

Heart pumps blood around body.

arm bones

strong muscles

**◄ INSIDE A GORILLA**
If you could look inside an ape, you would see its skeleton supporting and protecting the internal organs, such as the heart and lungs. Muscles join on to the bones and pull them into different positions. The insides of an ape are very similar to our own. Like most mammals, ape and human babies develop inside their mother's womb, or uterus, taking in food and oxygen from her blood.

**▲ NO TAIL**
Apes such as this chimpanzee do not have tails, but most monkeys do. Apes clamber and hang by their powerful arms. Monkeys walk along branches on all fours, using the tail for balance.

**EXTRA HAND ►**
Many of the monkeys that live in the dense rainforests of Central and South America have special gripping tails, called prehensile tails. The tails also have sensitive tips that work like an extra one-fingered hand, allowing them to cling to the branches when they gather fruit.

141

**western lowland gorilla** *(Gorilla gorilla gorilla)*

# Hairy Apes

Apes are mammals, like cats, bears, mice and deer. Mammals are warm-blooded animals, and most have hair-covered bodies. The hair grows out of little pits in the skin called follicles, forming a layer that traps warm air given off by the body. This helps to keep an ape warm.

Apes that live in colder places, such as mountain gorillas, have longer, thicker hair for extra warmth. Apes don't like the rain, because their hair is not very waterproof. Sometimes apes try to shelter from the rain or make umbrellas out of large leaves, but often they just sit hunched up, waiting for the rain to stop. Male and female chimpanzees both have black hair, and all orangutans have orange-red coats, but adult male gorillas have a distinctive silver back, and some male and female gibbons are totally different colours.

## ▲ SILVER LEADER

When a male gorilla is about 11 or 12 years old, he grows a saddle-shaped area of silvery grey hair on his back, and long, shaggy hair on his arms. He also loses his chest hair. He is called a silverback, and these changes show he is grown-up. Males whose hair has not yet changed are called blackbacks.

## GROOMING ▶

Chimpanzees regularly search through each other's hair with their fingers, carefully picking out any dirt and lice, and cleaning cuts and scratches. Grooming feels pleasant, and it helps the apes to relax and reassure each other. It also helps to strengthen friendships.

**◄ COLOUR CONTRAST**

In some species of gibbon, males and females have different coloured hair. For instance, male concolour and hoolock gibbons are black, and females are a golden colour. Male and female lar gibbons are the same colour, but populations living in different places may be different colours.

**white-handed gibbons**
*(Hylobates lar)*

**▲ TURNING GREY**

Chimpanzees can live for 40 or 50 years. As a chimpanzee grows older, its coat fades and may turn grey. Its hair also thins, and older chimps may start to go bald.

**▲ HAIRY SIGNALS**

This chimpanzee has made its hair stand on end to make itself look bigger and more frightening. A nervous or fearful chimp has flattened hair and a "fear grin".

**orangutan**
*(Pongo pygmaeus)*

**LONG HAIR ►**

Orangutans from Sumatra have longer, thicker hair than those from Borneo. Scientists now think that they are a separate species from their Bornean relatives. Sumatran males have shaggy faces, with long, rich beards and moustaches that extend out on to their cheeks. Even female Sumatran orangutans have impressive chin hair. The long hair of male orangutans makes them look bigger and helps to scare off their rivals.

# Hands and Feet

Can you imagine how difficult it would be to pick up something if your arms ended in paws, hooves or flippers? It would be impossible to grip the object, and you could not turn it around, carry it, throw it, pull it apart or put it together. An ape's hands and feet are remarkable. They are very adaptable, and the opposing thumb or big toe enables them to grasp firmly or hold delicately. Ape hands and feet are strong and flexible, allowing apes to climb, swing and jump through the treetops. They also allow apes to reach food, build nests, investigate their surroundings and groom their family and friends. With most apes, the feet look a lot like hands, but in humans, the feet look different, because human feet are adapted for walking rather than climbing.

▲ **SMILE, PLEASE**
Grasping a delicate camera lens, a gorilla demonstrates how it can pick up fragile objects without breaking them. A gorilla has thicker, sturdier hands than a person, with fingers the size of bananas and a smaller thumb. Its hands have to be strong so that they can support the weight of the gorilla's body when it walks around on all fours.

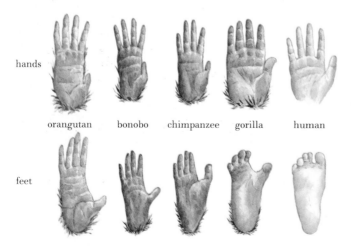

hands

orangutan   bonobo   chimpanzee   gorilla   human

feet

◄ **LOOK-ALIKE HANDS**
The hands of the great apes have several features in common, such as nails and long, sensitive fingers. The thumb on a great ape's hand turns at an angle and can press against each finger. The big toe on an ape's foot can also do this, except in humans. Bonobos have a unique feature not shared by the other apes – webbing between the second and third toes.

144

orangutan
(*Pongo
pygmaeus*)

## ▲ OPPOSABLE THUMB

Since a great ape's thumb can easily
touch, or oppose, its fingers, it is called an
opposable thumb. This special thumb gives
an ape's hand a precise pincer grip, allowing
it to pick up objects as small as berries.

*Did you know?*
*Humans have over 5 million hairs on their bodies.*

## ▲ POWER GRIP

An orangutan's arms and legs end
in huge hands and feet that work
like powerful clamps. Just
one hand or foot can take the
entire weight of the ape.

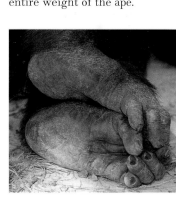

## ▲ HAND-FOOT

Unlike a human, a chimp can use its feet like hands to hold
and investigate things. The opposable big toe stretches out
around one side of a branch, and the toes reach around the
other side, forming a very strong grip.

## ▲ FLAT FEET

Chimpanzees are flat-footed, with
tough, hairless feet and long toes.
When they are upright, their feet
must take all of the body weight.

145

# Smart Apes

Apes appear to be the brightest of all the nonhuman animals, but it is difficult to measure intelligence. Scientists think an intelligent animal is one that can solve problems, investigate and adapt to new conditions, behave in a flexible way, remember things, use tools, pass on information from one generation to the next and even use language. Apes can do all these things, but their throats cannot make the sounds used by humans to produce a spoken language. Scientists have experimented with teaching apes signs and symbols in order to understand them better and to investigate their intelligence. There is much debate about whether chimpanzees, bonobos, gorillas or orangutans are the most intelligent of the great apes.

▲ ESCAPE ARTISTS
Captive orangutans are the master escapologists of the ape world. They use branches to ford deep moats full of water around their enclosures. They take out the centre pins from hinges to open doors the wrong way and they unravel chain-link fences.

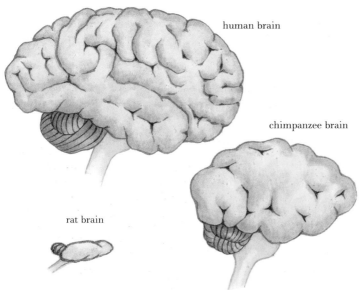

human brain

chimpanzee brain

rat brain

◄ BRAIN POWER
Humans and chimpanzees have much bigger brains than rats, even in relation to body size. The bigger the brain, the less tied an animal is to set ways of doing things. Humans and chimps have large areas of the brain for learning, memory, reasoning and judgment. This helps them to make decisions about what to do next, where to go and what to eat.

**▲ COMPUTER APE**

At Yerkes Regional Primate Centre near Atlanta, Georgia, bonobos and chimpanzees have been taught to communicate with a computer.

**◄ APE ART**

Many people have suggested that the way humans use art to express ideas is a measure of our intelligence. When captive apes have been allowed to experiment with pencils, paints and paper, they have produced a variety of interesting images.

**▲ HAND SPEAK**

All four great apes have been taught sign language for simple communication. The apes have even taught fellow apes. Bonobos, such as Kanzi (above), have learned to communicate by pointing to specific symbols on a large board.

*Planet of the Apes*

*In the film* Planet of the Apes *(1968), three astronauts find themselves on a planet where apes are in control and humans are hunted as stupid beasts. Orangutans are judges and priests, chimpanzees are scholars, and gorillas are the police. The hero realizes that this is an Earth of the future, where ape and human roles are reversed.*

147

# Living in a Group

Of all the apes, chimpanzees live in the largest groups — up to about 100 individuals. The chimps constantly change their friends and often drop out altogether to spend time on their own. A chimpanzee group is based around the most important male chimps, like gorilla groups, in which one of the male silverbacks leads his group. Bonobos live in smaller groups than chimpanzees, but their society is led by females instead of males. Orangutans tend to live on their own, although females and their young spend a lot of time together while the youngster is growing up. Gibbons have a completely different social system from that of the other apes — they live in family groups of a mother, father and their young.

## ▲ GENTLE GIANTS

Life in a gorilla group is mostly peaceful and friendly, and there is seldom serious fighting within the group. The silverback can stop most quarrels by strutting and glaring at the troublemakers. He is the group's leader, deciding where and when it will travel and when it will settle down.

Did you know? A silverback male is prepared to die to defend his group.

bonobos
(*Pan paniscus*)

## ▼ SOCIABLE SOCIETY

Bonobos are very sociable creatures. Most of the time they live in large, loose groups, called communities, which are split up into smaller groups of 15 or less when they forage for food.

juvenile male

male silverback leader

adult female

young gorilla

### ◄ HAPPY FAMILIES

Gorillas like to live in extended family groups, usually with between five and 30 members. A gorilla without a group will do its best to join one or start a new one. Each group is controlled and defended by a large adult silverback male.

### ▲ TREETOP FAMILIES

Gibbons are the only apes that live in pairs and mate for life. They may have several young with them, since they do not leave their parents until they are six or seven years old. The gap between births is two-and-a-half to three years.

### LONE ORANG ►

Orangutans spend most of their time alone. One reason for this may be that they need to eat a lot of fruit every day. If many orangutans lived together, they would not be able to find enough fruit to eat. Even when they do meet, they often ignore each other.

### GIRL POWER ►

Females form the backbone of a bonobo group. Adult female bonobos form strong friendships, which are reinforced by grooming and hugging each other. This group of female bonobos have been raised in captivity. Boredom in captivity leads some apes to pluck out their hair.

**bonobos**
*(Pan paniscus)*

# Communication

Although apes cannot speak, they communicate with a variety of sounds, facial expressions, and gestures. Scientists have even learned some of this ape-speak in order to reassure the apes they are studying, and avoid frightening the animals away. Orangutans and gibbons both call loudly to stake their claim to their territory, just as we would put up a fence and "keep out" signs around our property. In chimp and gorilla societies, body positions and gestures show which animals are the most important, or dominant, and which are the least important, or submissive. Chimps and gorillas also communicate through a variety of sounds, especially chimps, who can be very noisy apes.

▼ **GIBBON DUET**
Many pairs of adult gibbons sing to warn other gibbons to stay out of their territories. The duet may also help the pair to stay together. Singing gibbons fill the forest with a chorus of noisy whoops, hoots and calls.

siamang gibbon
*(Hylobates syndactylus)*

▲ **MAKING FACES**
Chimpanzees have a variety of different expressions for communication. A wide, open and relaxed mouth is a play face used to start, or during, a game. An angry chimp clenches his lips shut.

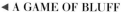

## ◀ A GAME OF BLUFF

Rising on his back legs, a male silverback gorilla slaps his cupped hands rapidly against his chest, making a "pat-pat-pat" sound. Then he charges forward, tearing up plants and slapping the ground. This display is really a bluff to scare away rivals. Gorillas hardly ever fight, and a male usually stops his charge at the last minute.

## ▲ GORILLA-SPEAK

Researchers observing gorillas in the wild have learned to make the same sounds and gestures as the gorillas. A content gorilla makes a rumbling, burping sound. A sharp, pig-grunt noise means that the gorilla is annoyed.

## ◀ KEEP OUT!

Fully grown male orangutans usually keep to their own area of forest – up to 15sq km/6sq miles. This is called their "home range". Every day, a male roars loudly to warn other orangutans to stay away. This long call lasts for about two minutes. By calling, males avoid meetings that might end in a fight.

## TOP CHIMP ▶

The dominant chimpanzee in a group shows off occasionally by charging around, screaming and throwing branches. He also hunches his shoulders and makes his hair stand on end.

## ▼ LOW RANK

To avoid fighting with important chimps, low-ranking chimps behave in a certain way. They flatten their hair, crouch down or bob up and down, and back toward the more important chimp, while they pant-grunt.

**▲ SILVER PROTECTION**
If a leopard or a similar predator threatens a group of gorillas, the silverback leader puts himself between his family and the danger. The females and youngsters in the group huddle together and rely on the silverback to drive away the intruder.

# Defence

The great apes are too big to be killed and eaten by most animals. Sometimes a tiger, leopard, snake or crocodile does succeed in catching an ape, although they probably pick on the old, the young and the sick. Apes can also be injured or even killed in battles with members of their own species. But their main enemy is people, who destroy their habitat, kill them for meat and capture them as pets or for medical research. Living in a group is a good defence, since members can warn each other of danger and help to defend each other. Apes that live in smaller groups or on their own, such as gibbons and orangutans, can escape danger by living high in the trees.

**◄ FRIEND OR FOE?**
This frightened chimpanzee is seeking reassurance by holding out her hand. When they are faced with human predators, chimps usually keep quiet and still, or slip away into the bush, but they will attack leopards with long branches and big stones. A chimp's sharp teeth can also inflict a nasty bite.

◀ **HUNTED**
Leopards are clever hunters, and especially dangerous because they hunt at night. Their spotted coats camouflage them well, and they are excellent tree

**leopard**
*(Panthera pardus)*

climbers. Leopards are very agile in trees, so they can spring on apes from overhead.

▲ **ILLEGAL KILLERS**
Apes are protected by law, but poachers (illegal hunters) break the rules because they hope to make money. Here, a pair of gorillas were shot so that their infant could be captured and sold.

▲ **CONFUSING GRIN**
This chimpanzee may look as if it is smiling, but in fact it is showing its teeth and gums in a fear grin. Chimps make this sort of face when they are frightened or nervous.

*Killer Orangutan*
*In 1841, the American writer Edgar Allan Poe published his story "The Murders in the Rue Morgue". In a mysterious and macabre tale, Poe describes how an orangutan escapes from its cage and finds shelter in the home of Madame L'Espanaye and her daughter. Terrified by the two women's cries of fear, the orangutan seizes a razor and cuts their throats.*

153

# Ape Habitats

▲ VANISHING APE
In the dark and dappled rain forest where orangutans live, their shaggy, orange hair blends in with the tangle of forest plants. This makes them surprisingly difficult to see.

GORILLA SIGNS ▶
It is often hard for scientists to watch gorillas in their forest habitats. Instead, the scientists study the signs left behind by the gorillas as they move around.

If you want to see wild apes in their natural habitats, you have to travel to tropical Africa or South-east Asia. Most apes live in tropical rainforests, but some chimpanzees are found in more open, deciduous woodlands or in wooded grasslands, and some gorillas prefer mountain forests, with their lush vegetation and misty atmosphere. In some places, gibbons live in deciduous forests, too. All the apes used to be more widespread, but over time they are being gradually squeezed into smaller and smaller areas, as people have hunted them and destroyed their habitats.

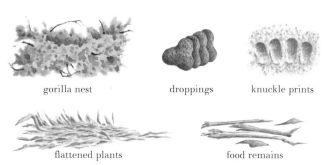

gorilla nest

droppings

knuckle prints

flattened plants

food remains

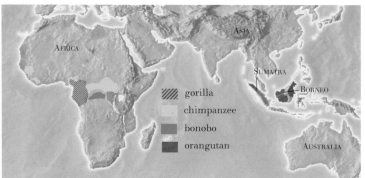

◀ WHERE APES LIVE
Gorillas, chimpanzees and bonobos live in Africa, while orangutans live only on the islands of Borneo and Sumatra. However, orangutans once lived in parts of mainland South-east Asia. Some people believe that they were hunted out by poachers.

gorilla
chimpanzee
bonobo
orangutan

AFRICA
ASIA
SUMATRA
BORNEO
AUSTRALIA

**▲ ROUTE MAP**

Chimpanzees travel around their own neighbourhoods on the ground, following a network of paths. They use a mental map in their heads to decide where to go. Each day they figure out where to get a good meal, climbing trees to find fruit and leaves, or to chase prey.

**▲ TREETOP APE**

Gibbons are totally at home in the tops of the trees and hardly ever go down to the ground. They are the only apes that do not build nests. They sleep sitting up in the forks of branches, resting on tough sitting pads. These pads act like built-in cushions.

**▼ NIGHT NESTS**

Every night, the adult great apes make nests in the trees or on the ground. They bend and weave together leafy branches, and pile more leaves and branches on top. This makes a warm, springy nest which keeps out the cold.

**▲ MOUNTAIN HOME**

Mountain gorillas live in dense, misty forests up to about 3,505m/11,500ft above sea level. At night, the temperature may drop to below freezing, but the long hair of the mountain gorillas helps them to keep warm.

chimpanzee
(*Pan troglodytes*)

# Ape Ancestors

**▲ HANDY MAN**
This is a model of *Homo habilis*, or handy man, an early human named after its ability to make simple stone tools. *Homo habilis* lived about two million years ago in Africa and was 1.3m/4ft tall. Although their brains were only half the size of modern humans, they could probably speak.

The first apes appeared on Earth some 20 million years ago, but their early evolution is difficult to trace accurately, because few of their fossils (preserved remains) have been discovered. Early apes were heavier than monkeys, swinging underneath branches and using their powerful arms for support. Some of these early apes died out, leaving just six groups to evolve through to the present day. Scientific tests suggest that chimpanzees and humans separated from six to eight million years ago, and then began to develop in their own ways. Gorillas branched out earlier, possibly six to nine million years ago, orangutans 12 to 16 million years ago, and gibbons 20 million years ago. However, there is debate about these dates.

**FOSSIL APES ▼**
*Apes probably evolved from a group called Aegyptopithecus (Egyptian ape), which lived in North Africa some 30 million years ago. Other fossil apes include Dryopithecus, or woodland ape (about 18 million years ago), Ramapithecus (8–15 million years ago), and Gigantopithecus (6–9 million years ago). The Gigantopithecus apes died out, but Dryopithecus and Ramapithecus evolved into modern apes, including humans.*

*Aegyptopithecus*

*Dryopithecus*

*Gigantopithecus*

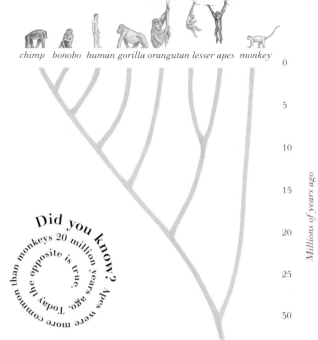

chimp   bonobo   human gorilla orangutan lesser apes   monkey

0

5

10

15

20

25

30

35

*Millions of years ago*

**Did you know?** Apes were more common than monkeys 20 million years ago. Today, the opposite is true.

◄ **FAMILY TREE**
There is a lot of debate about the evolution of the apes. This is just one family tree showing possible dates and routes taken by the different apes as they evolved over 20 million years. The human and ape lines of evolution may have separated about five to seven million years ago. Monkeys evolved earlier than apes, about 30 million years ago.

◄ **APE THEORY**
In 1871, Charles Darwin published a book called *The Descent of Man*, in which he suggested that humans had evolved from apelike ancestors. Many people were shocked by this idea and made fun of Darwin in cartoons such as this one. What Darwin meant was that people and apes evolved along separate lines from earlier, apelike animals.

▼ **A COMMON ANCESTOR?**
Some scientists have suggested that a small, tree-climbing animal, similar to modern tree shrews, may have been the ancestor of all primates, such as lemurs, monkeys, apes and humans. However, recent evidence suggests that they might not be as closely related.

**Treeshrew**
*(Tupaia lyonogale tana)*

# ELEPHANTS

Elephants are the longest lived,
largest and heaviest of all land animals,
and they are found in the forests,
swamps, deserts and bushland of both
Africa and Asia. As well as having big
ears, strong tusks and amazing trunks,
these giant herbivores are extremely
intelligent and they live in close-knit,
cooperative societies.

*Author*: Barbara Taylor
*Consultant*: Dr Adrian Lister
University College London

# What is an Elephant?

Elephants are the largest and heaviest creatures on land. An African bull (male) elephant weighs as much as 80 people, 6 cars, 12 large horses or 1,500 cats! Elephants are extremely strong and can pick up whole trees with their trunks. They are also highly intelligent, gentle animals. Females live together in family groups and look after one another. Like human beings, elephants are mammals. As with all mammals, they can control their body temperature and, like most mammals, they give birth to babies. After humans, elephants are the longest living mammals. Some live to be about 70 years old. Two species of elephant exist today – the African elephant and the Asian elephant. Both have a trunk, large ears and thick, grey skin. Not all elephants have tusks, however. Generally, only African elephants and male Asian elephants have tusks.

▲ **WORKING ELEPHANTS**
In India, domesticated (tamed) elephants are used by farmers to carry heavy loads. In some Asian countries they also move heavy logs by pulling them.

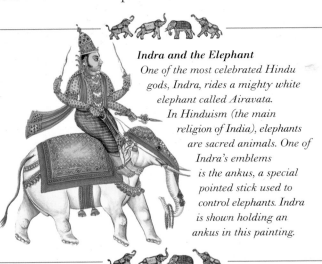

*Indra and the Elephant*
*One of the most celebrated Hindu gods, Indra, rides a mighty white elephant called Airavata. In Hinduism (the main religion of India), elephants are sacred animals. One of Indra's emblems is the ankus, a special pointed stick used to control elephants. Indra is shown holding an ankus in this painting.*

Tail, with a brush of thick hair at the end.

## ▼ UNUSUAL FEATURES

The mighty elephant is a record-breaking beast. Not only is it the largest land animal, it is also the second tallest (only the giraffe is taller). It has larger ears, teeth and tusks than any other animal. The elephant is also one of the few animals to have a nose in the form of a long trunk.

**FAMILY LIFE ▲**

Adult male and female elephants do not live together in family groups. Instead, adult sisters and daughters live in groups led by an older female. Adult bulls live on their own or in all-male groups.

The huge ear of an African elephant.

Small eyes, protected by long eyelashes.

Wrinkly skin with hardly any hair.

Long trunk, used as a nose and an extra hand.

Gently curved tusks, used for digging, fighting and lifting.

Strong legs and flat feet for support.

**BABY ELEPHANTS ▲**

An elephant baby feels safe between its mother's front legs. It spends most of the first year of its life there. Mother elephants look after their young for longer than any other animal parent except humans. All the members of the family group assist and protect the young.

*161*

# African or Asian?

How do you tell an African elephant from an Asian elephant? They seem alike, but they are not identical. The most obvious difference is the size of the ears — the African elephant's are larger. In Africa, too, elephants have longer legs and a more slender body than their Asian relatives. The back of the Asian elephant is arched, while the African species has a dip in its back. Another difference is tusks — in Asia usually only males have visible tusks, whereas in Africa both male and female elephants normally have them.

## ▲ AFRICAN SHAPE

You can always tell an African elephant from its large ears and the dip in its back. This species of elephant usually holds its head slightly lower than its shoulders. The male African elephant stands on average 3.5m/11ft at the shoulder, while females are about 2.7m/9ft tall. The male weighs about 5 tonnes/tons, which is about the same as a truck.

## ▶ CONTINENTAL EARS

Some people say that the large, triangular ears of the African elephant (*right*) are shaped like the continent of Africa, while the ears of an Asian elephant are shaped like India. In fact, ears are like finger-prints — they are different on each elephant. Scientists look closely at the pattern of veins, notches and tears on the ears to identify individual elephants.

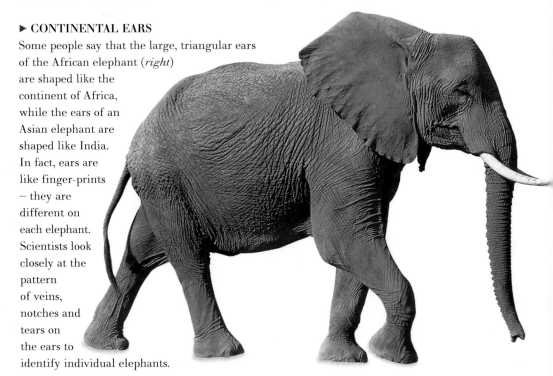

### ▶ HEAD UP

The Latin name of the Asian elephant, *Elephas maximus*, means huge arch. This refers to the upturned shape of its back. The Asian elephant usually holds its head above its body, so that the top of its head is the highest point of the body.

### ▲ ASIAN TUSKS

The tusks of a male Asian elephant are shorter and lighter than those of an African elephant. Female Asian elephants have very small tusks or none at all.

Did you know? The heaviest known African elephant weighed 7 tonnes/tons.

### ▼ SKIN SPOTS

Elephants are usually thought of as grey. However, some Asian elephants have pink patches of skin. These patches are commonly found on the ears, trunk, and face. They generally develop as the animal grows older. African elephants rarely have them.

### ▲ THE HAIRY ONE

Asian elephants have more hair than their African relatives, and baby Asian elephants (*above*) are hairier still. As baby elephants grow up, most of this protective hair is worn away.

# Big Bones

An elephant's legs are placed directly underneath its body, like a table's legs. This arrangement provides a firm support for its great weight. The leg bones stack one above the other to form a strong, tall pillar. As a result, an elephant can rest, and even sleep, while standing up. The pillar-like legs also help to hold up the backbone, which runs along the top of the animal and supports the ribs. The backbones of both African and Asian elephants arch upward in the middle. Their differently shaped backs are produced by bony spines that stick up from the backbone. The elephant's skeleton is not just built for strength, however. It is also flexible enough to let the elephant kneel and squat easily.

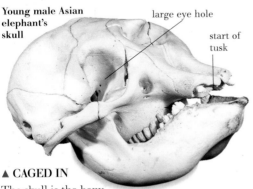

**▲ BONY BACK**
Long spines stick up from the backbone of the Asian elephant's skeleton. The muscles that hold up the head are joined to these spines and to the back of the skull.

**Young male Asian elephant's skull**

large eye hole

start of tusk

**▲ CAGED IN**
The skull is the bony box that protects the brain and holds the huge teeth and tusks. The skull above is that of a young elephant with undeveloped tusks. On an adult male the upper jaw juts out further than the lower jaw because it contains the roots for the heavy tusks.

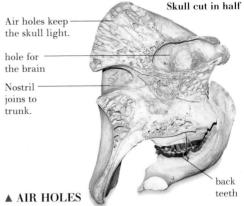

**Skull cut in half**

Air holes keep the skull light.

hole for the brain

Nostril joins to trunk.

back teeth

**▲ AIR HOLES**
An elephant has a large skull compared to the size of its body. However, a honeycomb of air holes inside the skull makes it lighter than it looks from the outside.

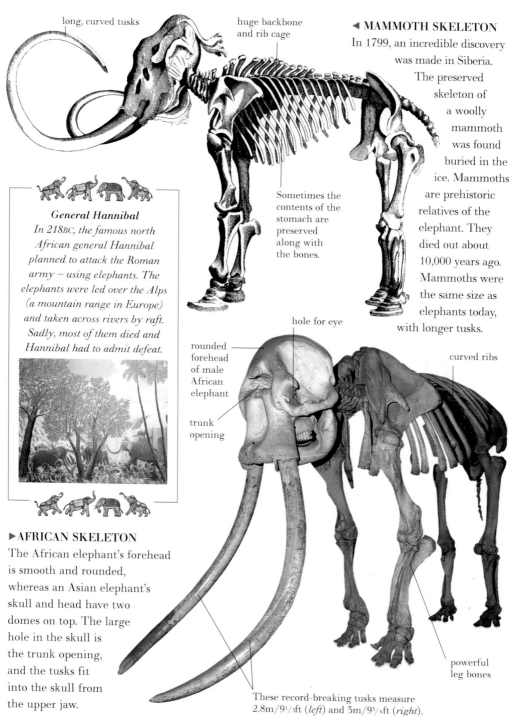

long, curved tusks

huge backbone
and rib cage

◀ **MAMMOTH SKELETON**
In 1799, an incredible discovery
was made in Siberia.
The preserved
skeleton of
a woolly
mammoth
was found
buried in the
ice. Mammoths
are prehistoric
relatives of the
elephant. They
died out about
10,000 years ago.
Mammoths were
the same size as
elephants today,
with longer tusks.

*General Hannibal*
*In 218BC, the famous north*
*African general Hannibal*
*planned to attack the Roman*
*army – using elephants. The*
*elephants were led over the Alps*
*(a mountain range in Europe)*
*and taken across rivers by raft.*
*Sadly, most of them died and*
*Hannibal had to admit defeat.*

Sometimes the
contents of the
stomach are
preserved
along with
the bones.

hole for eye

curved ribs

rounded
forehead
of male
African
elephant

trunk
opening

▶ **AFRICAN SKELETON**
The African elephant's forehead
is smooth and rounded,
whereas an Asian elephant's
skull and head have two
domes on top. The large
hole in the skull is
the trunk opening,
and the tusks fit
into the skull from
the upper jaw.

powerful
leg bones

These record-breaking tusks measure
2.8m/9¹/₅ft (*left*) and 3m/9³/₄ft (*right*).

# Tusks

An elephant's tusks are its front teeth. The part that we see is just two-thirds of the tusk's total length. The rest is hidden in the skull. Tusks are made from a very hard material called ivory. Elephants mainly use their tusks for feeding. The sharp ends are ideal for digging up edible roots and stripping bark from trees. Tusks are also used as weapons, and help to protect the trunk, like a car bumper. Elephants are born with milk tusks, which are replaced by permanent tusks when the elephant is between 6 and 12 months old. They grow continuously at the rate of about 18cm/7in a year. As the tip wears down, more tusk is pushed out from the skull.

## ▲ TINY TUSKS

Some female Asian elephants have small tusks called "tushes". They grow so slowly that they hardly stick out of the mouth. Some male Asian elephants have no tusks.

This elephant's left-hand tusk is shorter than the right-hand one because it has been used more.

Did you know? One rare elephant was found with four tusks instead of two.

Male elephant tusks weigh up to 59kg/132lb, or about the weight of two children. Female tusks are lighter and weigh 9kg/20lb on average.

## ◀ TUSK SHAPES

Elephants tend to be either right-handed or left-handed, just as human beings are. Their tusks are like hands, and elephants prefer to use one of them more than the other one. As a result, the favourite one becomes more worn. Tusks also come in different shapes and sizes. Some are slim and straight, while others stick out at different angles or even cross in front.

### ◄ USEFUL TUSKS

African elephants dig for salt with their tusks. They loosen the soil with the sharp points, just as we use a garden rake. On occasion, elephants also dig for salt in caves underground.

### ▼ MAMMOTH TUSKS

The tusks of extinct mammoths could be 2.4–3m/ 8–10ft long—half as long again as the tusks of most African elephants today. Mammoth tusks tended to curve first outward and then inward, although the females' tusks were more symmetrical and smaller than the males'. Early humans hunted mammoths for food. They also built huts from their bones.

African bull (male) tusk

African cow (female) tusk

Asian bull (male) tusk

### ▲ FIGHTING ELEPHANTS

In ancient India, humans trained elephants to help them fight battles. The elephant's sharp tusks were deadly when used as weapons. In ancient Rome, elephants were made to battle against gladiators (trained fighters) and other animals for sport. Cruelly, the elephants were usually forced to fight, against their own gentle nature.

### ◄ RAW MATERIALS

Tusks are made of solid ivory, which is a type of dentine. This is a hard material that forms the tusks of all tusked mammals. Nerves and blood vessels run through the tusks. The blood carries food to feed the growing tusk. Elephants feel pain and pressure in their tusks, just as we can in our teeth.

*167*

# Body Parts

An elephant's skin is thick, grey and wrinkly, and surprisingly sensitive. Some insects, including flies and mosquitoes, can bite into it. Often, elephants roll around in the mud to keep flies from biting them (as well as to cool themselves down). Underneath the skin, the elephant has typical mammal body parts, only much larger. The heart, for example, is about five times bigger than a human heart and weighs up to 20kg/44lb – the weight of a child. Also, an elephant's huge intestines can weigh nearly a ton, including the contents. The powerful lungs are operated by strong muscles. These let the elephant breathe underwater while using its trunk as a snorkel.

**▲ THICK SKIN**
An elephant's skin is 2.5cm/1in thick on the back and in some areas of the head. But in other places, such as around the mouth, the skin is paper thin.

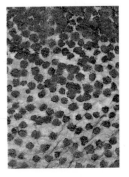

**▲ PINK SKIN**
An elephant gets its colour from dots of grey pigment (colouring) in the skin. As it ages, this grey pigment may gradually fade so that the skin looks pink.

*Did you know?*
*Some very rare Asian elephants have white skin.*

**◀ ELEPHANT HAIR**
The hairiest part of an elephant is the end of its tail. The tail hairs are many times thicker than human hair and grow into thick tufts. Apart from the end of the tail, the chin and around the eyes and ears, the elephant is not a particularly hairy animal.

## ▲ PINK TRUNKS

Some Asian elephants, particularly the Sri Lankan subspecies, have pink trunks. They may also have pink patches on their ears, face and belly, which are a sign of aging. This is comparable to human hair turning grey.

### Flying Elephants

*According to an Indian folktale, elephants could once fly. This ability was taken away by a hermit with magical powers when a flock of elephants woke him from a deep trance. The elephants landed in a tree above him, making a lot of noise and causing a branch to fall on his head. The hermit was so furious that he cast a magical spell.*

## ▼ INSIDE AN ELEPHANT

If you could look inside the body of an elephant, you would see its huge skeleton supporting the inner organs. The elephant cross section shown here is of a female elephant.

skull

brain

shoulder blade

ribs

small intestine

ovaries

backbone

kidney

eye

nostril

uterus

bladder

oesophagus (gullet)

trachea (windpipe)

lungs

heart

stomach

liver

large intestine

anus

nerve

nerve in trunk

wrist bone

blood vessel

ankle bone

169

# Elephant Senses

Elephants use their five senses to learn about their surroundings – hearing, sight, smell, touch and taste. The most important sense is smell, which they rely on more than any other. Elephants smell through their trunks, using them as directional noses. The trunk is also particularly sensitive to touch and has short hairs that help the elephant feel things. The tip of the trunk is used to investigate food, water and other objects. It can tell whether something is hot, cold, sharp or smooth. Elephants communicate with each other largely by sound. They make rumbling sounds, most of which are too low for humans to hear. Touch is also crucial for communication. When two elephants meet, each places the tip of its trunk in the other's mouth as a greeting.

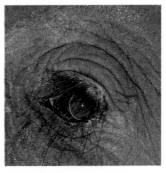

▲ **ELEPHANT EYES**
All elephants' eyes are brown with long lashes. They are small in relation to the huge head. Elephants are colour-blind and do not see well in direct, strong sunlight. Their eyesight is better in darker, more shadowy conditions.

**Did you know?** An African elephant's ear is as big as much as a single bed sheet and can weigh as a person.

◄ **SMELL**
An elephant raises its trunk like a periscope at the slightest scent of danger. It can tell who or what is coming towards it just from the smells picked up by the sensitive trunk. Its sense of smell is so powerful that an elephant can pick up the scent of a human being from more than 1.6km/1 mile away.

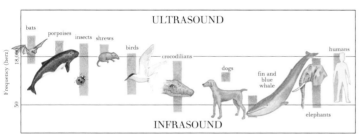

### ◀ USING EARS

An elephant strains to hear a distant noise by putting its ears forward to catch the sound. It also does this when it is curious about a certain noise. Elephants have a well-developed sense of hearing. Their enormous ears pick up the rumble of other elephants from up to about 8km/5 miles away. Male elephants also flap their ears to spread a special scent that lets other elephants know they are there.

### ◀ HEARING RANGE

Elephants can hear low sounds called infrasound. Human beings cannot hear infrasound, although we can sometimes feel it. Some animals, such as bats and mice, can hear very high sounds called ultrasound.

ULTRASOUND

bats   porpoises   insects   shrews   birds   crocodilians   dogs   fin and blue whale   humans   elephants

Frequency (hertz)

INFRASOUND

### ▲ SENSE OF TOUCH

A young elephant is touched by its mother or another close relative every few seconds. This constant reassurance keeps it from being frightened. Elephants also touch each other when they meet. They often stand resting with their bodies touching.

### ▲ QUICK LEARNERS

Some young working elephants learn to stop their bells from ringing by pushing mud inside them. This allows the clever animals to steal food from farmers' fields without being heard.

# Trunks

Imagine what it would be like if your nose and top lip were joined together and stretched into a long, flexible tube hanging down from your face. This is what an elephant's trunk must feel like. It can do everything your nose, lips, hand and arm can do – and more. An elephant uses its trunk to breathe, eat, drink, pick things up, throw things, feel, smell, fight and play, squirt water, hurl mud and dust, greet and touch other elephants and make sounds. Not surprisingly, a baby elephant takes a long time to learn all the ways to use its trunk.

## ▲ DRINKING

An elephant cannot lower its head down to the ground to drink, so it sucks up water with its trunk. Baby elephants drink with their mouths until they learn to use their trunks to squirt water into their mouths.

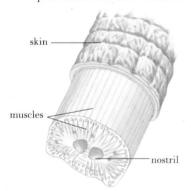

skin

muscles

nostril

## ▲ A CLOSER LOOK

The two holes in the centre of the trunk are nostrils, through which the elephant breathes. Thousands of muscles pull against each other in different directions to move the trunk.

## ▲ TRUNK POWER

An African elephant coils its trunk around a branch to lift it off the ground. Elephants can lift whole tree trunks in this way. The powerful trunk has more than 100,000 muscles, which enable an elephant to lift large, heavy objects easily.

172

## ▲ TAKING A SHOWER

An elephant does not need to stand under a shower to be sprayed with water, mud or dust. Its trunk is like a built-in shower, able to cover almost its whole body as it reaches backward over the head. Showering cools the elephant down and gets rid of insects.

## ▲ FLEXIBLE TRUNK

Elephants sometimes double up their trunks and rest them on their tusks. They can do this because the trunk has no bones inside it, just muscles, which makes it very flexible.

## ▶ TALL ORDER

African elephants use their long, stretchy trunks to pull leaves off the top branches of tall acacia trees. The highest leaves are the most juicy. The trunk is slightly telescopic, which means that, if necessary, it can be stretched out even longer than usual. The trunk can also be pushed into small holes or gaps between rocks to find hidden pools of water.

**Asian elephant**

**African elephant**

## ▲ TRUNK TIPS

The trunk of an African elephant has two fingers at the tip, while the Asian elephant has only one. These fingers can pick up an object as small as a leaf or a coin.

*173*

# Feeding

Elephants are herbivores (plant-eaters). They eat more than 100 different kinds of plants and enjoy almost every part – from the leaves, twigs, bark and roots to the flowers, fruit, seeds and thorns. However, most plants are not very nutritious, so an elephant has to eat huge amounts to survive. It spends about 16 hours a day choosing, picking and eating its food. Millions of microscopic organisms live inside an elephant's gut, which help to digest food. Even with the help of these organisms, half the food eaten by an elephant leaves the body undigested.

### ▲ STRIPPING BARK

An elephant munches on tree bark, which provides it with essential minerals and fibre. The elephant pushes its tusks under the bark to pull it off the tree trunk. Then it peels off a strip of bark by pulling with its trunk.

### ◀ EATING THORNS

Elephants do not mind swallowing a mouthful of thorns – as long as some tasty leaves are attached to them! Leaves and thorns make up an important part of an elephant's diet as they stay green in the dry season long after the grasses have dried up. This is because trees and bushes have long roots to reach water deep underground.

### ▼ GRASSY DIET

Marshes are packed full of juicy grasses. About 30–60 percent of an elephant's diet is grass. On dry land, an elephant may even beat grass against its leg to remove the soil before feeding.

► **BABY FOOD**

Baby elephants often feed on the dung of adult elephants. They do this to pick up microscopic organisms to live inside their guts and help them to digest food. Baby elephants learn what is good to eat by watching their mother and other relatives. They are also curious and like to try new types of food.

◄ **DUNG FOOD**

Elephant dung provides a feast for dung beetles and thousands of other insects. They lay their eggs in the dung, and the young feed on it when they hatch. Certain seeds only sprout in dung which has first passed through an elephant.

**FOOD IN CAPTIVITY** ►

People make meals for captive elephants from grasses and molasses (a type of sugar). Zoo elephants eat food such as hay, bread, nuts, fruit, leaves, bark and vegetables. They need a huge pile of food every day – in the wild they eat 99–198kg/220–440lb of plants every day.

# Living Together

An elephant family group is made up of related females and their offspring. Each family is led by an older, dominant female known as the matriarch. She makes all the decisions for the group. Her experience, learned over many years, is very important in keeping the family healthy and safe. Female elephants never leave the matriarchal unit unless it becomes too big. Then smaller groups break away and are led by the eldest daughters. Bulls (males) leave their family group when they are between 10 and 16 years old. When they are adults, only the strongest males mate with the females. Bulls spend most of their lives in small, all-male groups (comprising two or three animals) or wander on their own. Each family group has close links with up to five other families in the same area. These linked family units, together with groups of adult bulls, make up a herd.

## ▲ LITTLE LEARNERS

Young elephant calves copy the adults of the family to learn where to find water and food. If they are in trouble, a big sister, a cousin or an aunt is always around to help.

## ▼ THE MATRIARCH

Usually, the oldest and largest adult female becomes the matriarch (female leader). The rest of the group relies on her. She controls when they eat, drink and rest. She also protects them from danger and controls family members who misbehave.

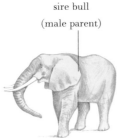

sire bull
(male parent)

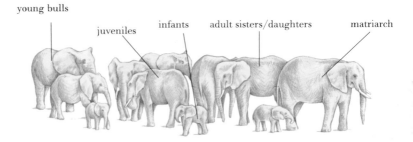

young bulls

juveniles

infants

adult sisters/daughters

matriarch

## ▲ AFRICAN FAMILY

A family of African elephants usually consists of a matriarch, her adult daughters and sisters, their calves and a number of young males and females. Bulls may sometimes join the family for mating, but they do not stay with it for long. They soon leave to resume their solitary lives.

## ◄ ASIAN FAMILIES

Elephants in Asia live in smaller groups than African elephants. Asian families have between four and eight members, although as many as 10–20 individuals may stay in touch.

## ◄ ALONE

Young bulls have a lot to learn once they leave the safety of their families. Often, they follow older males (patriarchs) around, and sometimes they have mock fights. However, males do not form strong social bonds with each other as the females in family groups do. As a result, some bulls lead entirely solitary lives.

177

# Elephant Habitats

The two main species of elephant are divided into smaller groups called subspecies. These subspecies each look a little different from one another and are named after their habitats. Africa has three subspecies – the bush elephant of the open grasslands, the forest elephant of west and central Africa and the desert elephant of Namibia. The main subspecies in Asia is the Indian and South-east Asian elephant. Asia is also home to the Sri Lankan elephant and the Sumatran elephant, which lives on the islands of Sumatra and Borneo (parts of Indonesia).

**▲ SUMATRAN ELEPHANT**
These elephants wade into swamps to find juicy grasses to feast on. They are the smallest of the three Asian subspecies. Sumatran elephants are also the lightest in colour, and they have fewer pink patches than the other Asian subspecies.

**SRI LANKAN ELEPHANT ▶**
The rare Sri Lankan elephant is the biggest and darkest of the three Asian subspecies. Many of the 2,500–2,700 elephants in Sri Lanka live in protected national parks or nature reserves.

Did you know? The desert elephant is the tallest elephant in the world, at up to 4.3m/14ft high.

**◀ FOREST ELEPHANTS**
The forest elephant (*Loxodonta africana cyclotis*) is the smallest African subspecies. Its size enables it to move easily through the trees. Generally, its ears are small and rounded and its tusks are less curved than those of other African elephants.

**◀ DESERT ELEPHANTS**
The hot, dry deserts of Namibia in south-west Africa are home to the rare desert elephant. This subspecies is very closely related to the African bush elephant, but it has longer legs. Desert elephants have to walk long distances to find food and water. Scientists think that this is why they have longer legs than any other subspecies.

**▶ ELEPHANT WORLD**
African elephants live in a scattered band across central and southern Africa. They became extinct in north Africa around AD300. Today, Asian elephants live in hilly or mountainous areas of India, Sri Lanka, South-east Asia, Malaysia, Indonesia and southern China. In the past, they roamed right across Asia.

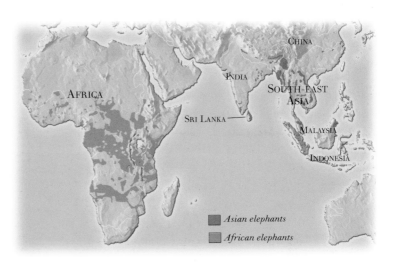

Asian elephants
African elephants

**▲ BUSH ELEPHANTS**
African bush elephants live on the savannah (areas of grassland with scattered trees). However, some live in forests or marshes and even on mountains.

**◀ SOLIDLY BUILT**
The African bush elephant, *Loxodonta africana africana*, is bulkier and heavier than any other elephant subspecies. Like all elephants, its large size is a useful weapon against lions, tigers and other predators.

179

# Elephant Migrations

protected areas ▪ ▪ planned extension to protected areas

## ▲ ANIMAL CORRIDORS

Much of the land in Sri Lanka is used for agriculture, so some elephants live in protected areas. They move between the regions along special corridors of land, in the same way that people travel between cities along highways.

Elephants do not have permanent homes. Every year they make long journeys called migrations to search for food and water. In the dry seasons, elephants gather in large groups for feeding migrations. They follow the same paths when moving from one place to another year after year. These paths are learned by one generation of elephants after another. Today, elephants have been squeezed into smaller areas as human beings take up more and more land. As a result, elephant migrations are much shorter than they used to be, although they may still cover hundreds of kilometres/miles.

**ELEPHANT RAIDERS ▶**
Farmers on the island of Sumatra try to chase a herd of elephants away from their corn fields. Migrating elephants can do a lot of damage to crops.

## ◀ ELEPHANT WELLS
During times of drought, elephants may dig holes in dry stream beds. They use their trunks, tusks and feet to reach water hidden underground. Elephants need to drink 68–90 litres/18–24 gallons of water each day and have been known to travel up to 30.5km/19 miles to reach a tiny patch of rainfall. Elephant wells can be lifesavers for other types of wildlife that come to drink the water after the elephants have gone.

**LONG JOURNEYS ▶**

African elephants on the savannah grasslands may wander over an area of more than 4,817sq km/1,860sq miles. The extent of their migrations depends on the weather and other conditions. Asian elephants living in forests migrate over smaller areas of about 155–466sq km/60–180sq miles.

**◀ WATCHING FROM ABOVE**

Migrating elephants can be followed by aeroplane in open country. Little or no rain falls during the dry season and the elephants tend to group together in places where water is available. The thirsty animals usually stay around a river valley or a swamp that still has water in it. In rainy seasons, elephants spread out over a wider area.

**◀ ELEPHANT BARRIERS**

Elephants will try anything to find a way through farmers' fences. They can use their tusks to break electric fence wires and even drop large rocks or logs on top of fences.

**KEEPING TRACK ▶**

Scientists in Africa fit a radio-collar to an elephant. This device tracks the animal's movements without disturbing its natural behaviour.

# Ancestors

The two species of elephant today are the surviving members of a once huge group of animals. However, the early members looked nothing like elephants. *Moeritherium*, which lived 50–60 million years ago, was a dog-sized animal with no trunk. This creature evolved into a larger animal called *Palaeomastodon*, with tusks, long lips and jaws for feeding. The first true elephant ancestor, *Stegodon*, evolved about 12 million years ago. It gave rise to the African and the Asian elephant, as well as the now extinct mammoth.

## ▲ EARLIEST ANCESTOR

*Moeritherium* was a small animal that lived in and around lakes and swamps about 50–60 million years ago. It had nostrils instead of a trunk, which were high on its face for breathing while submerged. Its eyes were also set quite high, similar to those of a hippo-potamus, to allow it to see easily while in the water. *Moeritherium* had sturdy legs, like an elephant, and small tusks.

## *GOMPHOTHERIUM* ▶

This distant elephant ancestor was up to 3m/10ft tall. Its skull was longer than that of a modern elephant, and it had tusks in both the top and bottom jaws. The lower jaw was longer, so the short lower tusks reached out as far as the upper ones.

## ◀ *STEGODON GANESA*

*Stegodon ganesa* lived in India and was named after the Hindu elephant-headed god Ganesh. It probably lived in forests and ate bamboo shoots and leaves. The long tusks of this animal were parallel along most of their length and grew very close together. The family to which this elephant belonged was similar to, but distinct from, true elephants. It died out about one million years ago.

### ▲ MASTODONS

Creatures known as
mastodons were
more common
than mammoths
in the woodlands of
North America. They lived more than 10,000 years ago and
were about the same size as Asian elephants, with long black-
brown hair. Some mastodons had two small tusks in the lower
jaw as well as the big, curved tusks in the top jaw.

### ► WOOLLY MAMMOTHS

These elephant relatives lived
in cold areas. They had long,
woolly coats to protect them
from freezing temperatures.
Mammoths
lived at the
same time as
early humans and died
out about 10,000 years ago.

### ▼ PRESERVED SKULL

Mammoth skeletons, including skulls, have
been found in Asia. From their preserved
flesh, we can determine that mammoths had
small ears. They would have
helped stop the animal
from losing
valuable body
heat in very
cold areas.

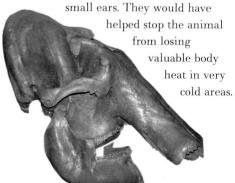

*The Cyclops*
*In Greek legend, Cyclops*
*were fierce giants with only*
*one eye. The legend may*
*have been based on the*
*fossilized skull of a*
*mastodon found in Greece.*
*The huge nose opening*
*could have been mistaken for*
*a large, central eye socket.*

### ▲ CAVE PAINTING

Stone Age people painted pictures of mammoths
on cave walls, many of which can still be seen
today. These early humans may have dug pits to
trap mammoths or driven them over cliffs.

# WHALES AND DOLPHINS

Whales and dolphins live in all of the oceans of the world, and are expert swimmers, divers and feeders. Although they live in the water they are, in fact, warm-blooded mammals which need to breath oxygen from the air. They range in size from the largest animal on Earth – the blue whale – to much smaller porpoises and dolphins.

*Author*: Robin Kerrod
*Consultant*: Michael Bright

# Whale Order

Like fish, whales and dolphins spend all their lives in the sea. But unlike fish, they breathe air, have warm blood and suckle their young. They are more closely related to human beings than to fish because they are mammals. Many whales are enormous – some are as big and as heavy as a train coach full of passengers. Dolphins are much smaller – most are about the same size as an adult human being. Porpoises, which look much like dolphins, are also roughly the same size as humans. Although smaller, dolphins and porpoises are kinds of whales, too. All whales belong to the major group, or order, of animals called Cetacea.

## ▼ BALEEN WHALES

These humpback whales are feeding in Alaskan waters. They belong to the group, or suborder, of whales known as the baleen whales. These are in general much larger than those in the other main group, the toothed whales.

## ▲ HEAVYWEIGHTS

The largest of the whales are the biggest animals ever to have lived. This leaping humpback whale is nearly 15m/50ft long and weighs over 25 tonnes/tons – as much as five fully-grown elephants. Some other kinds of whales, such as the fin and blue whales, are much bigger.

## ▶ WHALE ANCESTORS

More than 50 million years ago, creatures like this were swimming in the seas. They seem to have been ancestors of modern cetaceans. This creature, named Basilosaurus (meaning king lizard), grew up to over 20m/65ft long. It had a snake-like body with tiny front flippers and traces of a pair of hind limbs.

### Whale in the Sky

*This star map shows a constellation of stars named Cetus, meaning the sea monster or whale. In Greek mythology, Cetus was a monster that was about to eat Andromeda, a maiden who had been chained to a rock as a sacrifice. Along came Perseus, who killed the sea monster and saved Andromeda.*

### ▲ TOOTHED WHALES

A bottlenose dolphin opens its mouth and shows its teeth. It is one of the many species of toothed whales. Toothed whales have much simpler teeth than land mammals and many more of them. The bottlenose dolphin, for example, has up to 50 teeth in both its upper and lower jaws.

### ◄ BREATHING

Because they are mammals, whales and dolphins breathe air. This common dolphin breathes out through a blowhole on top of its head as it rises to the surface. It can hold its breath for five minutes or more when diving.

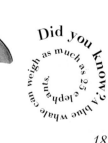

Did you know? A blue whale can weigh as much as 25 elephants.

187

# Whales Large and Small

Most large whales belong to the major group of cetaceans called the baleen whales. Instead of teeth, these whales have brush-like plates, called baleen, that hang from their upper jaw. They use the baleen to filter food from the water. The sperm whale does not belong to the baleen group. It belongs to the other major cetacean group, called the toothed whales. This group also includes dolphins, porpoises, white whales and beaked whales.

### ▲ GREY WHALE

The grey whale can grow up to nearly 15m/
50ft long, and tip the scales at 35 tonnes/tons or more.
It is a similar size to the humpback, sei, bowhead and right
whales, but looks quite different. Instead of the smooth skin
of other whales, the grey has rough skin and no proper dorsal
fin on its back.

Did you know? Some whales have as many as 3,000 baleen plates in their jaws.

### ▲ BLACK AND WHITE

The bowhead whale, which has a highly curved jaw, grows to 16m/52ft. It is closely related to the right whale. The bowhead is famous for its long baleen plates and thick layer of blubber. The toothed whales we call belugas *(above left)* grow to about 4.5m/15ft at most. The first part of the word beluga means white in Russian, and belugas are also known as white whales.

188

## ▶ SEI WHALE

At up to about 16m/52ft, the sei whale looks much like its bigger relatives, the blue whale and the fin. All are members of the group called rorquals, which have deep grooves in their throat. These grooves let the throat expand to take big mouthfuls of water for feeding. Seis have up to 60 grooves in their throat.

*Did you know? The blue whale's tongue weighs as much as an African elephant.*

## ▶ RELATIVE SIZES

Whales come in many sizes, from dolphins smaller than a human to the enormous blue whale, which can grow to 30m/98ft or more. In general, the baleen whales are much bigger than the toothed whales. The exception is the sperm whale, which can grow up to 19m/62ft.

porpoise

dolphin

narwhal

killer whale

beaked whale

grey whale

sperm whale

right whale

blue whale

## ▲ RISSO'S DOLPHIN

The dolphin pictured leaping here is a Risso's dolphin. It has a blunt snout and as few as six teeth. Most of the toothed whales that we call dolphins are on average about 2–3m/6–10ft long. Risso's dolphins can grow a little bigger – up to nearly 4m/13ft long.

189

# Whale Bones

Like all mammals, whales have a skeleton of bones to give the body its shape and protect vital organs like the heart. Because a whale's body is supported by water, its bones are not as strong as those of land mammals, and are quite soft. The backbone is made up of many vertebrae, with joints in between to give it flexibility. While providing some body support, the backbone acts mainly as an anchor for the muscles, particularly the strong muscles that drive the tail. Instead of limbs, a whale has a pair of modified fore limbs, called flippers.

**◄ BONE CORSET**
This advertisement for a "whalebone" corset dates from 1911, a time when women wore corsets to give them shapely figures. The corsets were, in fact, made from the baleen plates found in whales' mouths.

**► UNDERNEATH THE ARCHES**
Arches built from the jaw bones of huge baleen whales can be seen in some ports that were once the home of whaling fleets. This jaw-bone arch can be seen outside Christ Church Cathedral in Port Stanley, Falkland Islands. Nowadays, whales are protected species and building such arches is forbidden.

**► HANDS UP**
The bones in a sperm whale's flipper are remarkably similar to those in a human hand. A whale's flippers are a much changed version of a typical mammal's front limbs. Both hands have wrist bones, finger bones and joints.

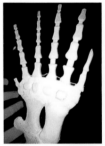
sperm whale flipper

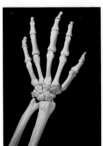
human hand

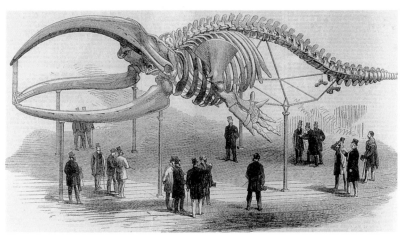

## ◄ BIG HEAD

This whale skeleton was displayed in London in 1830. Its large jaw bones tell us that it is a baleen whale, which needs a big mouth for feeding. Like other mammals, it has a large rib cage to protect its body organs. However, it has no hind limbs or pelvic girdle.

*Did you know? Whales are very oily and have a very strong smell.*

## ▼ TOOTHY JAW

This is the skeleton of a false killer whale, one of the toothed whales. The head is much smaller than that of the baleen whales, and its jaws are studded with teeth. Its long spine is made up of segments called vertebrae. The vertebrae in the whale's waist region are large, so that they are strong enough to anchor the animal's powerful tail muscles.

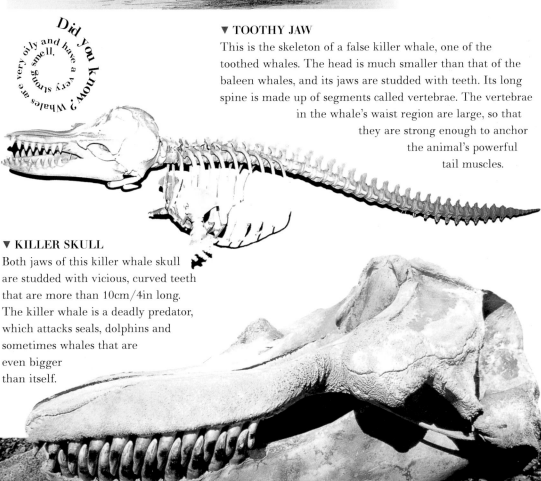

## ▼ KILLER SKULL

Both jaws of this killer whale skull are studded with vicious, curved teeth that are more than 10cm/4in long. The killer whale is a deadly predator, which attacks seals, dolphins and sometimes whales that are even bigger than itself.

# Whale Bodies

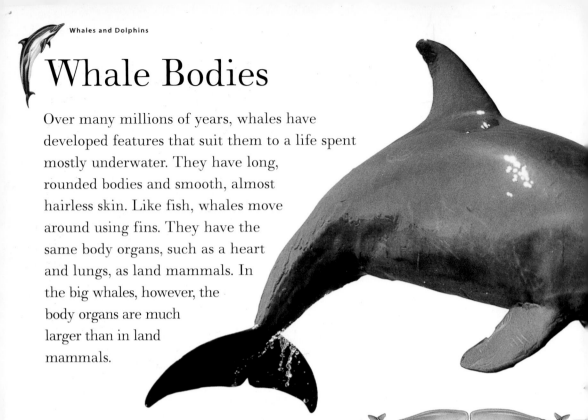

Over many millions of years, whales have developed features that suit them to a life spent mostly underwater. They have long, rounded bodies and smooth, almost hairless skin. Like fish, whales move around using fins. They have the same body organs, such as a heart and lungs, as land mammals. In the big whales, however, the body organs are much larger than in land mammals.

## ▼ BIG MOUTH

This grey whale is one of the baleen whales, and the baleen can be seen hanging from its upper jaw. Baleen whales need a big mouth so that they can take in large mouthfuls of water when they are feeding. Grey whales usually feed at the bottom of the sea.

baleen

### Jonah and the Whale

*This picture from the 17th century tells one of the best known of all Bible stories. The prophet Jonah was thrown overboard by sailors during a terrible storm. To rescue him, God sent a whale, which swallowed him whole. Jonah spent three days in the whale's belly before it coughed him up on to dry land. The picture shows that many people at this time had little idea of what a whale looked like. The artist has given it shark-like teeth and a curly tail.*

## ▼ LEAPING DOLPHINS

A pair of bottlenose dolphins leaps effortlessly several yards out of the water. Powerful muscles near the tail provide them with the energy for fast swimming and leaping. They leap for various reasons – to signal to each other, to look for fish or perhaps just for fun.

## ▲ HANGERS ON

This humpback whale's throat is covered with barnacles, which take hold because the whale moves slowly. They cannot easily cling to swifter-moving cetaceans, such as dolphins. A dolphin sloughs off rough skin as it moves through the water. This also makes it harder for a barnacle to take hold.

## ► LOUSY WHALES

The grey whale's skin is covered with light-coloured patches. These patches are clusters of ten-legged lice, called cyamids, about 2–3cm/¾–1¼in long. They feed on the whale's skin.

## ◄ BODY LINES

A pod, or group, of melon-headed whales swim in the Pacific Ocean. This species is one of the smaller whales, at less than 3m/10ft long. It shows the features of a typical cetacean – a well-rounded body with a short neck and a single fin. It has a pair of paddle-like front flippers and a tail with horizontal flukes.

Did you know? Whales have whiskers on their faces.

193

# Staying Alive

Whales are warm-blooded creatures. To stay alive, they must keep their bodies at a temperature of about 36–37°C/96.8–98.6°F. They swim in very cold water that quickly takes heat away from the surface of their bodies. To stop body heat from reaching the surface, whales have a thick layer of a fatty substance called blubber just beneath the skin. Whales must also breathe to stay alive and they do this through a blowhole, situated on top of the head. When a whale breathes out, it sends a column of steamy water vapour high into the air.

**▲ IN THE WARM**

Southern right whales feed in icy Antarctic waters in summer. The whales' size helps to limit the percentage of body heat they lose to the water.

epidermis

blood vessels

layer of blubber

**◄ SKIN DEEP**

This is a cross-section of a whale's outer layer. Beneath its skin, a thick layer of blubber insulates it from ice-cold water.

**► SMALL BODY**

The Atlantic spotted dolphin is about the size of a human. Because it is small, its body has a relatively large surface area for its size and so loses heat faster than its big relatives. This is probably why the Atlantic spotted dolphin lives in warm waters.

► **SKY HIGH**

A humpback whale surfaces and blows a column of warm, moist air. As it rises it cools, and the moisture in it condenses into a cloud of tiny water droplets.

▼ **DEEP DIVING**

Whales feed at different depths. Most dolphins feed close to the surface. The sperm whale holds the diving record and can descend to about 1,980m/ 6,500ft and stay under water for up to an hour.

| Depth | | Length of Dive |
|---|---|---|
| Surface | | common dolphin 15 minutes |
| 610m/ 2000ft | | fin whale 20 minutes |
| | | pilot whale 15 minutes |
| 1220m/ 4000ft | | |
| 1830m/ 6000ft | | sperm whale 60 minutes |
| 2440m/ 8000ft | | |

▼ **ONE BLOWHOLE**

Like all toothed whales, a bottlenose dolphin has only one blowhole. When the dolphin dives, thick lips of elastic tissue close it to stop water from entering, no matter how deep the dive.

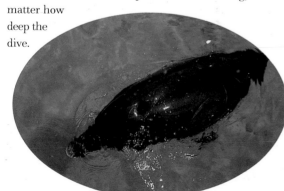

▲ **TWO BLOWHOLES**

The humpback whale breathes out through a pair of blowholes, located behind a ridge called a splashguard. This helps prevent water from entering the blowholes when the whale is blowing.

195

# Whale Brain and Senses

A whale controls its body through its nervous system. The brain is the control centre, carrying out functions automatically, but also acting upon information supplied by the senses. The size of whale brains varies according to the animal's size. However, dolphins have much bigger brains for their size. Hearing is by far a whale's most important sense. They pick up sounds with tiny ears located just behind the eyes.

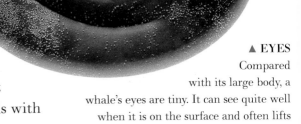

▲ EYES
Compared with its large body, a whale's eyes are tiny. It can see quite well when it is on the surface and often lifts its head out of the water to look around.

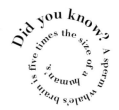

Did you know? A sperm whale's brain is five times the size of a human's.

◄ CLOSE ENCOUNTERS
A group of Atlantic spotted dolphins swims closely together in the seas around the Bahama Islands. Like most other cetaceans, the dolphins often nudge one another and stroke each other with their flippers and tail. Touch plays a very important part in dolphin society, especially in courtship.

A humpback whale slapping its tail, or lob-tailing, a favourite pastime for great whales. Lob-tailing creates a noise like a gunshot in the air, but, more importantly, it will make a loud report underwater. All the other whales in the area will be able to hear the noise.

### Cupids and Dolphins
*In this Roman mosaic, cupids and dolphins gambol (play) together. In Roman mythology, Cupid was the god of love. Roman artists were inspired by the dolphin's intelligence and gentleness. They regarded it as a sacred creature.*

### ◄ BRAINY DOLPHIN?
Some dolphins, such as the bottlenose, have a brain that is much the same size as our own. It is quite a complex brain with many folds.

### ► IN TRAINING
A bottlenose dolphin is shown with its trainer. This species has a particularly large brain for its size. It can be easily trained and has a good memory. It can observe other animals and learn to mimic their behaviour in a short amount of time. It is also good at solving problems – a sign of intelligence.

# Feeding Habits

Most baleen whales feed by taking mouthfuls of seawater containing fish and tiny shrimp-like creatures called krill or plankton, as well as algae, jellyfish, worms and so on. The whale closes its mouth and lifts its tongue, forcing water out through the bristly baleen plates on the upper jaw. The baleen acts like a sieve and holds back the food, which the whale then swallows. Toothed whales feed mainly on fish and squid. They find their prey by echolocation.

**▲ CRUNCHY KRILL**
These crustaceans, known as krill, form the diet of many baleen whales. Measuring up to 7.6cm/3in long, they swim in vast schools, often covering an area of several square miles. Most krill are found in Antarctic waters.

**◄ PLOUGHING**
A grey whale ploughs into the seabed, stirring up sand and ooze. It dislodges tiny crustaceans, called amphipods, and gulps them down. Grey whales feed mostly in summer in the Arctic before they migrate south.

**◄ SKIM FEEDING**
With its mouth open, a southern right whale filters tiny crustaceans, called copepods, out of the water with its baleen. It eats up to two tonnes/tons of these plankton daily. It eats so much because of its huge size – up to 80 tonnes/tons. Usually right whales feed alone, but if food is plentiful, several will feed cruising side by side.

**◀ SUCCULENT SQUID**

Squid is the sperm whale's favourite food and it is also eaten by other toothed whales and dolphins. Squid are molluscs, in the same animal phylum as snails and octopuses. Unlike octopuses, they have eight arms and two tentacles, and are called decapods (meaning "ten feet"). Squid swim together in dense schools, many thousand strong.

**◀ TOOTHY SMILE**

A Ganges river dolphin has more than 100 teeth. The front ones are very long. Ganges river dolphins eat mainly fish, and also take shrimp and crabs. They usually feed at night and find their prey by echolocation.

*Did you know? A blue whale eats nearly 990kg/2,200lb of krill in a single meal.*

**▶ LUNCH**

Belugas feed on squid and small fish, which are in plentiful supply in the icy ocean. Unlike common dolphins, belugas do not have many teeth. They may simply suck prey into their mouths. Many beaked whales, which also feed on squid, have no teeth suitable for clutching prey.

**▲ HUNT THE SQUID**

The sperm whale is the largest toothed whale, notable for its huge head and tiny lower jaw. It hunts the giant squid that live in waters around 1,980m/6,500ft deep. At that depth, in total darkness, it hunts its prey by echolocation.

# Sounds and Songs

Whales use sounds to communicate with one another and to find their food. Baleen whales use low-pitched sounds, which have been picked up by underwater microphones as moans, grunts and snores. The toothed whales make higher-pitched sounds, picked up as squeaks, creaks or whistles. Whales also use high-pitched clicks when hunting. They send out beams of sound, which are reflected by objects in their path, such as fish. The whale picks up the reflected sound, or echo, and figures out the object's location. This is called echolocation.

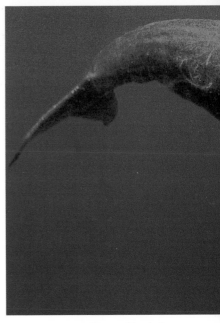

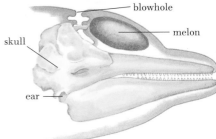

blowhole

melon

skull

ear

◀ **ECHO SOUNDINGS**
The Amazon river dolphin hunts by echolocation. It sends out up to 80 high-pitched clicks per second. The sound transmits in a beam from a bulge on top of its head. All toothed whales and dolphins hunt in this way.

▲ **MAKING WAVES**
A dolphin vibrates the air in its nasal passages to make high-pitched sound waves, which are focused into a beam by the melon – a bulge on its head. The sound beam transmits into the water.

▶ **SEA CANARIES**
A group of belugas, or white whales, swims in a bay in Canada. Belugas' voices can clearly be heard above the surface. This is why they are known as sea canaries. They also produce high-pitched sounds we cannot hear, which they use for echolocation.

### ◄ SUPER SONGSTER

This male humpback whale is heading for the breeding grounds where the females are gathering. The male starts singing long and complicated songs. This may be to attract a mate, or to warn other males away from its patch. The sound can carry for 30km/18 miles or more.

### ▼ LONG SONGS

This is a voice print of a humpback whale's song, picked up by an underwater microphone. It shows complex musical phrases and melodies. Humpback whales often continue singing for a day or more, repeating the same song.

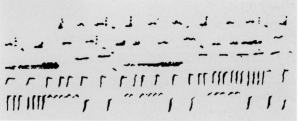

### ▼ SOUND ECHOES

A sperm whale can locate a giant squid more than 1.6km/1 mile away by transmitting pulses of sound waves into the water and listening. The echo is picked up by the teeth in its lower jaw and the vibrations are sent along the jaw to the ear.

Did you know? A dolphin picks up sounds through its lower jaw.

### ◄ ALIEN GREETINGS

The songs of the humpback whale travel not only through Earth's oceans, but also far out into space. They are among the typical recorded sounds of our world that are being carried by the two Voyager space probes. These probes are now many millions of miles away from earth and are on their way to the stars.

# Swimming

All whales are superb swimmers. All parts of the whale's body help it to move through the water. The driving force comes from the tail fin, or flukes. Using very powerful muscles in the rear third of its body, the whale beats its tail up and down, and the whole body bends. It uses its pectoral fins, or flippers, near the front of the body to steer with. The body itself is streamlined and smooth to help it to slip through the water easily. The body can change shape slightly to keep the water flowing smoothly around it. Little ridges under the skin help as well.

▲ STEERING

Among whales, the humpback has by far the longest front flippers. As well as for steering, it uses its flippers for slapping the water. Flipper-slapping seems to be a form of communication.

◄ TAIL POWER

The tail flukes of a grey whale rise into the air before it dives. Whales move their broad tails up and down to drive themselves through the water.

▼ MASSIVE FIN

The dorsal fin of a killer whale projects high into the air. The animal is a swift swimmer, and the fin helps keep its body well balanced. The killer whale has such a large dorsal fin that some experts believe it may help to regulate their body temperature, or even be used in courtship. Most whales and dolphins have a dorsal fin, although some only have a raised hump.

Did you know? A killer whale can swim up to 64kph/40mph.

### ◀ STREAMLINING

Atlantic spotted dolphins' bodies are beautifully streamlined – shaped so that they slip easily through the water when they move. The dolphin's body is long and rounded, broad in the front and becoming narrower toward the tail. Apart from the dorsal fin and flippers, nothing projects from its body. It has no external ears or rear limbs.

### ▼ HOW A DOLPHIN SWIMS

Dolphins beat their tail flukes up and down by means of the powerful muscles near the tail. The flukes force the water backward at each stroke. As the water is forced back, the dolphin's body is forced forward. Its other fins help guide it through the water. They do not provide propulsion.

### ◀ SMOOTH SKINNED

This bottlenose dolphin is tailwalking – supporting itself by powerful thrusts of its tail. Unlike most mammals, it has no covering of hair or hair follicles – the dimples in the skin from which the hair grows. Its smooth skin helps the dolphin's body to slip through the water.

### ▼ HOW A FISH SWIMS

It is mainly the tail that provides the power for a fish to swim. The tail has vertical fins, unlike the horizontal fins of the dolphin. It swims by beating its tail and body from side to side.

203

# Social Life

Every day we meet, work, play and communicate with other people. We are sociable animals. Some whales are also sociable and live together. Sperm whales live in groups of up to about 50. A group may be a breeding school of females and young or a bachelor school of young males. Older male sperm whales live alone, except in the breeding season. Beluga whales often live in groups of several hundred. Baleen whales are not as sociable. They move alone or in small groups, probably because of their huge appetite – they could not find enough food if they lived close together.

▲ **HERD INSTINCT**
Beluga whales gather together in very large groups, or herds, and they mostly stay in these herds for life. Many of the animals in this group, pictured in the Canadian Arctic, have calves. These can be recognized not only by their smaller size, but also by their darker skin colour.

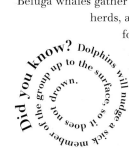

Did you know? Dolphins will nudge a sick member of the group up to the surface, so it does not drown.

▼ **NOSY ORCAS**
Two killer whales, or orcas, spy-hop in Antarctic waters. They rise out of the water together, as if on a signal. They are members of the same pod, which stays together all their lives. The bonds between the animals are very strong. This helps them coordinate their activities, especially when hunting for food.

**◄ STAYING CLOSE**

Two Atlantic spotted dolphins swim with their young. The young's spots will not start to appear until the animals are about a year old. As with many other species, the young stay very close to their parents most of the time.

**▼ HUMAN CONTACT**

A bottlenose dolphin swims alongside a boy. These dolphins live in social groups, but lone outcasts, or animals that have become separated from their group, often approach humans.

**▲ SOLITARY SWIMMER**

An Amazon river dolphin rests on the river bed. It spends most of its life alone, or with just one other. This solitary behaviour is typical of river dolphins, but not typical of most whales and ocean dolphins.

**► PILOT ERROR**

These long-finned pilot whales are stranded on a beach. Pilot whales usually live in large groups, with strong bonds between group members. One whale may strand itself on a beach. The others may try to help it and get stranded themselves.

# Where Whales are Found

Whales are found in all the world's oceans. Some kinds live all over, while others are found only in a certain area. They may stay in the same place all year long, or migrate from one area to another with the seasons. Some whales stick to shallow coastal areas, others prefer deep waters. Some live in the cool northern or southern parts of the world. Others are more at home in tropical regions near the Equator. Some species even live in rivers.

▼ **OCEAN WANDERER**

A humpback whale surfaces to blow while swimming at Cape Cod off the north-east coast of North America. In summer, the humpback feeds in high latitudes. It migrates to low latitudes to breed during the winter.

▲ **MUDDY WATERS**

The mud-laden waters of the Amazon River in South America are the habitat of the Amazon river dolphin. Here, one shows off its teeth. This species ranges along the Amazon and its tributaries.

**Did you know?** Some dolphins come and go between salt water and fresh water.

◄ **WORLDWIDE ORCA**

Among ice-floes in the Arctic Ocean, a killer whale, or orca, hunts for prey. Orcas are found in all the oceans. They live in coastal areas but may venture out to the open ocean. They also swim in the surf along the shore, and may beach to snatch their prey.

► **SNOW WHITE**
These belugas, or white whales, are in Hudson Bay, Canada. These cold-water animals live around coasts in the far north of North America, Europe and Asia. They venture into estuaries and even up rivers. In winter they hunt in the pack ice in the Arctic.

◄ **TROPICAL MELONS**
A pod of melon-headed whales is shown swimming in the Pacific Ocean. These creatures prefer warm waters and are found in subtropical and tropical regions in both the Northern and Southern Hemispheres. They generally stay in deep water, keeping well away from land.

► **WIDE RANGER**
A bottlenose dolphin lunges through the surf in the sunny Bahamas. This animal is one of the most wide-ranging of the dolphins, being found in temperate to tropical waters in both the Northern and Southern Hemispheres. It is also found in enclosed seas such as the Mediterranean and the Red Sea. Mostly it stays in coastal waters. When bottlenose dolphins migrate to warmer areas, they lose weight. When they return to colder climates, their blubber increases again.

207

# Migration

Grey whales spend the summer months feeding in the Arctic Ocean. Many of the females are pregnant. Before winter comes, the whales head south toward Mexico for warmer waters, where the females give birth to their calves, which stand a better chance of surviving in the warmer waters. Mating occurs in late winter. In the spring, the greys head north to the Arctic. Their annual journey between feeding and breeding grounds involves a round trip of some 19,955km/12,400 miles. The humpbacks also take part in long migrations. Most of the other large rorquals and the right whales seem to undergo similar migrations.

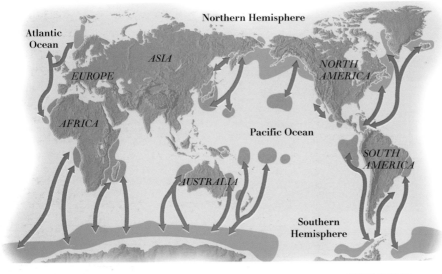

**Migration**
*This map shows the routes taken by humpback whales during their annual migrations between their summer feeding and winter breeding grounds. There are at least three main groups, two in the Northern and one in the Southern Hemisphere.*

KEY TO MAP

■ breeding grounds    ■ feeding grounds

◀ **SUMMER FEEDING**
Two Southern Hemisphere humpbacks feed in the Antarctic Ocean during the summer months. This is when the krill and other plankton they feed on thrive. The whales have taken huge mouthfuls of water, which they strain for plankton using the baleen on their upper jaws.

## ▼ RIGHT LOCATION

The tail fluke of a southern right whale is thrust into the air as the animal sails. This whale is one of a group of right whales in winter breeding grounds off the coast of Argentina. By summer the whales will have returned south to feed in the Antarctic Ocean.

Did you know? Grey whales make longer migrations than any other mammal.

## ▲ WINTER BREEDING

It is early winter, and two humpbacks have migrated north from the Antarctic to a shallow bay on the coast of eastern Australia. A large group of humpbacks will mate here and, about 12 months later, the females will give birth.

## ▼ MATING GREYS

In the winter breeding grounds of Baja California, a grey whale surfaces. They spend about three months in the region, where mating and (two years later) births take place.

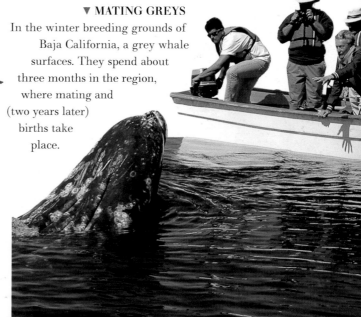

# SHARKS

There are over 400 different species of
shark, and they can be found at every
depth of every ocean. Despite their
reputation as man-eaters, attacks on
humans are extremely rare and
are limited to a small number of
species. All sharks are carnivores,
and their food ranges from tiny
plankton to large seals.

*Author*: Michael Bright
*Consultant*: Ian K. Fergusson
The Shark Trust

# What is a Shark?

There are about 400 different kinds of shark in the world. Some are as big as whales, others as small as a cigar. Whatever their size, they all eat meat. Some sharks eat tiny plants and animals called plankton. Others hunt down fish, squid and even seals. Many sharks will also feed off the remains of another's meal or eat animal carcasses. They live at all depths, in every ocean, from tropical waters to cold polar seas. Some sharks can survive in the fresh water of rivers and lakes. Like other fish, sharks take oxygen from the water as it passes over their gills. Although some sharks like to live alone, others survive as part of a group.

**▼ CLASSIC SHARK**
This blue shark (*Prionace glauca*) is how most people imagine sharks. However, there are many different families of sharks in the seas and oceans and they have a variety of body shapes.

no cover over the gill slits

blue shark's mouth filled with sharp teeth

Wing-like pectoral fins help keep the shark moving forward.

**◄ WHITE DEATH**
The great white shark (*Carcharodon carcharias*) is the largest hunting fish in the sea. It has an exaggerated reputation as a killer, partly because a killer shark appears in the film, *Jaws*. In reality great white sharks do often eat large prey, but they attack people only occasionally, in cases of mistaken identity.

## ▶ SHARK SCHOOL

Some sharks live alone,
others live in schools
(groups). Every day
schools of female
scalloped hammerhead
sharks (*Sphyrna lewini*)
like these gather off the
Mexican coast. At
night, the sharks
separate and hunt alone.

triangular
dorsal (back)
fin for stability

body packed
with muscles
for strength

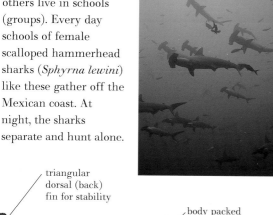

## ▲ GENTLE GIANT

Although the basking shark
(*Cetorhinus
maximus*) is the
second largest fish
after the whale
shark, it is not a
hunter. It funnels water
through its huge mouth,
using gill rakers (giant
combs) to filter out the tiny
plankton that it eats.

flattened tail to
help propel (push)
through water

## ▲ REEF HUNTERS

Whitetip reef sharks (*Triaenodon obesus*) are
one of the smaller species (kinds) of shark.
They rarely grow over 1.8m/6ft long and
hunt along tropical coral reefs at night.

*Maya Origins*
*This monkey head from
Central America has been
decorated with shark teeth.
It is thought that the word
shark comes from the Maya
people of Central America. It
may be based on the Maya
word* xoc *(fury). The
Maya symbol (word picture)
for* xoc *is a shark-like creature.*

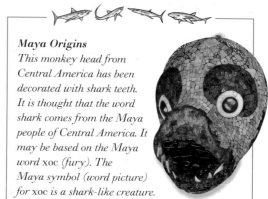

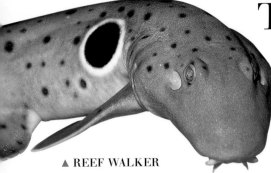

# The Eight Families

Sharks fall into eight main orders (groups) divided according to different features. The most primitive orders, including frilled and sevengill sharks, have more than five gill slits. Dogfish sharks have long, round bodies and include luminous (glow in the dark) sharks that live in very deep water. The seven or more species of sawshark have a saw-like snout. Angel sharks look like rays and lie hidden on the seabed. Bullhead sharks have spines on both of their dorsal fins, and carpet sharks, like the wobbegong sharks, have bristles on their short snouts. Mackerel sharks, with their special, warm muscles, are awesome hunters. These sharks include the great white and mako. The ground sharks include the widest range of all, from catsharks to bull sharks, hammerheads, blue sharks and oceanic whitetips.

▲ REEF WALKER
Two pairs of muscular pectoral fins allow the epaulette shark (*Hemiscyllium ocellatum*) to walk over its tropical reef home. It feeds on the seabeds of shallow waters around the Australian reefs.

▼ TYPES OF SHARKS
Modern sharks are divided into eight large family groups. These groups are divided into over 30 smaller families, and nearly 400 species. This number will probably rise, as more species of shark are discovered.

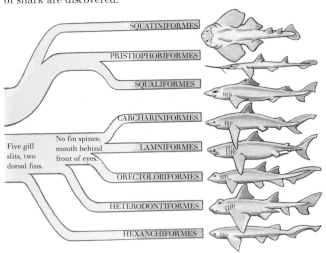

| | | |
|---|---|---|
| SQUATINIFORMES | | Body flattened, raylike. Mouth in front. |
| PRISTIOPHORIFORMES | | Snout elongated and sawlike. Mouth underneath. |
| SQUALIFORMES | | Snout short, not sawlike. |
| CARCHARINIFORMES | | Sliding flap that covers eyes. |
| LAMNIFORMES | No fin spines; mouth behind front of eyes. | No sliding flap over eyes. |
| ORECTOLOBIFORMES | | Mouth well in front of eyes. |
| HETERODONTIFORMES | | Dorsal fin spines. |
| HEXANCHIFORMES | | Six or seven gill slits. One dorsal fin. |

Five gill slits, two dorsal fins.

**◄ PRIMITIVE SHARK**
The broadnose sevengill shark
(*Notorynchus cepedianus*) is
one of five species of
primitive shark. Each has
six or seven gill slits. All
swim in deep waters.

**▲ GROUND SHARK**
The swell shark (*Cephaloscyllium ventriosum*) is
a ground shark. It blows up like a balloon by
swallowing water and storing it in
its stomach. When it is
threatened, this amazing
shark wedges itself
firmly inside the cracks
between rocks. It can be
very difficult to remove.

*Did you know?* Pacific Island children ride on nurse sharks' backs.

*Food for the sharks*
*The Carib peoples buried the bodies of*
*their dead relatives by ceremonially*
*putting them into Lake Nicaragua in*
*Central America. Many of the bodies were*
*then eaten by bull sharks in the lake. One*
*thief made a fortune by catching the*
*sharks, slitting them open and removing*
*jewels that had decorated the bodies of the*
*dead. Until he was caught, that is . . .*

**► REQUIEM SHARK**
The sandbar, or brown, shark
(*Carcharhinus plumbeus*) is a
requiem shark – here, requiem
means "ceremony for the
dead". All members of this
family are active hunters.
They rule tropical seas,
hunting fish, squid and sea
turtles. They are probably the
most modern group of shark.

# Shapes and Sizes

Many hunting sharks have long, rounded shapes, like the slim blue shark and the bulkier bull shark. Angel sharks have a flattened shape suited to hiding on the sea floor, while eel-like frilled sharks swim in the deep sea. Horn sharks have spines on their backs, and megamouths (big mouths) have big, blubbery lips! As their names suggest, hammerhead sharks have hammer-shaped heads, and sawsharks have elongated, saw-like snouts. Giant sharks, such as the whale shark, are as long as a school bus, and there are midget sharks, such as the Colombian lantern shark, that you could hold in the palm of your hand! Whatever the kind of shark, they are all perfectly adapted for the waters in which they live.

### ▲ GROTESQUE SHARK
The goblin shark (*Mitsukurina owstoni*) has an unusual horn-shaped snout. This shark seems to have also lived in the dinosaur age. A fossil of a similar shark has been found in rocks that were created about 150 million years ago. Today, the goblin shark lives in very deep waters found off continental shelves.

### ▶ DEEP SEA NIPPER
The pygmy shark is one of the smallest sharks in the world. When fully grown, it is no more than 20cm/8in. long, making it smaller than a whale shark embryo (baby). It roams the gloomy waters of the Caribbean Sea, hunting in packs.

**pygmy shark**
(*Europtomicrus bispinatus*)

### ▲ STRANGE HEAD
The amazing heads of the hammerhead, bonnethead and winghead sharks are shaped like the letter T. These sharks use their hammers to detect prey and to help when swimming.

zebra bullhead shark
(*Heterodontus zebra*)

## ▲ ROCK DISGUISE

Unlike many sharks, the spotted wobbegong shark (*Orectolobus maculatus*) has a flattened shape. It is a carpet shark (a family of camouflaged sharks that lie on the seabed), and disguises itself as part of the coral reef. The barbels (tassels) under its mouth look like seaweed.

## ▲ SAFETY SPINES

A striped pattern helps the colourful zebra bullhead shark to camouflage itself (blend in) among corals and seaweed. For further protection, at the front of each dorsal fin is a sharp spine. If swallowed, the shark's spines will stick into the throat of any attacker, forcing it eventually to spit out its prickly meal.

## ▶ UNDERWATER TIGER

A young tiger shark has pale stripes along its body, which fade as it grows older. The powerful tiger shark (*Galeocerdo cuvier*) has a long, rounded shape, typical of hunting sharks. Some can rival great whites in size.

## ◀ BIG GULP

The whale shark (*Rhincodon typus*) is aptly named. Bigger than any other shark, it is closer in size to the giant whales. It is the largest fish in the sea, can grow to 13–15m/ 40–50ft in length and weigh up to 3 tons. With its giant mouth and large gill slits, the whale shark, like the basking shark, is a filter feeder.

# Light and Strong

Although most fish are bony, the skeleton of a shark is made up almost entirely of cartilage, which is also found in the human nose. It is lighter and more elastic than bone, and it is this that makes the shark skeleton very flexible. This cartilage structure is strong enough to support a shark's huge muscles, and flexible enough to allow it to move with ease. Because sharks' skeletal cartilage and soft body parts decay (rot) so quickly after they die, it is unusual to find complete shark fossils (preserved bodies) in ancient rocks. Only the hard teeth and spines are fossilized.

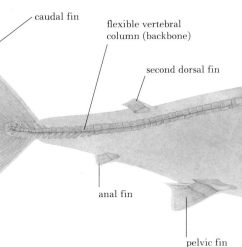

caudal fin

flexible vertebral column (backbone)

second dorsal fin

anal fin

pelvic fin

**▼ PROTRUDING JAWS**
A shark's jaws are attached to the skull by flexible ligaments. These allow some sharks to thrust their jaws forward when taking a bite.

teeth in upper jaw slice like a knife

**▲ DARK TRIANGLE**
Like the keel of a yacht, a shark's stiff dorsal fin helps it to balance in the water and stops it from slipping sideways. Most sharks have two dorsal fins, one at the front and one at the back.

► **AEROPLANE FINS**
A shark's pectoral fins, one on each side, act like the wings of an aeroplane. As water passes over them, the fins give lift.

◄ **SHARK SKELETON**
The skeleton of a great white shark. It is tough, flexible and typical of that found in most sharks, providing support and protection for the entire body. The great white's muscles are attached to a long backbone; the gills are supported by gill arches and a box-like skull protects the brain.

dorsal fin

Gill arches support shark's gills.

Compact skull protects brain and nasal capsules.

pectoral fin

▲ **CARTILAGE SOUP**
These fins have been cut from sharks and are drying in the sun. The cartilage in a shark's fin helps to make it stiff. When boiled in water it makes a gluey substance that is used in the Far East to make shark's fin soup.

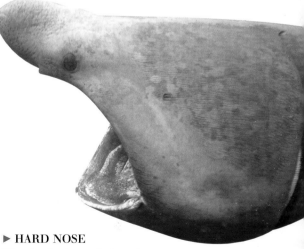

► **HARD NOSE**
The shark pictured above is an adult basking shark. At birth, this shark has a strange, hooked nose, like that of an elephant. When the basking shark starts to grow, the cartilage in its snout gradually straightens.

# Tough Teeth

A shark species can be identified by the shape of its teeth alone. Each species has its own distinctive shape, designed for the type of food it eats. Some have sharp, spiky teeth that can hold on to slippery fish and squid. Others have broad, grinding teeth that can crack open shellfish. The teeth of some species of shark change as they get older and hunt different prey. Although sharks lose their teeth regularly, the teeth are always replaced. Behind each row of teeth lie more rows. If a front tooth is dislodged, an extra tooth simply moves forward to take its place!

**▲ SHARK SAW MASSACRE**

The teeth of a tiger shark are shaped like the letter L. They can saw through skin, muscle and bone, and can even crack open the hard shell of a sea turtle. A tiger shark eats its prey by biting hard and shaking its head from side to side, slicing into its food like a chain saw.

**▼ AWESOME JAWS**

When it is about to grab its prey, a sandtiger shark opens and extends its awesome jaws. The rows of spiky teeth inside are perfect for grabbing and holding slippery fish and squid. Once caught, the prey is swallowed whole.

**sandtiger shark**
*(Eugomphodus taurus)*

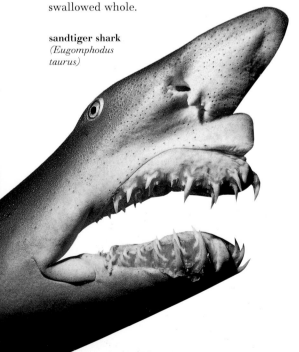

**▲ NEEDLE POINT**

This 1.8m/6ft-long leopard shark (*Triakis semifasciata*) has rows of small, needle-sharp teeth. Although it is thought to be harmless, in 1955 a leopard shark sank its tiny teeth into a skin diver in Trinidad Bay, California. This was an unprovoked attack, and the diver escaped.

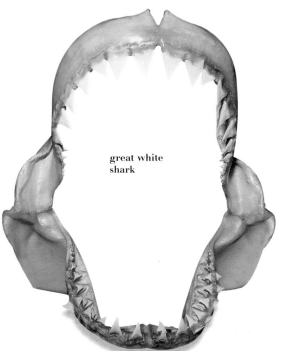

great white
shark

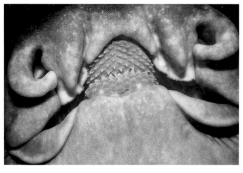

## ▲ DUAL SETS OF TEETH

The Port Jackson shark (*Heterodontus portusjacksoni*) has small, sharp teeth for catching small fish and broad, crushing teeth that can crack open shellfish.

## ▲ JAWS

The awesome jaws of a great white shark are filled with two types of teeth. The upper jaw is lined with large, triangular teeth that can slice through flesh. The lower jaw contains long, pointed teeth that are used to hold and slice prey.

## ▼ BIG TEETH

The cookie-cutter is a small shark, reaching only 50cm/20in long. However, for its body size, it has the biggest teeth of any shark known. It uses them to cut round chunks out of its prey, which includes dolphins, whales and large fish.

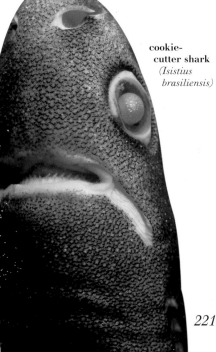

cookie-
cutter shark
(*Isistius
brasiliensis*)

**Shark Man**
*Ceremonial carvings such as this one were used in ritual dances performed in the South Pacific Solomon Islands. From one dance master to another, these traditional dances were passed down through many generations. They told of myths in which sharks turned into men, and men turned back into sharks again.*

221

# Shark Bodies

Sharks are incredible machines, packed with muscle. Some sharks, such as the great white and mako, can even keep their muscles, gut, brain and eyes warmer than the temperature of the seawater around them. They do this with special blood vessels, which work like a radiator to collect the heat in the blood and send it back into the body. These make muscles more efficient, allowing the sharks to swim faster. They also help these sharks to hunt in seas of different temperatures. Sharks have a huge, oil-filled liver that helps to keep them afloat. However, like an aeroplane, they must also move forward in order to stay up. Open ocean sharks must swim all the time, not only to stop them from sinking, but also to breathe. Some sharks can take a rest on the seabed by pumping water over their gills to breathe.

▲ GILL BREATHERS
Like this sixgill shark (*Hexanchus griseus*), most sharks breathe by taking oxygen-rich water into their mouths. The oxygen passes into the blood and the water exits the gill slits.

▲ OCEAN RACER
The shortfin mako shark (*Isurus oxyrinchus*) is the fastest shark in the sea. Using special muscles, it can travel at speeds of 32–48kph/20–30mph and catch fast-swimming swordfish.

◄ SUSPENDED ANIMATION
The sandtiger shark (*Eugomphodus taurus*) and a few others can hold air in their stomachs. The air acts like a life jacket, helping the shark to hover in the water. Sandtiger sharks stay afloat without moving, lurking among rocks and caves.

### ▶ KEEP MOVING

Like many hunting sharks, the grey reef shark (*Carcharinhus amblyrynchos*) cannot breathe unless it moves forward. The forward motion passes oxygen into its gills. If it stops moving, the shark will drown.

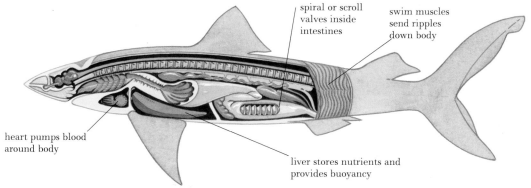

spiral or scroll valves inside intestines

swim muscles send ripples down body

heart pumps blood around body

liver stores nutrients and provides buoyancy

### ▲ INSIDE A SHARK

If you could look inside a shark, you would find thick muscles, an enormous liver, an intestine with a special spiral valve and a complicated system of blood vessels that supply the shark's gills.

Did you know? Mako sharks have been seen to leap 6m/20ft clear of the water.

### ◀ ABLE TO REST

The tawny nurse shark (*Nebrius ferrugineus*) pumps water over its gills by lifting the floor of its mouth. This allows it to rest on the seabed, yet still breathe. Whitetip reef sharks, lemon sharks, catsharks and nursehounds also do this.

223

# Brain and Senses

A shark's brain is small for its size, but its senses are highly developed. Sharks see well, and see in colour. They can also recognize shapes. Just as amazing are a different range of senses that allow sharks to pick up sounds and vibrations from miles around. They can detect changes in the ocean currents, recognize smells, and follow the trail of an odour right back to its source. Some species have shiny plates at the backs of their eyes that collect light to help them see as they dive into deep, dark water. They also have dark membranes that they draw across the shiny plates to keep from being dazzled by the light when they return to the surface. Sharks even have special nerves in their noses that can detect minute electrical fields, such as those produced by the muscles of their prey.

▲ **ELECTRICAL SENSE**
Like all sharks, sandtiger sharks have tiny pits in their snouts, known as the ampullae of Lorenzini. Inside these pits are special nerves. These help the shark to find food by detecting minute electrical fields in the muscles of its prey.

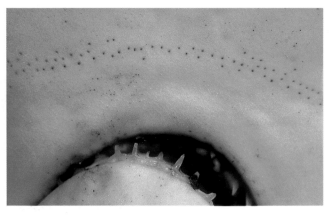

◄ **PREY DETECTOR**
In a hammerhead shark the special pits that can sense electrical fields in its prey are spread across the hammer of the shark's head, helping it to scan for prey across a wide area. The hammerhead searches for food by sweeping its head from side to side, as if it was using a metal detector. It can find any prey buried in the sand below.

## ◄ SIGHT, SMELL AND SOUND

The nostrils of the hammerhead shark are positioned on the sides of its head. This gives the shark "stereo smelling" with which it can more easily track odours to their source. But, because its eyes are at the ends of its hammer, it must turn its head from side to side in order to see forward.

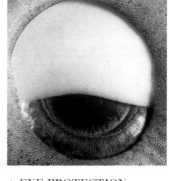

**scalloped hammerhead shark**
(*Sphyrna lewini*)

## ▲ EYE PROTECTION

When a shark bites, its eyes can easily be injured by the victim's teeth, spines or claws. To prevent this, sharks such as this tiger shark have a special membrane (sheath) that slides down across the eye during the attack.

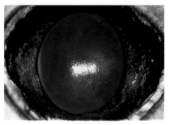

eye of blacktip reef shark
(*Carcharhinus melanopterus*)

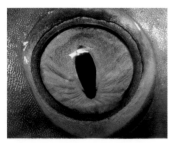

eye of bluntnose sixgill shark
(*Hexanchus griseus*)

## ◄ DEEP AND SHALLOW

The blacktip reef shark has a small eye with a narrow, vertical slit. This type of eye is often found in shallow-water sharks. Sharks that swim in deeper waters, such as the sixgill shark, tend to have large, round pupils.

Did you know? Sharks find their way through mazes as fast as rabbits.

*Shark Callers*

*On the islands of the south-west Pacific, sharks are the islanders' gods. To test their manhood, young shark callers attract sharks by shaking a coconut rattle under the water. Sensing the vibrations, a shark will swim close to the canoe. It is then wrestled into the boat, and its meat divided among the villagers as a gift from the gods.*

225

# Feeding

Sharks catch a variety of foods, eating whatever they can find in their area. Most sharks eat bony fish and squid, but they can be cannibalistic (eat each other). They often feed on other smaller sharks, sometimes even on their own species. Some sharks prefer particular kinds of food. Hammerheads like sting rays, while tiger sharks will crunch a sea turtle's shell for the meat inside. Shortfin mako sharks hunt bluefish and swordfish. Great white sharks eat fish, but as they get older will also hunt seals and sea lions. Sharks will scavenge (feed on dead animals) whenever they can. The bodies of dead whales are food for many sharks that swim in open waters, including tigers, blues and oceanic whitetips.

**▲ FEEDING FRENZY**
Large quantities of food will excite grey reef sharks, sending them into a feeding frenzy. When divers hand out food, the sharks will circle with interest, until one darts forward for the first bite. Other sharks quickly follow, grabbing at the food until they seem out of control.

**▲ FOREVER EATING**
A large school of mating squid will send blue sharks into a frenzy. The sharks feed until full, then empty their stomachs to start again!

**▲ FISH BALL**
A group of sharks will often herd schools of fish into a tight ball. The sharks will then pick off fish from the outside of the ball, one by one.

### ▶ BITE A BROTHER

Sharks do not take care of their relatives!
Big sharks will often eat smaller sharks,
and sharks that swim side by side in the
same school will take a nip out of each
other. The remains
of this blacktip
shark, caught on
a fishing line,
show that it has
been eaten by a
large bull shark.

*Did you know?*
*The great white shark sometimes eats crabs and lobsters.*

### ◀ OCEAN TRASH CAN

Tiger sharks are well known as
the sharks that eat more than just
living things such as fish, other
sharks, or dead animals floating
in the sea. Tiger sharks have
been known to eat coal, rubber
tyres and clothes. They are found
all over the world and grow to
a length of 5m/16½ft. Not
surprisingly, tiger sharks have
been known to try eating humans.

### ▼ BITE-SIZE CHUNKS

The cookie-cutter shark feeds by
cutting chunks out of whales and
dolphins, such as this spinner dolphin.
The shark uses its mouth like a
clamp, attaching itself to its
victim. It then bites
with its razor-sharp
teeth and swivels to
twist off a circle
of flesh.

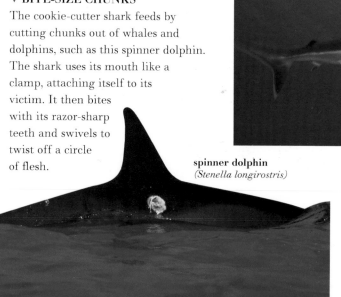

**spinner dolphin**
(*Stenella longirostris*)

### ▲ OPPORTUNISTS

Sharks will often follow fishing
boats, looking for a free meal.
This silvertip shark is eating
pieces of tuna that have been
thrown overboard.

227

**▲ FOOD CHAIN**

Eggs and sperm released on the same night by the corals of the Ningaloo Reef in Australia are eaten by the larvae (young) of crabs and lobsters. The larvae are eaten by fish and krill. The fish and krill in turn become food for the hungry whale sharks that swim off the coral reefs.

# Filter Feeders

Some of the biggest fish in the sea eat some of the smallest living things there. Giant species, like the whale shark and basking shark, use their gill rakers to comb plankton (tiny animals and plants) from the water. In the same way as hunting sharks, they use their sharp senses to track down huge areas of food. Whale sharks are often seen near coral reefs, where, at certain times of the year, large amounts of animal plankton can be found. Basking sharks often swim in the area between ocean currents, feeding on plankton that gather on the boundary. Whale and basking sharks swim in the upper layers of the sea. The giant megamouth shark lives deeper down, straining out the shrimps that live in the middle layers of the ocean.

**◄ WHALE OF A FEAST**

Exactly two weeks after the coral has spawned at Ningaloo, the whale sharks appear. By this time, each creature, from the smallest larvae to the reef's fish and krill, will have fed upon the coral's rich food. Each night, the whale sharks swim with their huge mouths wide open, scooping up food that they strain from the sea's surface.

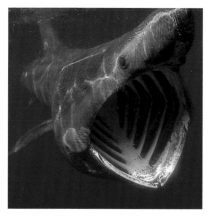

## ▲ BIG GULP

The basking shark swims slowly through the sea, funnelling food-filled water into its huge mouth. In one hour, it can filter 6,624 litres/7,000 quarts of seawater! When enough food has been trapped, the shark closes its mouth and swallows with one gulp.

## ▲ COLD WATER SKIMMERS

The basking shark has gill slits that almost encircle its gigantic body. These are used to filter food, such as shellfish larvae and fish eggs, from the water. The shark passes water through its gill chamber, where enormous gill rakers comb the food from the water.

## ▲ PLANKTON

Plankton is made up of tiny plants and animals that float together in huge clouds on and just below the sea's surface. Both animal and plant plankton are eaten by the basking shark.

## ▲ BIG MOUTH

Patrolling the middle waters of the deep, the megamouth shark scoops up tiny shrimps as they cross its path. Since this shark's discovery in 1976, another 13 examples have been discovered and some of these have been examined by scientists.

# Stay in Line

No shark is alone for long. Sooner or later, one shark will come across another, including those of its own kind. In order to reduce the risk of fights and injury, sharks talk to each other, not with sound, but with body language. Sharks have a clear pecking order. The bigger the shark, the more important it is. Not surprisingly, small sharks tend to keep out of the way of larger ones. Many species use a sign that tells others to keep their distance. They arch their back, point their pectoral fins down and swim stiffly. If this doesn't work, the offending shark will be put in its place with a swift bite to the sides or head. Bite marks along its gill slits can be a sign that a shark has stepped out of line and been told firmly to watch out.

▲ GREAT WHITE CHUMS

Great white sharks were once thought to travel alone, but it is now known that some journey in pairs or small groups. Some sharks that have been identified by scientists will appear repeatedly at favourite sites, such as California's Farallon Islands, 39km/24 miles off the coast of San Francisco. There they lie in wait for seals.

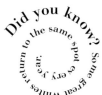

Did you know? Some great whites return to the same spot every year.

◄ BED FELLOWS

Sharks, like these whitetip reef sharks, will snooze alongside each other on the seabed. They search for a safe place to rest below overhanging rocks and coral, where, as fights rarely break out, they seem to tolerate each other. The sharks remain here until dusk, when they separate to hunt.

## ◀ PECKING ORDER

This grey reef shark has swum too close to another, larger shark and has been bitten on its gill slits as a punishment. The marks on its skin show that its attacker raked the teeth of its lower jaw across the sensitive skin of the grey reef's gill slits. A shark's injuries heal rapidly, so this unfortunate victim will recover quickly from its wounds.

## ▶ REEF SHARK GANGS

Sharks have their own personal space. As they patrol the edge of a reef, schools of blacktip reef sharks will tell others that they are too close by moving their jaw or opening their mouth. During feeding, order sometimes breaks down, and a shark might be injured in the frenzy.

## ◀ SHARK SCHOOL

Every day schools of scalloped hammerhead sharks gather close to underwater mountains in the Pacific Ocean. They do not feed, even though they come across schools of fish that would normally be food. Instead, they swim repeatedly up and down, as though taking a rest.

*231*

# Look in any Ocean

Sharks live throughout the world's oceans and seas, and at all depths. Some sharks, like bull sharks, even swim in rivers and lakes. Whale, reef and nurse sharks are all tropical species that prefer warm waters. Temperate-water sharks, such as the mako, horn and basking sharks, live in water that is 10–20°C/50–68°F. Cold-water sharks often live in very deep water. The Portuguese shark, frilled shark and goblin shark are all cold water sharks. A few species will swim in extremely cold waters, such as the Greenland shark, which braves the icy water around the Arctic Circle.

NORTH AMERICA

ATLA OCH

PACIFIC OCEAN

SOUTH AMERICA

### ▶ SWIMMING POOLS
This map shows the main parts of the world's seas in which different kinds of sharks live. The key beneath the map shows which sharks live where.

### ▶ OCEAN WANDERER
The oceanic whitetip shark swims the world's deep, open oceans, in tropical and subtropical waters. It is also one of the first sharks to appear at shipwrecks.

### KEY
| | |
|---|---|
| | whale shark |
| | basking shark |
| | bull shark |
| | tiger shark |
| | white tip shark |
| | Greenland shark |
| | great white shark |

### ◀ ISLAND LIVING
The Galapagos shark (*Carcharhinus galapagensis*) swims in the waters of the Galapagos islands, on the Equator. It also swims around tropical islands in the Pacific, Atlantic and Indian oceans.

### ◀ UNDER THE ICE

The Greenland shark (*Somniosus microcephalus*) is the only shark known to survive under polar ice in the North Atlantic seas. It has a luminous parasite attached to each eye that attracts prey to the area around its mouth.

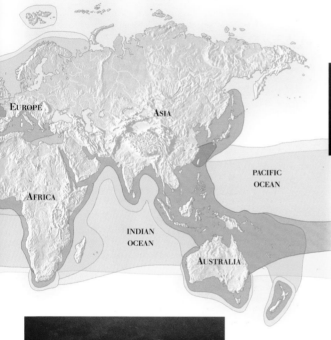

EUROPE

ASIA

AFRICA

PACIFIC
OCEAN

INDIAN
OCEAN

AUSTRALIA

### ▲ TEMPERATE PREDATOR

The great white shark lives in temperate, subtropical and tropical seas, including the Mediterranean. It usually swims in coastal waters.

### ▲ TIGER OF THE SEAS

The tiger shark swims in mainly tropical and warm temperate waters, both in open ocean and close to shore. Tiger sharks have been seen off Morocco and the Canary Islands.

### ◀ REEF SHARK

The blacktip reef shark patrols reefs in the Indian and Pacific oceans. It also lives in the Mediterranean and Red Sea, and as far west as the seas off Tunisia, in North Africa.

233

# TURTLES AND TORTOISES

Turtles, tortoises and terrapins have
lived on Earth for more than 220
million years, and together they form a
group of reptiles called Chelonians.
There are over 300 species and
they can be found in warm climates all
over the world, where they live in the
sea, in fresh water and on land.

*Author*: Barbara Taylor
*Consultants*: Andy and Nadine Highfield
Tortoise Trust

# What are Turtles and Tortoises?

Turtles, tortoises and terrapins make up a group of reptiles called chelonians. They have lived on the Earth for more than 220 million years, since the days of the earliest dinosaurs.

There are about 300 different kinds of chelonian, living in warm places all over the world. Those types that live in the ocean are called turtles. Other types of chelonian have different names in different countries. In the U.K., for example, those that live on land are tortoises, and those that live in fresh water are called terrapins. In the U.S.A., however, most freshwater chelonians are called turtles, while in Australia they are called tortoises.

**▲ OCEAN FLYERS**
The green sea turtle is the largest of the sea turtles with hard shells. There are seven types of sea turtle, and they all have flattened, streamlined shells and powerful front flippers. They "fly" gracefully through the water but move clumsily on land and cannot pull their head and neck back into the shell as many land chelonians can.

**STAR TURN ▼**
With its high, domed shell, this Indian star tortoise looks like a walking tank. Only the head, legs and tail stick out of the shell, which has a top and a bottom part and goes right around the body. The stumpy legs are strong, like an elephant's, to support its weight. Land chelonians usually have these pillar-like legs. Those that live in water usually have webbed toes or flippers.

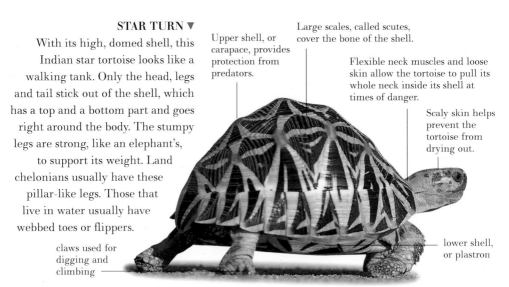

Upper shell, or carapace, provides protection from predators.

Large scales, called scutes, cover the bone of the shell.

Flexible neck muscles and loose skin allow the tortoise to pull its whole neck inside its shell at times of danger.

Scaly skin helps prevent the tortoise from drying out.

claws used for digging and climbing

lower shell, or plastron

*236*

### Turtle Who Taught Us

*In the children's book* Alice's Adventures in Wonderland, *by Lewis Carroll, Alice meets a character called the Mock Turtle, who is often upset and cries easily. He tells Alice a story about his school days, when he had an old turtle as a teacher. Alice is puzzled as to why the old turtle was called Tortoise. The Mock Turtle explains that the teacher was called Tortoise because he "taught us".*

### ▲ BRAVE NEW WORLD

All chelonians lay shelled eggs on land, even those that live in the ocean. This is because the young need to breathe oxygen from the air. When the baby chelonian is ready to hatch, it uses an egg tooth on its snout to cut through the shell. The egg tooth is a hard scale, not a real tooth. Even with the help of the egg tooth, escaping from the shell is a slow process.

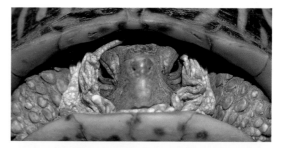

### ▲ STRAIGHT BACK OR SIDES

Chelonians are divided into two groups according to the way they tuck their heads inside their shells. Some fold the neck straight back on itself in a tight S-shape (top). The others bend their necks sideways under the lip of the top shell, leaving the neck and head slightly exposed at the front (bottom).

### ▼ TASTY TERRAPIN

The diamond-backed terrapin lives in the shallow marshes along North America's Atlantic coast, where fresh water and salt water mix together. For a hundred years or so, this terrapin was hunted for its tasty meat. Much of its habitat was also destroyed, and the terrapin almost became extinct. Today, thanks to conservation and changes in eating habits, numbers are recovering.

# Familiar Faces

There are hundreds of different kinds, or species, of chelonian. These are grouped into twelve families, based on the features that they have in common. The biggest of these families has about 90 species, but four families contain only one species because there are no other chelonians that are quite like them. Chelonians such as land tortoises and sea turtles may be quite familiar to you. The largest and smallest chelonians belong to these families. The largest is the leatherback sea turtle, which tips the scales at 1,675kg/1,500lb or more, while the tiny speckled padloper tortoise weighs less than 229g/9oz and would easily fit into your hand.

## ▲ LAND TORTOISES

Land tortoises, such as this leopard tortoise, belong to the family Testudinidae. This is the second largest family, with more than 50 species, living mainly in hot areas of Africa, India, South-east Asia and South America. A few species live in cooler areas of southern Europe, western Asia and southern North America. The land tortoise family includes the giant tortoises of the Galapagos Islands and Aldabra. Land tortoises generally have a domed, bony shell and strong, stocky legs equipped with claws for digging. They eat mainly plants.

## SEA TURTLES ▶

Six species of hard-shelled sea turtle belong to the Cheloniidae family. These are the hawksbill (*right*), green, flatback, loggerhead, Kemp's Ridley and olive Ridley turtles. The giant leatherback turtle, with its soft, leathery shell, is so unusual that it is placed in a separate family. Sea turtles spend most of their lives in the ocean, but females lay their eggs on land. Their legs are shaped like flippers, and they cannot pull the head and neck back inside the shell.

## POND TURTLES ▶

This slider, or red-eared terrapin, belongs to the largest and most varied group of chelonians, the Emydidae. There are more than 90 species in this family of pond turtles, members of which live on all continents except Australia and Antarctica. The top shell is shaped like a low arch, and some species have a movable hinge in the bottom shell. The legs of pond turtles are developed for swimming and some are slightly webbed between the toes.

## ◀ POND TURTLE GROUPS

The pond turtle family, the Emydidae, is divided into two smaller subfamilies. The Batagurinae live in Europe, Africa and Asia. The Indian black turtle (*left*) belongs to this group, as do the spiny turtle, the Asian leaf turtle and the European pond turtle. The other group, the Emydinae, lives in parts of North, Central and South America. It includes species such as the slider, the spotted turtle, the wood turtle, the ornate box turtle and the painted turtle.

## MUD OR MUSK TURTLES ▼

Members of the mud or musk turtle family, including the loggerhead musk turtle (*below*), live in an area ranging from Canada to South America. These small chelonians are named after the musky-smelling substances they produce when they are disturbed. These strong smells drive away any enemies. These turtles live in fresh water, and one of their special characteristics is webs between their toes. Their legs are specially adapted for crawling along the muddy bottom of marshes, swamps and rivers. The bottom shell may have one or two movable hinges.

Did you know? The green turtle is named after the colour of its body fat.

# Strange Species

Did you know that there is a turtle with a face like a pig? This is just one of the many strange and surprising species of chelonians. They include the formidable snapping turtles and unusual softshells, and a turtle with a head too big for its own shell. There are also the strange side-necked turtles, which bend their necks sideways under their shells. Side-necked turtles were more common in the past, and one extinct species may have been the largest freshwater turtle that ever lived. It grew to a length of 230cm/90in, which is twice as long as the largest side-necked turtle alive today – the Arrau river turtle.

## ▲ SNAPPING TURTLES

The two types of the North American snapping turtle are the only chelonians that can be dangerous to people. They are named after their powerful, snapping jaws, and have terrible tempers when provoked, which makes them very hard to handle. The bottom shell of snapping turtles is small and shaped like a cross, which makes it easier for them to move their legs in muddy water and among thick water plants.

Did you know? Pig-nosed turtles in Australia have been known to eat giant fruit bats.

## ▼ SOFTSHELL TURTLES

The 22 species of softshell turtle have a flattened top shell covered with a leathery skin instead of a hard, horny covering. Their aggressive nature makes up to some extent for the poor protection given by their softer shells. Softshell turtles are agile, expert swimmers, with legs like paddles. The tip of the turtle's nose is a long tube with the nostrils at the very end. This allows it to stay under water and breathe by just pushing its nostrils above the water's surface. Softshell turtles live in Africa, Asia and North America.

◄ BIG-HEADED TURTLE

The unique big-headed turtle is the only member of its family, Platysternidae. Its huge head is almost half the width of its top shell, far too big to be drawn back inside the shell. The skull has a solid bony roof for protection, and the head is covered by an extra-tough horny layer. Living in cool mountain streams in South-east Asia, the big-headed turtle comes out at night to catch small fish and other water creatures in its hooked jaws.

PIG-NOSED TURTLE ▼

The weird pig-nosed turtle has a snout that sticks out, like softshell turtles, but its nose is shorter, wrinkled and has the nostrils at the side, making it look like a pig. Another extraordinary feature is its front legs, which look like the flippers of sea turtles. The pig-nosed turtle lives in the rivers and lakes of Papua New Guinea and northern Australia. One river it inhabits is called the Fly River, so it is also named the Fly River turtle. It is the only member of the Carettochelyidae family.

◄ SIDE-NECKED TURTLES

There are about 60 species of side-necked turtles, such as the yellow-spotted Amazon River turtle (left). Some of them have such long necks that they are called snake-necked turtles. Side-necked turtles are divided into two groups. One group, Pelomedusidae, lives only in South America, Africa and on some of the Indian Ocean islands. The other group, Chelidae, inhabits South America and the Australian region. They all live in freshwater habitats, such as streams, rivers, lakes and swamps, and their back feet are strongly webbed for swimming.

*241*

# The Turtle Shell

No other animal has body armour quite like a chelonian's shell. The shell protects the animal from the weather and also from predators, and it will regrow if it is damaged. It also supports soft muscles and organs, such as the heart and lungs, inside the body. The shell is made of bony plates, which are covered by giant scales called scutes. Land chelonians typically have high-domed or lumpy shells to protect them from predators. Water chelonians have lighter, streamlined shells.

**▲ TOPS AND BOTTOMS**

Every turtle shell has a top part, known as the carapace, and a bottom part, the plastron. You can clearly see these on this upside-down Florida box turtle. The two parts of the shell are locked together on each side by bony bridges.

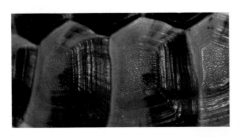

**◄ HOW OLD?**

Many chelonians have growth rings on their scutes. The rings represent a period of slow growth, such as during a dry season. However, it is not a very reliable method to work out the age of a chelonian by counting the rings, because more than one ring may form in a year, and some rings may be worn away.

**SOFTSHELLS ►**

Named after their soft, leathery shells, softshell turtles also have a bony shell underneath. The bones have air spaces in them, which help the turtle to float in water. Their flat shells make it easier for softshells to hide in soft mud and sand as they lie in wait for their prey.

## ▲ SHELL PROBLEMS

This young marginated tortoise has a deformed shell because it has been fed on the wrong food. Pet chelonians should be given mineral and vitamin supplements as well as the correct food in order to keep them healthy.

## ▲ FLAT AS A PANCAKE

The shell of the African pancake tortoise lives up to its name, being much flatter than those of other land species. This allows the tortoise to squeeze into narrow crevices under rocks to avoid predators and the hot sun. The flexible carapace also helps with this, and the tortoises use their legs and claws to fix themselves firmly in position. Once the tortoise has wedged itself in between the rocks, it is extremely difficult to remove it.

## ▲ TURTLE IN A BOX

Some chelonians, such as this box turtle, have a hinge on the plastron. This allows them to pull the head, legs and tail inside and shut the shell completely. In some species, this gives protection from predators, but protection against loss of moisture may also be important. African hinge-back tortoises have a hinge on the carapace rather than on the plastron.

### Turtle World

*Turtle shells are very strong. The strongest ones can support a weight over 200 times heavier than the body of the turtle – that's like you having nine cars on your back! According to Hindu beliefs, the Earth is supported by four elephants standing on the back of a turtle that is floating in the Universal Ocean.*

*243*

# How the Body Works

Chelonians have a skeleton both inside and outside their bodies. There is the bony shell on the outside, and on the inside there is a bony skeleton made up of the skull, backbone and ribs, and the leg, hip and shoulder bones.

Just like humans, chelonians use oxygen from the air to work their muscles, and this gets into the blood through the lungs. When we breathe in, our chest moves out to draw air into our lungs, but chelonians' ribs are fused to their shells, so they cannot expand their chests in this way. Instead, they use muscles between the front legs to force air in and out of the body.

scute

spine bones

carapace

plastron

### ▲ SPECIAL SKELETON

The shell of a chelonian is its outside skeleton, while inside the body is a framework of bones that provides an anchor for the muscles and protects the delicate internal organs. Apart from in the leatherback turtle, the spine bones and ribs are fused to the carapace (the top part of the shell).

### SWIMMING BONES ▼

The most obvious features of a sea turtle's skeleton are the extremely long toe bones that support the front flippers. The toe bones of the back feet are also long and slim. Chelonians have eight neck bones (mammals have seven) and between 40 and 50 bones in the backbone (you have 33 of these bones). You can see how the shoulder and hip bones fit inside the ribs so the shell can cover the whole body. Most other animals have their shoulder and hip bones outside their ribs.

hip bones

shoulder bones

244

## WINDOW ON THE BODY ▶

If you could see inside a chelonian's body, you would be able to see its heart, lungs and other internal organs. A three-chambered heart pumps the blood around the body. (Most reptiles have hearts with three chambers, while mammals' hearts have four chambers.) The digestive system works fairly slowly, and food takes days to pass through the body. The digestive, excretory and reproductive systems all end in one chamber called the cloaca.

The hole where the cloaca opens to the outside may be called the cloaca, anus or vent.

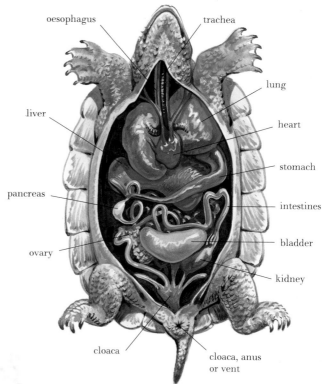

oesophagus
trachea
liver
lung
pancreas
heart
ovary
stomach
intestines
bladder
kidney
cloaca
cloaca, anus or vent

## ◀ TURTLE TAILS

Chelonian tails come in a variety of lengths and thicknesses, and are particularly long in snapping turtles. The big-headed turtle also has a long tail, which it uses as a brace to help it climb. Male chelonians (shown here on the left) often have longer and heavier tails than females (on the right), which usually have short, stubby tails. This is one way of telling the sexes apart.

## SNORKEL NOSE ▶

Some freshwater chelonians, such as this snake-necked turtle, have a long neck and a tube-like nose that works like a snorkel. They can stay under water and just push their nostrils up above the surface to breathe air. As well as breathing air into their lungs, some freshwater chelonians also extract oxygen from the water. The oxygen is absorbed through areas of thin skin inside the throat and rear opening, or cloaca.

245

# Temperature Check

Chelonians are cold-blooded, but this does not mean that chelonians are cold. They need heat to keep their bodies working properly, but they cannot produce this heat themselves as mammals and birds do. Instead, their body temperature rises and falls with that of their surroundings. They control body temperature by basking in the sun to warm up and moving into the shade or water to cool down. In places with very cold or very hot seasons, chelonians may take shelter and go into a long sleep.

## ▼ SUNBATHING

On sunny days chelonians, such as these side-necked turtles, often bask in the sun to warm up. The extra warmth from the sunlight can speed up digestion and may help turtles to make Vitamin D, which is needed for healthy bones and shells. Females bask more than males because they need extra warmth for making eggs.

## ▲ CHILLY SWIMMER

The leatherback sea turtle swims farther into the cold northern and southern oceans than any other sea turtle. It has special ways of keeping warm in the cold water. Its dark body probably helps it to absorb the sun's heat. The leatherback's muscles also produce heat, and this is trapped in the body by its thick, oily skin, which has a layer of fat underneath it. These turtles also have an ingenious system that keeps their flippers colder than the rest of the body, so heat is not lost as the turtle swims.

**SUN SHELTER ▶**

In hot climates, many land tortoises, such as this Mediterranean tortoise, need to shelter from the heat of the sun. They seek out the shade cast by bushes or trees, or retreat into underground burrows. The tortoises dig out the burrows with their front legs, often making large chambers for resting or sleeping. Sometimes they sleep in their burrow throughout a hot season – this is called aestivation. The cool, moist tortoise burrows may also provide a refuge for other animals, such as mice, frogs and lizards.

**◀ HOW TO HIBERNATE**

Tortoises that sleep throughout the cold season in the wild also need to do so when in captivity. This deep winter sleep is called hibernation. Before hibernating your pet tortoise, make sure it is fit, that it has enough body fat and that there is no food in its gut. During hibernation, the tortoise must be dry and neither too hot nor too cold. To find out more, contact an organization such as the Tortoise Trust.

**DRYING IN THE SUN ▶**

A basking yellow-bellied turtle stretches its neck and legs and spreads its toes wide to soak up as much sunshine as possible. Basking makes a turtle drier as well as warmer. This may help it to get rid of algae and parasites growing on its shell. A thick covering of algae would slow the turtle's movement through the water, and it could also damage the shell.

247

# Plodders and Swimmers

From slow, plodding land tortoises to graceful, swimming sea turtles, chelonians have developed a variety of types of legs and feet to suit their surroundings. On land, the heavy shell makes running impossible. It takes a land tortoise about five hours to walk just 1.6km/1 mile! Sea turtles, with their powerful flippers, can reach the greatest swimming speeds of any living reptile. Some swim as fast as 32kph/20mph, which is as fast as humans can run on land. Freshwater chelonians have webbed feet for speed in swimming. Some chelonians make regular migration journeys to find food or nesting places.

**▲ ELEPHANT LEGS**

Land chelonians, such as this giant tortoise, have back legs like sturdy columns, which help to support them. The front legs may be like clubs, or flattened and more like shovels, which helps with digging.

**◀ FLIPPER FEET**

The strong, flat flippers of sea turtles have no toes on the outside, although inside the flippers are five long toe bones bound together into one stiff unit. The front flippers are used to propel the turtle through the water, while the back ones act as rudders and brakes. There are only one or two claws on each flipper, and leatherback turtles have no claws at all. This makes the flippers more streamlined.

◄ SEASONAL WALKABOUT

Some freshwater chelonians, such as the spotted turtle (left) and wood turtle of North America, migrate on to land in the summer for feeding and nesting. In winter they return to swamps, pools and rivers to hibernate during the cold weather. On these short migrations, the turtles often have to cross roads. They run the risk of being run over, especially as they move so slowly.

WEBBED TOES ►

The feet of freshwater turtles have long toes joined together by webs, creating a bigger surface area to push against the water. They use all four legs to paddle along, but the back ones provide most of the pushing power. Freshwater chelonians also have gripping claws for walking on land and on the bottom of ponds and streams.

▲ FRESHWATER FLIPPERS

The pig-nosed turtle is the only freshwater turtle with flippers. Like a sea turtle, it flies through the water, moving both front flippers at the same time. Other freshwater turtles mainly use their back legs to swim, and move their front legs alternately. The pig-nosed turtle has two claws on the edge of each paddle-like leg. The back claws are used for digging nests.

*Slow and Steady Winner*

*In Aesop's fable* The Hare and the Tortoise *a speedy hare boasted about how fast he could run. He made fun of the tortoise, with his short feet and slow walk. But the tortoise just laughed and challenged the hare to a race. The hare thought there was no need to hurry because the tortoise was so slow. Instead of racing, he took a nap by the side of the road. The tortoise just kept plodding slowly along. As the tortoise approached the finish, the loud cheering woke up the hare, but he was too late to win the race.*

249

# Eyes, Ears and Noses

A chelonian's most important senses are sight, taste and smell. The shell and skin are also sensitive to touch. Chelonians probably do not hear very well, although they can pick up vibrations through an ear inside the head. They do not have an ear opening on the outside of the head, as we do. Their eyesight is best at close range, and they can see in colour. Good eyesight is useful for finding food, avoiding predators and navigating on long journeys. As well as smelling through their noses, chelonians have a structure in the mouth called the Jacobson's organ. This allows them to detect tiny chemical particles in the air.

**▲ VIBRATION DETECTORS**

The extraordinary matamata lives in murky waters where it is hard to see clearly. Its eyes are very small and it does not seem to detect its prey by sight. Instead, it relies on the flaps of skin on its head, which have lots of nerve endings and are very sensitive to vibrations in the water. The flaps pick up signs of prey as the matamata moves through the water, and this helps it to get ready to attack.

Did you know? A chelonian can feel pressure on its shell just as you can on your fingernails.

**◄ ON THE CHIN**

Many freshwater turtles, such as this side-neck turtle, have fingers of skin, called barbels, dangling under their chins. Snapping turtles have four pairs. Scientists are not sure exactly what the barbels are for, but they seem to be sensory structures. Some Australian side-necks touch each other's barbels during their courtship display.

### Robot Turtle

*These girls are joining the electrical leads to a robot called a Turtle. Schoolchildren are able to program the Turtle robot to make simple movements and draw lines and patterns across a large sheet of paper. Inside the Turtle's see-through shell are the wheels it uses to move about. Working with the Turtle robot helps children learn how computers work and how to give them simple instructions.*

### ▲ THE EYES HAVE IT

Sea turtles have good vision under the water but are short-sighted on land. Their large upper eyelids protect the eyes while they are swimming. Chelonians also have a third eyelid, called a nictitating membrane. This cleans the eye and keeps it moist, protecting it like a pair of goggles.

### ▼ TASTY TONGUE

A chelonian's tongue is broad and flat and firmly attached to the bottom of the mouth, which stops it from moving around. Taste buds on the tongue and in the throat are used for tasting food, although the sense of taste is also linked to the sense of smell. This leopard tortoise comes from Africa, and in the wild it eats grasses, prickly pear cacti and thistles.

### ▼ MR RED-EYE

Adult male box turtles often have red eyes, while the eyes of the females are yellow or brown. A few females also have red eyes, but they are less bright than the males'. Scientists have shown that turtles seem to prefer certain colours, such as orange and blue. Japanese turtles can even be trained to tell the difference between red and blue.

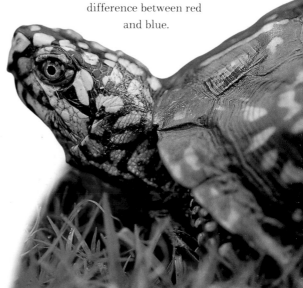

# What Chelonians Eat

Chelonians may be herbivores (plant-eaters) or carnivores (meat-eaters), but many of them are omnivores, which means they eat all kinds of food. Some herbivores, such as the cooters of North and Central America, have jaws with jagged edges. This helps them to crush plant food, such as stems and fruits.

The diet of omnivores often changes with age. Young ones tend to eat more insects, while adults either eat more plants or have a more specialized diet. Many chelonians pick up extra nutrients by feeding on dung or dead animals. Also, after eggs have hatched, female offspring may eat the eggshells to help them to build a store of calcium for producing the shells of their own eggs.

**▲ GRASS FOR LUNCH**
A giant Galapagos tortoise uses its horny jaws to bite off pieces of grass. Galapagos tortoises also eat other plants, such as cacti and other fleshy, water-filled plants. In the dry season, these tortoises have to get all of their water from their plant food.

**NOT A FUSSY EATER ▶**
The hawksbill sea turtle is an omnivore that seems to prefer invertebrates (animals without backbones) such as coral, sponges, jellyfish, sea urchins, shrimps and molluscs. Plants in its diet include seaweeds and mangrove fruits, leaves, bark and wood. The hawksbill has a narrow head with jaws meeting at an acute angle. This helps it to reach into narrow cracks in coral reefs and pull out food.

*252*

## ▲ CHANGING DIET

Many chelonians, such as this slider, change their diet as they grow up. Young sliders eat more insects, while adults feed on mainly plants. Some chelonians switch to a whole new diet when they reach adulthood. When males and females are different sizes, they may also have different diets. Female Barbour's map turtles are more than twice the size of the males. They eat mainly shellfish, whereas the males feed mostly on insects.

## OPEN WIDE ▶

Chelonians never need to visit the dentist, because they do not have teeth! Instead of teeth, their jaws are lined with hard keratin – the material fingernails are made of. The keratin is either sharpened into cutting edges or broadened into crushing plates. Cutting edges slice through animal bodies, while plates are used to grind plant food. Some ancient turtles had a set of teeth on the roof of the mouth, but did not have proper ones along the edges of the jaws, like most reptiles and other vertebrates.

## Feeding Pets

*Feeding pet tortoises or turtles is not as simple as you might think. An incorrect diet can lead to growth problems such as soft or deformed shells, and eggs with thin walls that break during laying. It is best to find out what your pet eats in the wild and try to feed it a similar, and varied, diet. Land chelonians eat mostly plants, while those that live in water have more animal food in their diets. High-fat foods, such as cheese, will make your pet overweight, and this is not good for its health. Ask the advice of an organization such as the Tortoise Trust for more information. Most pet chelonians need extra vitamins and minerals to make up for those missing in the prepared foods available in stores. Water is also important. Without enough to drink, your pet chelonian may suffer from kidney problems.*

# *Focus on*

Of the seven species of sea turtle, six have hard shells. These are the green, flatback, hawksbill, loggerhead, Kemp's Ridley and olive Ridley turtles. Most of these gentle and mysterious creatures are found in warm waters worldwide. The seventh sea turtle is the leatherback. This soft-shelled giant swims in both warm and cold ocean waters. Sea turtles use their strong flippers to "fly" through the water. Only the females come on to land to lay their eggs. A male sea turtle may never touch dry land again after hatching from its egg and heading out to sea. In a few places, such as Hawaii, green turtles bask in the sun on beaches.

**MYSTERIOUS LIVES**
Once a loggerhead hatchling reaches the sea, its movements are not well known. In places such as Florida, they seem to rest on mats of floating seaweed (above). The babies are reddish brown above and below, which gives them good camouflage among the brown seaweed. This helps them to hide from predators.

**BIGGEST CHELONIAN**
This nesting turtle is being observed by a conservation scientist. The enormous leatherback can weigh as much as 653kg/1,450lb. It is the fastest growing of all chelonians, increasing its body weight by about 8,000 times between hatching and growing into an adult. A leatherback's shell has a leathery skin with thousands of small bones embedded in it, rather than horny scutes. It feeds on soft prey such as jellyfish.

254

# Sea Turtles

## NESTING TOGETHER

This olive Ridley turtle will join a large group for nesting. More than 100,000 females nest each year on the east coast of India alone. Most sea turtles nest alone or in small groups.

## STREAMLINED SHELL

Sea turtles, such as this green sea turtle, have a very streamlined shell to allow the water to flow smoothly over it. They do not have the overhang at the front of the shell, into which other chelonians withdraw their heads, as a ridge would slow a sea turtle down. Instead, its head is protected by thick, horny scales and the solid bony roof of the skull.

AFRICA

ASCENSION ISLAND

SOUTH AMERICA

MIGRATION OF GREEN TURTLES

## MIGRATIONS

Sea turtles, both young and adults, swim along ocean migration routes as they move to new feeding sites. Adults also travel to beaches to mate and lay eggs. Scientists are not sure how the turtles find their way. They may smell their route, find their way by the Sun or stars, or use Earth's magnetism.

## TORTOISESHELL

The scutes of the hawksbill turtle are a beautiful mixture of amber, brown, black, white, red and green. It is these scutes that are used to make "tortoiseshell" combs, jewellery and spectacle frames. Sadly, the turtle is usually killed before the scutes are removed. This practice is entirely unnecessary, especially now that so many synthetic alternatives are available.

# Ancient Chelonians

**▲ FORMING FOSSILS**
This fossil tortoise was found in the badlands of South Dakota, in the United States. It lived about 35 million years ago, when that area was covered in a shallow sea. Rock and minerals have filled in the spaces inside the tortoise's shell and then turned into hard stone, preserving the tortoise's body for millions of years.

**► LARGEST TURTLE**
About 100 million years ago there was an ancient turtle called *Archelon*, which was bigger than a rowing boat. It swam in an inland sea that once covered the grassy prairies of North America. *Archelon* looked like modern leatherback turtles, with a leathery, streamlined carapace and wing-like front flippers. It had very weak jaws and may have fed on jellyfish and other animals with soft bodies, such as squid. The most complete fossil of *Archelon* is of an animal that was about 100 years old when it died. It measured 4.5m/ 15ft long and 52m/17ft from one outstretched front flipper to the other.

Scientists have different ideas about which group of animals chelonians evolved from. The oldest known chelonian, called *Proganochelys*, lived about 220 million years ago, but this ancient turtle probably did not give rise to modern chelonians. These are most likely to have developed from a group called the Casichelydia, which lived between 208 and 144 million years ago. Ancient chelonians lived alongside the dinosaurs – giant reptiles that roamed the Earth until 65 million years ago, when they all died out. Unlike the dinosaurs, many chelonian species survived and are still around today.

| Triassic 251–200 mya | Jurassic 200–144 mya | Cretaceous 144–65 mya | Paleocene to present 65 mya–present | | mya – millions of years ago |
|---|---|---|---|---|---|
| Proganochelydia (extinct) | | | Trionychoidea (Cretaceous–recent) | Kinosternidae | mud or musk turtles |
| | | | | Dermatemydidae | Central American river turtle |
| | | | | Carettochelyidae | pig-nosed turtle |
| | Cryptodira (Late Jurassic) | | Chelonioidea (Jurassic–recent) | Trionychidae | softshell turtles |
| | | | | Dermochelyidae | leatherback turtle |
| Casichelydia (dominant during Jurassic) | | | | Cheloniidae | sea turtles |
| | | | Testudinoidea (Paleocene–recent) | Chelydridae | snapping turtles |
| | | | | Platysternidae | big-headed turtle |
| | | | | Emydidae | pond turtles and relatives |
| | | | | Testudinidae | land tortoises |
| | | | Pleurodira (Late Cretaceous–recent) | Chelidae | side-necked turtles |
| | | | | Pelomedusidae | side-necked turtles |

## ▲ EVOLUTION PATHWAYS

This diagram shows how chelonians may have evolved over a period of 220 million years. A group called the Casichelydia became dominant about 208 million years ago and gave rise to the 12 families of chelonians alive today. They are listed at the top right of the chart above.

### Island Evolution

*On the Galapagos Islands, the English scientist Charles Darwin found some of the most important evidence for his theory of how evolution happens. During his visit in 1835, he collected information about how the giant tortoises and other animals varied between islands. He suggested that these differences had come about because the animals had adapted to suit the unique conditions on each island.*

*The best-adapted animals survived to produce the next generation, an idea that Darwin called "natural selection".*

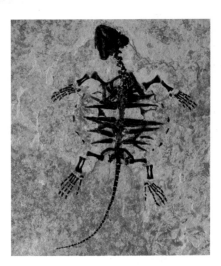

## ▲ SNAPPING FOSSILS

This is a fossil of a young snapping turtle that lived between 58 and 37 million years ago. You can see the outline of its shell and its long tail. From fossils, we know that there were more species of snapping turtles in the past. Today, only the common snapping turtle and the alligator snapping turtle are still alive.

*257*

# CROCODILES

The first crocodilians lived about
200 million years ago, and today they
are the largest reptiles alive on Earth.
These amazing cold-blooded reptiles
are fierce predators with highly
developed senses, powerful bodies
and remarkable social skills, all of which
have helped them to survive where
others have perished.

*Author*: Barbara Taylor
*Consultant*: Dr Richard A. Griffiths,
Durrell Institute of Conservation and Ecology

# What is a Crocodilian?

Crocodilians are scaly, armour-clad reptiles that include crocodiles, alligators, caimans and gharials. They are survivors from a prehistoric age – their relatives first lived on the Earth with the dinosaurs nearly 200 million years ago. Today, they are the dinosaurs' closest living relatives, apart from birds.

Crocodilians are fierce predators. They lurk motionless in rivers, lakes and swamps, waiting to snap up prey with their enormous jaws and strong teeth. Their prey ranges from insects, frogs and fish to birds and large mammals, such as deer and zebras. Very few crocodilians regularly attack and kill humans. Most are timid. Crocodilians usually live in warm, tropical places in or near fresh water, and some live in the sea. They hunt and feed mainly in the water, but crawl on to dry land to sunbathe, build nests and lay their eggs.

▲ SCALY TAILS
Like many crocodilians, an American alligator uses its long, strong tail to swim through the water. The tail moves from side to side to push the alligator along. The tail is the same length as the rest of the body.

Long, strong tail has flat sides to push aside water for swimming.

▶ CROCODILIAN CHARACTERISTICS
With its thick, scaly skin, huge jaws and powerful tail, this American alligator looks like a living dinosaur. Its eyes and nostrils are on top of its head so that it can see and breathe when the rest of its body is underwater. On land, crocodilians slither along on their bellies, but they can lift themselves up on their four short legs to walk.

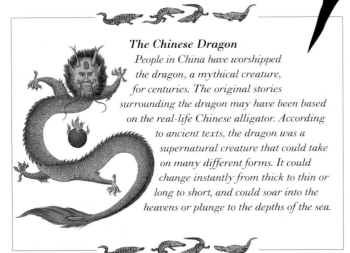

### The Chinese Dragon
*People in China have worshipped the dragon, a mythical creature, for centuries. The original stories surrounding the dragon may have been based on the real-life Chinese alligator. According to ancient texts, the dragon was a supernatural creature that could take on many different forms. It could change instantly from thick to thin or long to short, and could soar into the heavens or plunge to the depths of the sea.*

## ▲ TALKING HEADS

Huge, powerful jaws lined with sharp teeth make Nile crocodiles killing machines. They are some of the world's largest and most dangerous reptiles. The teeth are used to attack and grip prey, but are useless for chewing. Prey has to be swallowed whole or in chunks.

## ► SHUTEYE

Although this spectacled caiman has its eyes shut, it is probably dozing rather than sleeping. Two butterflies are basking in safety on the caiman's head. Predators will not dare attack it because the caiman is still sensitive to what is going on around it, even though its eyes are shut.

## ► SOAKING UP THE SUN

Nile crocodiles sun themselves on a sandbank. This is called basking and warms the body. Crocodilians are cold-blooded, which means that their body temperature is affected by their surroundings. They have no fur or feathers to keep them warm, nor can they shiver to heat up. They move into and out of the water to warm up or cool down.

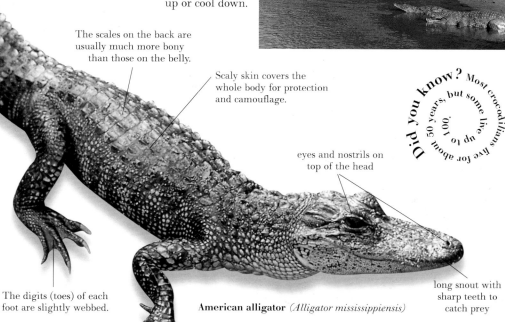

The scales on the back are usually much more bony than those on the belly.

Scaly skin covers the whole body for protection and camouflage.

Did you know? Most crocodilians live for about 50 years, but some live up to 100.

eyes and nostrils on top of the head

The digits (toes) of each foot are slightly webbed.

**American alligator** (*Alligator mississippiensis*)

long snout with sharp teeth to catch prey

261

# Croc or Gator?

There are 13 species (kinds) of crocodile, two species of alligator, five species of caiman and two species of gharial. Gharials have distinctive long, slender snouts, but crocodiles and alligators are often more difficult to tell apart. Crocodiles usually have longer, more pointed snouts than alligators. Crocodiles also have one very large tooth sticking up from each side of the bottom jaw when they close their mouths.

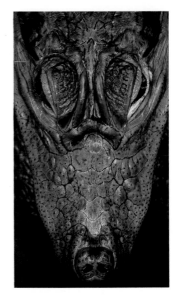

KEY
crocodiles
alligators
gharials

▲ **CAIMAN EYES**
Most caimans have bonier ridges between their eyes than alligators. These ridges help to strengthen the skull and look like glasses people wear to help them see. Caimans are usually smaller than alligators.

▲ **WHERE IN THE WORLD?**
Crocodiles are the most widespread crocodilian and live in Central and South America, Africa, southern Asia and Australia. Caimans live in Central and South America, while alligators live in the south-eastern United States and China. The gharial is found in southern Asia, while the false gharial lives in South-east Asia.

*Chinese alligator*
(*Alligator sinensis*)

▼ **A CROCODILE'S SMILE**
With its mouth closed, a crocodile's fourth tooth in the lower jaw fits into a notch on the outside of the upper jaw. No teeth can be seen on the bottom jaw of an alligator's closed mouth.

▲ **COOL ALLIGATOR**
There are two species of alligator, the Chinese alligator (*above*) and the American alligator. Alligators are the only crocodilians that can survive cooler temperatures and live outside the tropics.

### ▶ DIFFERENT SNOUTS

Crocodilian snouts are different shapes and sizes because of the food they eat and the way they live. Gharials and crocodiles have narrow, pointy snouts suited to eating fish. Alligators and caimans have wider, rounder snouts that can manage larger prey, such as birds and mammals. Their jaws are strong enough to overpower victims that are even larger than they are.

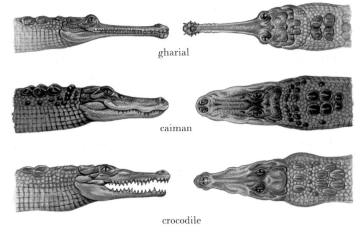

gharial

caiman

crocodile

### ◀ OUT TO SEA

The enormous saltwater crocodile, often called the saltie, has the largest range of all the crocodilians. It is found from the east coast of India through South-east Asia to the Philippines, New Guinea and northern Australia. Saltwater crocodiles are one of the few species found far out at sea, but they do live in freshwater rivers and lakes as well.

### ▶ POT NOSE

Two species of gharial, the gharial (or gavial) and the false gharial, live in the rivers, lakes and swamps of southern Asia. The name comes from the bump on the nose of the male gharial, which is called a *ghara* (pot) in the Hindi language. Some experts say the false gharial is a species of crocodile and is therefore not really part of the gharial family.

Adult male gharials have a conspicuous bump at the tip of the snout.

**gharial**
(*Gavialis gangeticus*)

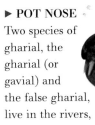

# Large and Small

Can you imagine a crocodile that weighs as much as three cars? A big, 7m/23ft-long saltwater crocodile is as heavy as this. It is the heaviest living reptile in the world. Other enormous crocodilians include Nile crocodiles, gharials and American alligators, which can reach lengths of 5.5m/18ft or more. Very large crocodiles and alligators are now rare because many are hunted and killed for their meat and skins before they grow to their maximum size. The smallest species of crocodilian are the dwarf caimans of South America and the African dwarf crocodile. These forest-dwelling reptiles grow to about 1.5m/5ft long.

**▲ BIGGEST CAIMAN**
The black caiman is the largest of the caimans. It can grow to over 5.8m/19ft long and is the biggest predator in South America. Black caimans live in the flooded Amazon forest, around lakes and slow-flowing rivers. They hunt at night for capybara, turtles, deer and fish.

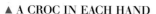

**▲ A CROC IN EACH HAND**
A person holds a baby Orinoco crocodile (*top*) and a baby spectacled caiman (*bottom*). As adults, the Orinoco crocodile will be twice the length of the caiman, reaching about 5m/16ft. You can clearly see how the crocodile has a longer, thinner snout than the caiman.

*Crocodile God*
*The ancient Egyptians worshipped the crocodile-headed god Sebek. He was the god of lakes and rivers, and is shown here with Pharaoh Amenhotep III. A shrine to Sebek was built at Shedet. Here, a Nile crocodile decorated with gold rings and bracelets lived in a special pool. It was believed to be the living god. Other crocodiles were also treated with great respect and hand-fed on meat, cakes, milk and honey.*

### ◄ SUPER-SNOUTED CROCODILE

The mugger crocodile of India and surrounding lands has the broadest snout of all crocodiles, making it look more like an alligator. Adult males reach about 4m/13ft long. The name mugger comes from its habit of snatching fish out of people's fishing nets.

### ◄ SMALLEST CROCODILIAN

Cuvier's dwarf caiman is about a fifth of the size of a giant saltwater crocodile, yet it would still only just fit on your bed! It lives in the rainforests of the Amazon basin in South America. It has particularly tough, armoured skin to protect it from rocks in fast-flowing rivers. It has a short snout and a high, smooth skull. Its short snout does not prevent it from eating a lot of fish.

*Did you know? Male alligators keep growing until they are 15 years old.*

### ► MONSTER CROC

The huge Nile crocodile is the biggest and strongest freshwater predator in Africa. It can grow up to 5.8m/19ft long and eats any prey it can overpower, including monkeys, antelopes, zebras and sometimes people. Nile crocodiles probably kill at least 300 people a year in Africa. Despite its name, the Nile crocodile is not just found along the Nile but also lives in rivers, lakes and swamps through most of tropical Africa.

# Scaly Skin

The outside of a crocodilian's body is completely covered in a suit of leathery armour. It is made up of rows of tough scales, called scutes, that are set into a thick layer of skin. Some scutes have small bony discs inside them. Most crocodilians have bony scutes only on their backs, but some, such as caimans, have them on their bellies as well. The tail never contains bony scutes, but it does have thicker tail scutes. As crocodilians grow, bigger scutes develop under the old ones. Crocodilians do not get rid of their old scaly skin in a big piece, like a snake, or in patches like a lizard. Old scutes drop off one at a time, just as humans lose flakes of skin all the time. On the head, the skin is fused directly to the bones of the skull without any muscles or fat in between.

***Tricky Alligator***
*A Guyanese myth tells how the Sun was tricked by an alligator into letting him guard his fish ponds from a thief. The thief was the alligator, and to punish him the Sun slashed his body, forming the scales. The alligator promised the Sun his daughter for a wife. He had no children, so he carved her from a tree. The Sun and the woman's offspring were the Carob people.*

## ▲ COLOUR CHANGE

Most crocodilians are brightly coloured or patterned as babies, but these features usually fade as they grow older. They have more or less disappeared in fully-grown adults. The colours and patterns may help with camouflage by breaking up the outline of the body.

## ▲ NECK ARMOUR

Heavy, bony scutes pack tightly together to create a rigid and formidable armour on the back and neck of an African dwarf crocodile. Even the scutes on the sides of its body and tail are heavily armoured. This species lives in the dwindling rainforests of west and central Africa. The small size and bony armour of the dwarf crocodile has saved it so far from being hunted for its skin.

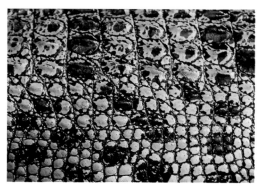

## ▲ MISSING SCALES

The gharial has fewer rows of armoured scutes along its back than other crocodilians. Adults have four rows of deeply ridged back scutes, whereas other crocodilians have two or four extra rows in the middle of the back. The scutes on the sides and belly are unarmoured.

## ▲ BONY BACK

The belly of a saltwater crocodile does not have bony plates in the scutes. You can see the difference in this close-up. Large, bony back scutes are shown at the top of the picture, and the smaller, smoother belly scutes are at the bottom. The scutes are arranged in rows.

## ► EXTRA ARMOUR

This close-up shows the skin of a dwarf caiman – the most heavily armoured crocodilian. It has strong bones in the scutes on its belly as well as its back. This provides protection from predators. Even its eyelids are protected by bony plates.

*Did you know?* The scales of the black caiman are as tough as the head of a tool.

## ► ALBINO ALLIGATOR

An albino crocodilian would not survive long in the wild. It does not blend in well with its surroundings, making it easy prey. Those born in captivity in zoos or crocodile farms may survive to adulthood. True albinos are white with pink eyes. White crocodilians with blue eyes are not true albinos.

**American alligator**
(*Alligator mississippiensis*)

267

# Bodies and Bones

The crocodilian body has changed very little over the last 200 million years. It is superbly adapted to life in the water. Crocodilians can breathe with just their nostrils above the surface. Underwater, their ears and nostrils close, and a transparent third eyelid sweeps across the eye for protection. Crocodilians are the only reptiles with ear flaps. Inside the long, lizard-like body a bony skeleton supports and protects the lungs, heart, stomach and other soft organs. The stomach is in two parts, one for grinding food, the other for absorbing (taking in) nutrients. Unlike other reptiles, which have a single-chambered heart, a crocodilian's heart has four chambers, like a mammal's. This allows the heart to pump more oxygen-rich blood to the brain during a dive. The thinking part of its brain is more developed than in other reptiles. This enables a crocodilian to learn things rather than act only on instinct.

▲ **THROAT FLAP**
A crocodilian has no lips, so it is unable to seal its mouth underwater. Instead, two special flaps at the back of the throat keep water from filling the mouth and flowing into the lungs. This enables the crocodile to open its mouth underwater to catch and eat prey without drowning.

Did you know? A saltwater crocodile can stay underwater for more than an hour.

◄ **PREHISTORIC LOOKS**
These American alligators look much like their crocodilian ancestors from the age of the dinosaurs. Crocodilians are the largest living reptiles. The heaviest is the saltwater crocodile which can weigh up to 1,089kg/2,420lb.

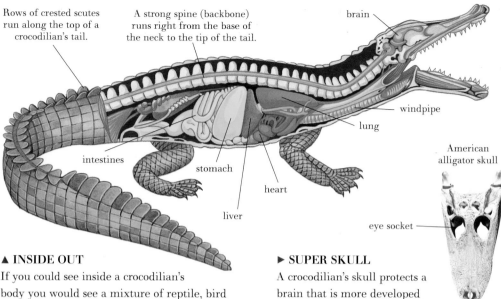

Rows of crested scutes run along the top of a crocodilian's tail.

A strong spine (backbone) runs right from the base of the neck to the tip of the tail.

brain

windpipe

lung

intestines

stomach

heart

liver

American alligator skull

eye socket

## ▲ INSIDE OUT

If you could see inside a crocodilian's body you would see a mixture of reptile, bird and mammal features. The crocodilian's brain and shoulder blades are like a bird's. Its heart, diaphragm and efficient breathing system are similar to those of mammals. The stomach and digestive system are those of a reptile, as they deal with food that cannot be chewed.

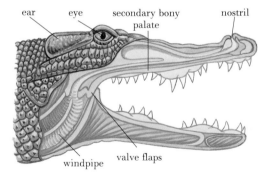

ear    eye    secondary bony palate    nostril

windpipe

valve flaps

## ▲ WELL-DESIGNED

A view inside the head of a crocodilian shows the ear, eye and nostril openings set high up in the skull. The bones in the mouth are joined together to create a secondary bony palate that separates the nostrils from the mouth. Flaps of skin form a valve, sealing off the windpipe underwater.

## ▶ SUPER SKULL

A crocodilian's skull protects a brain that is more developed than any other reptile's. The skull is wider and more rounded in alligators (*top*), and long and triangular in crocodiles (*bottom*). Behind the eye sockets are two large holes where jaw muscles attach to the skull.

## ▶ STOMACH STONES

Crocodilians swallow objects, such as pebbles, to help break down their food. These gastroliths (stomach stones) churn around inside part of the stomach, helping to cut up food so it can be digested. Some very unusual gastroliths have been found, such as bottles, coins, a whistle and a vacuum flask.

# Jaws and Teeth

The mighty jaws of a crocodilian and its impressive rows of spiky teeth are lethal weapons for catching prey. Crocodilians have two or three times as many teeth as a human. The sharp, jagged teeth at the front of the mouth, called canines, are used to pierce and grip prey. The force of the jaws closing drives these teeth, like a row of knives, deep into a victim's flesh. The short, blunt molar teeth at the back of the mouth are used for crushing prey. Crocodilian teeth are useless for chewing food, and the jaws cannot be moved sideways to chew either. Food has to be swallowed whole, or torn into chunks. The teeth are constantly growing. If a tooth falls out, a new one grows through to replace it.

▲ **MEGA JAWS**
The jaws of a Nile crocodile close with tremendous force. They sink into their prey with tons of crushing pressure. Yet the muscles that open the jaws are weak. A thick rubber band over the snout can easily hold a crocodile's jaws shut.

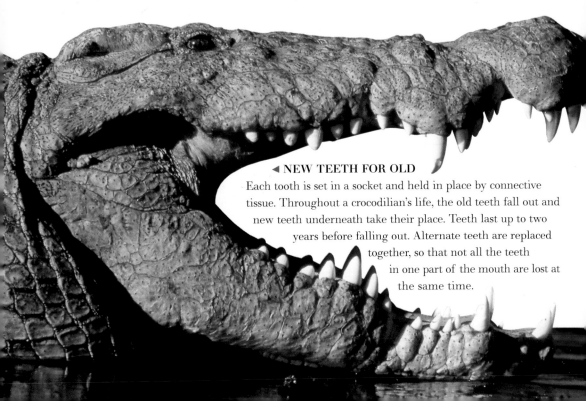

◄ **NEW TEETH FOR OLD**
Each tooth is set in a socket and held in place by connective tissue. Throughout a crocodilian's life, the old teeth fall out and new teeth underneath take their place. Teeth last up to two years before falling out. Alternate teeth are replaced together, so that not all the teeth in one part of the mouth are lost at the same time.

◀ **LOTS OF TEETH**

The gharial has more teeth than any other crocodilian – around 110. Its teeth are also smaller than those of other crocodilians and are all the same size. The narrow, beak-like snout and long, thin teeth of the gharial are geared to grabbing fish with a sweeping sideways movement of the head. The sharp teeth interlock to trap and impale the slippery prey.

**CHARMING**

Crocodilian teeth are sometimes made into necklaces. People wear them as decoration or lucky charms. In South America, the Montana people of Peru believe they will be protected from poisoning by wearing a crocodile tooth.

▲ **BABY TEETH**

A baby American alligator is born with a full set of 80 teeth when it hatches from its egg. Baby teeth are not as sharp as adult teeth and are more fragile. They are like tiny needles. In young crocodiles, the teeth at the back of the mouth usually fall out first. In adults, it is the teeth at the front that are replaced more often.

▶ **GRABBING TEETH**

A Nile crocodile grasps a lump of prey ready for swallowing. If prey is too large to swallow whole, the crocodile grips the food firmly in its teeth and shakes its head hard so that any unwanted pieces are shaken off.

A Nile crocodile has 68 teeth lining its huge jaws.

**Did you know?** A Nile crocodile may use 45 sets of teeth by the time it is 3.5m/13ft long.

# Temperature Check

Soon after the Sun rises, the first alligators heave themselves out of the river and flop down on the bank. The banks fill up quickly as more alligators join the first, warming their scaly bodies in the Sun's rays. As the hours go by and the day becomes hotter, the alligators open their toothy jaws wide to cool down. Later in the day, they may go for a swim or crawl into the shade to cool off. As the air chills at night, the alligators slip back into the water again. This is because water stays warmer for longer at night than the land.

Crocodilians are cold-blooded, which means their body temperature varies with outside temperatures. To warm up or cool down, they move to warm or cool places. Their ideal body temperature is 29–35°C/85–95°F.

▲ MUD PACK
A spectacled caiman is buried deep in the mud to keep cool during the hot, dry season. Mud is like water and does not get as hot or as cold as dry land. It also helps to keep the caiman's scaly skin free from parasites and biting insects.

◄ SOLAR PANELS
The crested scutes on the tail of a crocodilian are like the bony plates on armoured dinosaurs. They act like solar panels, picking up heat when the animal basks in the sun. They also open to let as much heat as possible escape from the body to cool it down.

### ◄ UNDER THE ICE

An alligator can survive under a layer of ice if it keeps a breathing hole open. Only alligators stay active at temperatures as low as 12–15°C/53–59°F. They do not eat, because it is too cold for their digestive systems to work.

### ▼ OPEN WIDE

While a Nile crocodile suns itself on a rock it also opens its mouth in a wide gape. Gaping helps to prevent the crocodile from becoming too hot. The breeze flowing over the wide, wet surfaces of the mouth and tongue dries the moisture and, in turn, cools the blood. If you lick your finger and blow on it softly, you will notice that it feels a lot cooler.

### ▲ ALLIGATOR DAYS

Alligators follow a distinct daily routine when the weather is good, moving in and out of the water at regular intervals. They also enter the water if they are disturbed. In winter, alligators retreat into dens and become sleepy because their blood cools and slows them down.

### ► MEAL BREAKS

Being cold-blooded is quite useful in some ways. These alligators can bask in the sun without having to eat very much or very often. Warm-blooded animals such as mammals have to eat regularly. They need to eat about five times as much food as reptiles to keep their bodies warm.

# Crocodilian Senses

The senses of sight, sound, smell, taste and touch are much more powerful in a crocodilian than in other living reptiles. They have good eyesight and are able to see in colour. Their eyes are also adapted to seeing well in the dark, which is useful because they hunt mainly at night. Crocodilians can smell their prey from as far as 3.2km/2 miles away and they also have an acute sense of hearing. They sense the sounds of danger or prey moving nearby and listen for the barks, coughs and roars of their own species at mating time. Crocodilians also have sensitive scales along the sides of their jaws, which help them to feel and capture prey.

**▲ NOISY GATOR**

An American alligator bellows during courtship. Noises such as hissing or snarling are made at enemies. Young alligators call for help from adults. The animal keeps small ear slits behind the eyes open when it is out of the water. Flaps close to protect the ears when it submerges.

Did you know? Crocodiles shake their ear flaps up and down when they are angry.

**▲ SMELL DETECTORS**

A Nile crocodile picks up chemical signals through the nostrils at the tip of its snout. These messages help it to detect prey and others of its kind. Crocodiles can smell food over long distances. They are known to have come from as far away as 3.2km/2 miles to feed on the carcass of a large animal.

*Crocodile Tears*

*According to legend, crocodiles cry to make people feel so sorry for them that they come near enough for the crocodiles to catch them. Crocodiles are also supposed to shed tears of remorse before finishing a meal. It is said that people cry crocodile tears when they seem to be sorry for something but really are not. Real-life crocodiles cannot cry but sometimes look as if they are.*

## ▶ TASTY TONGUE

Inside the gaping mouth of an American crocodile is a wide, fleshy tongue. It is joined to the bottom of the mouth and does not move, so it plays no part in catching prey. We know that crocodilians have taste buds lining their mouths because some prefer one type of food to another. They can tell the difference between sweet and sour tastes. They also have salt glands on their tongues that get rid of excess salt. Salt builds up in the body over time if the animal lives in the sea or a very dry environment.

## ◀ GLOW-IN-THE-DARK EYES

A flashlight shone into a crocodile farm at night makes the dark glow eerily with a thousand living lights. The scientific explanation is that a special layer at the back of the eye reflects light back into the front of the eye. This ensures that the eye catches as much light as possible. Above water, crocodilians see well and are able to spot prey up to 90m/295ft away. Underwater, an inner, transparent lid covers the eye, making vision foggy, like looking through thick goggles.

## ▶ A PREDATOR'S EYE

The eye of a spectacled caiman, like all crocodilians, has both upper and lower lids. A third eyelid at the side, called a nictitating (blinking) membrane, moves across to clean the eye's surface. The dark, vertical pupil narrows to a slit to stop bright light from damaging the eye. At night, the pupil opens wide to let any available light into the eye. A round pupil, such as a human's, cannot open as wide.

# Food and Hunting

How would it feel to wait up to two years for a meal? Amazingly, a big crocodile can probably survive this long without eating. It lives off fat stored in its tail and other parts of its body. Crocodilians eat a lot of fish, but their strong jaws will snap up anything that wanders too close, from birds, snakes and turtles to raccoons, zebras, cattle and horses. They also eat dead animals. Young crocodilians eat small animals such as insects, snails and frogs.

Most crocodilians sit and wait for their food to come to them, which saves energy. They also catch their meals by stalking and surprising prey. The three main ways of capturing and killing food are lunging toward prey, leaping up out of the water, and sweeping their jaws open from side to side through the water. Most crocodilians hunt at night. They eat every part of their prey, including the bones.

▲ **SURPRISE ATTACK**
A Nile crocodile lunges from the water at an incredible speed to grab a wildebeest in its powerful jaws. It is difficult for the wildebeest to jump back, as the river bank slopes steeply into the water. The crocodile will plunge back into the water, dragging its prey with it in order to drown it.

▼ **BOLD BIRDS**
Large crocodiles feed on big wading birds, such as this saddlebill stork. However, birds often seem to know when they are in no danger from a crocodile. Plovers have been seen standing on the gums of crocodiles and even pecking at their teeth for leftovers. A marabou stork was once seen stealing a fish right out of a crocodile's mouth.

## ▶ SMALLER PREY

A dwarf caiman lies in wait to snap up a tasty bullfrog. Small species of crocodilian like this caiman, as well as young crocodilians, eat a lot of frogs and toads. Youngsters also snap up beetles, spiders, giant water bugs and small fish. They will leap into the air to catch dragonflies and other insects hovering over the water. Small crocodilians are also preyed upon by their larger relatives.

Crocodilians have varied diets and will eat any animal they can catch.

## ◀ SWALLOWING PREY

A crocodile raises its head and grips a crab firmly at the back of its throat. After several jerky head movements the crab is correctly positioned to be crushed between the crocodile's jaws. High levels of acid in the crocodile's stomach help it break down the crab's hard shell so that every part is digested.

Did you know? A Nile crocodile has a stomach that is about the size of a basketball.

## ▶ FISHY FOOD

A Nile crocodile swallows a fish head first. This stops any spines it has from sticking in the crocodile's throat. About 70 percent of the diet of most crocodilians is fish. Crocodilians with narrow snouts, such as the gharial, Johnston's crocodile and the African slender-snouted crocodile, feed mainly on fish. Fish are caught with a sideways, snapping movement that is easier and faster with a slender snout.

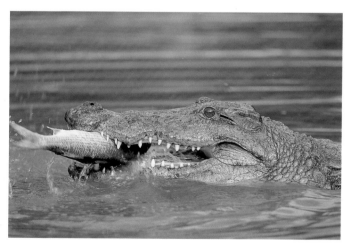

# Communication

Crocodilians pass on messages to each other by means of sounds, body language, smells and touch. Unlike other reptiles, they have a remarkable social life. Groups gather together for basking, sharing food, courting and nesting. Communication begins in the egg and continues throughout life. Adults are particularly sensitive to hatchling and juvenile distress calls and respond with threats or actual attacks. Sounds are made with the vocal cords and with other parts of the body, such as slapping the head against the surface of the water. Crocodilians also use visual communication. Body postures and special movements show which individuals are strong and dominant. Weaker individuals signal to show that they recognize a dominant individual to avoid fighting and injury.

▲ HEAD BANGER
A crocodile lifts its head out of the water, jaws open. The jaws slam shut just before they smack the surface of the water. This is called the head slap and makes a loud pop followed by a splash. Head slapping is often used during the breeding season, and may be a sign of dominance.

**The Fox and the Crocodile**
*In this Aesop's fable, the fox and the crocodile meet one day. The crocodile boasts at length about its cunning as a hunter. Then the fox says, "That's all very impressive, but tell me, what am I wearing on my feet?" The crocodile looks down and there, on the fox's feet, is a pair of shoes made from crocodile skin.*

▲ GHARIAL MESSAGES
The gharial does not head slap, but claps its jaws underwater during the breeding season. Sound travels faster through water than air, so sound signals are very useful for aquatic life.

### ▶ INFRASOUNDS

Some crocodilians make sounds by rapidly squeezing their torso muscles just beneath the surface of the water. The water bubbles up and bounces off the back. The sounds produced are at a very low level, so we can hardly hear them. At close range, they sound like distant thunder. These infrasounds travel quickly over long distances through the water and may be part of courtship. Sometimes they are produced before bellowing, roaring or head slaps.

*Did you know?* The bellow of an alligator can be heard at least 150m/490ft away.

### ◀ I AM THE GREATEST

Dominant animals are usually bigger and more aggressive than submissive ones. They show off their importance by swimming boldly at the surface or thrashing their tails from side to side on land. Weaker individuals usually only lift their heads out of the water and expose their vulnerable throats. This shows that they submit and do not want to fight.

### ▶ GETTING TOGETHER

These caimans are gathering together at the start of the rainy season in Brazil. Crocodilians often come together in loose groups – for example, when they are basking, nesting or sharing food. They tend to ignore each other once dominance battles have been established. During a long, dry spell, large numbers of crocodilians often gather together at water holes to share the remaining water. Young crocodilians stay in a close group for the first months of life, as there is safety in numbers.

# On the Defensive

By the time a crocodilian has grown to about 1m/3ft long, very few predators will threaten it. The main dangers to adult crocodilians come from large animals, such as jaguars, lions, elephants and hippopotamuses, who attack to protect their young. Giant snakes called anacondas will attack and kill crocodilians for food. Adults may also be killed during battles with other crocodilians during the breeding season. People are the main enemy of crocodilians. They kill them for their skins, for food or when they become dangerous. Crocodilians are protected by their powerful jaws, strong tail and heavy armour. They can also swim away from danger and hide underwater, in the mud or among plants.

▲ **KEEP AWAY!**
An American alligator puffs up its body with air to look more threatening. It lets out the air quickly to make a hissing sound. If an enemy is still not scared away, the alligator will then attack.

▶ **THE HIDDEN EYE**
What sort of animal is peeping out from underneath a green carpet of floating water plants? It is hard to tell that there is a saltwater crocodile lurking just beneath the surface. Crocodilians feel safer in the water because they are such good swimmers. They may spend hours almost completely underwater, keeping very still, waiting for prey to come by or for danger to pass. They move so quietly and smoothly that the vegetation on top of the water is hardly disturbed.

## ► CAMOUFLAGE COLOURS

The colour of crocodilians blends in well with their surroundings. Many species change colour all the time. For example, at warmer times of the day, they may become lighter in colour. During cool parts of the day, such as the morning, they may look duller and are often mistaken for logs.

## ◄ CAIMAN FOR LUNCH

A deadly anaconda squeezes the life out of an unfortunate caiman. The anaconda of South America lives partly in the water and can grow up to 9m/30ft long. It can easily kill a caiman by twisting its strong coils around the caiman's body until the victim cannot breathe any more. The caiman dies slowly, either from suffocation or shock. However, anacondas only kill caimans occasionally – they are not an important part of the snake's diet.

### Ticking Croc

*One of the most famous crocodiles in literature is in* Peter Pan, *written by J.M. Barrie in 1904. Peter Pan's greatest enemy is Captain Hook. In a fair fight, Peter cuts off Hook's left hand, which is eaten by a crocodile. The*

*crocodile follows Hook's ship, hoping for a chance to gobble up the rest of him. He makes a ticking noise as he travels because he swallowed a clock. At the end, Hook falls into the water where he is chased by the crocodile, but we do not find out if it eats him.*

## ▲ HUMAN DANGERS

People have always killed small numbers of crocodilians for food, as this Brazilian family has done. However, the shooting of crocodilians through fear or for sport has had a much more severe impact on their population. Of the 22 species of crocodilian, 17 have been hunted to the verge of extinction.

# Ancient Crocodiles

The first alligators and crocodiles lived at the same time as the dinosaurs. Some were even powerful enough to kill the biggest plant-eating dinosaurs. Unlike the dinosaurs, the crocodilians have managed to survive to the present day, possibly because they were so well adapted to their environment. The first crocodiles, the protosuchians, lived about 200 million years ago. They were small land animals with long legs and short snouts. From 200 to 65 million years ago, long-snouted mesosuchians lived mainly in the sea, while the dinosaurs dominated the land. The closest ancestors of today's crocodilians were the early eusuchians, which developed about 80 million years ago. They looked much like gharials, with long snouts, and probably lurked in the shallow fresh waters of rivers and swamps. Like today's crocodilians, the eusuchians could breathe through their nostrils even when their mouths were open underwater. This made it possible for them to catch their prey in the water.

▲ **FIRST CROCODILE**
The name of this ancient crocodile, *Protosuchus*, means "first crocodile". It lived about 200 million years ago in Arizona and looked much like a lizard. *Protosuchus* was small, probably no more than 1m/3ft long, with a small, flat skull and a short snout.

▼ **BACK TO THE SEA**
Swimming along the shores and estuaries in Jurassic times, from about 200 to 145 million years ago, the most widespread crocodilian was *Stenosaurus*. It looked like modern-day gharials, although it is not related to them. *Stenosaurus* had a flexible body and a powerful tail, which allowed it to swim after fast-moving prey.

long, slender snout and up to 200 piercing teeth for trapping fish

### ▶ DINOSAUR DAYS

*Goniopholis*, shown here, was more dependent on land than many of its fellow mesosuchians. It looked much like a broad-snouted crocodile of today. *Goniopholis* had two or more rows of armour on its back and well-developed armour on its belly as well. Most mesosuchians lived in the sea. They were long-snouted with many piercing teeth for catching fish.

### ◀ MONSTER CROCODILE

Lurking in rivers and lakes 70 million years ago was a gigantic crocodile called *Deinosuchus*, which is believed to have grown to perhaps 15m/50ft long. It was a similar size to *T. rex* and ig enough to eat quite large dinosaurs, such as the duck-billed dinosaurs. It had strong teeth and legs, vertebrae (spine bones) that were each 30cm/12in long, and heavy protective scales shielding the body and the tail.

### ▶ SURVIVORS

Crocodilians are survivors from a world inhabited by dinosaurs. However, the origins of both crocodilians and dinosaurs date back much further, to a group of animals called thecodontians, which lived some 200 million years ago.

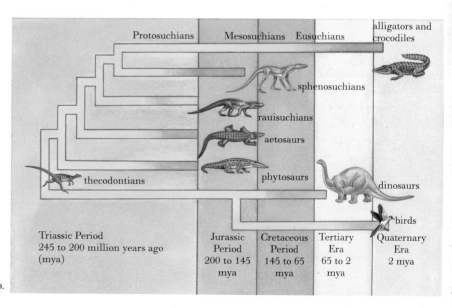

# LIZARDS

Lizards are incredibly adaptable and live
almost everywhere in the world – from
rocky mountains and Arctic tundra, to
arid desert and the forest canopy. They
first appeared on Earth more than 260
million years ago, and today there are
almost 4,000 different known species,
making them the largest
group of reptiles.

*Author*: Mark O'Shea
*Consultant*: Dr Richard A. Griffiths
Durrell Institute of Conservation and Ecology

# Top Reptiles

Lizards form the largest group of reptiles — there are nearly 4,000 different species known. They are found in more places than any other type of reptile, and they live everywhere, from deserts to the Arctic tundra, and exposed mountain slopes to isolated islands. A lizard's habitat can be anything from the highest branches in a forest's trees to the soil underneath its leaf litter. Like all living reptiles, lizards are cold-blooded, which means that their body temperature varies with that of their surroundings. Most are small and feed on insects, but some have become large, dangerous carnivores. A few eat only plants. Lizards are very varied in shape and colour. Most have four legs, but some have lost their legs and look like snakes.

**▲ FIVE TOES, FOUR LEGS**
This green lizard is a typical lizard. It is active by day and has four legs, each with five toes. Most lizards are fairly small; in the food chain, they sit between insects and the predatory birds, mammals and snakes.

**▼ LIZARD EGGS**
Reptiles lay their eggs on land. Their eggs are cleidoic, which means "closed-box" — the baby develops inside the egg, isolated from the outside world and often protected by a tough, leathery shell. Nutrition is supplied by the yolk sac, and waste products are stored in a membrane called the allantois. The amnion, a protective, fluid-filled membrane, surrounds the growing baby lizard and the yolk sac.

**▲ SCALY SKIN**
Lizards are covered in scales made of a substance called keratin, which is also the basis of human hair. Lizard scales vary in size, from the tiny grainlike scales on geckos to the large, fingernail-like scales, or scutes, of plated lizards. Scales offer protection from injury and against drying out.

## MEGA MONITORS ▶

Lizards first appeared 100–150 million years ago. *Megalania priscus* was a giant Australian monitor lizard that would have made a Komodo dragon, the world's largest living lizard, look very puny. Adults reached 7m/23ft and may have weighed more than half a ton. They probably ate prehistoric kangaroos and giant wombats. *Megalania* lived until 25,000 years ago, and they may have met Australia's first humans.

7m/23ft

*Megalania priscus*

1.8m /6ft

man

3m/10ft

Komodo dragon

## ◀ GIANT DRAGONS

The heaviest lizard in the world is the Komodo dragon from the group of islands of the same name in Indonesia. Although there are stories of 5m/16½ft-long Komodo dragons, the longest specimen ever accurately measured was 3m/10ft. It can weigh up to 70kg/155lb. The Salvador's monitor lizard from New Guinea, a more slimline and lighter relative, may grow longer, to over 4m/13ft.

## MINI MARVELS ▶

The Nosy Be pygmy chameleon from Northern Madagascar grows to no more than 4cm/1½in long, but it is not the smallest living lizard. Even smaller is the Jaragua gecko from the Dominican Republic, in the Caribbean. It grows to a maximum length of just 1cm/½in and was discovered in 2001. It is the world's smallest lizard and the smallest land-living vertebrate (animal with a backbone) known to science.

287

# Hard Tongues

All lizards not contained in the Iguania belong to a group known as the Scleroglossa, or hard-tongued lizards. Their tongues are tough and flat. There are more than 2,700 species of hard-tongued lizard, ranging in size from the tiny insectivorous Caribbean least geckos to large carnivorous monitor lizards. Many of the 17 families have become burrowers and have lost their legs, after millions of years of them getting smaller and smaller to make burrowing easier. Hard-tongued lizards are the ancestors of amphisbaenians and snakes. They include a huge variety of species, among them geckos, lacertid lizards, zonures, skinks, anguid lizards and monitor lizards.

**▲ STICKY FINGERS**

Most geckos are nocturnal and hunt insects. The larger species, such as this tokay gecko, include other lizards in their diet. Geckos are well known for their ability to walk up walls and tree trunks, and across ceilings. They do this with the help of flattened toes that have special plates called scansors underneath. Not all geckos can climb like this, however.

**SUN LOVERS ▶**

Europe's eyed lizard preys on many smaller lizards, insects and spiders. Like most of the lizards that are commonly seen in Europe, it belongs to the lacertid family. Indeed the green lizards, wall lizards and ruin lizards often seen basking in the sun are all lacertids. The most widespread European species is the viviparous lizard. Other lacertids live in Africa and Asia. All lacertids are active and alert hunters of insects and spiders.

**◄ REAR GUARD**

The sungazer is the largest of the zonures, which are also called girdled lizards because their spiny scales are arranged in rings, or girdles, around the body. The sungazer has extremely spiny scales on its tail. The scales are used to defend the lizard when it dives headfirst down a hole or wedges itself into a rocky crevice.

**SMOOTHLY DOES IT ►**

Most skinks, including this Müller's skink, have smooth shiny scales. Skinks make up the largest lizard family. Most skinks are small, active by day, live on the ground and eat insects. However, the Solomon's monkey-tail skink breaks all the rules by being a tree-living plant-eater that is active by night.

**▲ WORM, SNAKE OR LIZARD?**

The European slowworm is a legless lizard that feeds on slugs and other soft-bodied creatures. It is the best-known anguid lizard, but not all anguids lack limbs – the American alligator lizards have short legs, but they still wriggle along. The longest anguid is the 1m/3ft European glass lizard. It looks like a snake, but it is a true lizard with eyelids and ear openings.

**▲ ALMOST INVISIBLE**

This Indo-Malay water monitor is almost invisible against the rock it is lying on. Like other monitor lizards, it is a good climber and swimmer. It is found in Africa and Asia, but most live in Australia, and range in size from the 25cm/10in-long short-tailed monitor to the giant Komodo dragon. Most eat insects or vertebrates, but Grey's monitor also eats fruit.

289

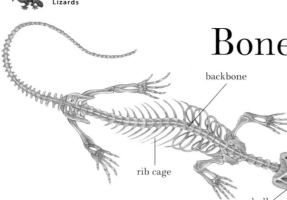

# Bone and Cartilage

The scaffolding that supports a lizard's body is called bone. This is a living tissue that develops as a lizard matures from juvenile to adult. In hatchlings, the body is supported by flexible cartilage. As a lizard ages, calcium is deposited in the cartilage and it hardens, thickens and becomes bone. Lizards obtain calcium from their food. Different lizards have different skeletons, and scientists have divided lizards into families based mostly on skeletal features and the way bones develop.

backbone

rib cage

skull

## ▲ LIZARD SKELETON

Most lizards have four legs, each ending in five toes. As with all reptiles, the body is supported by the backbone, which stretches from the neck to the tail. The backbone is actually not one bone but many small bones, or vertebrae. Important organs, such as the heart and lungs, are protected by the rib cage. The skull forms a tough case around the brain.

## ▼ FASCINATING HORNS

Many lizards have extra structures that stick out from their body. Johnston's chameleon has three large horns on the front of its head. The horns are made of soft tissue, and they grow from raised structures on the skull. All Johnston's chameleons have these horns, but they are larger on males than females. Male use their horns to intimidate rivals, and they may also be helpful in attracting a female mate.

## ▲ LOST LIMBS

Some lizards have less than five toes; others have lost all their limbs. Scaly-feet lizards have completely lost their front legs, and all that remains of their hind limbs is a small scaly flap. Despite the small size of the scaly flaps, they are used for gripping and moving across rock.

monitor lizard skull

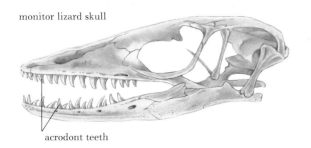

monkeytail skink skull
(*not to scale*)

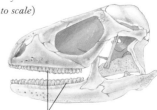

acrodont teeth

pleurodont teeth

## ▲ SKULL AND TEETH

Monitor lizards, chameleons, iguanas and agamas have their
teeth on top of the jawbone, which is known as acrodont. Other
lizards, such as the monkeytail skink, have pleurodont teeth,
positioned on the side of the jawbone. The lower jawbones are
linked to the back of the skull by a ball and socket joint.

*Did you know? Many lizards are classified by the structure of the bones in their skull.*

## ◀ DEFENSIVE UMBRELLA

When the Australian frilled lizard feels
threatened, it opens its mouth. This
action causes a wide frill of skin
around its neck to open like an
umbrella. The frill is supported
by special bones but is poorly
developed in juveniles. It is intended
to frighten an enemy and give the
lizard time to turn and run away. At rest,
or when the lizard is running or climbing,
the frill is folded along the body.

## SPECIAL SAILS ▶

Some lizards have a sail-like fin on their
back. Supported by cartilage or bony
extensions from the backbone, these
fins may serve more than one
purpose. In chameleons, they may
aid balance or help with camouflage
by making the lizard look more like
a leaf. They also increase a lizard's
body surface area to make it easier
to warm up quickly in the sun.

291

# Skin and Scales

All reptiles have tough and almost completely waterproof skin. Lizard skin is made of three layers. The outer layer, or epidermis, is usually transparent and is shed regularly as the lizard grows. Under the epidermis is a layer called the stratum intermediate, which contains the pigments that give the lizard colour. Beneath that is the inner layer, or dermis. In many hard-tongued lizards, this layer contains rigid plates called osteoderms ("bone skin"), which add strength to the skin. Scales vary in shape and texture from the smooth, rounded scales of skinks to the sharp, keeled (ridged) scales of zonures. Lizards don't have sweat glands as mammals do, but they have special glands between the scales.

## ▲ ARMOUR PLATES

Plated lizards, such as this southern African, rough-scaled, plated lizard, have rectangular platelike scales arranged in regular overlapping rows around the body. These scales are strengthened by the presence of protective osteoderms. Along each of the lizard's flanks is a long fold of skin containing small granular scales. This allows the lizard to expand its body when it breathes, in what would otherwise be a very constricting suit of armour.

## SMOOTH AND SHINY ▶

This slowworm and many ground-dwelling skinks have bodies covered in small, rounded, smooth scales that give little resistance when the reptile is burrowing and moving underneath debris. The slowworm is legless, so when it sheds its epidermis, the entire layer often comes off in one large piece, not inside out like a snake. The skin of the slowworm contains protective osteoderms.

## ▲ TINY BEADS

The Salvador's monitor lizard, which is a large, tree-climbing lizard from New Guinea, has numerous tiny scales. The smaller and more regular a lizard's scales are, the more flexible its body is. The Gila monster and beaded lizard have scales that look even more like beads.

## ▲ MOBILE FOLDS

The small scales of South America's northern tegu are arranged in a series of overlapping triangular folds. The northern tegu is a speedy hunter, and this arrangement of scale groups, which move over each other as the lizard runs, gives the tegu both protection and agility.

## ▲ SHARP RIDGES

The back of the Bosc monitor lizard from the African savannahs has numerous interlocking but non-overlapping, keeled scales. Those on the lizard's underside are smaller and not keeled. Keeled scales may help dew condense on the lizard's back at night, giving it water to drink in an otherwise arid environment.

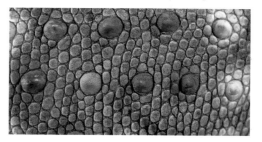

## ▲ SCATTERED SCALES

Geckos have granular, velvety or papery skin. The tokay gecko has scattered conical scales surrounded by smaller, granular scales. The skin of smaller geckos is usually much more fragile. One species from Madagascar sheds all three layers of its skin if it is grasped.

## OFF WITH THE OLD ▶

Lizards must shed the outer layer of their skins in order to grow. Unlike snakes, they tend to shed their skin in pieces. This wonder gecko has begun to shed its old skin. Since the cells that produce pattern and colour are in the second layer, the old skin looks colourless. The original colours are visible in the new gecko that emerges.

# Getting Around

The typical lizard has four well-developed legs, each with five clawed toes. The legs stick out from the side of the body. This means that the body is thrown into S-shaped curves when the lizard walks and runs. Lizard backbones are flexible to let the lizard move easily as its stride lengthens. Some lizards run very fast on all fours. Others run even faster using just their hind legs with the front of the body raised and the tail for balance. In tree-dwelling species, the feet and tail may be adapted for climbing.

### ▲ A FIFTH LIMB
Some tree-living lizards have prehensile tails, which they can use when climbing. The monkey-tail skink is a large lizard from the Solomon Islands that uses its powerful tail when clambering in the forest canopy.

### ▲ SPIDER MEN
Geckos are famous for their ability to run up walls and glass, but not all geckos can do this. Only the geckos with expanded digits, such as house geckos and tokay geckos, can climb sheer surfaces. Under their toes are a series of flattened plates called "scansors", which mean they can stick onto almost any flat surface.

### ▼ WALKING ON WATER
Basilisks escape predators by running very fast on their long-toed hind-limbs. They can sprint across water for quite a while before they break the surface of the water and fall in. This unusual ability to run on water has earned them the nickname of "Jesus lizard". Some other long-legged lizards can also run on water.

## ▲ LEAP FOR FREEDOM

Flying lizards and flying geckos do not actually fly but glide down from trees to avoid predators. The flying gecko has webs of skin between its toes and also along the side of its body to slow its descent, but this flying lizard is more elaborate. It has a pair of "wings" spread out by false ribs to produce the lizard equivalent of a parachute.

## ▲ LIFE UNDERGROUND

Many desert lizards spend part of their lives underground, where they can escape from enemies and the heat of the sun. Africa's sand fish disappears into loose sand extremely rapidly, digging with its legs and flattened snout. Other lizards have developed an elongated body and lost their limbs, so that they can swim through the sand like eels in water.

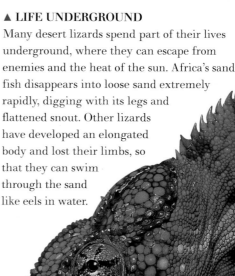

### Night Fighters

*"Gecko" is an onomatopoeic word – a word that sounds like what it describes. This comes from the Malay word "gekok," which is derived from the noise that some geckos make when they call. The tokay gecko has another call that sounds like "tow-kay." Geckos are active after dark, and this led the Japanese to give the name "Gekkoh" to their night-fighter aircraft in World War II.*

### HOLDING ON ▶

Chameleons' toes are fused together. Each foot has three toes opposing two toes. The toes grip in the same way as a human's opposing thumb and other four fingers. This makes the chameleon such an expert climber that it can walk along slender twigs.

295

# Sensing the Surroundings

Lizards have a variety of finely tuned sense organs to allow them to move around, locate and capture prey, avoid predators and find a mate. Eyesight is an important sense for most lizards, but the structure of the retina (the back of the inside of the eye) varies a lot. The retinas of day-living lizards are dominated by cells called cones, giving them detailed vision, and those of nocturnal species have far more light-sensing rod cells, which increases their ability to see by moonlight. Lizards that are active at dusk and dawn have vertical pupils that close down to protect the sensitive retina from bright daylight. Day-living lizards may also possess colour vision.

▲ EAGLE EYES
Lizards that are active by day, such as the green iguana, have excellent vision. Focusing for studying close detail is accomplished by changing the shape of the soft, deformable lens of the eye. Many lizards need to be able to focus rapidly, because they move around quickly and with agility, so that they can catch fast-moving insects. Vision is also important for basking lizards, since they must be able to locate approaching predators.

◀ LOOKING TWO WAYS AT ONCE
Chameleons are the only land vertebrates with eyes that move independently. This Parson's chameleon can use its turret-eyes to look in two directions at the same time. When an insect is located, both eyes converge on the prey and, working like a telephoto lens, they focus quickly and precisely to enlarge the image. The turret-eyes and the long sticky tongue evolved to work together, making chameleons expert shots when they shoot out their tongues to capture insects.

296

## ▼ A THIRD EYE

Green iguanas and many other lizards have a small circular object in the middle of their heads. This is the pineal eye, a third eye with a lens, retina, and a nerve feeding back into the brain, but it has no muscles, making it unable to focus. The pineal eye may help basking lizards to monitor how much sunlight they are receiving, but the way in which it works is not yet fully understood.

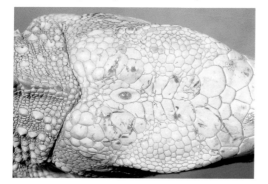

## ▲ LISTENING LIZARDS

Lizard ears are made up of three parts: the outer, middle and inner ear. The eardrum of this bearded dragon is visible on the side of its head, because the outer ear is absent. In other species, the eardrum is hidden by a deep, outer ear opening. Most lizards have external ears, but some have scales over them, and others have no eardrum at all.

## SEEK WITH FORKED TONGUE ▶

Some hard-tongued lizards have a Jacobson's organ that allows them to "taste" the air and track prey from a long way away. The forked tongue of this water monitor lizard is picking up odour particles and delivering them to the Jacobson's organ to be analysed. The forks of the tongue help it tell direction – if more interesting particles are on the right fork, the lizard turns right.

## ◀ PECULIAR TASTES

The herbivorous monkey-tail skink has a bulbous tongue with a slightly bi-lobed tip that contains many taste buds. This skink does not eat insects or meat so it does not have to track down any prey, but probably uses its sensitive tongue to discriminate between suitable and unsuitable leaves. Monkey-tail skinks are social lizards, and tongue-licking may also be a way of recognizing other members of the colony.

# Body Temperature

A lizard's body temperature depends on the temperature of its surroundings. Unlike birds and mammals, which produce their own body heat, cold-blooded lizards need to bask on hot surfaces such as sun-heated rocks, or have warm air around them. In the hot tropics, lizards can be active day or night. Elsewhere, they need the heat of the sun to raise their body temperature. Most lizards speed up this process by basking in the sun, but they must be careful not to get too hot.

**▲ ON GUARD**

A lizard in the sun has to keep its eyes open for predators. Birds of prey are a particular threat to this African ground agama – the slightest shadow will send it dashing back to its refuge, a hole at the base of the bush. A basking lizard may look like a dozing sunbather, but it is usually alert.

**▲ TOO HOT TO HANDLE**

If you have ever walked barefoot on sand in the summer, you know how hot it can be. Desert lizards have to face this problem every day. The African ground agama gets around it by standing on the balls of its feet. Other species do a balancing act, standing on two feet with two raised before swapping over.

**◀ SUN-POWERED COLOUR**

Some male lizards adopt very bright colours to attract a female. The male common agama is bright blue and red, but only during the daytime. At night, the sleeping lizard is much drabber and duller, but it quickly becomes more colourful as the day warms up. After a minute or so of basking in the sun, the lizard changes from grey to glowing red and blue again.

## ▲ BASKING IN THE RAINFOREST

Not much sunlight reaches the ground in
a rainforest, yet some lizards warm up by
basking on the rainforest floor. When a
rainforest tree falls, it creates a natural gap
in the canopy, and a patch of sunlight appears
on the ground. In tropical America, ameivas
look for these sunny patches, and are usually
the first lizards to arrive after a tree has fallen.

## ▲ WARM AT NIGHT

Lizards that hunt at night still need to be warm
to be active. The granite night lizard from
California spends the day in a rocky crevice,
venturing forth to capture insects and scorpions
only after dark. It manages to do this by seeking
places where the rocks are still warm from the
sun's rays. It is also able to remain active at
temperatures too low for most lizards.

## CATCHING THE RAYS ▶

So that they can get warm quickly,
basking lizards flatten themselves to
expose their bodies to the sun or the
warm ground. They do this by expanding
their ribs outward and making themselves
more rounded. Some desert lizards are
naturally rounded and can present almost
half their body surface to the sun.

## ON TIPTOES ▶

This northern desert
horned lizard is round
and flattened – the ideal
shape for basking, since it
can present a large surface area to
the sun. When it gets too hot, it lifts
its underside and tail off the sand.
Horned lizards spend long periods of
time almost motionless, waiting
for the ants that they eat to
swarm into reach.

# Defence Methods

**▲ BOLD DEFENCE**

The toad-headed agama of Iran and southern Russia puts on a bold defence display. When it is threatened, it raises its front, opens its mouth wide and extends flaps at both sides to make it look threatening. It then hisses, waves its tail like a scorpion and jumps towards its enemy.

Many lizards are small and looked upon as food by other animals. To escape being eaten, lizards have evolved a wide array of defensive mechanisms. One of the most effective is simply being well camouflaged and staying still to avoid detection. When this fails, the lizard may have to adopt a more active method of defending itself. Running away, diving off a branch or even gliding to freedom are all simple escape procedures. But many lizards have evolved more elaborate defensive behaviour, including displays intended to intimidate or confuse potential predators. Some of these are among the most extreme seen anywhere in the animal kingdom.

**◄ PUTTING ON A SHOW**

The Australian frilled lizard's first reaction to danger is to open its mouth wide to spread its neck frill. All of this makes the lizard seem suddenly less like an easy meal and more like a large, dangerous opponent. If this display fails to scare a predator, the lizard turns tail and runs, the frill trailing around its neck like a partially closed umbrella. The frilled lizard uses its display to scare rivals as well as predators.

## THREATENING DISPLAY ▶

The shingleback skink from Australia tries to frighten predators by opening its mouth and sticking out its bright blue tongue. These lizards have short legs so they cannot run away, and must stand their ground. The rolling tongue, combined with a flattening and curving of the body, and a hiss, is enough to intimidate most animals.

### ▲ SEEING RED

The horned lizards of Mexico and the U.S.A. have one of the strangest defence mechanisms of any animal – they squirt foul-tasting blood from the corners of their eyes. They use this defence only against large predators. Birds and rodents are usually chased away by the lizard's prickly spines.

### ▼ FIGHTING TINY ENEMIES

New Guinea's green-blooded skinks have a pigment in their blood that makes it bright green. This is thought to be a defence against the tiny blood parasites that cause a disease called malaria. Lizards suffer from seven types of malaria. The skinks' blood is believed to be so toxic, the malarial parasite cannot survive.

### ▼ CHAMPION WRESTLER

Monitor lizards have powerful jaws, which can deliver a painful bite. They use their tails as whips, dealing rapid blows to their enemies. When the argus monitor is threatened, it makes itself look bigger by standing on its hind feet and inflating its throat. If this fails, it attacks, wrestling fiercely until its opponent flees.

Did you know? The frilled lizard can run on its back legs at speeds of more than 20kph / 12½mph.

# Colour and Camouflage

A lizard's colour is usually dictated by the habitat in which it lives: most desert lizards are sandy brown, most tree-living species are bark-coloured or green. By matching themselves to the colour of their background, they become well camouflaged, which protects them from animals that want to eat them. Some lizards take camouflage one step further and actually look like objects from their surroundings. Colour is also important socially. Many male lizards adopt bright colours in the mating season, or change colour or expose bright parts of the body when confronted by a rival.

▲ DEAD LEAF

Not all chameleons are green or camouflaged like living leaves. The West African pygmy chameleon lives in low vegetation in forests and is a drab brown with a series of darker lines making it look like a dead leaf. When the pygmy chameleon feels threatened, it just falls to the forest floor and lies still, disappearing among the leaf litter.

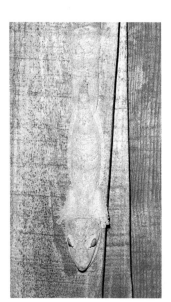

◄ WOODEN PERFORMANCE ►

Chameleons are not the only lizards capable of changing their pattern or colour. The Malagasy flat-tailed gecko can also alter its appearance, shown here as it matches the wooden planks of a hut (left) and the bark of a tree (right). By combining camouflage with a flattened body edged with thin fringes of skin, this nocturnal gecko can sleep unseen during the day. Its gripping toes allow it to merge into the background on vertical surfaces or even the undersides of branches. At night, it wakes up again to feed.

## ▲ LEGS LIKE STICKS

The Sri Lankan kangaroo lizard has legs that look like fine twigs, and body and head patterns that look like a dead leaf or fern frond. When a predator approaches, the kangaroo lizard skips across the forest floor and then disappears into the dead leaves. It is often found near forest streams and can run across water.

### Omen of Evil

*Chameleons are considered evil omens in Africa, but nowhere are they feared as much as on the island of Madagascar, where the giant panther chameleon is avoided at all costs. Drivers who would not think twice about hitting a dog or a chicken swerve to avoid chameleons, preferring to risk a serious accident rather than incur the wrath of an angry spirit. Chameleons are also believed by some Malagasy people to be poisonous, so they are never handled or eaten, even when other meat is scarce.*

## ◄ SPOTLIT SIDES

In 1938, a British naturalist captured a small, cave-dwelling lizard in Trinidad and reported that it had white spots on its flanks that glowed like a ship's portholes. Recently, a male lizard was caught, and the 1938 report was proved correct. The purpose of the spots is unknown, but it is thought they might be used to startle predators.

## STANDING OUT ►

Four-fingered skinks are usually brown and blend in with the leaf litter, but this individual is an albino. Being born an albino can make life more dangerous. Albinos lack coloured pigment and stand out from their surroundings, making them easy targets for predators. Not only are they more likely to be eaten, but they are also thought to be vulnerable to sunburn.

# Where in the World?

Lizards are the most numerous of all reptiles, and they are also among the most adaptable – they live in regions where even snakes are absent. Lizards have adapted to cope with cold on mountains and inside the Arctic Circle and can endure the heat of any desert. They are excellent colonizers – especially those species that give birth to live young – and can adapt in time to feed on anything that is available. In fact, almost everywhere you look on land, there is a good chance that a lizard lives there. Unlike amphibians, which lived on Earth before reptiles, some lizards have learned to live in or near the sea, and have adapted to high levels of salt in their diets.

▲ **DUSTY DESERT**
Many lizards live in deserts, but surviving there is hard. Desert lizards are often nocturnal to avoid the heat. They rarely drink, and many survive on the water they get from their food alone. Some desert lizards, such as this Namib gecko, have webbed feet or fringes on their toes to help them run over sand.

▲ **ICY COLD**
The Arctic is not an ideal place for reptiles, but a few lizards do live in this cold region and are active in the short summers. The viviparous lizard is common throughout Europe, but unlike other European lizards, it is also found well inside the Arctic Circle. Viviparous means live-bearing, and most reptiles that live in cold climates give birth to live young.

▲ **SEASHORE SALT**
The swollen-snouted, side-blotch lizard is one of the few lizards that live on the seashore. It lives on the tiny island of Isla Colouradito, off Mexico, where it eats shore-living crustaceans called slaters and the sea lice that infest the sea lion colony. The salt level in its diet is 20 times the lethal level of other lizards. Special glands in its nostrils help it get rid of some of the salt.

## ◀ WHERE DO LIZARDS LIVE?

Lizards inhabit every continent apart from Antarctica, and have colonized most island groups. Some species, such as house geckos, have even used human transportation to reach and colonize islands a long way from land. Lizards are not found in areas of very high altitude and latitude, because it is too cold for them. The five species shown on these two pages are from different continents and different habitats. The only thing these lizards have in common is that they all survive in difficult conditions.

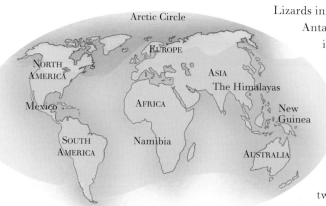

Lizards live on every continent except the Antarctic

### MOUNTAIN HIGH ▶

The mountains are tough places for reptiles, which rely on the sun to keep them warm and active. Few lizards can survive in these conditions, but one exception is the rock agama from the southern Himalayas. It is found as high as 2,286m/7,500ft, basking on rocks along the freezing rivers that pour from glaciers. The rock agama hibernates in winter to save energy and avoid the worst of the cold.

### ◀ STEAMY RAINFOREST

Lizards are everywhere in rain-forests: in the canopy, on the tall trunks, down on the ground and underneath the leaf litter. There is plenty of food in the forest, but there are also many predators, so lizards have to be alert. New Guinea's twin-crested anglehead lizard lives in rain-forests, but it is seldom seen because it is well camouflaged.

*305*

# Lizard Relatives

The first reptiles appeared on Earth over 260 million years ago. Most types that lived in the distant past, such as dinosaurs and flying pterodactyls, are extinct today. Even so the Class Reptilia currently contains over 7,000 living species, ranging from turtles to crocodiles and geckos to snakes. All reptiles have scaly or leathery protective skin, which allows them to survive in salty, hot or dry conditions that would kill many other animals. Most lay leathery-shelled eggs, but a few lizards and snakes bear live young – an adaptation to living in colder climates where eggs would die. This versatility makes reptiles excellent survivors. Even though we now live in the Age of Mammals, reptiles are still a very successful group.

▲ **RELATION WITH A SHELL**
Turtles and tortoises belong to an ancient order of reptiles that split from the main reptile line shortly after the ancestors of mammals did. They are distantly related to other modern reptiles – in fact, lizards are related less to turtles and tortoises than they are to dinosaurs or birds. Turtles live in the sea and fresh water, while tortoises live on land.

▲ **DINOSAUR DINNER**
In this reconstruction, a plant-eating *Iguanodon* is being stalked by two meat-eating *Deinonychus*. Although dinosaurs might look like giant lizards they were more closely related to crocodiles and birds. Unlike modern reptiles, many dinosaurs walked on two legs. Most of these ancient reptiles were plant-eaters, but some ate meat.

▲ **FIERCE HUNTER**
Crocodiles and alligators include the largest reptiles alive today. Nile crocodiles such as this can grow to 6m/20ft long and weigh almost a tonne/ton, and the Indo-Pacific crocodile is even larger. Crocodilians eat meat and spend most of their time in water. They are distantly related to lizards and, like all egg-laying reptiles, they lay eggs on land.

## Congo Monster

*People living in the Congo rainforest claim it is inhabited by a giant Diplodocus-like creature that they call Mokele-mbembe. Do dinosaurs still walk the Earth, or could the monster be a large monitor lizard standing on its hind feet and stretching out its long neck? Several expeditions have set out in search of Mokele-mbembe but the mystery remains unsolved.*

### THE FAMILY TREE ▼

As this tree shows, reptiles are a very diverse group. Turtles split away from the main reptilian line millions of years ago. Reptiles then divided into two main groups. The Archosauria (ancient reptiles) became dinosaurs, crocodilians and birds. The Lepidosauria (scaled reptiles) includes tuataras, and modern lizards, snakes and amphisbaenians (worm-lizards).

### ▲ TWO TUATARAS

These reptiles live on islands off the coast of New Zealand. Although they look like lizards, they have their own reptile group. They have hardly changed their appearance and behaviour since dinosaurs walked the Earth. Only two species of tuatara are alive in the world today.

### ▼ LEGLESS LIZARDS

Amphisbaenians, or worm-lizards, are legless reptiles that evolved from lizards. There are around 130 species, living in Florida, north-western Mexico, the West Indies, South America, Africa and Mediterranean Europe. Burrowers in soil and sand, amphisbaenians feed on earthworms and other invertebrates.

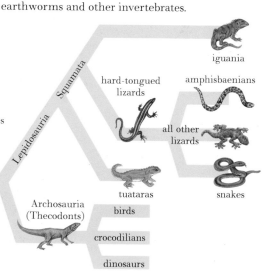

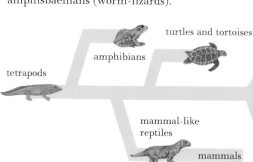

# SNAKES

Snakes are among the most feared and
least understood of all predators. They
vary in size from the tiny blind snake
that can fit into the palm of your hand
to the enormous Burmese python. Some
snakes kill their victims by squeezing
them to death in seconds, while others
swallow their live prey whole.

*Author*: Barbara Taylor
*Consultant*: Michael Chinery

long, thin,
flexible body
with no legs

Tough scales
protect the
body and
keep it from
drying out.

# Snake Life

Snakes are a kind of reptile
related to lizards, crocodiles and
turtles. Altogether, there are about
2,700 different kinds of snake, but only
300 or so are able to kill people. In North
America or Europe, you are more likely to
be struck by lightning than to be bitten by a
poisonous snake. All snakes have long bodies covered
with waterproof scales. They are flesh eaters and
swallow their prey whole. Snakes have always had
a special place in myths and legends, being used
as symbols of both good and evil.

### ◀ A SNAKE'S TAIL
The tail of a snake is the part behind a small opening
called the cloaca, where the body waste passes
out. The snake narrows slightly where
the tail begins.

tail, the part
of the body
that tapers
off to a point

**grass snake**
*(Natrix natrix)*

### ◀ SNAKE HEADS
Most snakes have a definite head and neck.
But in some snakes, one end of the body looks
very much like the other end!

### ◄ FORKED TONGUES

Snakes and some lizards have forked tongues. A snake flicks its tongue to taste and smell the air. This gives the snake a picture of what is around it. A snake does this every few seconds if it is hunting or if there is any danger nearby.

**rattlesnake**
*(Crotalus)*

**Colombian rainbow boa**
*(Epicrates cenchria maurus)*

### ▲ SCALY ARMOUR

A covering of tough, dry scales grows out of a snake's skin. The scales usually hide the skin. After a big meal, the scaly skin stretches so that the skin becomes visible between the scales. A snake's scales protect its body while allowing it to stretch, coil and bend. The scales may be either rough or smooth.

**red-tailed boa**
*(Boa constrictor)*

Did you know? Snakes never feel slimy to the touch.

Did you know? A boa squeezes its prey to death in its coils.

Eye has no eyelid.

forked tongue

### Medusa

*An ancient Greek myth tells of Medusa, a monster with snakes for hair. Anyone who looked at her was turned to stone. Perseus managed to avoid this fate by using his polished shield to look only at the monster's reflection. He cut off Medusa's head and carried it home, dripping with blood. As each drop touched the earth, it turned into a snake.*

# Snake Families

Scientists have divided the 2,700 different kinds of snake into about ten groups, called families. These are the colubrids, the elapids, the vipers, the boas and pythons, the sea snakes, the sunbeam snakes, the blind snakes and worm snakes, the thread snakes, the shieldtail snakes and the false coral snakes. The snakes in each family have features in common. The biggest family is the colubrid family, with over 1,800 different species of snake.

*Did you know?* The viper family includes rattlesnakes, adders, asps and pit vipers.

**▲ COLUBRIDS**
About three-quarters of all the world's snakes, including this milk snake, belong to the colubrid family. Most colubrids are not poisonous. They have no left lung or hip bones.

**▲ VIPERS**
Snakes in this family, such as the sand viper, have long, hollow fangs that can be folded back inside the mouth when they are not needed.

**► ELAPIDS**
Elapids, such as this cobra, are poisonous snakes that live in hot countries. They have short, fixed fangs at the front of the mouth.

Indian cobra
*(Naja naja)*

| Classification Chart | | |
|---|---|---|
| | Kingdom | Animalia |
| | ⇩ | ⇩ |
| | Phylum | Chordata |
| | ⇩ | ⇩ |
| | Class | Reptilia |
| | ⇩ | ⇩ |
| | Order | Squamata |
| | ⇩ | ⇩ |
| | Suborder | Ophidia |
| | ⇩ | ⇩ |
| | Family | Boidae |
| | ⇩ | ⇩ |
| | Genus | Boa |
| | ⇩ | ⇩ |
| | Species | Boa constrictor |

*This chart shows how a boa constrictor is classified within the animal kingdom.*

312

**Colombian
rainbow boa**
*(Epicrates cenchria
maurus)*

▶ **BOAS
AND
PYTHONS**
This family
includes snakes
that kill by
constriction rather than
poisoning. They have curved teeth,
hip bones and tiny back leg bones.

▶ **SEA SNAKES**
Some sea snakes are born in the sea
and spend all their lives there, and
others spend part of their time on
land. Sea snakes have flattened tails
for swimming and nostrils that can
be closed off underwater. Most
live in warm waters, from the Red
Sea to New Zealand and Japan.

◀ **SUNBEAM SNAKES**
The two members of the sunbeam family are burrowing
snakes that live in South-east Asia and southern China.
Unlike most other snakes, they have two working lungs.

*313*

# Shapes and Sizes

Can you imagine a snake as tall as a three-storey house? The reticulated python is that big. The biggest snakes' bodies measure almost 0.9m/1yd around. Other snakes are as thin as a pencil and small enough to fit into the palm of your hand. Snakes also have different shapes to suit their environments. Sea snakes, for example, have flat bodies and tails like oars to help them push through the water and move forward.

## ▼ THICK AND THIN

Vipers mostly have thick bodies with much thinner, short tails. The bags of poison on each side of a viper's head take up a lot of space, so the head is quite large.

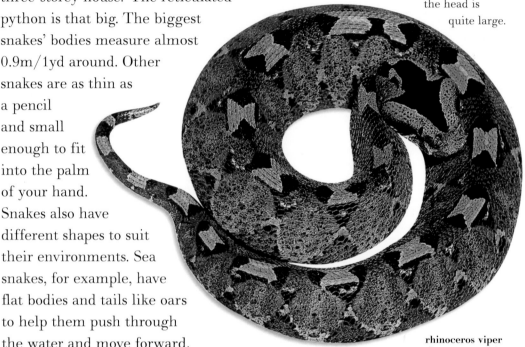

rhinoceros viper
(*Bitis nasicornis*)

## ◄ LONG AND THIN

A tree snake's long, thin shape helps it slide along leaves and branches. Even its head is long, pointed and very light so that it does not weigh the snake down as it reaches for the next branch.

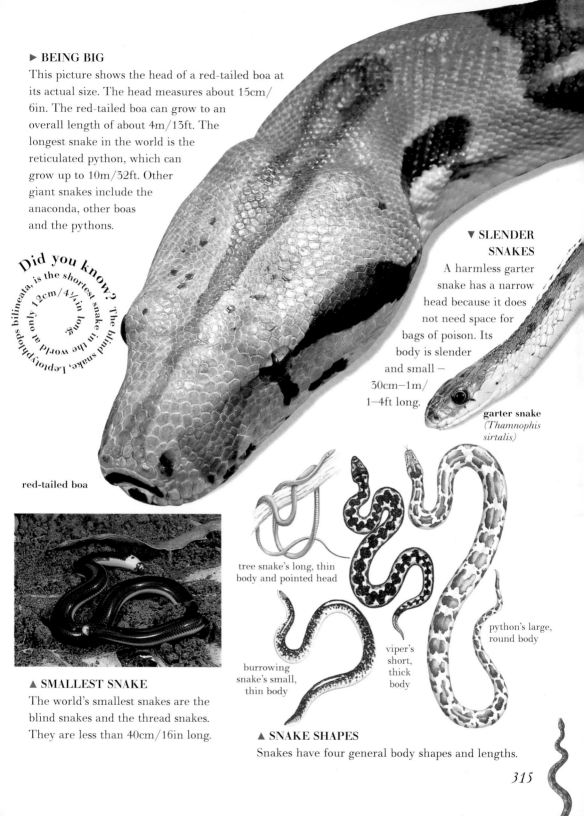

► **BEING BIG**

This picture shows the head of a red-tailed boa at its actual size. The head measures about 15cm/ 6in. The red-tailed boa can grow to an overall length of about 4m/13ft. The longest snake in the world is the reticulated python, which can grow up to 10m/32ft. Other giant snakes include the anaconda, other boas and the pythons.

*Did you know?* The blind snake, Leptotyphlops bilineata, is the shortest snake in the world at only 12cm/4¾in long.

red-tailed boa

▼ **SLENDER SNAKES**

A harmless garter snake has a narrow head because it does not need space for bags of poison. Its body is slender and small – 30cm−1m/ 1−4ft long.

**garter snake** (*Thamnophis sirtalis*)

▲ **SMALLEST SNAKE**

The world's smallest snakes are the blind snakes and the thread snakes. They are less than 40cm/16in long.

tree snake's long, thin body and pointed head

burrowing snake's small, thin body

viper's short, thick body

python's large, round body

▲ **SNAKE SHAPES**

Snakes have four general body shapes and lengths.

315

egg-eating
snake
(*Dasypeltis
fasciata*)

◄ **STRETCHY STOMACH**
Luckily, the throat and digestive tract of the egg-
eating snake are so elastic that its thin body
can stretch enough to
swallow a whole
egg. Muscles in the
throat and first part of
the tract help force food
down into the stomach.

# How Snakes Work

A snake has a stretched-out inside to match
its long, thin outside. The backbone extends
along the whole body with hundreds of ribs joined
to it. There is not much room for organs such as the
heart, lungs and liver, so these are thin so that they fit
inside its body. Many snakes have only one lung. The
stomach and intestines are stretchy so that they can
hold large meals. When a snake swallows big prey, it
pushes the opening of the windpipe up from the floor
of the mouth in order to keep breathing. Snakes
are cold-blooded, which means that their body
temperature is the same as their surroundings.

Right lung is
very long and
thin and does
the work of
two lungs.

Liver is very
long and thin.

flexible tail bone,
which extends
from the back
bone

▼ **INSIDE A SNAKE**
This diagram shows
the inside of a male
snake. The organs are
arranged to fit the
snake's long shape. In
most species, paired
organs, such as the
kidneys, are the
same size and
placed opposite
each other.

▲ **COLD-BLOODED CREATURE**
Like all snakes, the banded rattlesnake is cold-blooded.

rectum
through
which
waste is
passed to the
cloaca

316

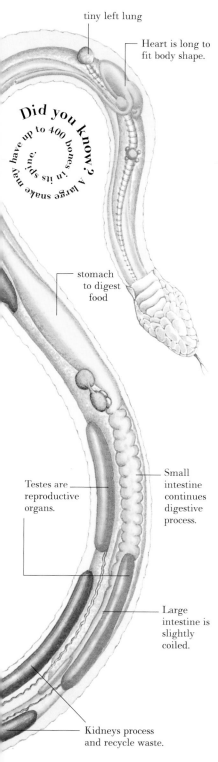

tiny left lung

Heart is long to fit body shape.

Did you know? A large snake may have up to 400 bones in its spine.

stomach to digest food

Testes are reproductive organs.

Small intestine continues digestive process.

Large intestine is slightly coiled.

Kidneys process and recycle waste.

## ▲ SNAKE BONES

This X-ray of a grass snake shows the delicate bones that make up its skeleton. There are no arm, leg, shoulder or hip bones. The snake's ribs do not extend into the tail.

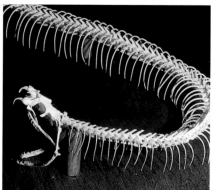

## ◀ SKELETON

A snake's skeleton is made up of a skull and a backbone with ribs arching out from it. The free ends of the ribs are linked by muscles.

317

# Scaly Skin

## ▼ HORNED SNAKE

As its name suggests, the European nose-horned viper has a strange horn on its nose. The horn is made up of small scales that lie over a bony or fleshy lump sticking out at the end of the nose.

nose-horned viper
(*Vipera ammodytes*)

A snake's scales are extra-thick pieces of skin. Like a suit of armour, the scales protect the snake from bumps and scrapes as it moves. They also allow the skin to stretch when the snake moves or eats. Scales are usually made of a horny substance called keratin. Every part of a snake's body is covered by a layer of scales, including the eyes. The clear, bubble-like scale that protects each eye is called a brille or spectacle.

## ▼ SCUTES

Most snakes have a row of broad scales, called scutes, underneath their bodies. The scutes go across a snake's body from side to side, and end where the tail starts. Scutes help snakes to grip the ground.

corn snake's
scutes

## ▼ WARNING RATTLE

The rattlesnake has a number of hollow tail-tips that make a buzzing sound when shaken. The snake uses this sound to warn enemies. When it sheds its skin, a section at the end of the tail is left, adding another piece to the rattle.

rattlesnake's
rattle

## ► SKIN SCALES

The scales of a snake grow out of the top layer of the skin, called the epidermis. There are different kinds of scales. Keeled scales may help snakes to grip surfaces, or break up a snake's outline for camouflage. Smooth scales make it easier for the snake to squeeze through tight spaces.

*Look closely at the rough scales of the puff adder (left) and you will see a raised ridge, or keel, sticking up in the middle of each one.*

**Did you know?** *Most snakes get their colours from pigments in the scale.*

**corn snake's scale**

*The wart snake (right) uses its scales to grip its food. Its rough scales help the snake to keep a firm hold on slippery fish until it can swallow them. The snake's scales do not overlap.*

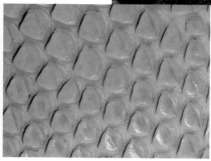

*The green scales and stretched blue skin (left) belong to a boa. These smooth scales help the boa to slide over leafy branches. Burrowing snakes have smooth scales so that they can slip through soil.*

### Eternal Youth
*A poem written in the Middle East about 3,700 years ago tells a story about why snakes can shed their skins. The hero of the poem is Gilgamesh (shown here holding a captured lion). He finds a magic plant that will make a person young again. While he is washing at a pool, a snake eats the plant. Since then, snakes have been able to shed their skins and become young again. But people have never found the plant – which is why they always grow old and die.*

**Did you know?** *The hairy bush viper has pointed scales with curled tips, making it look hairy.*

**1** In the days before its skin peels, a snake is sluggish and its colours become dull. Its eyes turn cloudy as its skin loosens. About a day before moulting, the eyes clear.

# *Focus on New Skin*

About six times a year, an adult snake wriggles out of its old, tight skin to reveal a new, shiny skin underneath. Snakes shed their worn-out skin and scales in one piece. This process is called moulting or sloughing. Snakes only moult when a new layer of skin and scales has grown underneath the old skin.

**2** The paper-thin layer of outer skin and scales first starts to peel away around the mouth. The snake rubs its jaws and chin against rocks or rough bark, and crawls through plants. This helps to push off the loose layer of skin.

*Did you know? A baby snake may shed its skin when it is only a few days old.*

320

**3** The outer layer of skin gradually peels back from the head over the rest of the body. The snake slides out of its old skin, which comes off inside-out. Imagine grasping a long sock at the top and peeling it down over your leg and foot!

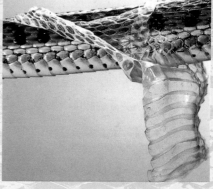

Did you know? Female snakes often shed their skin just before giving birth.

**4** A snake usually takes several hours to shed its whole skin. The old skin is moist and supple soon after shedding but gradually dries out to become crinkly and brittle. The moulted skin is a copy of the snake's scale pattern. It is very delicate, and if you hold it up to the light, it is almost transparent.

**5** A shed skin is longer than the snake itself. This is because the skin stretches as the snake wriggles free.

321

# Snakes on the Move

For animals without legs, snakes move around very well. They can glide over or under the ground, climb trees and swim through water. A few snakes can even parachute through the air. Snakes are not speedy – most move at about 3kph/2mph. Their flexible backbones give them a wavy movement. They push themselves along using muscles joined to their ribs. The scales on their skin also grip surfaces to help with movement.

*Did you know? A person can walk faster than a snake can move.*

**corn snake**
*(Elaphe guttata)*

**▶ S-SHAPED MOVER**
Most snakes move in an S-shaped path, pushing the side curves of their bodies backward against the surface they are travelling on or through. The muscular waves of the snake's body hit surrounding objects and the whole body is pushed forward from there.

**▲ SWIMMING SNAKE**
The banded sea snake's stripes stand out as it glides through the water. Snakes swim using S-shaped movements. A sea snake's tail is flattened from side to side to give it extra power, like the oar on a rowboat.

**▼ ACCORDION SNAKE**
The green whip snake moves with an action much like an accordion. The accordion is played by squeezing it in and stretching it out.

322

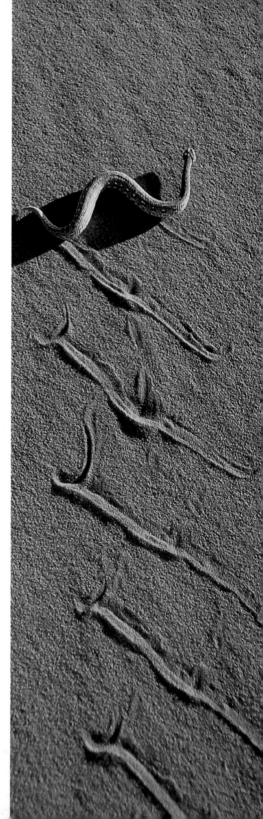

► **SIDEWINDING**

The way snakes that live on loose sand move along is called sidewinding. The snake anchors its head and tail in the sand and throws the middle part of its body sideways.

*Did you know? The fastest land snake is the black mamba, moving at up to 11kph./7mph.*

▼ **HOW SNAKES MOVE**

Most land snakes move in four different ways, depending on the type of terrain they are crossing and the type of snake.

**1** S-shaped movement: the snake wriggles from side to side.

**2** Accordion movement: the snake pulls one half of its body along first, then the other half.

**3** Sidewinding movement: the snake throws the middle part of its body forward, keeping the head and tail on the ground.

**4** Caterpillar movement: the snake uses its belly scutes to pull itself along in a straight line.

# Snake Senses

To find prey and avoid enemies, snakes rely more on their senses of smell, taste and touch than on sight and sound. Snakes have no ears, but they do have one ear bone joined at the jaw. The lower jaw picks up sound vibrations travelling through the ground. As well as ordinary senses, snakes also have some special ones. They are one of the few animals that taste and smell with their tongues.

**▲ EYESIGHT**
Snakes have no eyelids to cover their eyes. The snakes with the best eyesight are tree snakes, such as this green mamba, and day hunters.

**▲ NIGHT HUNTER**
The horned viper's eyes open wide at night (*above*). During the day, its pupils close to narrow slits (*below*).

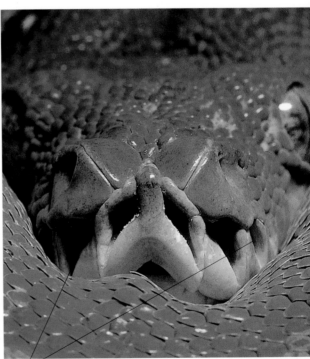

heat pits

**▲ SENSING HEAT**
The green tree python senses heat given off by its prey through pits on the sides of its face.

## ◄ THE FORKED TONGUE

When a snake investigates its surroundings, it flicks its tongue to taste the air. The forked tongue picks up tiny chemical particles of scent.

## ▲ HEARING

As it has no ears, the cobra cannot hear the music played by the snake charmer. It follows the movements of the pipe, which resemble a snake, and rises up as it prepares to defend itself.

## ► JACOBSON'S ORGAN

As a snake draws its tongue back into its mouth, it presses the forked tip into the two openings of the Jacobson's organ. This organ is in the roof of the mouth and it analyses tastes and smells.

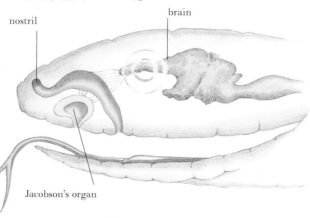

nostril

brain

Jacobson's organ

325

# Food and Hunting

Snakes eat different foods and hunt in different ways depending on their size, their species and where they live. Some snakes eat a wide variety of food, while others have a more specialized diet. A snake has to make the most of each meal because it moves fairly slowly and does not get the chance to catch prey very often. A snake's body works at a slow rate, so it can go for months without eating.

**▲ TREE HUNTERS**
A rat snake grasps a baby bluebird in its jaws and begins the process of digestion. Rat snakes often slither up trees in search of baby birds, eggs or squirrels.

rat snake
*(Elaphe)*

**▲ FISHY FOOD**
The tentacled snake lives on fish. It probably hides among plants in the water and grabs fish as they swim past.

**▼ TRICKY LURE**
The Australasian death adder's colourful tail tip looks like a worm. The adder wriggles the "worm" to lure lizards, birds and small mammals to come within its range.

**◀ EGG-EATERS**
The African egg-eater snake checks an egg with its tongue to make sure it is fresh. Then it swallows the egg whole. It uses the pointed ends of the bones in its backbone to crack the eggshell. It eats the egg and coughs up the crushed shell.

**▶ SURPRISE ATTACK**
Lunch for this gaboon viper is a mouse! The gaboon viper hides among dry leaves on the forest floor. Its colouring and markings make it very difficult to spot. It waits for a small animal to pass by, then grabs hold of its prey in a surprise attack. Many other snakes that hunt by day also ambush their prey.

Did you know? Sometimes a snake coughs up its prey – alive!

**smooth snake**
*(Coronella austriaca)*

**◀ SNAKE EATS SNAKE**
This smooth snake is eating an asp viper. The viper fits neatly inside the body of the smooth snake. This makes it easier to swallow than animals that are different shapes.

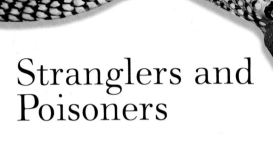

# Stranglers and Poisoners

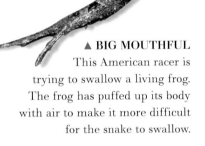

**American racer**
*(Coluber constrictor)*

Most snakes kill their prey before eating it. Snakes kill by using poison or by squeezing their prey to death. Snakes that squeeze, called constrictors, stop their prey from breathing. Victims die from suffocation or shock. To swallow living or dead prey, a snake opens its jaws wide. Lots of slimy saliva helps the meal to slide down. After eating, a snake yawns widely to put its jaws back into place. Digestion can take several days, or even weeks.

▲ **BIG MOUTHFUL**
This American racer is trying to swallow a living frog. The frog has puffed up its body with air to make it more difficult for the snake to swallow.

▲ **AT FULL STRETCH**
This fer-de-lance snake is at full stretch to swallow its huge meal. It is a large pit viper that kills with poison.

▲ **SWALLOWING A MEAL**
The copperhead, a poisonous snake from North America, holds on to a dead mouse.

## ▲ KILLING TIME

A crocodile is slowly squeezed to death
by a rock python. The time it takes for a
constricting snake to kill its prey depends
on the size of the prey and how strong it is.

**spotted python**
(*Liasis maculosus*)

Did you know? King cobras sometimes kill Indian elephants by biting them on the trunk.

## ► COILED KILLER

The spotted python
sinks its teeth into its
victim. It throws coils
around the victim's body,
and tightens its grip until
the animal cannot breathe.

## ▼ BREATHING TUBE

An African python shows its breathing
tube. As the snake eats, the windpipe
moves to the front of the mouth so
that air can get to and from the lungs.

## ▲ HEAD-FIRST

A whiptail wallaby's legs disappear inside a carpet python's
body. Snakes usually try to swallow their prey head-first so
that legs, wings or scales fold back. This helps the victim
to slide into the snake's stomach more easily.

# Where Snakes Live

Snakes live on every continent except Antarctica. They are most common in deserts and rainforests. They cannot survive in very cold places because they use the heat around them to make their bodies work. This is why most snakes live in warm places where the temperature is high enough for them to stay active day and night. In cooler places, snakes may spend the cold winter months asleep. This is called hibernation.

**▲ GRASSLANDS**
The European grass snake is one of the few snakes to live on grasslands, where there is little food or shelter.

**◄ MOUNTAINS**
The Pacific rattlesnake is sometimes found in the mountains of the western United States, often on the lower slopes covered with loose rock.

In general, however, mountains are problem places for snakes because of their cold climates.

**▲ WINTER SLEEP**
Thousands of garter snakes emerge after their winter sleep.

## ◄ TROPICAL RAINFORESTS

The greatest variety
of snakes live
in tropical
rainforests,
including this Brazilian
rainbow boa. There is
plenty to eat there,
from insects, birds
and bats to frogs.

## ▲ LIVING IN TREES

The eyelash viper lives in
the Central American
rainforest. The climate
in rainforests is warm all year
round, so snakes can stay active
all the time. There are also
plenty of places to live – in
trees, on the forest floor,
in soil and in rivers.

**Brazilian rainbow boa**
(*Epicrates cenchria*)

## ► BURROWERS

Yellow-headed worm
snakes live under tree
bark. Many worm, or
thread, snakes live
underground where
the soil is warm.

## ◄ DESERTS

This African puff adder lives
in the Kalahari desert of
southern Africa. Many
snakes live in deserts because
they can survive with little
food and water.

331

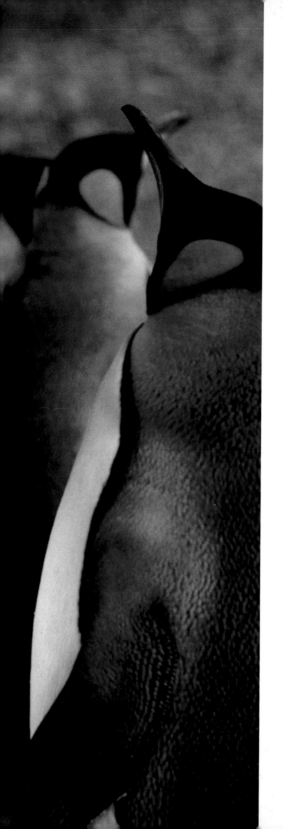

# PENGUINS

Penguins are warm-blooded, flightless
birds which are found only in the
Southern Hemisphere, where they feed
on the rich array of fish living in these
nutrient-packed waters. They spend the
vast majority of their time in the water,
where they are fast and graceful
swimmers and divers, and they only
come on to dry land to mate.

*Author*: Barbara Taylor
*Consultant*: Michael Chinery

# What Makes Penguins Special?

Penguins are flightless birds that mostly live in the cooler parts of the southern oceans. There are no other birds quite like them. On land, they waddle along upright like small, clumsy people, but in the water, they are transformed into graceful, speeding torpedoes. Penguins spend up to three quarters of their lives in the water, only coming to land or sea ice in order to breed. Most of them nest in vast colonies of as many as a million individuals. They have complex courtship displays and many aspects of their lives and behaviour are still a mystery, especially the time they spend at sea. Even the origin of the name penguin is not clear. Penguigo means "fat" in Spanish; Spanish sailors were probably first to use the word for the fat auks and divers of the Northern Hemisphere, which look like penguins.

**▲ FLYING UNDERWATER**

Most other diving birds push themselves through the water using their feet, but penguins use their wings, called flippers. When it swims fast, a penguin draws its head into its shoulders and presses its feet close to the body.

**BUILT TO SWIM ▶**

With their compact, streamlined bodies, short, stiff wings and rudderlike feet and tail, penguins are superbly suited to swimming. Their legs are far back on their bodies, so they do not stick out and interrupt the streamlined shape. The feet are strong and webbed, each with three hooked toes for gripping slippery rocks and ice. Short, densely packed feathers form a waterproof coat over the whole body.

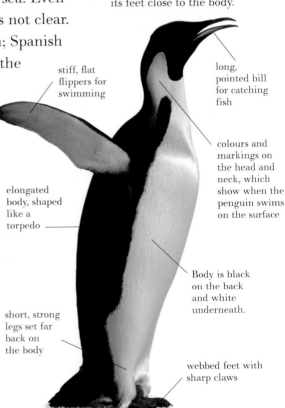

stiff, flat flippers for swimming

long, pointed bill for catching fish

colours and markings on the head and neck, which show when the penguin swims on the surface

elongated body, shaped like a torpedo

Body is black on the back and white underneath.

short, strong legs set far back on the body

webbed feet with sharp claws

## ▼ CHAT SHOW

When penguins come to land to breed, they communicate with a variety of calls and displays. These Gentoo penguins are performing an "ecstatic display", during which they stretch up and call loudly. All penguins, except the Emperor and the Little penguin, perform this display. It helps penguins to reinforce their claim to a nest site, to attract mates, and to deter rivals.

## ▲ LITTLE LAND LUBBERS

Even though penguins are most at home in the water, they depend on land for breeding, raising their young and moulting. Most penguins breed once a year, laying one or two eggs in the spring and rearing chicks during the summer. After the chicks have grown their feathers, most penguin parents moult their own feathers.

## ▼ NORTHERN LOOK-ALIKES

Birds in the auk family, such as puffins, guillemots and this little auk, all look a bit like penguins because they have a similar lifestyle. Both auks and penguins have small wings that they use to swim underwater as they chase prey. The difference is that auks can also use their wings for flying. Auks and penguins never meet, because auks only live north of the Equator.

## FLIGHTLESS GIANT ▼

Penguins are not the only birds that cannot fly. Other flightless birds include the ostrich, the kiwi and the flightless cormorant. Their ancestors were able to fly, millions of years ago, but lost the power to fly, either because they had few enemies or became too heavy.

335

# How the Body Works

Beneath a penguin's feathers is a thick layer of fatty blubber, which keeps it warm and stores energy. Energy stores are particularly important to penguins because they have to go for long periods without food while they look after their eggs and chicks, and when moulting their feathers on land. A penguin's bony skeleton supports and protects its internal organs, such as the heart and lungs. The bones are solid and heavy, helping penguins to dive under the water. (Flying birds have hollow bones to reduce their weight.) The bones inside the flipper are wide and flat, to push the water aside as the penguin swims. The breastbone has a strong ridge, to which the powerful flipper muscles are attached.

## ▲ COLD COMFORT

Like all birds, penguins are warm-blooded. They keep their body temperature at a warm 38°C/100°F or so, no matter how cold or hot it is around them. To help them keep warm, penguins rely on their dense, overlapping feathers and a thick layer of fat, or blubber, beneath the skin. Blubber is a bad conductor of heat, so it stops the bird's body heat from leaking out into the air.

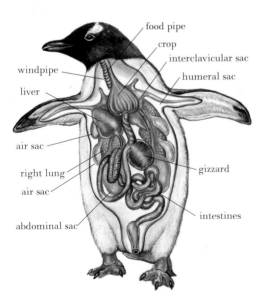

food pipe
crop
interclavicular sac
windpipe
humeral sac
liver
air sac
right lung
air sac
gizzard
abdominal sac
intestines

## ◄ INSIDE A PENGUIN ▼

These two diagrams show the internal organs of a typical penguin. The one on the left shows the breathing system and the digestive system. The diagram on the right shows the position of the penguin's heart and kidneys, along with some of its blood vessels.

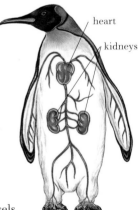

heart
kidneys

### HAPPY LANDINGS ▶

Penguins that live in colder places have longer
feathers and thicker blubber than those in
warmer places. Emperor penguins live in the
coldest places of all and are particularly
chubby. Their fatty blubber is useful as a
shock absorber when they leap out of the
sea on to land. It also serves as an energy
store, useful when the Emperors are caring
for their eggs and chicks and cannot get
back to the sea to feed. The large size of
Emperors helps them to stay warm, because
they have a smaller surface area compared
to their body volume than a smaller penguin.

### ◀ AIR TRAVEL

When penguins are travelling to
and from their feeding grounds,
most swim like dolphins and
porpoises, plunging in and out
of the sea. This behaviour, called
"porpoising", lets the penguins
breathe without stopping and
may help to confuse predators.
Porpoising may help penguins to
travel faster, since there is less
drag in the air to hold them back
than there is under the water.

### SALTY SOLUTION ▶

Penguins can drink sea water, because
they have special glands in their bills
that help get rid of extra salt from the
blood. The glands produce a salty
liquid, which is more salty than sea
water and drips out of the nose. Salty
droplets often collect at the tip of the
bill, and the penguins shake them off,
as this Adélie penguin is doing. Many
other seabirds, including gulls,
cormorants, shearwaters and petrels,
also have these salt glands.

# Fantastic Feathers

Like all birds, penguins are covered in feathers, but their feathers look very different from those of other birds. Penguins' feathers are small, stiff structures that look more like fur or scales, and are tightly packed above a layer of fine down. This arrangement means that they are smooth and waterproof on top to make swimming easier, but warm underneath to stop the penguin from getting cold. Penguins preen their own feathers and each other's to keep them in good condition. They spend hours a day preening, especially when they leave the water.

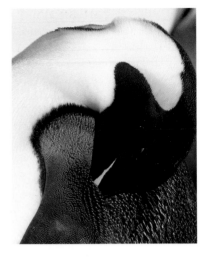

▲ THERMAL PADDING
A penguin's feathers are very stiff and turn at the tip. They have a fluffy outgrowth near the base, which creates a double layer of protection for the skin that is like a fluffy fleece (comforter) with a vest (undershirt) on top. The fluffy base of the feathers stops body heat from escaping, and the outer "vest" stops wind blowing warmth away from the body. If penguins need to cool down, they ruffle and separate feathers to allow heat to escape.

◄ WASH AND BRUSH
Penguins must look after their feathers so that they stay waterproof and keep out the cold. To preen its feathers, a penguin spreads oil over them with its bill. The oil comes from a preen gland at the base of the tail. A penguin also uses its bill to tidy its feathers.

#### ▼ YOU SCRATCH MY BACK…

Some species, such as Rockhoppers, preen each other's feathers. This is called allopreening, and it occurs between males and females, as well as between penguins of the same sex. Allopreening helps penguins to remove parasites, such as ticks, and is important in strengthening pair bonds.

#### ▲ FLUFFY CHICKS

When young penguins hatch, they are covered with warm, downy feathers that make them look very different from the adults. As the chicks grow up, the fluffy down is soon replaced by true feathers.

#### ▼ FINE NEW FEATHERS

While penguins are growing new feathers, they have to stay on land and cannot feed. Penguins need lots of energy to grow new feathers so, before they moult, they spend weeks at sea feeding and storing energy in the form of fat. New feathers start to grow under the skin while the penguins are still at sea. After they come ashore to moult, the new feathers push out the old ones.

#### ▲ CHECKING THE RUDDER

On land, penguins use their short, stubby tail feathers to prop themselves upright and help them to keep their balance when bending backwards to preen their feathers. Under the water, the short, stubby tail makes a useful rudder to help with the steering.

# Different Colour

Most penguins have black backs and white fronts, except for the Little penguin, which has a dark blue back and a white front. Other sea creatures, such as killer whales and sharks, are also dark on top and light underneath. This "countershading" helps penguins and other creatures to blend in with their environment so they can catch prey and avoid predators. When penguins are on land, their black back helps them to soak up the sun's warmth and their white front reflects heat away from them. From the chest up, each species has different colours, skin patterns and crests, which help them to recognize each other and are also used for display and courtship.

## ALL BLACK AND WHITE
These Adélie penguins show the clear difference between a penguin's black back and white front. These colours help to camouflage the penguin in the water. To a predator or prey looking upward, the white belly is hard to see against white ice on the surface or the lighter sky above the water. Looking down on a penguin, the black back blends better with the dark depths of the sea below.

## CHARACTERISTIC "HELMET"
Chinstrap penguins are very easy to recognize because of the narrow band of black-tipped feathers that extends from ear to ear under their chin. This looks like the strap on an English guardsman's helmet, which is worn under the chin.

# and Crests

## COLOURFUL MAKE-UP

King penguins have a golden-orange ear patch, which extends as a narrow stripe around the sides of the neck to the upper breast. There the colour fades downward to yellow and merges with the white of the breast. When King penguins first grow their proper feathers, they are still less colourful than those of adults.

## STRIPY FACE

The Yellow-eyed penguin has distinctive face markings as well as an unusual eye colour. In the adult, the crown of the head, the sides of the face and the chin are all pale yellow. Each feather here has a black streak down the middle. There is a broad yellow band that extends from the base of the bill, around the eyes, to the back of the head.

## MOVEABLE HEADGEAR

The Erect-crested penguin is the only penguin with a crest that stands up rather than flops down. The crest is very stubby and brushlike, and no part of it comes below the bird's eye level. This species is also the only penguin that can raise and lower its crest. No one knows exactly why Erect-crested penguins do this, although it is probably a way of communicating their mood to others. When young birds first grow their feathers, they have a smaller crest than the adults.

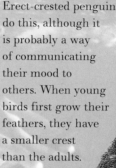

341

# Flightless Wonders

Swift and graceful swimmers and divers, penguins are probably better adapted for life at sea than any other group of birds. They usually travel around 6–8kph/4–5mph, using their flippers to "fly" underwater, and their tails and feet for steering, and possibly braking. The small size of penguin flippers helps to reduce drag. On the surface, penguins swim slowly with a small flipper stroke. A large stroke would bring the flipper out of the water, and therefore not push the penguin forward very far. Penguins usually stay underwater for only a few minutes at a time.

**▲ DIVING CHAMPIONS**
The best penguin divers are also the biggest – Emperor penguins. Emperors can dive down over 396m/1,300ft, although most dives are less than 107m/350ft. The record dive for an Emperor penguin lasted about 18 minutes.

surface

90m/ 300ft — Chinstrap penguin

Little penguin

Gentoo penguin

180m/ 600ft

King penguin

275m/ 900ft

365m/ 1,200ft

Emperor penguin

**◄ HOW DEEP DO PENGUINS DIVE?**
This chart shows the diving depths of five species of penguin. Larger species can dive to greater depths, because they are able to store greater reserves of oxygen to keep their muscles working. King penguins dive underwater for about seven and a half minutes, and medium-sized penguins dive for three to six minutes. Little penguins rarely dive for more than one minute.

### ◄ JUST AFLOAT

Penguins' bodies are quite dense – they are heavy for their size – so they float very low in the water. If they were less dense (lighter), they would float higher, but would find it hard to push their way under the water and stay below the surface. A penguin's darker colours and markings are only on the top part of the body, partly because this is the part that shows above the surface of the water.

### FLIPPER SWIMMING ►

A penguin's flippers are more like an aeroplane's wings than those of birds that fly in air. The long, narrow shape gives a strong propelling action in water, which is much denser than air and needs more effort to push through. The weight of a penguin is cancelled out in water, so the wings just have to propel it forward.

### OUT TO DRY ▼

The flightless cormorants of the Galapagos Islands are the only other sea birds apart from penguins that cannot fly. Their small, ragged wings are too weak for flying and swimming, and they push themselves through the water using their powerful legs and webbed feet. Flightless cormorants hold their wings out to dry their feathers after they have been swimming.

### ▲ PADDLE STEAMBOAT

Two kinds of South American duck have such short wings that they cannot fly. They are called steamer ducks because of their habit of flapping over the surface of the water with a great deal of spray, like an old-fashioned paddle steamboat. These diving ducks use their wings and legs to splash across the surface at a speed of over 20kph/20mph.

Did you know? When they are chased by predators, penguins can swim at speeds of up to 12kph/7½mph.

# Waddle, Hop, Slide and Jump

Although penguins may look clumsy and awkward on land, they are actually quite agile. In addition to waddling around at 4–5kph/2½–3mph, they can leap high out of the water, and some can jump over rocks. Uphill, penguins use their flippers to help propel themselves. On the snow, they can slide on their fronts like living toboggans. Some penguins walk long distances to reach their breeding colonies. Emperor penguins travel hundreds of miles over the sea ice to reach their breeding sites. Adélie penguins also make long journeys. They cannot wait for the ice to melt and allow them to swim to their nest sites, because the Antarctic summer is so short, and there is not much time for breeding. Instead, they walk long distances over the ice, and they are very good at navigating from the angle and position of the sun.

## ▼ THE LONG MARCH

Long columns of Emperor penguins march from their feeding grounds out at sea to reach their breeding areas. The side-to-side waddle of a penguin may look awkward, but it helps to save energy, like a clock pendulum storing energy at the end of each swing, ready for the next swing. Once Emperor penguin parents have chicks, they must travel to and from the sea to catch food for them.

## ▲ STANDING UP STRAIGHT

When penguins walk on land, they have to stand up straight, with the weight of the body balanced over the feet. This King penguin is stretching up to make itself very tall, probably to display to another penguin. The short, stubby tail of a penguin is not much use for balance, but it can be used to prop up its body on land.

## Race to the Pole

*Members of Captain Scott's expedition to the South Pole struggle to pull a heavy sled over the ice. In 1910, Scott planned to be the first person to reach the South Pole, but found polar travel and survival much more difficult than the penguins. His expedition arrived at the Pole only to find that the Norwegian explorer Roald Amundsen had reached it weeks before them. Tragically, Scott and four companions – Wilson, Bowers, Oates and Evans – all died on the journey home.*

## ▲ BOUNCING BACK

As penguins leap out of rough seas on to hard, sharp rocks and ice shelves, their bodies have to withstand many knocks and bangs. Penguins' squishy blubber helps to cushion the landing, but their feathers are also tough, and their skin is strong and leathery. This helps the birds to avoid injury when they enter and leave the sea.

## ◄ LOOK BEFORE YOU LEAP

Rockhoppers get their name from the way they jump from rock to rock with both feet held together. These Crested penguins lean forward to look at gaps and work out the distance between rocks before they jump. Rockhopper penguins are a bit like human mountaineers; they have the ability to climb, bound and claw their way up even steep rocky slopes. Sometimes they use their bill like a third leg to give them a stronger grip on the rocks and ice.

## TOBOGGAN IN THE SNOW ►

Penguins that live in snowy places often lie down on their chests and slide along. They row themselves with their flippers and push with their feet or use their feet to act as brakes. In this way, penguins can move faster than they can walk and can travel faster than a person over short distances.

# Eyes, Ears and Noses

Penguins rely on their senses of sight, hearing, smell and taste to help them catch food, escape danger and interact with other penguins. They can see well in both air and water, and they see in colour. Like most birds, penguins look forward with both eyes. The view they see with one eye overlaps that seen by the other eye. This is called binocular vision – people have it, too. It helps penguins to judge distances and catch prey. Penguins have good hearing, but their hearing is not as sharp as that of sea mammals, such as dolphins and seals.

penguin eye in air

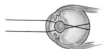
eye of water creature in air

penguin eye in water

eye of land creature in water

## ▲ COLOURFUL EYES ▶

The coloured part of a penguin's eye is called the iris. Many species, such as King penguins (*above, middle*) have brown eyes. Little penguins (*right*) have blue-grey eyes. Penguins with brighter eye colours include red-eyed Rockhoppers (*above, bottom*) and the Yellow-eyeds (*top*).

## ▲ GETTING IN FOCUS

Penguins have large eyes with a circular pupil to let in plenty of light. Their eyes are adapted for seeing in both air and water. To see a clear image in air, penguins have strong eye muscles to change the shape of the lens and a relatively flat layer at the front of the eye. This stops their eyes from bending light too much and causing things to look blurred in the distance.

346

**EXTRA EYELID ▶**

Penguins, like all birds, have a clear third eyelid called the nictitating membrane, usually held open at the side of the eye. This is sometimes called the blinking membrane and is also found in reptiles, amphibians and some mammals. Penguins move their third eyelid across the surface of the eye to keep it clean. It also helps to protect the eye from injury.

**◀ MAKING A RACKET**

The Maoris of New Zealand call the Yellow-eyed penguin *hoiho*, meaning "noise shouter", after its loud trumpet call. Sound is important to this species, because it nests in dense vegetation and cannot see its neighbours and rivals very easily. Most calling happens in the breeding season and includes the trumpeting of mated pairs at the nest site, a yelling threat or alarm call and grunting chuckles, which are used as a threat signal.

**ODOUR DETECTION ▶**

Most birds have a poor sense of smell, but a penguin's sense of smell may be good. A large area of the brain is taken up with the matter used to process odours. Humboldt penguins that are kept in captivity have been shown to have a sense of smell. A penguin's nostrils are partway along the top half of its bill, which can clearly be seen in this Jackass penguin.

**▲ GRIPPING STUFF**

Penguins have efficient weapons with which to deal with their prey. The gristly, backward-pointing spines on the tongue and roof of the mouth, plus the powerful beak, help them to grip slippery, wriggling prey. They can also swallow without fear of drowning. Macaroni penguins may use their bills to stun their prey before they start to eat. Magellanic and Humboldt penguins have sharp, heavy bills, which can wound fish.

# Food and Feeding

Penguins are all meat-eaters that feed in cool waters. Some swallow stones to help grind up their food. Penguins feed on three main types of food: small fish, squid and shrimplike krill, which are rich in vitamins and oils. Some penguins take all three types of prey, while others vary their diet according to where they hunt. King and Emperor penguins dive to deeper levels to feed mainly on squid. Emperors can eat up to 14kg/31lb of food at a time. Smaller penguins, such as Adélies, Gentoos, and Chinstraps live mostly on krill, which rise toward the sea's surface at night. Little and African penguins feed more on fish than krill, because there are more fish than krill in the warmer waters where they live.

**CHAIN OF LIFE ▶**

Penguins are in the middle of the Antarctic marine food chain. Their food chain starts with tiny floating plants, called phytoplankton, which are eaten by tiny animals, such as krill, as well as fish and squid. Penguins are the next link in the chain, but they themselves are eaten by seals, which in turn are eaten by killer whales, the top predators.

phytoplankton
krill
small fishes and squid
penguin
seals
large fishes
killer whale
leopard seal

## ▲ I'M HUNGRY

Penguin parents store the food they catch out at sea in their stomachs, then bring up the food to feed their chicks on land. This is called regurgitation. The parent bends over, and the chick puts its head into the parent's mouth to take the food.

## ▲ THE CHASE IS ON

Penguins, such as these Galapagos penguins, dive underwater to catch their prey. They dart to and fro, grabbing individual fish in mouthfuls of water. Fish are caught sideways and then turned around in the bill to be swallowed headfirst. Some penguins swim in circles around a group of fish to drive them into a dense mass before diving in for the kill.

## ▲ BIG MOUTH

Humpback whales feed on the same prey as penguins. They use long fringes of baleen that hang from their top jaws to strain krill and fish from the water. When people killed a lot of baleen whales in the nineteenth and early twentieth centuries, more food was left for the penguins, so their numbers increased dramatically.

## ▲ FEEDING TIME

The correct diet is vital to the survival of penguins in zoos. The smaller species need about 0.5kg/1lb of fresh fish daily, whereas the larger Kings and Emperors are fed 1–2kg/2–4½lb. More food is given before the penguins moult.

349

# Warming Up, Cooling Down

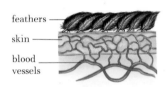

feathers
skin
blood vessels

Normal temperature – feathers lying down and narrow blood vessels.

High temperature – feathers ruffled and wide blood vessels near skin surface.

### ▲ HOT AND COLD
Penguins cannot cool down by sweating. Instead, they open blood vessels near the surface of their flippers, feet and face, and ruffle their feathers to let heat escape.

### ▼ THICK COAT OF FEATHERS
Adélie penguins must survive temperatures below freezing. They need to stay active in the water to generate body heat, which helps them to keep warm. Adélies have lots of long feathers, which hold a thicker layer of warm air close to the skin than those of other penguins.

From the tropical heat of the Galapagos to the bitter cold of Antarctica, penguins have to work hard to keep their temperature steady. Like all birds, they generate their own heat instead of relying on the sun to warm them up. Fatty blubber and air trapped by a penguin's feathers help to keep warmth in. Penguins can also shiver to create heat, hold their flippers close to their bodies or huddle together for warmth. They can even reclaim about 82 percent of the heat from the air they breathe out through the nose. Penguins are so good at keeping warm that they sometimes have trouble with overheating. Adélies even seem to suffer from the heat if the temperature gets much above freezing.

### ▲ COMPLETELY WATERPROOF
A penguin's feathers can be pulled into different positions by small muscles. On land, the feathers are raised to trap a thick layer of air next to the skin, which stops body heat from escaping. In water, feathers flatten to form a watertight barrier, forcing out air.

## ▼ SHADY CHARACTERS

These Magellanic penguins are huddled in the welcome shade of a bush to stay out of the direct sun. They are holding their flippers away from their bodies so they act as radiators to let heat escape. African elephants use their large ears in a similar way to help them cool down.

## ▲ BARE SKIN RADIATORS

Penguins that live in warmer places, such as these African penguins, can lose heat from bare patches on the face, flippers and feet. These act as radiators, allowing excess body heat to escape into the air, which cools the penguin down.

## ▼ COOL BURROW

Magellanic penguins nest in burrows, which gives them somewhere private to escape from the heat. It is much cooler underground than out in the hot sun. These penguins go to sea to catch food during the hottest parts of the day, which also helps them to avoid overheating on land.

## COLD FEET ▶

When they are resting on land, Emperor and King penguins turn up their feet and put their whole weight on their heels and tail. This reduces the amount of bare skin in contact with the ice and stops the penguin's feet from getting too cold. The way a penguin's blood circulates inside its feet also helps to retain heat inside the penguin's body. It keeps the penguin's feet at around the same low temperature as its surroundings, so it does not lose too much heat through its feet.

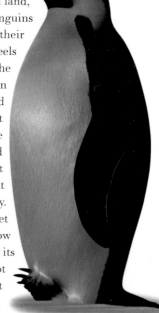

# Penguin Talk

Penguins communicate with calls, as well as behaviour patterns called displays. These displays may involve head and flipper waving, bowing and pointing with the bill. There are three main kinds of penguin calls: contact calls to recognize colony members at sea; display calls between breeding partners; and threat calls to defend nests and chicks and warn against predators. Males and females have different calls. Calls and displays in the breeding season help penguins to attract mates, recognize partners and stay together in order to raise the chicks. Penguin communication involves just two individuals at a time, though there may be thousands nesting together.

**▲ WARNING DISPLAY**

Most penguins are noisy and aggressive, and the majority of species nest in open ground, so threat behaviour is very important. When birds do not recognize each other or lay claim to the same nest site, they perform an aggressive display. This acts as a warning, telling rivals to "get out". If the rival does not take the hint, fighting may follow.

**◄ I AM THE GREATEST**

All male penguins, except for the Emperor and the Little penguin, advertise themselves with an "ecstatic display". This is their way of saying "I am the greatest, and I am available." This display is used by male penguins to attract a mate. Those with the best displays are most likely to impress females. The ecstatic display incorporates just about everything that a penguin can do. The bill points toward the sky, the flippers beat in a steady rhythm, the eyes roll and the bird calls loudly. Head feathers may be raised and the bill opened for greater effect. King penguin males and females both use a display like this.

*Did you know?* The contact call of Emperor and King penguins can be heard 1km/¾ mile away.

## ▲ STRENGTHENING BONDS

A pair of penguins may perform a mutual display together. In Crested penguins such as these Rockhoppers, this involves swinging the head between raised flippers with the bill gaping wildly, after bowing while making loud throbbing sounds. Mutual displays happen just before eggs are laid and when one partner arrives to take over care of the eggs or chicks.

### TAKING TURNS TO SPEAK ▶

Penguin calls range from the trills and trumpeting of the Emperor and the scratchy cooing of the Adélie, to the harsh braying of the African penguin. When a pair calls together, as these Chinstrap penguins are, they take turns. One bird calls in reply to the other.

## ▼ THIS IS MY NEST

To lay claim to a nest site out in the open, Gentoos perform a display with simple bowing, head raising movements, and calling. Little penguins do this, too, even though they mainly nest in burrows and crevices. Penguins that always nest in holes do not have displays to claim nest sites, because their nests are better protected from attack.

## ◀ A GIFT FOR THE LADY

This Chinstrap penguin is bringing a stone to his mate to impress her and show that he is serious about bringing up a family. This is part of a whole sequence of displays that leads to a pair of penguins building a nest and rearing a family. First the male advertises that he is ready and drives rivals away, then he brings gifts and sings and bows with the female, and finally, he waits to see if the female accepts or rejects him.

# Where Penguins Live

Penguins live only in the southern half of the world, where cold water currents carry nutrients along the coasts of South America, southern Africa, Australia, New Zealand and the Falkland Islands. Four species – Emperor, Adélie, Gentoo, and Chinstrap penguins – breed on the Antarctic continent, but more than half of all penguin species never visit Antarctica at all. The greatest variety of penguins live on the mainland and islands of southern New Zealand and the Falkland Islands.

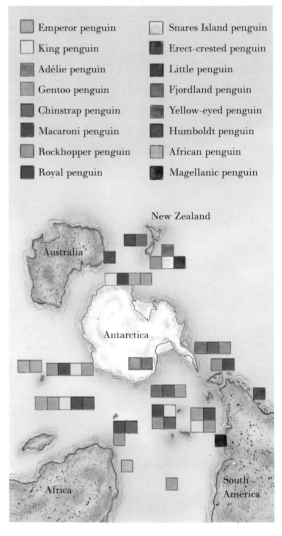

- Emperor penguin
- King penguin
- Adélie penguin
- Gentoo penguin
- Chinstrap penguin
- Macaroni penguin
- Rockhopper penguin
- Royal penguin
- Snares Island penguin
- Erect-crested penguin
- Little penguin
- Fjordland penguin
- Yellow-eyed penguin
- Humboldt penguin
- African penguin
- Magellanic penguin

New Zealand · Australia · Antarctica · Africa · South America

## ▲ THE ICE PENGUINS

Emperor penguins are truly the penguins of ice and snow. They live within the ice that floats around Antarctica and usually avoid the open waters beyond it. Sometimes they dive into seal holes or cracks in the ice to feed. Even their breeding colonies are usually on the ice.

## ▲ SOUTH OF THE EQUATOR

Penguins are found on every continent in the Southern Hemisphere, and each continent has its own unique species. Penguins may have originally spread from the area around New Zealand, gradually moving south towards Antarctica and north towards the Equator.

### ◀ A PLACE OF THEIR OWN

Royal penguins are found only on Macquarie Island, which is in the Southern Ocean between New Zealand and Antarctica. Here they nest among the lush, tussock grasses, using the same areas every year. Royal penguins are very similar to Macaronis, but have white feathers on their face and throat.

### ▼ DRY ROCK

Humboldt penguins live along the dry coasts of Peru and Chile. They nest on rocky shores, in sea caves and among boulders. The Humboldt penguin range overlaps that of Magellanic penguins by nearly 322km/200 miles. Usually, the two species breed in separate colonies.

### ▲ AT HOME ON THE BEACH

The African, or Jackass, penguin lives only in the coastal waters around southern Africa. It breeds on the mainland and offshore islands, and stays in the same area out of the breeding season. Most African penguins do not go farther than 13km/8 miles from land.

### SOME LIKE IT HOT ▼

The Galapagos penguin is a most unusual penguin, breeding on the hot desert islands of the Galapagos. It lives only on these islands and nowhere else in the world. Both adults and young remain at their breeding sites throughout much of the year and do not travel away from the islands.

355

# Prehistoric Penguins

It is believed that penguins evolved over 65 million years ago from flying birds that were similar to modern diving petrels, which "fly" underwater. No fossils of anything in between a flying ancestor and a typical penguin have ever been found. There are very few fossils of penguins that have been found, but over 40 different species of fossil penguin have been discovered so far. This means that penguins were once more varied than they are today. The evolution of seals and small whales about 15 million years ago may have contributed to the extinction of large penguins and many of the small ones.

**▲ DID ANCIENT PENGUINS FLY?**
The short answer to this question is yes! Some extinct species have features similar to those of modern albatrosses and petrels, both of which can fly. The modern penguin's flipper bones were modified from a flying wing. Its breastbone has areas for anchoring muscles that were developed originally for flying, and its tail bones have a structure that supports tail feathers in all modern flying birds.

**▼ EXTINCT RECORD-BREAKERS**
Some ancient penguins were much taller and heavier than the Emperor penguin, the largest penguin alive today. The first fossil penguin to be discovered, *Palaeeudyptes antarcticus*, was about 18cm/7in taller than the Emperor. The two largest fossil penguins discovered so far were much larger than this. *Pachydyptes ponderosus* was up to 56cm/22in taller than the Emperor penguin. A fossil penguin even smaller than the Little penguin has also been discovered.

1.8m/6ft

1.8m/6ft man     fossil penguin     largest known living penguin     smallest modern penguin     guillemot     Least auklet

mya = millions of years ago

Present day

Pliocene (5–2 mya)

Miocene (24–5 mya)

Oligocene (37–24 mya)

Eocene (58–37 mya)

Paleocene (65–58 mya)

Cretaceous (144–65 mya)

Jurassic (208–144 mya)

Archaeopteryx

Paleognathae

Anseriformes

Galliformes

Gruimorphae

Charadriiformes

Ciconiiformes

Pelecaniformes

Procellariiformes

Graviidae

Spheniscidae

ostriches, rheas, cassowaries, emus

ducks, geese, swans

pheasants, grouse

cranes, rails, coots

auks, waders, skuas

herons, storks, flamingos

pelicans, cormorants, gannets, frigate birds

albatrosses, petrels, shearwaters

loons, divers

penguins

## ▲ CHARTING PENGUIN EVOLUTION

This chart shows how penguins may have evolved from ancient shearwaters, petrels and albatrosses. Divers and loons probably evolved from the same ancestors but they form a separate group from penguins. Penguins, divers and loons are more closely related to the shearwaters and petrels, from which they descended directly, than they are to each other.

357

# BIRDS OF PREY

There are around 400 different species
of birds of prey, and they differ from
other birds because they hunt prey or
scavenge carrion rather than just
eating nuts, seeds, small insects and small
animals. They have amazing eyesight,
fearsome talons, hooked beaks and
awesome speed, which helps them to
locate, kill and rip apart larger animals.

*Author*: Robin Kerrod
*Consultant*: Jemima Parry Jones, M.B.E.
The National Birds of Prey Centre

# What is a Bird of Prey?

There are nearly 9,000 different species of birds in the world. Most of them eat plant shoots, seeds, nuts and fruit, or small creatures such as insects and worms. However, about 400 species, called birds of prey, hunt prey with their feet or scavenge carrion (the flesh of dead animals). Birds of prey are called raptors, from the Latin *rapere* meaning "to seize", because they grip and kill their prey with sharp talons and hooked beaks. The majority of raptors hunt by day. They are called diurnal birds of prey. Day hunters include eagles, falcons and hawks, and vultures (which are scavengers). Other raptors, such as owls, are nocturnal, which means they are active at night.

▼ **HANGING AROUND**

The outstretched wings of the kestrel (*Falco tinnunculus*) face into the wind, as the bird hovers above a patch of ground in search of prey. The bird also spreads its broad tail to supplement the air-catching effect of its wings.

large, forward-facing eyes

hooked, powerful bill

▼ **IN A LEAGUE OF THEIR OWN**

Five young tawny owls cluster together on a branch. Owls are not closely related to the other birds of prey. They usually hunt at night instead of during the day. However, they do share certain features with the other birds of prey. They have excellent eyesight for spotting prey; sharp, hooked beaks (bills) for ripping flesh; and strong legs, with pointed, curled claws (talons) for gripping their prey.

**tawny owls**
(*Strix aluco*)

### ◀ HAWKEYE
The sparrowhawk has large eyes that face forward. The bill is hooked, for tearing flesh. These are typical features of daytime hunters.

**Eurasian sparrowhawk**
(*Accipiter nisus*)

Wings lift in the flow of air and support the bird's weight. The primary feathers on the wing fan out.

long, sharp, curved talons

Tail guides the bird through the air and also acts as a brake.

### ▲ BUILT FOR SPEED
The peregrine falcon is the one of the swiftest birds in the world, able to dive at up to 225kph/140mph. Its swept-back wings help it cut through the air at speed. Their shape has been copied by aircraft designers for the wings of fighter planes.

### ▼ THE EAGLE HAS LANDED
In the snow-covered highlands of Scotland, a golden eagle stands over a rabbit it has just killed. Eagles kill with their talons. They are so long, sharp and deeply curved that one swipe is usually enough to kill a rabbit.

**golden eagle**
(*Aquila chrysaetos*)

*God of the Sky*
*Horus was one of the most important gods in ancient Egypt. He was the god of the sky and the heavens. His sacred bird was the falcon, and Horus is often represented with a human body and a falcon's head. The Egyptian hieroglyph (picture symbol) for "god" in ancient Egyptian is a falcon.*

# Orders and Families

There are more than 400 species of birds of prey. Each is different in size, colouring, behaviour and feeding pattern from every other species. Birds of prey fall into two major groupings, or orders. The diurnal raptors, the day-time hunters, belong to the order Falconiformes. The owls, the night-hunters, belong to the order Strigiformes. Within each order, similar kinds of birds are classed together in family groups. In the Falconiformes, there are five families. The secretary bird and the osprey have a family each. New World vultures form another family, and the falcons and caracaras another. But by far the largest family, containing more than 200 species, is the accipiters, which include eagles, Old World vultures, kites, hawks and buzzards.

**▲ NIGHT-HUNTERS**
This great grey owl is one of about 130 species of owls. Most, but not all, are nocturnal (night) hunters. Owls belong to the order Strigiformes and are not related to the other birds of prey.

*Roman Eagle*
*To the ancient Romans, the eagle symbolized power, nobility, strength and courage. When the Roman army marched into battle, one soldier at the head of each legion (group of soldiers) carried a golden eagle on a standard (see left). The Roman name for the eagle was aquila. Today, this name is given to a family of eagles, including the magnificent golden eagle.*

**▶ THE CARACARAS**
This striated caracara lives in the Falkland Islands. It is the member of a group within the falcon family. Caracaras are large, long-legged birds found from the southern United States to southern South America. Unlike true falcons, they often hunt on the ground.

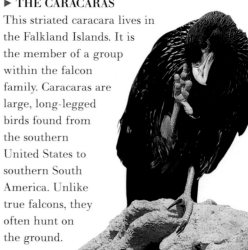

## ▼ ALL ALONE

There is only one species of osprey in the world. This one is nesting in Maryland, in the eastern United States, where it is known as a fish hawk. Some of the largest colonies of ospreys are found in north-eastern Africa.

## ▲ TALL SECRETARY

The secretary bird looks like no other bird of prey, so it is not surprising that it has a family all to itself. Its distinctive features are a crest on its head, a very long tail and legs, and short, stubby toes.

## ▼ OLD WORLD VULTURES

These white-backed vultures live in southern Africa. They belong to a family of some 14 species of vultures, found in the Old World, that is, Europe, Asia and Africa. Like all vultures, they live largely on carrion, often the remains of prey killed by big cats like lions.

**king vulture**
(*Sarcoramplus papa*)

## ▲ VULTURES OF THE NEW WORLD

The king vulture displays its impressive 17m/55ft wingspan. This bird is the most colourful and maybe the most handsome vulture of all. It is one of the seven species of New World vultures, found in the Americas. The Andean and Californian condors are two other members of this group.

**white-backed vulture**
(*Gyps africanus*)

363

# Shapes and Sizes

There are huge differences in size among birds of prey. As many as 40 pygmy falcons could perch on the outstretched wings of one Andean condor. Pygmy falcons are the smallest birds of prey, measuring as little as 20cm/8in from head to tail. The Andean condor is the biggest bird of prey, with a wingspan of about 3m/10ft. In most species, the female is larger than the male. In fact, in some hawk and falcon species the females are up to 50 percent bigger than the males. This is called reverse sexual dimorphism. Most raptors look quite similar when they perch. When they fly, however, there is a great variation in wing size and shape. This usually reflects the different techniques they adopt when hunting prey, and the nature of their habitat. For example, the huge wings of the Andean condor allow it to soar high above the Andes mountains.

**little owl**
(*Athene noctua*)

▲ **WELL-ROUNDED**
The little owl, like other owls, has a round head and broad, rounded wings. Its body, too, has a well-rounded shape, because of its fairly loose covering of feathers. It appears to have no neck at all. The little owl is about 23cm/9in from head to tail.

▲ **AMERICAN SCAVENGER**
The turkey vulture (or turkey buzzard) is a small vulture that lives in North and South America. It grows up to 76cm/30in from head to tail.

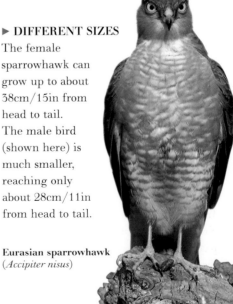

▶ **DIFFERENT SIZES**
The female sparrowhawk can grow up to about 38cm/15in from head to tail. The male bird (shown here) is much smaller, reaching only about 28cm/11in from head to tail.

**Eurasian sparrowhawk**
(*Accipiter nisus*)

## ▶ THE BIGGEST

The magnificent Andean condor is the biggest of all birds of prey. The males grow up to 1.2m/4ft from head to tail and can weigh more than 11kg/25lb. The condor is a scavenger, which means that it feeds on dead animals rather than hunting live prey.

**Andean condor** (*Vultur gryphus*)

Did you know? A pygmy owl's body is as long as an eagle owl's ear tuft.

## ▲ COMMON BUTEOS

This common buzzard (*Buteo buteo*) is typical of the family of birds of prey known as buteos. Buteos are about 50cm/20in from head to tail and have long, broad wings up to 4.3m/14ft from wing tip to wing tip. This bird is commonly found gliding high above the grasslands and woodlands of Europe and Asia in search of small mammals and reptiles.

## ▲ FISH-EATING EAGLE

The bald eagle (*Haliaeetus leucocephalus*) is instantly recognizable by its snowy white head and tail. It is an impressive bird, growing up to 1m/3ft from head to tail. The bird's long talons enable it to pluck fish from the surface of rivers and lakes in North America.

## ▶ STANDING TALL

The tallest and most unusual bird of prey is the secretary bird of Africa. It stands up to 1.2m/4ft tall, and its wings can span more than 1.8m/6ft. It can soar in the sky like other birds of prey, but most of the time it walks on the ground on its long legs.

**secretary bird** (*Sagittarius serpentarius*)

365

# How the Body Works

Birds of prey are supreme fliers. Like other birds, they have powerful chest and wing muscles to move their wings. Virtually the whole body is covered with feathers to make it smooth and streamlined and able to slip easily through the air. The bones are very light, and some have a honeycomb structure, which makes them lighter still. Birds of prey differ from other birds in a number of ways, particularly in their powerful bills (beaks) and feet, which are well adapted for their life as hunters. Also unlike most other birds, they regurgitate (cough up) pellets. These contain the parts of their prey they cannot digest.

▲ **NAKED NECK**
A Ruppell's vulture feeds on a zebra carcass in the Masai Mara region of eastern Africa. Like many vultures, it has a naked neck, which it can thrust deep inside the carcass. As a result, it can feed without getting its feathers too covered in blood.

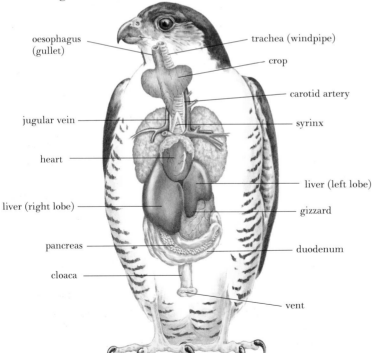

oesophagus (gullet)
trachea (windpipe)
crop
carotid artery
jugular vein
syrinx
heart
liver (left lobe)
liver (right lobe)
gizzard
pancreas
duodenum
cloaca
vent

◀ **BODY PARTS**
Underneath their feathery covering, birds of prey have a complex system of internal organs. Unlike humans, most birds have a crop to store food in before digestion. They also have a gizzard to grind up hard particles of food, such as bone, and to start the process of making a pellet. Birds also have a syrinx (the bird equivalent of the human vocal cord).

*366*

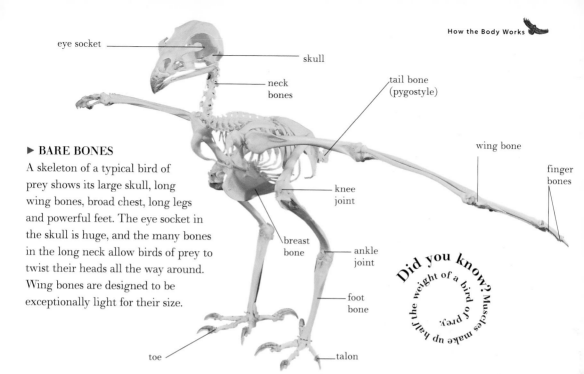

eye socket

skull

neck bones

tail bone (pygostyle)

wing bone

finger bones

knee joint

breast bone

ankle joint

foot bone

toe

talon

### ► BARE BONES

A skeleton of a typical bird of prey shows its large skull, long wing bones, broad chest, long legs and powerful feet. The eye socket in the skull is huge, and the many bones in the long neck allow birds of prey to twist their heads all the way around. Wing bones are designed to be exceptionally light for their size.

*Did you know? Muscles make up half the weight of a bird of prey.*

### ▼ BACK TO FRONT

This peregrine falcon appears to have eyes in the back of its head! Its body is facing away, but its eyes are looking right into the camera. All birds of prey can twist their heads around like this, because they have many more vertebrae than mammals. They can see in any direction without moving their body, but they cannot move their eyeballs in their sockets.

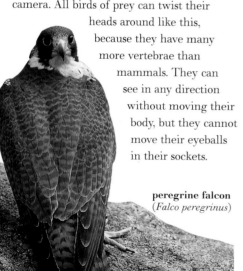

**peregrine falcon**
(*Falco peregrinus*)

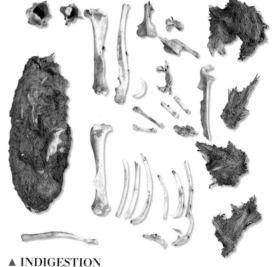

### ▲ INDIGESTION

On the left of the picture above is the regurgitated pellet of a barn owl, and on the right are the indigestible parts it contained. The pellet is about 5cm/2in long. From its contents we can tell that the owl has just eaten a small mammal, because the pellet contains scraps of fur and fragments of bone.

367

# The Senses

Humans rely on five senses to find out about the world. They are sight, hearing, smell, taste and touch. However, most birds live using just the two senses of sight and hearing. In birds of prey, sight is by far the most important sense for finding and hunting the prey they need to survive. Their eyes are exceptionally large in relation to the size of the head, and they are set in the skull so that they look forward. This binocular (two-eyed) forward vision enables them to judge distances accurately when hunting. Owls have particularly large eyes that are well adapted for seeing in dim light. They are equally dependent on hearing to find prey in the dark. Some harriers and hawks use their keen sense of hearing to hunt, too. Birds' ear openings are quite small. They are set back from the eyes and cannot be seen because they are covered in feathers.

common buzzard (*Buteo buteo*)

### ▲ OPEN WIDE

A common buzzard opens its mouth wide to make its distinctive mewing call. This bird has extremely large eyes in relation to its body, so it has excellent eyesight. The forward-facing eyes give it good stereoscopic (3D) vision and the ability to pinpoint the exact position of a mouse in the grass 100m/330ft away.

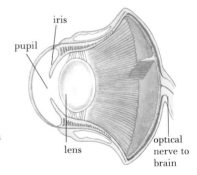

iris
pupil
lens
optical nerve to brain

### ▲ OWL EYE

The owl has exceptional eyesight. Its eye is very long, unlike the spherical human eye. The tubular shape of the owl's eye allows it to spot its prey from far away.

### ◄ NOT TO BE SMELLED AT

The turkey vulture of North and South America, like all New World vultures, has nostrils that you can see right through. Its nose is very sensitive. This enables the turkey vulture to smell carrion on the ground while it is flying above the forest canopy.

**turkey vulture** (*Cathartes aura*)

spotted eagle owl (*Bubo africanus*)

### ◄ FORWARD FACE

The African spotted eagle owl has big eyes. The pupil (centre) and lens are especially large to allow more light to enter and provide the owl with good night vision. The eyes are set in a flat facial disc. The earlike projections on top of the owl's head are actually ornamental tufts of feathers used for display. The true ears are hidden under stiff feathers at either side of the facial disc. They are sensitive to the slightest noise, which helps the owl locate its prey in the dark.

### ► ON THE LOOKOUT

This large falcon, called a lanner, is soaring high in the sky on outstretched wings, looking down with its sharp eyes on the scene below. If the lanner sees a flying bird, it will fold back its wings and dive on the unsuspecting bird. The lanner will hit the bird at high speed and usually break its neck. Then it will either snatch the bird in midair or pick it up off the ground.

### ◄ MONTAGU'S EYEBROW

Montagu's harrier is a slender, long-legged hawk with an owl-like facial ruff. The eyes are surrounded by a small, bony ridge covered in feathers, called a supraorbital ridge. It probably helps protect the harrier's eyes from attack when the bird goes hunting, and may also act as a shield against the sun's rays when it is flying.

Montagu's harrier
(*Circus pygargus*)

369

# Wings and Flight

The wings of most birds work in the same way. Strong pectoral (chest) muscles make the wings flap and drive the bird through the air. As it moves, the wings lift in the flow of air and support the bird's weight. The bird is now flying. All birds have differently shaped wings that are adapted to their way of life. Large birds of prey, such as vultures, spend much of their time soaring high in the sky. These birds have long, broad wings that glide on air currents. The smaller hawks, such as the sparrowhawk, have short, rounded wings and a long tail for rapid, zigzagging flight through woodland habitats. A bird's tail is also important for flying. It acts much like a ship's rudder, steadying the bird's body and guiding it through the air. It can be fanned out to give extra lift and also helps the bird to slow down when landing.

**▲ WING FINGERS**
An African fish eagle takes to the air. Like other eagles, it has broad wings and fingered wing tips, seen plainly here. The "fingers" reduce air turbulence around the wings, giving better lift.

**Mauritius kestrel**
(*Falco punctatus*)

◀
**AGILE BIRD**
The Mauritius kestrel has a broad tail and, for a falcon, fairly short wings. These two features help it to manoeuvre well in the woodland habitat in which it lives. It lives on the island of Mauritius, in the Indian Ocean.

**▲ DROPPING IN**
A sparrowhawk (*Accipiter nisus*) is poised to seize a bird it has just spotted. It has short, rounded wings and a long tail. The sparrowhawk's wings beat rapidly and provide enough speed to surprise its unsuspecting prey.

*370*

**Eagle of the Gods**
In Greek mythology, the eagle was the favoured bird of the mighty Zeus. Zeus was god of the sky, lord of the winds and rains, and king of the gods. He is often depicted holding a thunderbolt in his right hand, with an eagle standing at his feet. Here we see him riding in a chariot, drawn by a pair of his sacred birds.

## ▼ LIKE AN ARROW

The sharply pointed wings tell us that this bird is a falcon. In fact, it is a lanner falcon. A bird can fly extremely fast with pointed wings because the wings cut through the air and offer less wind resistance. Lanner falcons hunt in open ground and use pure speed to catch slower-flying birds.

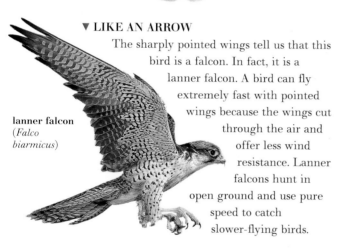

**lanner falcon** (*Falco biarmicus*)

## ▲ BUILT TO SOAR

A white-backed vulture soars high in the sky with its broad wings fully outstretched, on the lookout for carcasses on the ground. In the right climate, the vulture can remain in the air for a long time, because its wings provide plenty of lift.

## ▶ READY, SET, GO

A young male kestrel takes off in a multiple-exposure photograph. First the bird thrusts its body forward and raises its wings. Its wings extend and beat downward, pushing slightly backward. As the air is forced back, the bird is driven forward. At the same time, air moving past the wings gives the bird the lift it needs to keep itself airborne.

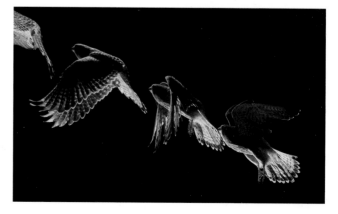

*371*

# Focus on

**1** A Harris' hawk (*Parabuteo unicinctus*) perches on a branch on the lookout for prey such as reptiles and small mammals. This native of South and Central America and the southern United States is also called the bay-winged hawk because of the reddish-brown (bay) bars on its shoulders. It has the relatively short, rounded wings and long tail typical of most small hawks.

Most of the smaller species of hawk have developed wings that enable them to fly at fast speeds over short distances. Larger hawks have broader, longer wings. These allow the birds to soar and glide in the air while scanning the ground below for their prey. Every species favours a different flying technique. For example, sparrowhawks twist and turn with ease as they manoeuvre among the many trees in the woodlands in which they are found. High-speed photography allows us to follow the action as the Harris' hawk shown here takes to the air.

**2** Now the hawk is getting ready to fly. It leans forward and begins to raise its wings. It tenses its leg muscles, ready to thrust itself from the perch. The bird's distinctive red thighs and white rump, and the white patches on the underwing, are clearly visible.

**3** The hawk lifts its wings, and the primaries (the flight feathers at the end of the wings) fan out. It pushes its legs against the perch to take off.

# Hawk Flight

4 With a powerful downbeat of its wings and a final push with its legs, the hawk thrusts its body from the perch and begins to travel forward through the air. As the air flows past the wings, it makes them lift and so supports the bird's body. The tail fans out and downward to provide extra lift. The bird is now airborne.

5 The hawk continues beating its wings and gathers more speed. However, the bird's feet are hanging below the body, causing air resistance, or drag, which slows it down. Consequently, the bird will soon tuck its feet up under its body and become a perfectly streamlined, magnificent flying machine.

Did you know? Sacs in a bird's body fill with air to help it stay airborne.

# Bill and Talons

The bill and talons of birds of prey are well-adapted for killing and feeding on prey or scavenging on the remains of carcasses. Typically the bill is hooked and sharp. However, it is not generally used for killing, but for tearing flesh. Raptors also use their bills to pluck the feathers from birds they catch. Most birds of prey use their feet for the kill. Their toes are tipped with long, sharp, curved talons. When a bird swoops down on its prey, the toes clamp around the prey's body and the talons sink into the flesh. The prey is quickly crushed to death. Small birds of prey, such as many falcon species, have less powerful leg muscles and may not always kill their prey this way. So the bird may have to finish it off with a bite. For this purpose, they have a notch (called a tomial tooth) in the upper part of the bill.

**Indian honey buzzard**
(*Pernis ptilorhyncus*)

### ▲ INSECT-EATER

The bill of the Indian honey buzzard is relatively small and delicate compared to that of most other birds of prey. The honey buzzard does not need a strong bill because it feeds mainly on insects and the larvae of wasps and bees.

### ▶ EGG HEAD

The Egyptian vulture's hooked bill is too weak to break into a large carcass without the aid of larger vultures. However, its long bill is ideal for breaking eggs, one of its favourite foods. In contrast to this bird's fine head plumage, other vultures have bare heads and necks. This prevents them from covering their feathers with blood when they reach deep inside a carcass to feed.

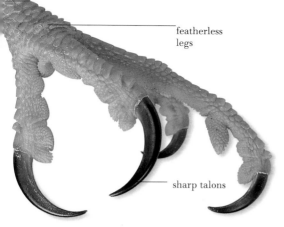

featherless
legs

sharp talons

## ▲ SPINDLY LEGS

The legs of the sparrowhawk are long and
slender and lack feathers. Both the toes and
talons are long. As it hones in on a small bird,
the sparrowhawk thrusts its legs forward, with
both feet spread wide. It then snaps its toes and
talons around the prey's body, and captures it in
a deadly grip. The sparrowhawk then flies off
to land and feed on its catch.

## ▲ FEATHER PANTS

Like most owls, the great horned owl of North
America has soft feathers covering its legs and feet,
as well as its body. They help keep its flight silent.

## ▲ FEET FIRST

The strong feet of the American bald eagle
are geared to catching fish, the main part
of the bird's diet. Its talons are sharp and
curved. The bald eagle can comfortably hold
a salmon weighing as much as 3kg/7lb in its
large, powerful talons.

*Horrific Harpies*
*The harpy*
*eagle is one*
*of the most*
*formidable*
*birds of prey.*
*It takes its*
*name from*
*the Harpies*
*of Greek*
*mythology. These were*
*winged monsters that brought*
*violent winds. They*
*had women's heads,*
*pale with hunger, and*
*the bodies and sharp*
*claws of eagles. They attacked*
*people and stole or dirtied their food.*

*375*

# The Hunted

Birds of prey hunt all kinds of animals. Many prey on other birds, including sparrows, starlings and pigeons, which are usually taken in the air. Certain birds prey on small mammals, such as rabbits, lemmings, rats, mice and voles, and some of the larger eagles will even take bigger mammals. The Philippine eagle and the harpy eagles of South America pluck monkeys from the rainforest canopy. These eagles are massive birds, with bodies 1m/3ft long. Serpent eagles and secretary birds feast on snakes and other reptiles. Small birds of prey often feed on insects and worms. Most species will also supplement their diet by scavenging on carrion (dead animals) whenever they find it.

**▲ INSECT INSIDE**
A lesser kestrel prepares to eat a grasshopper it has just caught on a rooftop in Spain. This kestrel lives mainly on insects. It catches grasshoppers and beetles on the ground, and all kinds of flying insects while in flight. When there are plenty of insects, flocks of lesser kestrels feed together. Unlike the larger common kestrel, the lesser kestrel does not hover when hunting.

**golden eagle**
(*Aquila chrysaetos*)

**◄ GOLDEN HUNTER**
A golden eagle stands guard over the squirrel it has just caught. The golden eagle usually hunts low to the ground. It flushes out prey — mainly rabbits and grouse, which it catches and kills on the ground. Whenever they get the chance, golden eagles will also eat carrion.

**martial eagle**
(*Polemaetus bellicosus*)

*The Fabulous Roc*
*In the famous tales of* The Arabian Nights, *Sinbad the Sailor encountered enormous birds called rocs. They looked like eagles, but were gigantic in size, and preyed on elephants and other large beasts. In this picture, the fearsome rocs are dropping huge boulders on Sinbad's ship in an attempt to finally destroy him.*

## ▲ REPTILIAN SNACK

A martial eagle stands over its lizard kill in Kruger National Park in South Africa. This is Africa's biggest eagle, capable of taking prey as big as a kuda (a small antelope).

*Did you know? 12 species of birds of prey eat only insects.*

## ▼ SNAIL DIET

A snail kite eyes its next meal. This is the most specialized feeder among birds of prey, eating only freshwater snails. It breeds in the Everglades National Park in Florida.

## ▲ COBRA KILLER

A pale chanting goshawk has caught and killed a yellow cobra. The chanting goshawks earned their name because of their noisy calls in the breeding season. The African plains are the hunting grounds of both the pale and the dark chanting goshawks, which feed mainly on reptiles, such as lizards and snakes.

**snail kite**
(*Rostrhamus sociabilis*)

377

# Building Nests and Laying Eggs

Courtship displays help the male and female birds bond. They also help to establish the pair's territory, the area in which they hunt. Within this territory, the birds build a nest in which the female lays her eggs. Birds of prey usually nest far apart, because they need a large hunting area. However, some species, including griffon vultures and lesser kestrels, nest in colonies. Birds of prey choose many different nesting sites, in caves and on cliffs, in barns and the disused nests of other birds, on the ground or high up in trees. The nests themselves may be simple scrapes on a ledge, no more than a bare place for the eggs to rest in. Other nests are elaborate structures built from branches and twigs. Many birds return to the same nest with the same mate every year, adding to it until it becomes a massive structure.

▲ CAMOUFLAGE COLOURS
This hen harrier is nesting on the ground among vegetation. The female, pictured brooding (sitting on her eggs), has the typical mottled-brown plumage of ground-nesting birds. This makes her hard to spot on the nest. The male often feeds the female in the air. He calls her to him, then drops the prey for her to catch.

Bonelli's eagle
(*Hieraaetus fasciatus*)

◀ SETTING UP HOME
A female Bonelli's eagle repairs her clifftop nest, keeping a careful watch over her young chick. If there are no cliffs in her territory, the female will build her nest at the top of a tall tree. The nests measure just under 2m/7ft in diameter, and they are used year after year. You can see that scientists have ringed this chick's leg.

## ▶ GO AWAY!

With its wings spread wide to make it look bigger, a barn owl adopts a threatening pose to protect his nest. The female has already laid several eggs, which she will incubate for just over a month. During this time, the male feeds her, usually with rats, mice or voles, but sometimes with insects and small birds. If food is plentiful, the pair may raise two broods a year.

## ◀ IN A SCRAPE

On a cliff ledge, this peregrine falcon has made a simple nest called a scrape, clearing a small patch of ground to nest on. Many peregrines use traditional nesting sites, where birds have made their homes for centuries. Others have adapted to life in the city, making their scrapes on the ledges of skyscrapers, office buildings and churches.

## ◀ NO VACANCY

A secretary bird comes in to land on the huge tree-top nest of a colony of social weaver birds in search of its own nesting site. As this tree is full, the bird will have to choose another site in which to nest. It prefers low thorny trees such as the acacia. It makes its nest out of sticks, lining it with soft grass.

**secretary bird**
(*Sagittarius serpentarius*)

## ▲ SECONDHAND

A disused raven's nest has been adopted by this peregrine falcon. Peregrines do not build their own nest but often lay eggs in nests abandoned by other birds. These are incubated by both parents. Falcon eggs are pale reddish-brown, unlike those of most other raptors, which are white or speckled.

*379*

# On the Move

Every bird of prey maintains a territory in which it can feed and breed. There is usually no room for the parents' offspring, so they have to forge a new territory themselves. The parents may stay in their breeding area all year long if there is enough food. If not, they may migrate (move away) to somewhere warmer in winter, sometimes because their prey have themselves migrated. For example, peregrines that breed on the tundra in northern Europe fly some 14,000km/8,700 miles to spend winter in South Africa.

EUROPE

ASIA

AFRICA

AUSTRALIA

**◀ ESCAPING SOUTH**
The rough-legged buzzard is slightly larger than its cousin, the common buzzard. It breeds in far northern regions of the world in the spring, both on the treeless tundra and the forested taiga. In the autumn, it migrates south to escape the cold Arctic winter.

**▲ FLIGHT PATHS**
Birds avoid migrating over large stretches of water. There are fewer uplifting air currents over water than there are over land, so many migration routes pass through regions where there is a convenient land bridge or a short sea crossing. Panama, in Central America, is one such area. Gibraltar, in southern Europe, is another.

**▼ JUST PASSING**

This sooty falcon was spotted on its way south to the island of Madagascar, where it spends the winter. In spring, it will return to north-east Africa or Israel to breed.

sooty falcon (*Falco concolor*)

**KEY**

➡ migration routes of birds of prey

**▲ KITE FLYING**

The red kite is unmistakable, with its reddish-brown belly and white wing patches. There are about 100 red kites in Wales. Unlike their continental European cousins, those that breed in Wales do not usually migrate south in winter.

**▲ GRACEFUL FLOCK**

Graceful kites fly over an Indian village during their annual migration from Asia to warmer winter quarters in southern Africa. They will cover hundreds of miles a day.

381

# TROPICAL BIRDS

Birds live all over the world and can
vary enormously in size, shape, habitat
and behaviour. From tiny, agile
hummingbirds to giant, flightless
ostriches, these amazing creatures
display a staggering range of plumage
colour, songs, flying skills, hunting
abilities, social behaviour and
migratory patterns.

*Author*: Tom Jackson
*Consultant*: Michael Chinery

# What are Tropical Birds?

More birds live in the tropics than anywhere else on Earth. The tropics are the warm regions that lie north and south of the Equator. The Equator is the imaginary line that divides the planet into the Northern Hemisphere and the Southern Hemisphere. The tropics include some of the hottest places on Earth, as well as some of the wettest and driest. In some places, it rains every day, and lush jungles or rainforests grow there. Other areas receive no rain for months on end and are covered by searingly hot, dry deserts. Tropical birds include many different species, from tiny hummingbirds to giant ostriches. They have all evolved in many extraordinary ways to survive in these habitats.

**▲ LUSH JUNGLE**
A blue and yellow macaw flies through a rainforest in South America. Rainforests contain more living things than any other habitat in the world. The plants grow very thickly because of the combination of the high temperatures and the amount of rain that falls. Forest birds, such as this macaw and many other parrots, live alongside all sorts of forest animals.

**◄ WET AND WILD**
An African flock of red-winged pratincoles takes off from a wetland in the Okavango Delta, in Botswana. Tropical wetlands are a magnet for many birds. Some birds spend all year wading through the shallows, searching for food, while other wetland birds choose to migrate from colder places far away, to avoid the cold winter back home.

### DRY LAND ▶

Many parts of the tropics are dry and receive very little rain. In some of the drier areas, open grasslands or savannahs form.

Water is scarce in these dry grasslands, so all animals, birds and reptiles must gather at the water holes to drink their fill. Grasslands are well known for their large herds of animals, such as antelopes and elephants, but many birds live there, too.

### ◀ IN THE CLOUDS

Tropical forests that grow high up the sides of mountains are often shrouded in mist. These habitats are called cloudforests. Because the forests are so high up and often gloomy, the bird life that lives there is rarely seen. However, many of the most stunning tropical birds, such as the bird of paradise, with its marvellous tail, and the resplendent quetzal, make their homes in these remote regions.

### GOOD NEIGHBOURS ▶

Because they live in such a crowded place, many tropical animals have had to learn how to get along with other animals and birds. These cattle egrets often hitch a ride on the backs of buffaloes. They feast on the many biting insects that also accompany the buffalo herds.

# Rainforest Birds

Tropical rainforests grow in Africa, India, South-east Asia, northern Australasia and South America. Rainforests are very wet. The Amazon Basin, in South America, receives enough rain to fill two billion Olympic swimming pools in just one year! All this rainwater comes from storm clouds that form over the oceans near the Equator. With so much rain, the tropical forests grow very quickly and thickly and provide plenty of opportunities for birds to make a living. Parrots, toucans and other plant-eating birds feed on seeds and fruits in the upper branches. Further down, insect-eaters, such as barbets and sicklebills, pick at the insects that pass up and down the trunks. On the ground, doves and tinamous scratch for food in the leaf litter of the forest floor.

## ▲ THROUGH THE UNDERGROWTH

Cassowaries are flightless birds related to emus that live in the forest of northern Australia and New Guinea. They can run at about 45kph/28mph to escape predators.

## ◄ MASSIVE BEAK

Great Indian hornbills are plant-eating birds that live high up in the forests of South-east Asia. Their most striking feature is the large horn, or casque, on the bill. This is not as heavy as it looks, since it is hollow. These hornbills feed on fruits such as figs, using the saw-toothed edge of their bills to cut into food. They also eat small frogs and other animals, hopping sideways along branches to get at their food.

## CUTTING EDGE ►

Toucans are not related to the hornbills they resemble but to woodpeckers. They live in South America. This particular toucan feeds on insects, small reptiles and soft fruits.

**AMAZING PLUMAGE** ▶

The resplendent quetzal is a very colourful bird that lives in the mountain forests of Central America. This small, rare bird flies around the trees looking for fruits and insects to eat. Once it finds a meal, it hovers as it plucks the food from the branch. The quetzal then returns to its perch to eat. Both males and females are brightly feathered, but there are differences. Males have crests of spiky feathers on their head, and their tails are very long.

◀ **SOCIAL CHATTER**

The scarlet macaw (left) and the blue and yellow macaw (right) are large and noisy rainforest birds in Central and South America. They feed on hard fruits in the treetops, using their tough bills to crack them open. Macaws are very sociable birds, and they form strong bonds with each other. Some pairs of birds may live together for life.

**FIG FEAST** ▶

There are no real seasons, as we know them, in a rainforest, but less rain falls at some times of the year than at others. In drier times of the year, there is often less fruit available for birds to eat. Many birds, such as this pale white-eye, rely on figs to see them through the lean times. Fig trees are hardy plants that do well in drier conditions.

# Grassland Birds

Tropical grasslands receive much less rain than the forests. Trees need a large amount of water to grow, and few trees can survive in the drier parts of the tropics. Instead of trees, tall grasses grow in these conditions. These tropical grasslands or savannahs include the Serengeti in East Africa and the Matto Grosso in Brazil. Life out in the open is very different from that of the forest. Grassland birds are much less brightly coloured than forest ones. They rely on drab brown and grey plumage to help them stay hidden from predators. For many grassland birds, being able to run fast is just as useful as flying, as there are few high perches around. Ostriches and some other grassland birds cannot fly at all. Instead, they run away at high speed from any danger.

## ▲ MIGHTY STRUTTER

The kori bustard lives on the savannahs of eastern and southern Africa. At over 1m/3ft tall and 20kg/44lb, it is one of the largest birds in the world that is capable of flight. However, the kori bustard spends most of its time on the ground. It often runs beside migrating herds of animals and feeds on the insects that are disturbed by the passing herds.

## SCRATCHING A LIVING ▶

A flock of helmeted guineafowl gather at a muddy watering hole in Africa. These birds are the tropical relatives of pheasants and other gamebirds, which are more common in the chillier parts of the globe. Guineafowl do not fly well and only take to the air to escape danger. They use their thin toes to scratch around in the ground for seeds to eat.

### ◀ MEAT-EATERS

A pair of ground hornbills perch above African grassland. These birds are not much like their forest relatives. They are much larger, and they do not have a casque on their bill. Instead, they have a bright red wattle of loose skin on their neck. These birds are chiefly carnivores (meat-eaters). The ground hornbill on the left is holding a chameleon lizard and a large insect in its bill.

### ▲ IN THE OPEN

This male sandgrouse is incubating eggs in a semidesert in Namibia. This region is even drier than grassland, and only the toughest plants can survive here. Food is hard to find. Sandgrouse travel around in search of areas that have just been rained on. The rain causes buried seeds to begin to sprout, and the birds are able to feed on these sprouting seeds.

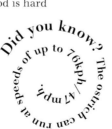

Did you know? Of up to 76kph/47mph, The ostrich can run at speeds

### ▲ GROUP LIVING

A colony of carmine bee-eaters perch outside their communal nest in a sandy cliff. When the breeding season is finished, the bee-eaters will travel long distances looking for food. Despite their name, these birds feed mainly on locusts and other grasshoppers. They catch insects on the wing, using their long, pointed bills.

*389*

# Wetland Birds

While too little water turns a region into a grassland or even a desert, a lot of water will change the habitat as well. Tropical wetlands, such as the Tonle Sap in Cambodia, are havens for bird life. Tropical wetlands are often seasonal, shrinking or vanishing altogether in dry seasons. However, when flooded, they are a good source of food, and many migrating birds travel thousands of miles to feed there.

**▲ SIFT AND SCOOP**

The African spoonbill is named after its oddly shaped beak. This bird spends most of its life in water. It feeds at night and during the day, wading through the shallows, swinging its beak from side to side. The swirls in the water attract small fish, which the spoonbill then scoops up.

**▲ IN HUGE NUMBERS**

Flamingos, such as these lesser flamingos from Africa, feed in huge flocks, which sometimes number more than a quarter of a million birds. They normally live in and around shallow tropical lakes, where the water is very salty or filled with other chemicals that make it inhospitable to other birds. Flamingos wade in these salty lakes and feed on the microscopic plants and animals that grow there.

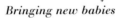

*Bringing new babies*

*European legend has it that newborn babies are brought to families by storks. White storks are migrating birds that arrive in Europe in the spring, when many babies are born. Ancient Europeans believed that the souls of new-born babies dwelled in the marshes and other wetlands where the storks feed, and that the birds carried the souls with them when they came from the wetlands and dropped them down the chimney.*

### ◄ RED WADERS

Scarlet ibises are unusual for wetland birds because they have such conspicuous plumage. They nest in trees in large numbers and feed in coastal swamps and mangroves.

### ▼ WALK ON WATER

African jacanas are also known as lily-trotters because they walk on flat lily pads that float on the surface of water. These small birds have extremely long toes that spread their weight over a large area. This prevents the birds from pushing the plants under the water and allows them to pick off insects and other food.

### ▲ SKIM AND GLIDE

African skimmers are related to seabirds that live on coastlines. The lower bill of a skimmer is longer than the upper one. They catch fish by dragging their longer lower bill through the water as they fly above the surface.

### ODD-LOOKING BILL ▶

As its name suggests, the shoebill, or whale-headed stork, has a large bill when compared to other waterbirds. Natives of central Africa, these unusual storks specialize in feeding on fish and frogs at pools that are drying out. They catch their prey as the water level falls.

# Sight and Sound

**▼ SEEING IN COLOUR**

Colour vision is very important for tropical birds that feed on flowers and fruits. When fruits ripen and flowers bloom, they change colour. Here, a sugarbird is preparing to feed on the nectar in the red flowers of an aloe plant.

Birds have excellent hearing and vision because these are the most useful senses that flying birds can have. Although all birds can smell and touch, few rely on these senses. Smelling food while speeding through the air is ineffective. Handling objects with wings and beaks is difficult.

Birds have large eyes compared to their body size, and most have their eyes on the side of the head. Each eye looks at a separate view, so the images are not as clear as those created by human binocular vision. Our eyes look forward and make a detailed three-dimensional view of the same thing.

Birds do not have outer ears. Sound waves get into the inner ear through small holes on either side of the head. These holes are covered by feathers.

**▼ SEEING WITH SOUND**

South American oilbirds spend the day inside dark caves and cannot rely on their eyes to find their way. Instead they use echolocation (see right) to work out where they are and to allow them to fly in the dark. Each bird makes its own unique clicking sound so that it does not get confused in crowded caves.

## HEARING LIKE BATS ▶

Echolocation is an orientation system that uses sound. A few birds that live in caves use echolocation, but nocturnal bats are the true masters of the art. Echolocating animals find their way around by producing loud and high-pitched sounds that bounce off objects as echoes. A near object produces a loud echo that returns quickly, while a more distant object will cause a weaker echo that takes a much longer time to come back.

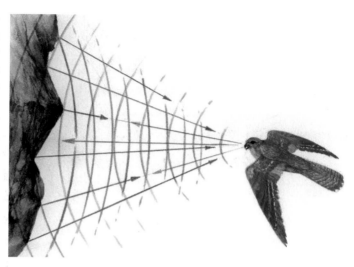

## ▼ SING A SONG

This black-lored babbler is singing to attract a mate or to defend its territory. Like most songbirds, this Kenyan species belongs to a large group of birds called the passerines. This group also includes sparrows and tits. Passerine songs are produced in the bird's well-developed voice box, called a syrinx. The songs have very complex melodies and are unique to each species. Male passerines sing more often, but the females can sing just as well.

## ▲ DISH FACE

Like all owls, this great horned owl, which lives in North and South America, hunts in the dark. It uses its large eyes and sensitive ears to locate its prey before swooping in for the kill. The disk of feathers around the face acts like a satellite dish, which channels even the tiniest sounds made by the prey into the ears.

*393*

# Built for Flight

Birds are the best flyers in the animal kingdom. They do not fly in exactly the same way as aeroplanes or helicopters. The inner section of each wing flaps ups and down, while the outer parts rotate, so that the tips draw a circle in the air. On the downstroke, the long flight feathers are flattened, so they overlap and make a solid surface to push air down and back. This pushes the bird up and forward. After the wing has flapped downward, the flight feathers are twisted to make slits in the wing. During the upstroke, air can rush through the wing so it can be raised easily and does not create a drag force that would slow the flight and make the bird lose height.

▲ AGILE FLYERS
Parrots such as these red and blue macaws have long, quite narrow wings that taper toward the tip. These allow parrots to be fast and agile fliers, but also make them able to glide well, when necessary. The position of a macaw's flight feathers, like those of other birds, can be adjusted to change the shape of the bird's wings.

◄ AIR CIRCULATION
Birds need a lot of oxygen to power their bodies when flying, so they have a very efficient lung system. Our lungs suck in air, extract the oxygen and breathe out used air. However, air passes through bird lungs in one direction, so that oxygen can pass continuously into the blood. Air breathed in goes straight into air sacs at the back, and is then pushed through the lungs and into the forward air sacs before being breathed out.

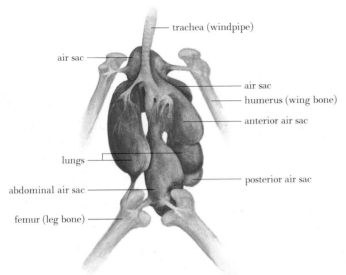

trachea (windpipe)

air sac

air sac

humerus (wing bone)

anterior air sac

lungs

posterior air sac

abdominal air sac

femur (leg bone)

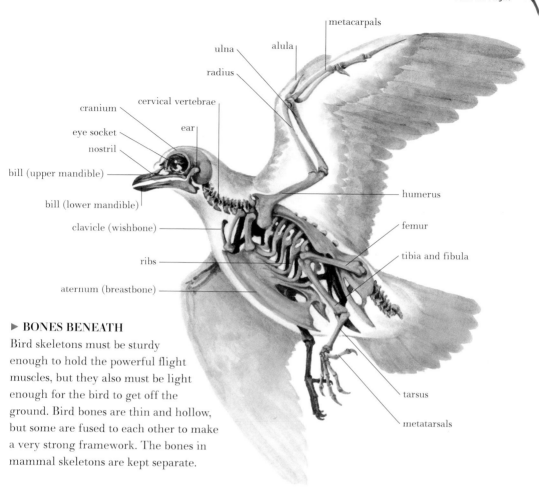

metacarpals

alula

ulna

radius

cervical vertebrae

cranium

eye socket

ear

nostril

bill (upper mandible)

bill (lower mandible)

clavicle (wishbone)

ribs

aternum (breastbone)

humerus

femur

tibia and fibula

tarsus

metatarsals

## ► BONES BENEATH

Bird skeletons must be sturdy enough to hold the powerful flight muscles, but they also must be light enough for the bird to get off the ground. Bird bones are thin and hollow, but some are fused to each other to make a very strong framework. The bones in mammal skeletons are kept separate.

## DELTA WINGS ►

This buff-tailed coronet hummingbird has triangular-shaped wings that make it especially good at performing fast and acrobatic manoeuvres in the air when it flies. Hummingbirds can flap their wings so quickly that they can hover in the air as they feed on the sugary nectar in flowers.

395

# How They Fly

Although most birds can fly, they use this ability in different ways, depending on how they live. Some birds fly huge distances while other birds make only short, fast flights. Grassland birds, such as pheasants, do not need to fly long distances because they scratch out their living on the ground. However, they will use their wings to make an escape should they be ambushed by a predator. Different ways of life require very different wing shapes. Many birds of prey, such as eagles and vultures, soar high above the ground for many hours, and they have developed long, broad wings to help them do this. Smaller, faster flying hunters, such as falcons, have sleeker wings that can be folded back to allow the bird to dive at great speeds toward its prey.

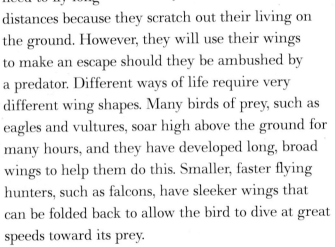

**▲ STRONG MUSCLES**

As this time-lapsed photograph of a Java dove shows, pigeons and other doves are very strong flyers. They have large breast muscles that pull the wings down. The lift force that keeps the bird in the air is generated during the downstroke of each wing-beat. When frightened, pigeons will take off with several noisy wing-beats in an attempt to scare the predator away. This defence behaviour can be very effective indeed.

**◄ SWOOP AND SWALLOW**

Swallows breed in the cooler regions, but when autumn comes they fly to the tropics. Their long, tapered wings are adapted for making long migration flights. Swallows are insect hunters, snapping up their flying prey out of the sky. Consequently swallows' wings are also thin and pointed enough to be good for the acrobatic twists and turns that they need to perform to catch their prey.

## ▼ SOARING ON THERMALS

Vultures can spend all day in the air. They use
their long and broad wings to catch thermals,
streams of hot air that rise up from hot tropical
hillsides. The vultures soar effortlessly upward
on this rising air and then circle around,
looking for food on the ground far below.
A flap of their mighty wings
prevents them from losing
too much height.

Did you know? The peacock, weighed down by its tail feathers, can only fly short distances.

## FLYING UNDER WATER ▶

Although penguins are more associated with the
cold ice floes of Antarctica, one species actually
lives in tropical waters. Galapagos penguins live
on the islands of that name on the Equator in the
Pacific Ocean, where they feed on fish like their
southern cousins. Like other penguins, this
species cannot actually fly through the air, but
Galapagos penguins flap their wings to push
themselves along under water. They are not
really swimming, but flying through the water.

## ◀ HOVER AND DIVE

A pied kingfisher, a fish-
hunting resident of Africa and
India, hovers over open water
while it prepares to dive under
the water to snatch a fish.
Kingfishers are one of the few
types of bird that can actually
hover in the air. Once the pied
kingfisher has dived, it floats up
to the surface. A single stroke
of its small but powerful wings
is enough to clear the water and
get back into the air.

# On the Ground

Several species of tropical bird have lost all power of flight. The world's heaviest bird, the ostrich, has tiny wings that cannot lift its mighty frame off the ground at all. An adult ostrich weighs 155kg/344lb, twice as much as an adult person, and its wings would have to be enormous to lift such a large body. The ostrich and other grassland birds such as the emu and rhea make up for their lack of flying ability with their powerful running legs. The ostrich can reach speeds of 76kph/47mph across the African savannah. Not all flightless birds live out in the open – the cassowary is a large forest bird, and the flightless kiwi lives in the fern forests of New Zealand – but they all find their food on the ground. Kiwis use their long bills to poke about in the soil for worms and insect larvae.

**▲ TINY WINGS**
A flightless cormorant from the Galapagos Islands spreads its wet wings to help them to dry. As you can see, this bird's wings are too small and weak for flight. This diving bird has no predators on land, so it does not need to be able to fly.

**◀ STAND ON ONE FOOT**
The flightless kagu lives on the island of New Caledonia in the South Pacific. It is related to cranes and other waterbirds. It has unique flaps over its nostrils that prevent it from breathing in soil when it digs for food. It spends its days standing almost motionless on one leg looking and listening for insects. The kagu has no defence against newly introduced animals, such as cats and dogs, and it is now threatened with extinction.

**▲ GROUND PARROT**
The flightless New Zealand kakapo is the heaviest of all parrots. It is most active at dusk, when it waddles across the forest floor, chewing plants and drinking their juices. The kakapo is extinct in the wild and under 100 survive in zoos.

## AMERICAN GIANT ▶

The greater rhea is the largest bird in South
America, where it roams in large groups across
grasslands and deserts. The rhea eats a range of
foods, from shoots to worms and lizards. The
bird's shaggy feathers provide camouflage
among tall grasses. Rheas have a claw at the
tip of each of their small wings. The birds use
these claws as weapons against predators,
such as pumas and
other large cats.

*Did you know? The flightless kakapo digs out roots with its bill.*

## WALKING DOWN UNDER ▶

An emu runs through grassland in
southern Australia. These birds are the
largest in Australia, reaching 1.9m/
5ft 6in tall. Emus are closely related to
cassowaries, which are smaller, also flightless,
birds. Emu feathers are not like those of flying
birds. Their feathers are more like thick hairs,
since they are made up of just a long central
shaft. Emus defend themselves from predators by
kicking backwards with their three-toed feet.

## ◀ FLIGHTLESS WANDERERS

Ostriches generally live in large groups, which
wander across lowland plains feeding on grass,
seeds and small animals. Unusually, these huge
birds have feet with two very sturdy toes. With
their thick, almost hoof-like claws, these feet are
well suited to walking and running over long
distances and are powerful defensive weapons.

*399*

# Foot and Mouth

The bills and feet of tropical birds vary enormously according to how they live. Bills are unique to birds. They are made up of two flexible mandibles, horny extensions that grow from the jaw. Birds of prey have a hooked bill that can rip into flesh, while the bills of other birds are shaped to dig out insects or crack nuts. Most birds have four toes, with three pointing forward and one backwards. Claws are used for fighting, gripping perches and digging.

## ▲ UPSIDE-DOWN FEEDERS

Flamingos, such as this one from the Caribbean, are filter feeders. The flamingo dips its bill upside down into the water and pumps water in and out of its mouth to trap food.

## ▲ WIDE MOUTHS

Tawny frogmouths are insect-eating birds that live in Australia. These birds use their wide mouths to catch insects on the wing and scoop their prey up off the ground.

| BASIC FOOTWORK | |
|---|---|
|  | Scratching: Pheasants and many other ground-living birds have a long middle toe, which they can use as a tool to scratch seeds and other food out of the ground. |
|  | Swimming: Ducks and other swimming birds have webbed feet that are good for propulsion, helping the birds push against water as they paddle on the surface. |
|  | Perching: Perching birds, such as song birds, have a fourth toe that points backward. This toe wraps around the back of the perch, while the front three grip the front. |
|  | Running: Most running birds have lost at least one toe. Ostriches have lost two, and their claws are thick and short, which helps them run at great speed up to 76kph/47mph. |
|  | Climbing: Birds, such as parrots, that climb well have zygodactyl feet, with two toes pointing back and two forward. This stops them falling backward when climbing. |

**UPTURNED BILL ▶**

This pied avocet is a wading bird. It has webbed feet that help it to stand on lake beds without sinking. It also has an unusual upturned bill. The avocet feeds by sweeping the tip through the water from side to side, and it may end up with its head under water as it grabs at its prey.

**▲ FLEXIBLE FEET**

Mousebirds get their name from their ability to scamper through flimsy branches, a little like small rodents. They live in central Africa and eat leaves, fruits and buds. They are so agile thanks to their unique feet. The two outer toes are reversible and they can point forward or backward. Mousebirds can use their feet to hang upside down or grasp onto perches.

## ALL KINDS OF BEAKS

| | |
|---|---|
|  | Chisel: Woodpeckers have a pointed bill that is used to get food by pecking through bark to get at insects living in wood. Many fruit-eating birds have a similar chisel-like bill. |
|  | Prober: Spiderhunters and many other insect-eating birds have a long curved bill, which they use to probe into crevices in trees and plants to get at their prey. |
|  | Cracker: Parrots have a distinctive, powerful bill, which they use for cracking open the shells of nuts and seeds. The strong jaws crush food between the sharp curved bill. |
|  | Scoop: Skimmers and other birds that scoop up their food have a longer lower bill. The shape of a bird's bill can tell you a great deal about how the bird gathers its food. |
|  | Sensor: While most birds do not have a well-developed sense of touch, a few use their bill to detect the slightest movements in water. This spoonbill beak does just that. |

# Wings and Feathers

Feathers are made from a protein called keratin, which is also used to make bird claws, mammal hair and reptile scales. Feathers have a very complex structure. The small downy feathers preserve body heat. The next layer of contour feathers creates the streamlined shape of a bird's body. The wings and tail are covered in flight feathers. These feathers are much longer and more rigid than the others on the body. Birds use their feathers for more than just flight. The plumage may keep them hidden from predators or it may attract the attention of mates.

▲ **STREAMING BEHIND**

This male standard-winged nightjar has two hugely long streamer feathers that stick out like flags from each wing. This truly remarkable plumage is meant as a signal to females that the male is a good mate. A weaker bird would not be able to cope with the long streamers, which make it harder to fly.

Did you know? Chemicals known as pigments produce the colours in feathers.

◄ **STAYING HIDDEN**

The common potoo's brown and grey plumage helps it to stay hidden as it roosts during the day. It sits motionless on stumps and broken branches and tries to look as much like a piece of wood as possible. It often keeps its large yellow eyes shut to help it blend in.

## ◄ POISONOUS FEATHERS

Two young hooded pitohuis from New Guinea perch on a branch. They have only just become old enough to leave their nest, and they still have some of the downy feathers that they were born with. These songbirds are unusual because their feathers and skin are naturally poisonous. Like many other poisonous animals, they smell unpleasant. The poison is a defence against predators. If a hawk or a snake eats a bird, it will become sick and quickly learn not to eat another bird with the same coloured plumage.

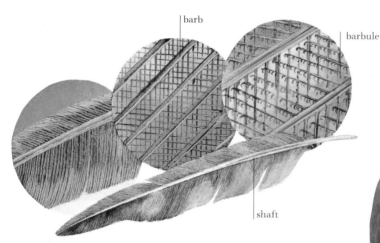

barb

barbule

shaft

## ▲ A CLOSER LOOK

A feather consists of a central shaft with hundreds of thin branches called barbs. The barbs on the flight feathers are linked to their neighbours by smaller branches called barbules. Tiny hooks on the barbules cling to the barbules of the next barb to form a flat, light surface. When barbs become detached, the bird reshapes them with its beak.

## SHOWING OFF ►

This male red cardinal uses his colourful feathers and impressive head crest to make an eye-catching exhibition of himself. Female red cardinals are not red at all. They have olive-grey plumage, which is much better for staying hidden when they sit on their eggs to hatch them. The males use their crest and colourful plumage to attract females. Pairs live together for the spring and summer.

*403*

# Migration

Many birds, such as storks, swallows and ducks, are winter visitors to the tropics. Since the tropics are warm all year, they are the perfect place for many birds to go when winter begins in the colder regions. Birds take their cue to begin their journey from the length of the day. As winter approaches, the days get shorter, and this causes the birds to set out. A regular journey made by an animal is called a migration. In cooler areas, nature reawakens in spring and summer, and this rapid spurt in growth creates a huge supply of foods for the birds to exploit. Therefore, the migrating birds take to the wing again, leave the tropics and head back to their summer feeding grounds.

▲ **GRASSLAND VISITORS**
Barn swallows spend summer in northern Europe, Siberia and North America, where they feast on flying insects that swarm during the long, warm summer days. However, as winter approaches and the days shorten, this insect food becomes more scarce, and the swallows head south to the tropics, where insects can be found all year around.

◄ **FINDING THE WAY**
Scientists are not sure how migrating birds, such as these rainbow lorikeets, find their way when they migrate. It is possible that birds are able to navigate by detecting the Earth's magnetic field with some kind of inbuilt compass. Birds that have never migrated before know in which direction to fly. However, young birds that hatch far away from the traditional nesting grounds end up in the wrong place.

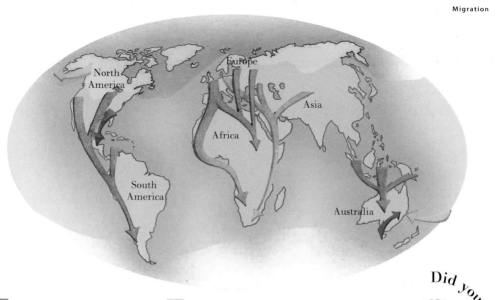

swift parrot

barn swallow

ruby-throated hummingbird

white stork

rainbow lorikeet

golden plover

Did you know? Migrating birds can learn how to recognize landmarks on their routes.

## ▲ MIGRATION MAP

As this map shows, migrating birds tend to fly over the land masses of the great continents rather than taking to the open ocean. This protects them from the worst storms, and means many more birds complete their journeys safely.

## ▲ OVER LAND AND OCEAN

A male American golden plover incubates eggs among the moss of the Alaskan tundra. When the chicks hatch out, they will grow quickly on a diet of insects that are abundant here.

## LONG JOURNEY ▶

The ruby-throated hummingbird lives in Canada and the U.S.A. in summer and then travels up to 3,219km/2,000 miles to the Amazon rainforest in winter. Some fly across the Gulf of Mexico.

*405*

# ANTS, BEES, WASPS AND TERMITES

Ants, bees, wasps and termites make up a group of insects called social insects, which live and work together in massive colonies. Within these colonies there are complex social hierarchies, which means that different insects do different jobs whilst all working together to ensure the survival of the whole group.

*Author*: Dr Jen Green
*Consultant*: Dr Sarah A. Corbet

# What are Social Insects?

Insects are the most successful group of animals on Earth. They make up about three-quarters of all animal species. Most insects have a solitary life, but a few kinds are called social insects because they live and work together in a group known as a colony. Some insect colonies hold hundreds, thousands or even millions of insects. Different members of the colony do different jobs. All ants and termites, some types of bees and a few kinds of wasps are social. For centuries, people have been fascinated by these insects because their colonies seem similar to human societies. Some types of social insects are also important because they make useful products such as honey, and they help to pollinate flowers. For these reasons, social insects are among the world's best-known insect groups.

**▲ LONELY LIVES**

Most insects, such as these tortoiseshell butterflies, do not live in colonies. They spend almost all of their lives on their own. After mating, the female lays her eggs on a plant that will feed her young when they hatch. Then she flies away, leaving her young to fend for themselves.

**▲ ONE LARGE FAMILY**

This scene inside a honey bee's nest shows a fertile (breeding) female bee, called the queen, in the centre, surrounded by her daughters who are called workers. Social insect colonies are like overgrown families. Each colony is made up of a parent or parents and lots of their offspring, who help bring up more young.

**Royal Emblem**
*This stained-glass window from Gloucester Cathedral, England, shows a fleur-de-lys, the emblem of the French royal family. "Fleur-de-lys" is a French term for an iris or lily flower. Originally, however, the symbol represented a flying bee with outstretched wings. French kings chose the bee as their symbol because bee colonies function like well-run, hard-working human societies. Bees also represented riches because they made precious honey.*

### ◄ TEAMWORK

These weaver ant workers are pulling leaves together to make a nest to protect the colony's young. Like all adult insect workers in a colony, they help rear the young but do not breed themselves. One ant working alone would not be strong enough to pull the leaf – the task needs a group of ants working as a team.

### DIFFERENT JOBS ►

These two different types of termites are from the same species. The brown insects with large heads and fierce jaws are soldiers. They are guarding the smaller, paler workers, who are repairing damage to the nest. The insects in all social insect colonies are divided into groups called castes. Different castes have different roles, for example worker termites search for food while soldiers guard the nest. In some species, the castes look quite different from each other because they have certain features, such as large jaws, that help them to do their work.

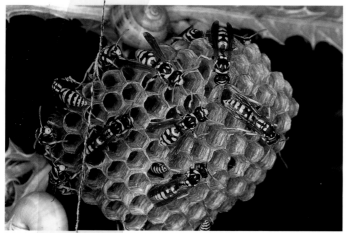

### ◄ NEST BUILDERS

Paper wasps are so-called because they build nests made of chewed wood fibres, or "paper". Like these wasps, most social insects live and rear their young inside a nest built by colony members. Some nests, such as those made by some wasps and bees, are complicated, beautiful structures. Some nests, such as those made by certain termites, are huge in size and tower some 6m/20ft high.

*409*

# Body Parts

Like other insects, adult social insects have six legs. Bees and wasps have wings, but non-breeding ants and termites (workers and soldiers) have no wings. As with other insects, the bodies of social insects are protected by a hard outer case that is called an exoskeleton. This tough covering is waterproof and helps to prevent the insect from drying out. An insect's body is divided into three main sections: the head, thorax (middle section) and abdomen (rear).

Social insects differ from non-social insects in some important ways. For example, they possess glands that produce special scents that help them to communicate with one another. The various castes also have special features, such as stings.

▲ PARTS OF AN INSECT
An insect's head holds the main sense organs, including the eyes and antennae. Its wings, if it has any, and legs are attached to the thorax. The abdomen holds the digestive and reproductive parts.

▲ BEE
A bumble-bee's body is covered with dense hairs. She collects flower pollen in special pollen baskets, surrounded by bristles, on her back legs.

▲ WASP
A wasp has narrow, delicate wings and a long body. In many wasp species, the abdomen and thorax are brightly striped.

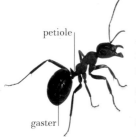

◄ ANT
An ant's abdomen is made up of the petiole (narrow waist) and the gaster (large rear part). The thorax contains strong muscles that move the six legs.

TERMITE ►
Unlike other social insects, termites do not have a narrow waist between their thorax and abdomen. They are less flexible than other social insects.

410

KEY

◼ circulatory system

◼ digestive system

◼ nervous system

wing

head

thorax

brain

antenna

pharynx

labrum

mandible

tongue

oesophagus

ganglion

honey
stomach

pollen basket

heart

mid gut

malpighian
tubes

hind
gut

sting

ventral
nerve cord

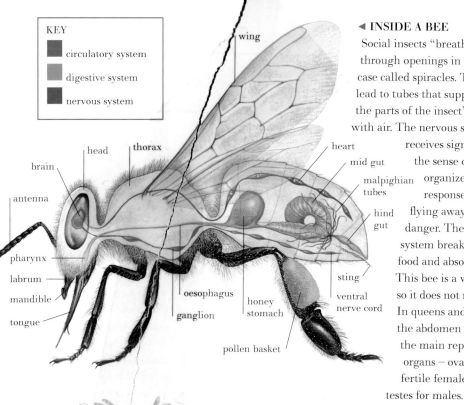

## ◀ INSIDE A BEE

Social insects "breathe" through openings in their body case called spiracles. These holes lead to tubes that supply all of the parts of the insect's body with air. The nervous system receives signals from the sense organs and organizes a response, such as flying away from danger. The digestive system breaks down food and absorbs it. This bee is a worker, so it does not reproduce. In queens and males, the abdomen contains the main reproductive organs – ovaries for fertile females and testes for males.

### Wasp Waist

*In the late 19th century, it became fashionable for women to **have a narrow "wasp waist."** Well-to-do ladies achieved this shape by wearing corsets like the one shown in this advertisement. However, the corsets were very tight and pressed on the ribs and lungs. They were very uncomfortable and even caused some women to faint from lack of oxygen.*

## ▲ COLD-BLOODED CREATURES

A queen wasp spends the winter in a sheltered place, such as a woodpile. Like all insects, social insects are cold-blooded, which means that when they are still, their body temperature is the same as the temperature outside. In winter, worker wasps die, but the queen enters a deep sleep called hibernation. She wakes up when the weather gets warmer again in spring.

*411*

# On the Wing

All adult wasps and bees have two pairs of narrow, transparent wings. They fly to escape their enemies and to get to food that cannot be reached from the ground. Honey bees fly off in swarms (groups) to start a new nest.

The wings of a bee or a wasp are attached to its thorax. Like other flying insects, bees and wasps may bask in the sun to warm their bodies before take-off. They also warm up by exercising their flight muscles. Flying uses up a lot of energy, so bees and wasps eat high-energy foods such as nectar. Most ants and termites are wingless, but young queens and males have wings, which they use during mating.

**▲ HOW BEES FLY**
Inside the thorax, bees and wasps have two sets of muscles that make their wings move. One set of muscles pulls down on the domed top of the thorax, which makes the wings flip up. Another set pulls on the ends of the thorax, so the top clicks back into its original shape. This makes the wings flip down.

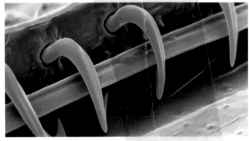

**▲ BUZZING BEES**
A group of honey bees approaches a flower. Flying bees beat their wings amazingly quickly – at more than 200 beats per second. The beating movement produces a buzzing sound, which becomes more high-pitched the faster the wings flap up and down.

**▲ HOOKING UP**
This row of tiny hooks is on the edge of a bee's front wing. Wasps have wing hooks, too. The hooks attach the front wings to the hind ones when the insect is flying. The large surface area of the combined wings helps the bee to fly faster.

412

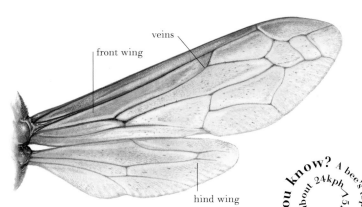

veins

front wing

hind wing

## ◀ DELICATE WINGS

The front wings of bees and wasps are bigger than their hind (back) wings. The wings are made up of the same hard material, called chitin, that covers the rest of the body, but the wings are thin and delicate. They are supported and strengthened by a network of veins.

*Did you know? A bee's top flying speed is about 24kph/15mph.*

**French wasp** (*Dolichovespula media*)

## ▲ SKILFUL FLIER

A brown bumble-bee hovers in front of a flower. Bees are very agile in the air. They can move their wings backwards and forwards, as well as up and down, so they can fly forward, reverse and also hover in one place.

## ▲ KEEPING CLEAN

This queen is cleaning her wings using tiny combs on her back legs. Bees and wasps clean their wings regularly to keep them in good working order. When not in use, they fold their wings over their backs to protect them from damage.

### The Sound of a Bee

*"Flight of the Bumble Bee" is a piece of piano music that was written by the Russian composer Nikolai Andreyevich Rimsky-Korsakov (1844–1908). The piece was inspired by the buzzing sound that is made by these flying insects. The fast pace and quavering melody suggest the buzzing noise made by the bee as she moves from flower to flower, gathering nectar. The piece is well known for being very difficult to play.*

# Lively Legs

Most ants and termites cannot fly, but they move around and even climb trees using their six legs. Social insects use their legs to groom (clean) their bodies as well.

All insects belong to a larger group of animals called arthropods, which means "jointed leg". True to this name, adult insects have many-jointed legs. An insect's legs have four main sections – the coxa, femur, tibia and tarsus. The coxa is the top part of the leg, where it joins to the thorax. The femur corresponds to the thigh, and the tibia is the lower leg. The tarsus, or foot, is made up of several smaller sections. Insects' legs do not have bones. Instead, they are supported by hard outer cases, like hollow tubes.

*Did you know? All adult insects have six legs, but young bees, wasps and ants have no legs at all.*

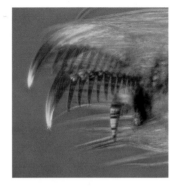

▲ **GRIPPING CLAWS**
This magnified photograph of a bee's foot shows clearly the tiny claws on the end of the foot. Claws help the insects to grip smooth surfaces such as shiny leaves, stems and branches without slipping. Ants can walk along the underside of leaves with the help of their claws.

**WALKING ON STILTS ▶**
Like other ants, this Australian bulldog ant has legs made up of several long, thin sections. In the hot, dry areas of Australia, the ant's stilt-like legs raise her high above the hot, dusty ground, helping to keep her cool. As well as walking, climbing and running, social insects' legs have other uses. Some ants and termites use their legs to dig underground burrows. Bees carry food using their hind legs.

## ▲ MULTIPURPOSE LEGS

Bees use their legs to grip on to flowers and also to walk, carry nesting materials and clean their furry bodies. Their front legs have special notches to clean their antennae. They use their hind legs to carry pollen back to the nest.

## ▲ ON THE MOVE

Army ants spend their whole lives on the move. Instead of building permanent nests as other ants do, they march through the forest in search of prey, attacking any creature they find and scavenging from dead carcasses.

## ▼ EXPERT CLIMBERS

Termites swarm along a tree branch in Malaysia, South-east Asia. Many termites nest underground, but some build their nests high in trees. They climb vertical surfaces such as trees by digging their claws into the bark.

## ▲ THREE-LEGGED RACE

A running ant keeps three of her legs (shown in black) on the ground at the same time, but does not move all the legs on one side together. The front and hind legs touch the ground at the same time as the middle leg on the opposite side, helping to keep the ant steady.

*415*

# Amazing Senses

Social insects find food, escape from danger and communicate with their nestmates with the help of their keen senses. However, the world their senses show them is very different from the one we humans know.

Antennae are the main sense organs for many insects. These long, thin projections on the insect's head are used to smell and feel, and sometimes to taste or hear. Sight is important to wasps, bees and most ants, but many termites have no eyes and are blind. Their world is a pattern of scents and tastes.

Social insects have no ears, so they cannot hear as people do. Instead, they "hear" using special organs that pick up tiny air currents, or vibrations, produced by sounds. Sensitive hairs all over their bodies help the insects know when danger is near.

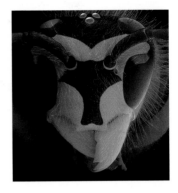

▲ **TWO TYPES OF EYE**
This close-up of a wasp shows the large compound eyes that cover much of the head. The curving shape of the eyes allows the wasp to see in front, behind and above at the same time. Compound eyes make out colours and shapes, and are good at detecting movement. On top of the wasp's head are three simple eyes, arranged in a triangle. These detect light and help the wasp know what time of day it is.

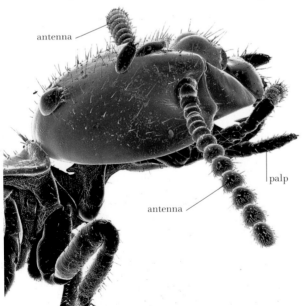

antenna

palp

antenna

◀ **TOUCHY-FEELY**
This close-up of a soldier termite clearly shows its antennae — the main sense organs. They are divided into bead-like segments, which are covered with tiny hair that send signals to the insect's brain. Shorter feelers, called palps, on the mouth give the termite a better sense of touch. The palps help it to find and guide food to its mouth. This termite has tiny parasites called mites crawling on its head.

## ▲ BRISTLING WITH SENSES

Honey bee workers have compound eyes, simple eyes, and short but sensitive antennae that pick up the scents of flowers. Hairs on the head detect wind speed and tell the bee how fast she is flying.

## ▲ ELBOW ANTENNAE

A bull ant worker uses her feet to clean her antennae. Ant antennae have a sharp-angled "elbow" joint, which can be seen here.

human's-eye view

possible bee's-eye view

## ◄ MANY LENSES

A bee's compound eyes are made up of many small, six-sided lenses. Bees and wasps have thousands of these lenses in each eye. Some ants have only a few. Each lens lies at a slightly different angle from its neighbours on the curved surface of the eye, and each gives a slightly different picture. The insect's brain may combine all these little images to build up a big picture of the world.

Did you know? Only the termite king and queen have eyes – workers and soldiers are blind.

## ON THE ALERT ►

Ants don't have ears, so they use special organs on their antennae, body and feet to "listen" for prey. This Caribbean ant is lying in wait to pounce on passing small creatures. It is in a special ambush position.

417

# How Insects Eat

The mouthparts of insects are shaped to tackle the particular food they eat. Most social insects eat plant matter, but some species, such as army ants, eat meat and actively hunt their prey. Bees feed on sugary nectar and pollen from flowers. They also use nectar to make honey, which they eat in winter. Bee larvae are fed the same food as adults, but young wasps eat different food. Adult wasps feed mainly on liquid foods, but their larvae eat chewed-up insects.

Many ants eat liquid plant food. Some species lick sweet honeydew from aphids. Other ant species prey on caterpillars and worms, or even lizards, birds and mammals. Most termites and their young eat plant matter. They absorb the goodness in their food with the help of tiny organisms in their guts.

▲ NECTAR COLLECTOR

A honey bee's tongue forms a long, flexible tube that can be shortened or made longer and pointed in any direction. The worker bee uses her tongue like a drinking straw to suck up nectar. She stores most of the liquid in her honey stomach until she returns to the nest.

▲ DUAL-PURPOSE MOUTH

A common wasp laps up juice from an apple. Worker wasps have mouthparts designed to tackle both fluid and insect food. They slurp up liquid food for themselves with their sucking mouthparts, and use their strong jaws to chew up the bodies of insects for the young wasps in the nest.

◄ FEEDING TIME

A honey bee feeds another worker at the nest. As the bee laps flower nectar, strong muscles inside her mouth pump the sweet fluid into her honey stomach. Back at the nest, the worker regurgitates (brings up) the nectar to feed a nestmate, or stores the nectar in special larder cells.

## ▲ STRONG-JAWED ANT

A red carpenter ant shows her large, powerful, toothed jaws, called mandibles. An ant's jaws, which move from side to side, not up and down, are used to break off chunks of plant food.

## ▲ DAIRYING ANTS

These red ant workers are "milking" black aphids for the sweet liquid called honeydew that the aphids give off as a waste product. Some types of ants keep the aphids like miniature cattle. They "milk" their captives by stroking them with their antennae to get them to release the honeydew. The ants protect the aphids from their enemies, and, in return, have a ready supply of food.

## ◄ WOOD-MUNCHERS

Termites feed mainly on soft, decaying wood in fallen trees and in human settlements. In tropical countries, they can damage wooden houses and destroy furniture, books, and other wood products. They also cause great damage in farm fields and orchards if they infest trees or crops.

## HELP WITH DIGESTION ►

Inside a termite's body live even smaller creatures. These strange, pear-shaped forms are called protozoans and they live inside the guts of termites. This photo was taken using a microscope and has been magnified 65 times. Inside the termite's gut, the protozoans digest cellulose, a tough material that forms the solid framework of plants. In this way, the protozoans, and other tiny organisms called bacteria, help termites to break down and absorb the goodness in their food.

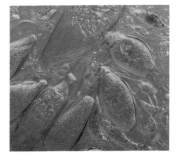

*419*

# How Social Insects

Communication is the key to the smooth running of social insect colonies. Colony members interact using smell, taste, touch and sound. Social insects that can see also communicate through sight. Powerful scents called pheromones are the most important means of passing on information. These strong smells, given off by special glands, are used to send a wide range of messages that influence nestmates' behaviour. Workers release an alarm pheromone to rally their comrades to defend the colony. Ground-dwelling ants and termites smear a scent on the ground to mark the trail to food. Queens give off pheromones that tell the workers she is alive and well.

**THE QUEEN'S SCENT**
Honey bee workers lick and stroke their queen to pick up her pheromones. If the queen is removed from the nest, her supply of pheromones stops. The workers rear new queens who will produce the vital scents.

**TERMITE PHEROMONES**
A queen termite spends her life surrounded by workers who are attracted by her pheromones. The scents she releases cause her workers to fetch food, tend the young and enlarge or clean the nest.

**FRIEND OR FOE?**
Two black ants meet outside the nest and touch antennae to identify one another. They are checking for the particular scent given off by all colony members. Ants with the correct scent are greeted as nestmates. "Foreign" ants will probably be attacked.

# Communicate

## THIS WAY, PLEASE

A honey bee worker exposes a scent gland in her abdomen to release a special scent that rallies her fellow workers. The scent from this gland, called the Nasonov gland, is used to mark sources of water. It is also used like a homing beacon to guide other bees during swarming, when the insects fly in search of a new nest.

## ALARM CALL

These honey bees have come to the hive entrance to confront an enemy. When alarmed, honey bees acting as guards give off an alarm pheromone that smells like bananas. The scent tells the other bees to come to the aid of the guards against an enemy. In dangerous "killer bee" species, the alarm pheromone prompts all hive members to attack, not just those guarding the nest.

## SCENT TRAIL

This wood-ant worker has captured a worm. The ant is probably strong enough to drag this small, helpless victim back to the nest herself. A worker that comes across larger prey returns to the nest to fetch her comrades, rubbing her abdomen along the ground to leave a scent trail as she does so. Her fellow workers simply follow the smelly trail to find the food. Ants can convey as many as 50 different messages by releasing pheromones and through other body language.

421

# The Search for Food

Social insects work in teams to bring back food for the colony. Experienced workers acting as scouts search for new food sources. When they are successful, they return to the nest and communicate their information to their comrades. The workers are then able to visit the same food source. Ants mark the trail to the food with pheromones.

Bees and wasps fly back to the nest with their food. Some ants carry food to the nest in long lines, guarded by soldiers. They may need to cut up the food into manageable pieces, or work together to lift heavy loads. Worker wasps feed their young on chewed-up insects. In return, the larvae produce a sweet saliva that the adults feed on.

▲ **STORING BUDS**
These harvester ants live in the Sonoran Desert in the western United States. They take seeds and buds to the nest to store in chambers called granaries. Ants that live in dry places put food aside for the times when there is nothing to eat.

▲ **MAKING MEATBALLS**
A wasp converts her caterpillar prey to a ball of pulp, which will be easier to carry back to the nest. Social wasps kill their insect prey by stinging them or simply chewing them to death. The wasp then finds a safe perch and cuts off hard parts such as the wings. She chews the rest of the body into a moist ball.

▲ **LARGE PRIZE**
This column of Central American army ants has captured a katydid, a type of grasshopper. Soldiers hold down the struggling insect while a group of workers arrives to cut it into pieces. Army ants spend most of their lives on the move, but sometimes stay in one place while the colony's newly hatched young grow up.

422

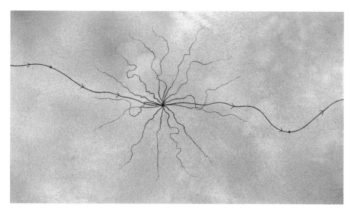

**◄ RAIDING PATTERN**

This diagram shows the temporary camp of a colony of army ants. When camping, a column of ants marches out to raid for food. Each day, the ants take a different direction, which varies about 120 degrees from the route of the previous day. Their routes form a star pattern radiating from the nest. Army ants camp for about three weeks.

**▼ AN ARMY OF TERROR**

Army ants are feared forest hunters. They mainly hunt small creatures, such as this insect, but will also kill large animals such as dogs, goats and even horses that are tied up and unable to escape.

**▲ KEPT IN THE DARK**

Termites scurry along a hidden highway they have built inside a fallen log. These insects forage widely in search of food, but seldom move into the open because bright sunlight harms them. Instead, they excavate long tunnels by digging through soft wood or earth. When moving above ground, they roof over their highways with moistened soil.

**SWEET FOOD ▶**

A European hornet sucks nectar from a hogweed flower. This sweet liquid forms a staple food for both adult bees and wasps. The young wasps produce a sweet saliva that the adult workers also feed on. In autumn, no more eggs are laid, so the supply of saliva stops. Deprived of this food, the wasp workers wander in search of other sweet fluids to drink, such as fruit sap.

423

# Insect Enemies

Bees, wasps, ants and termites provide a rich source of food for many animal predators, ranging from large mammals to birds, lizards, frogs, toads and small creatures. A bees' nest, in particular, contains a feast of different foods – stored honey and pollen, young bees and even beeswax. Bears, badger and bee-eater birds tear into the nest to eat the contents. Some insects, such as waxmoths, are specialized to feed on particular bee products, including, as their name suggests, wax.

Bees try to defend the nest with their stings, but may not manage to fight off their enemies. Wasp, ant and termite nests contain large numbers of only young insects, but they provide a good meal.

**▲ FOREST FEAST**
Silky anteaters live in the forests of Central and South America. They feed on forest-dwelling ants and termites. Like other mammals that eat ants, they have long snouts, sticky tongues and sharp claws.

**▲ GRASSLAND ANTEATER**
This giant anteater is probing a termite mound with its long, sticky tongue. These bushy-tailed mammals, which live in Central and South American grasslands, are major enemies of ants and termites.

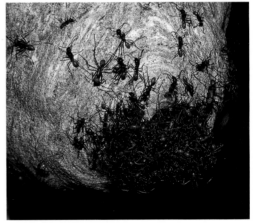

**▲ INVASION FORCE**
These army ants are invading a wasps' nest. They will break into the wasps' nest to steal – and later feast on – the young wasps. Army ants are enemies of many social insects, including other types of ants and termites.

### ◄ FOLLOW THE BIRD

This bird is a honey guide, and it is found in Africa and western Asia. Its favourite foods are found in bees' nests. It can't attack a nest by itself, so it enlists the help of a mammal called a honey badger, or ratel. The honey guide makes a special call, and the badger follows the bird to the bee's nest. The ratel breaks open the nest to get to the honey, allowing the bird to feed on the bee larvae, the wax and the remains of the honey. Honey guides also lead people to bees' nests for the same reason.

### BLOOD-SUCKING PARASITE ►

One of a bee colony's worst enemies is a tiny creature called the varroa mite. This photograph of the mite has been magnified many times. This eight-legged creature lives on the bee's skin and sucks its blood. Some varroa mites carry disease.

Another type of mite, the tracheal mite, infests the bee's breathing tubes. The two types of mite have destroyed thousands of bee colonies worldwide in the last ten years.

### ◄ EATEN ALIVE

This solitary wasp, called a bee-killer, has captured and paralyzed a worker bee and is dragging it to its burrow. In the burrow, the bee-killer wasp will lay an egg on the unlucky worker. When the young wasp larva hatches out, it feeds on the still-living bee, and so the bee becomes food for the wasp's young.

*425*

# Social Insect Habitats

Huge numbers of social insects live in tropical regions, where the climate is hot all year round. They include most termites and many different types of ants, wasps and bees. Rainforests are home to a greater variety of insects, including social species, than any other habitat on Earth. Many termite species live in dry grasslands, or savannahs. Scrublands on the edges of deserts are home to some hardy social insects, such as honeypot ants. The world's temperate regions have warm summers and mild or coolish winters. They provide many different habitats, which are home to particular kinds of social insects. The polar regions are generally too cold for insects to survive.

▲ FOREST BIVOUAC
Driver ants spend their lives on the move through the South American rainforests. At night, the workers lock claws and form a ball, called a bivouac, to make a living nest.

◄ LIVING CUPBOARD
Honeypot ants live in dry parts of the world, including the south-western United States, Mexico and Australia. During the rainy season, the ants gather nectar. They store the sweet food in the crops (honey stomachs) of ants called repletes, whose bodies swell to form living honeypots. The repletes hang from the roof of the nest and feed the other ants during the dry season.

KEEPING COOL AND DRY ►
Some African termites nest in tropical forests where rain falls almost every day. These species build broad caps on their ventilation chimneys to prevent rain dripping into the nest. The chimneys provide a vital cooling system. Being wingless, termites cannot keep their nests cool by fanning them with their wings, as tropical wasps and bees do.

### ◄ TREETOP TERRITORY

These ants are making a nest by binding leaves together with silk. Some tree-dwelling ants establish large treetop territories that include many nests. African weaver ant colonies, for instance, can contain up to 150 nests in 20 different trees. The ants patrol a territory of 1,337sq km/1,600sq yd − one of the largest insect territories ever known.

### PINEFOREST HOME ►

A wasp queen perches on her home. In rainy parts of the world, wasps' nests with open cells are constructed with the cells sloping downward, so rainwater can't collect in them. Other species build an outer covering around the nest to protect the young wasps from the elements.

### ▲ MOUNTAIN-DWELLER

Bumble bees live mainly in northern temperate regions, where the climate is coolish. They also live in mountainous parts of the tropics, where the height of the land keeps the air cool. In winter, the queen hibernates in a burrow, where the temperature is warmer than above ground. Her thick coat helps her to keep warm.

### ▲ HONEY BEES IN THE RAIN

Honey bees normally shelter on the comb inside the hive or nest cavity in rainy weather and do not venture outside to forage. If the comb becomes exposed to the elements for any reason, the bees will adopt a heads-up position when it rains, so the water drains off their bodies.

*427*

# How Insects Evolved

Insects are a very ancient group of creatures.
They started to evolve from common ancestors
about 400 million years ago and developed into
around 30 or so orders (types). Insects were the
first creatures to fly, and some evolved wings
more than 350 million years ago.

Relatively few fossils of prehistoric insects
survive because insects are so small and fragile.
However, some fossils have been preserved in
amber (hardened tree resin). Experts believe
that modern ants, wasps and bees all evolved
from the same wasp-like, meat-eating ancestors.

### ▲ FOSSILIZED IN AMBER
This prehistoric bee has been
preserved in amber. About
40–50 million years ago, the
bee landed on the trunk of a
pine tree and became trapped
in the sticky resin. Later, the
resin slowly hardened to
become clear, golden-coloured
amber, which is often used to
make jewellery.

### ◄ INSECT EVOLUTION
This diagram shows the time
period when some insect
orders evolved and how they
are related to each other.
There are more than a million
different insect species divided
into about 30 orders. Bees,
wasps and ants belong to the
order Hymenoptera. Termites
belong to a separate order,
Isoptera. As this diagram
shows, termites developed
earlier than many other
insects. They are more closely
related to earwigs than they
are to bees, wasps and ants.

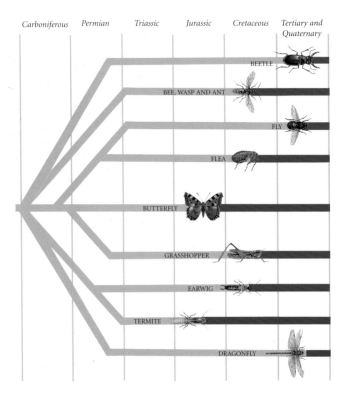

Carboniferous  Permian  Triassic  Jurassic  Cretaceous  Tertiary and Quaternary

BEETLE

BEE, WASP AND ANT

FLY

FLEA

BUTTERFLY

GRASSHOPPER

EARWIG

TERMITE

DRAGONFLY

## ◀ ANCIENT TERMITE

This winged male termite became trapped in tree resin about 30 million years ago. As you can see, the insect's delicate wings, legs and even its antennae have been preserved in the amber. The oldest amber fossils date back to about 100 million years ago, but termites are thought to have evolved long before that.

**brown bumble bee**
(*Bombus pascuorum*)

## A NEW PARTNERSHIP ▶

The ancestors of bees and wasps were meat-eaters. About 100 million years ago, bees began to feed on pollen and nectar from newly evolved flowers. Experts think that plants developed the flowers to lure insects into helping them with pollination. The partnership between insects and flowering plants flourished, and the number of both species increased greatly.

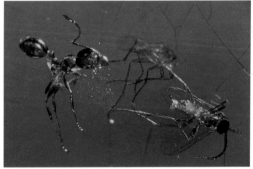

## ▲ TERROR OF THE PAST

About 45 million years ago, giant ants roamed the forests of Europe. This picture shows how a worker may have looked. The ants probably lived in large colonies and were carnivorous, just like many ants today. The queens were the largest ants ever to have lived and had a wing-span of up to 13cm/5in, which is larger than some hummingbirds.

## ▲ PREHISTORIC HUNTER

This amber fossil contains an ant with two mosquito-like insects. The ant, a meat-eating hunter, became trapped in the resin while preying on one of the mosquitoes, whose leg can still be seen between the ant's jaws. Experts believe ants were originally ground-dwelling insects. Later, they became social and began to live in underground nests.

# BUTTERFLIES AND MOTHS

Butterflies and moths make up one
of the largest insect groups, and there
are over 20,000 types of butterfly
and 145,000 types of moth. These
glorious insects begin their lives as tiny
eggs, before hatching into hungry
caterpillars, becoming pupae and
eventually emerging as fully formed,
nectar-loving, winged beauties.

*Author*: John Farndon
*Consultant*: Michael Chinery

# Winged Beauties

Butterflies and moths are the most beautiful of all insects. On sunny days, butterflies flit from flower to flower. Their slow, fluttering flight often reveals the full glory of their large, vividly coloured wings. Moths are usually less brightly coloured than butterflies and generally fly at night. Together, butterflies and moths make up one of the largest orders (groups) of insects, called Lepidoptera. This order includes more than 165,000 different species, of which 20,000 are types of butterfly and 145,000 are types of moth. The richest variety is found in tropical forests, but there are butterflies and moths in fields, woods, grasslands, deserts and mountains in every area of land in the world – except Antarctica.

geometrid moth
(*Hypochrosis bifurcata*)

body cover
in thick h

feathery
antennae

## ▲ MOTHS

Most moths fly only at dusk or at night. They rest on tree trunks and leaf litter by day, where their generally drab colours make them difficult to see. Moths tend to have plump bodies covered in thick hair, and their antennae are feathery or thread-like.

## ▼ RESTING BUTTERFLY

You can usually tell a butterfly from a moth by the way it folds its wings when it is resting. A moth spreads its wings back like a tent, with only the upper sides visible. However, a butterfly settles with its wings folded flat, with the uppersides together, so that only the undersides show.

green-veined white butterfly
(*Pieris napi*)

*Psyche and Aphrodite*
*The ancient Greeks believed that, after death, their souls fluttered away from their bodies in the form of butterflies. The Greek symbol for the soul was a butterfly-winged girl called Psyche. According to legend, Aphrodite (the goddess of love) was jealous of Psyche's beauty. She ordered her son Eros to make Psyche fall in love with him. Instead, Eros fell in love with her himself.*

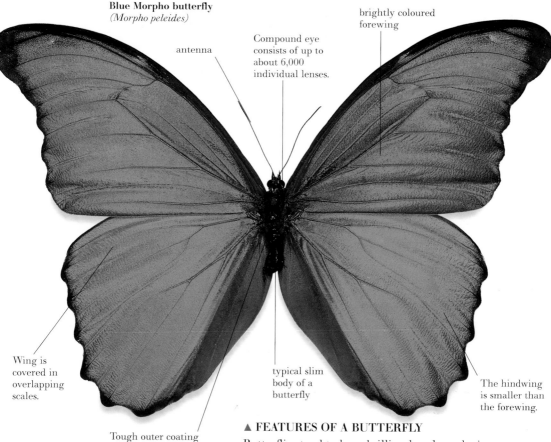

**Blue Morpho butterfly**
*(Morpho peleides)*

antenna

Compound eye
consists of up to
about 6,000
individual lenses.

brightly coloured
forewing

Wing is
covered in
overlapping
scales.

typical slim
body of a
butterfly

The hindwing
is smaller than
the forewing.

Tough outer coating
supports the body,
instead of an
internal skeleton.

## ▲ FEATURES OF A BUTTERFLY

Butterflies tend to have brilliantly coloured wings
and fly only during the day. They have slim bodies
without much hair, and their antennae are shaped
like clubs, with lumps at the ends. However, the
distinction between butterflies and moths is very
blurred, and some countries do not distinguish
between them at all.

## ▶ CATERPILLARS

A many-legged caterpillar hatches from
a butterfly's egg. When young, both
moths and butterflies are
caterpillars. Only
when they are big
enough do the
caterpillars go
through the
changes that
turn them into
winged adults.

**privet hawk moth caterpillar**
*(Sphinx ligustri)*

Did you know? Tiger moths make high-pitched clicks at night to warn bats they taste bad.

433

# Superfamilies

Scientists group butterflies and moths into 24 groups known as superfamilies. All but two of these superfamilies are moths, ranging from the tiny Micropterigoidea to the huge Bombycoidea. This latter group contains the giant Atlas moths. Butterflies belong to the other two superfamilies. The first, Hesperoidea, includes all 3,000 or so species of Skippers. The second, Papilionoidea, consists of about 15,000 species, divided among several families. These families include Papilionidae (Swallowtails, Apollos and Festoons), Pieridae (Whites and Yellows), Lycaenidae (Blues, Coppers and Hairstreaks) and Nymphalidae (Fritillaries, Morphos, Monarchs, Browns and Satyrs).

**▲ FEATHERY FAMILY**
The Plume moths (Pterophoridae) are small but very distinctive. They get their name from the way their wings are branched in feathery fronds, making them look almost like craneflies.

**European Swallowtail butterfly** *(Papilio machaon)*

**Garden Tiger moth** *(Arctia caja)*

**◄ ARCTIIDAE**
Tiger moths belong to a family of moths called the Arctiidae. Many of them are protected from predators by highly unpleasant body fluids and coats of irritating hairs, which they announce with their striking colours and bold patterns.

**▲ GREAT BEAUTIES**
Swallowtail butterflies belong to a family called Papilionidae. This family contains about 600 species. It includes some of the largest and most beautiful of all butterflies, such as the Birdwings of South-east Asia and the African Giant Swallowtail, whose large wings reach about 25cm/10in across.

### ◄ THE BRUSH-FOOTS

The Fritillaries belong to one of the largest families of butterflies, called the Nymphalidae. This family is sometimes known as the brush-foots, because their front legs are short and covered in tufts of hair. The Fritillaries get their name from *fritillaria*, the ancient Roman game of chequers.

### ▼ AN EXCLUSIVE BUNCH

The Japanese Oak Silk moth has brown wing markings, unlike the famous white Silk moth of China. Silk moths belong to a family of moths called the Bombycidae. Only 300 species of Bombycidae are known to exist. Silk moths are among the best known of all moths because of the ability of their caterpillars to spin large amounts of silk.

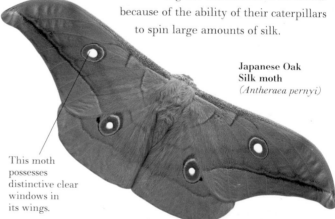

**Japanese Oak Silk moth**
(*Antheraea pernyi*)

This moth possesses distinctive clear windows in its wings.

### ▲ TROPICAL RELATIVES

The beautiful and aptly named Glasswing butterfly of South America is a member of a group called the Ithomiids. This group forms part of the larger Nymphalidae (or brush-foot) family, which is found all over the world. Ithomiids, however, live only in the tropics.

### ► SMALL WONDERS

The Longhorn moths belong to a family of tiny moths called the Incurvariidae. These European moths are often metallic in colour. Longhorn moths are easily recognized by their unusually long antennae.

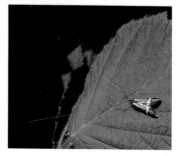

# How Butterflies Look

A male Queen Alexandra's Birdwing has brightly coloured wings.

Butterflies vary enormously in size and shape. In regions such as Europe and the United States they range from big butterflies such as the Monarch, which has a wingspan of 10cm/4in, to the Small Blue, which is smaller than a postage stamp. The variation among tropical species is even greater. The largest butterfly in the world is the rare Queen Alexandra's Birdwing. The female has a wingspan of 28cm/11in, which is more than 25 times the size of the minute Western Pygmy Blue. The shape of butterfly wings can be deceptive. In photographs and drawings, butterflies are usually shown with both pairs of wings stretched out fully. However, they are not always seen like this in nature. For example, sometimes the forewings may hide the hindwings.

**Monarch butterfly**
*(Danaus plexippus)*

◀ **MONARCH MIGRATIONS**
The Monarch is one of the biggest butterflies outside of tropical regions. In North America, it makes long journeys, called migrations, to spend the winter in warm areas such as California, Florida and Mexico. Some Monarch butterflies fly from as far away as Canada.

▼ **COMMA BUTTERFLY**
Each species of butterfly has its own distinctive wing markings. The Comma butterfly gets its name from the small white C, or comma-shape, on the undersides of its hindwings.

**Comma butterfly**
*(Polygonia c-album)*

## ▼ BIG AS A BIRD

The Queen Alexandra's Birdwing is a rare butterfly that lives only in the Northern Province of Papua New Guinea. Its wings are wider than those of many birds. Females can grow up to 28cm/11in across.

**Small Blue butterfly**
*(Cupido minimus)*

**Queen Alexandra's Birdwing butterfly**
*(Ornithoptera alexandrae)*

## ▲ SMALL BLUE

The Small Blue is the smallest butterfly in Great Britain. It is barely 2.5cm/1in across, even when fully grown. However, the tiny Pygmy Blue butterfly of North America is even smaller with a wingspan of 11–18mm/½–¾in.

**Peacock butterfly**
*(Inachis io)*

## ► PEACOCK EYES

The Peacock butterfly is easily identified by the pairs of markings on both the front and hindwings. These large spots look like eyes. It is one of the most common and distinctive butterflies in Europe and parts of Asia, including Japan.

The bright yellow body warns predators that the butterfly is poisonous.

## ► A TAIL OF DECEPTION

The wing shapes of butterflies can vary dramatically from species to species. Many butterflies in the family called Papilionidae have distinctive tails on their wings, resembling swallows' tails. Some species of Swallowtail use them to confuse predators. When the wings are folded, the tails look like antennae, so a predator may mistake the butterfly's tail-end for its head.

**Swallowtail butterfly**
*(Papilio machaon)*

437

# How Moths Look

American Moon moth
(*Actias luna*)

Like butterflies, moths come in all shapes and sizes. There is also more variety in wing shape among moths than among butterflies. In terms of size, some of the smallest moth species have wingspans no wider than 3mm/0.1in. The biggest have wings that are almost as wide as this book, for example the Hercules moth of Australia and New Guinea and the Bent-wing Ghost moth of south-east Asia. The larvae (caterpillars) of small moths may be tiny enough to live inside seeds, fruits, stems, leaves and flowers. The caterpillars of larger moths are bigger, although some do live inside tree trunks and stems.

### ▲ MOON MOTH

The American Moon moth shows just how delicate and attractive large moths can be. Its wingspan is about 30cm/ 12in and it has long, slender tails on its hindwings. When it is resting on a tree, its body and head are so well hidden by its big wings that any predatory bird will peck harmlessly at its tails. This allows the moth time to escape.

### ▼ ELEPHANT HAWK MOTH

Many moths are less colourful than butterflies, but they are not all drably coloured. For example, the Elephant Hawk moth is a beautiful insect with delicate pink wings that blend in well with its favourite flowers (valerian and pink honeysuckle). The Elephant Hawk moth, however, flies at night, so it is not often seen in its full glory.

Garden Tiger moth
(*Arctia caja*)

### ◄ COLOUR RANGE

Identifying moths can be quite difficult, as some species show a wide range of colouring. For example, many Garden Tiger moths are slightly different colours from each other. As a result of this variety, scientists often use the Garden Tiger moth for breeding experiments.

Elephant Hawk moth (*Deilephila elpenor*)

### ▶ INDIAN MOTH

This moth belongs to the family Pyralidae and comes from southern India. This tiny moth has a wingspan of just 2cm/⅜in. The distinctive white bands on its wings break up the moth's outline and make it more difficult to spot when at rest.

*Lepyrodes neptis*

**Did you know?** The Big Beet Borer moth (*Melitta gloriosa*) has a furry striped abdomen and looks like a bee.

### ▼ WIDE WINGS

The Giant Atlas moth of India and South-east Asia is one of the world's largest moths. Only the Giant Agrippa moth of South America has wider wings, with a span of up to 30cm/12in. Some Atlas moths grow almost as big as this entire double page when their wings are opened fully. They have shiny triangles on their wings that are thought to confuse predators by reflecting light.

**Giant Atlas moth**
(*Archaeoattacus edwardsii*)

### ▲ MANY PLUME MOTH

The beautiful feathery wings of this unusual looking moth give it its name, the Many Plume moth (*Alucita hexadactyla*). Each of its fore and hindwings is split into six slender feathery sections, or plumes.

### ▼ LARGE CATERPILLAR

Caterpillars have many different shapes and sizes, just like moths. The young Acacia Emperor moth is one of the biggest caterpillars. Although they are generally sausage-shaped, some caterpillars are twig-like, making them hard to see in a bush or tree.

439

European Map butterfly
(*Araschnia levana*)

# Scaly Wings

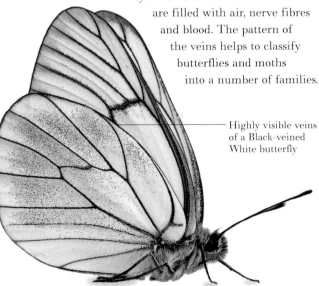

The scientific name for butterflies and moths, Lepidoptera, refers to the minute scales covering their wings. *Lepis* is the ancient Greek word for scale, and *pteron* means wing. The scales are actually flattened hairs, and each one is connected to the wings by a short stalk. These delicate scales give butterfly wings their amazing colours, but can rub off easily like dust. Underneath the scales, butterfly and moth wings are transparent like the wings of other insects. The vivid colours of the scales come either from pigments (coloured chemicals) in the scales or the way their structure reflects light.

▲ **SCENTED SCALES**
Many male butterflies have special scales called *androconia* that help them to attract mates. These scales scent the wings with an odour that stimulates females.

▲ **OVERLAPPING SCALES**
Tiny scales overlap and completely coat the wings. They are so loosely attached that they often shake off in flight.

▲ **CELL SPACE**
The areas between the wing veins are called cells. All the cells radiate outward from one vein at the base of the wings.

Black-veined
White butterfly
(*Aporia crataegi*)

▼ **WING VEINS**
Butterfly and moth wings are supported by a framework of veins. These veins are filled with air, nerve fibres and blood. The pattern of the veins helps to classify butterflies and moths into a number of families.

Highly visible veins of a Black-veined White butterfly

440

► **SCALING DOWN**

A Large White butterfly takes off from a buttercup. Butterflies in flight naturally lose scales from time to time. The loss does not seem to harm some species. However, others find themselves unable to fly without a reasonable coating of scales to soak up the sun and warm their bodies.

*Did you know? The wings of the Glasswing butterfly are transparent, making it almost invisible.*

◄ **MORPHO WING**

The metallic blue wings of the South American Morpho butterfly shimmer in the sunlight. This effect is produced by the special way the surface texture of their wings reflects light. When filmed by a video camera that is sensitive to invisible ultraviolet light, these scales flash like a beacon.

► **EYE TO EYE**

The patterns of scales on some butterflies form circles that resemble the bold, staring eyes of larger animals. Scientists think that these eyespots may have developed to startle and scare away predators such as birds. However, the eyespots on other butterflies may be used to attract mates.

**Butterfly Ball**
*The butterfly's fragile beauty has always inspired artists. In the 1800s, many European artists portrayed them as fairies, with human bodies and butterfly wings.*

# Focus on

## SUN LOVERS

Butterflies and moths can only fly if their body temperature reaches at least 24–29°C/75–85°F. If they are too cold, the muscles powering the wings do not work. To warm up, butterflies bask in the sun, so that the wing scales soak up sunlight like solar panels. Night-flying moths shiver their wings to warm them instead.

Butterflies and moths fly in a different way from other insects. They fly in a similar way to birds. Most insects simply beat their wings very rapidly to move through the air. Since they can only stay aloft if they beat their wings fast enough, they soon run out of energy. However, many butterflies ripple their wings slowly up and down. Some, such as the White Admiral, can even glide on currents of air with just an occasional flap to keep them aloft. This enables them to fly amazing distances. Flight patterns vary from the fluttering of the Wood White to the soaring of the Purple Emperor butterflies. Wingbeat tends to be faster in the smaller species, with the skipper family having the fastest wingbeat of all. Moths, such as the hawk moths with their jet plane-like wings, fly at fast speeds in a generally straight line.

## TWISTERS

To the human eye, the wings of butterflies and moths appear simply to flap. However, freeze-frame photography reveals that the bases of the wings twist as they move up and down, so that the wing tips move in a figure eight.

Butterflies look like clumsy fliers, but their acrobatic twists and turns enable them to escape sparrows and other predatory birds. Some moths can fly at up to 48kph/30mph when frightened.

# Flight

The wings push air backwards.

The butterfly is propelled forwards.

A butterfly lifts its wings upwards.

As the wings come down again, they provide lift to keep the butterfly up.

## UP, UP AND AWAY

The wings are stiff along the front edges and at the bases, but the rest of the wing is flexible. The stiff front edges of the wing give the butterfly lift, like the wings of an aircraft, as it flies forward. The flexing of the rest of the wing pushes air backwards and drives the butterfly forwards.

## GRACEFUL GLIDERS

Butterflies in the family Nymphalidae, such as this Painted Lady (*Vanessa cardui*), flap their wings occasionally when in flight. They glide along, with just the odd beat of their wings.

443

**▲ ANTENNAE**

The feathery side branches on an Atlas moth's antennae increase the surface area for detecting scent, like the spikes on a TV aerial. They allow the male moth to pinpoint certain smells, such as the scent of a potential mate, from huge distances away.

# Senses

Butterflies and moths have a very different range of senses from humans. Instead of having just two eyes, they have compound eyes made up of hundreds or even thousands of tiny lenses. They also have incredibly sensitive antennae (feelers) which they use not only to smell food, but also to hear and feel things. The antennae play a vital part in finding a mate and deciding where to lay eggs. They may even detect taste and temperature change. Butterflies and moths have a good sense of taste and smell in their tarsi (feet), too. Moths hear sounds with a form of ears called tympanal organs. These little membranes are situated on the thorax or abdomen and vibrate like a drum when sound hits them.

**▲ SMELL THE WIND**

A butterfly's antennae act like an external nose packed with highly sensitive smell receptors. They can pick up minute traces of chemicals in the air that are undetectable to the human nose.

**◄ ATTRACTIVE ANTENNAE**

Male Longhorn moths have very long antennae. These antennae are used to pick up scent, but they also have another, very different, job. They shine in the sunlight and attract females when the males dance up and down in the afternoon.

moth's head

## ▲ HEARING BODY

Many moths have "ears" made up of tiny membranes stretched over little cavities. These ears are situated on the thorax. When the membranes are vibrated by a sound, a nerve sends a signal to the brain. These ears are highly sensitive to the high-pitched sounds of bats, which prey on moths.

A noctuid moth showing the position of the ears at the rear of the thorax.

Did you know? The male Emperor moth can smell a female at 11km/7 miles – upwind!

## ◄ MULTI-VISION

The compound eyes of an Orange-tip butterfly are large. The thousands of lenses in a compound eye each form their own picture of the world. The butterfly's brain puts the images together into one picture. Although butterflies are quite nearsighted, they can see all around using their multiple eyes.

## ▼ FEELING FOR FLOWERS

Butterflies and moths find the flowers they want to feed on mainly by the incredibly sensitive sense of smell their antennae give them. This enables them to pick up the scent of a single bloom from some distance away.

## ▼ A CASE OF THE BLUES

Butterflies don't see flowers such as this evening primrose the way we do, because their eyes are not very senstive to red and yellow light. But they can see ultraviolet light, which we cannot see. They see flowers in the colours shown here.

445

# Focus on

Rear claspers grip a silken pad.

Pupation (changing from a caterpillar to a butterfly or moth) is one of the most astonishing transformations undergone by any living creature. Inside the chrysalis, or pupa, the body parts of the caterpillar gradually dissolve. New features grow in their place, including a totally different head and body, and two pairs of wings. This whole process can take less than a week. When these changes are complete, a fully-formed imago (adult moth or butterfly) emerges almost magically from the nondescript pouch.

1 The Monarch butterfly caterpillar (*Danaus plexippus*) spins a silken pad on a plant stem and grips it firmly with its rear claspers. It then sheds its skin to reveal the chrysalis, which clings to the silken pad with tiny hooks.

2 The chrysalis of the Monarch is plump, pale and studded with golden spots. It appears lifeless except for the occasional twitch. However, changes can sometimes just be seen through the skin.

fully formed chrysalis

Chrysalis darkens before opening.

3 The chrysalis grows dark just before the adult emerges. The wing pattern becomes visible through the skin. The butterfly then pumps body fluids to its head and thorax. Next, the chrysalis cracks open behind the head and along the front of the wing.

446

# Metamorphosis

**5** The newly emerged adult slowly pumps blood into the veins in its wings, which begin to straighten out. The insect hangs down with its head up so that the force of gravity helps to stretch the wings. After about half an hour, it reaches its full size.

split skin of chrysalis

**4** The butterfly swallows air to make itself swell up, which splits the chrysalis even more. The insect emerges shakily and hangs down, clinging tightly to the chrysalis skin.

Wings are soft and crumpled.

wing veins with blood pumping into them

**6** The butterfly basks in the sun for an hour or two while its wings dry out and harden. After a few trial flaps of its wings, it is ready to fly away and begin its life as an adult butterfly.

The adult butterfly tests its wings before its maiden flight.

# Nectar and Food

Butterflies and moths cannot chew food. Instead, they suck up liquids through their long proboscises (tongues), which act like drinking straws. Their preferred food is nectar. This sugary fluid is produced in the nectaries of flowers in order to attract insects such as butterflies and bees. Most species of butterfly survive on nectar alone and spend most of their brief lives flitting from flower to flower in search of this juice. Some woodland species extract sweet liquids from a wide variety of sources, including rotting fruit and sap oozing from wounds in trees. A few species even suck on dung. However, these sources do not provide much real sustenance, which is why butterflies rarely live for more than 20 days.

▲ **LONG LIFE**
*Heliconius* butterflies of the tropical forests of South America are among the few relatively long-lived butterflies. They are able to live for 130 days or more, compared with barely 20 for most temperate species. *Heliconius* butterflies feed on passion fruit flowers.

**Red Admiral butterfly**
(*Vanessa atalanta*)

▼ **CIDER DRINKING**
In autumn, butterflies such as the Red Admiral and the Camberwell Beauty often feed on rotting fruit. Sometimes the juice has fermented to alcohol, and the Red Admiral may be seen reeling around as if drunk.

▲ **FRUIT EATERS**
The first generation of Comma butterflies appears each year in early summer. These insects feed on the delicate white blossoms of blackberries, because the fruit has not yet ripened at this time. The second generation appears in autumn and feeds on the ripe blackberries.

**Did you know?** The Purple Emperor butterfly often survives by sucking juice from the rotting bodies of dead animals.

### ◀ DRINKING STRAW

Many flowers hide their nectaries deep inside the flowers in order to draw the butterfly right on to their pollen sacs. Many butterflies have developed very long proboscises to reach the nectar. They probe deep into the flowers to suck up the juice.

### ▲ HOVERING HAWK MOTHS

The day-flying Hummingbird Hawk moth gets its name from its habit of hovering in front of flowers like a hummingbird as it sips nectar, rather than landing on the flower. Moths from the hawk moth family have the longest proboscises of all. One member, known as Darwin's Hawk moth, has a proboscis that reaches 30–35cm/12–14in – about three times the length of its body.

### ▶ WOODLAND VARIETY

Many woodland butterflies extract juice from a variety of sources. The Speckled Wood butterfly sometimes sips nectar from bluebells, although it feeds mainly on honeydew. This is the sugary secretion of tiny insects called aphids. The leaves of flowers are often coated with honeydew.

### ▲ NIGHT FEEDER

Noctuid moths often sip nectar from ragworts in meadows by moonlight. In temperate countries, these moths mostly feed on warm summer nights. They get their name from the Latin word *noctu*, which means "by night".

**Speckled Wood butterfly**
*(Pararge aegeria)*

449

# Around the World

Butterflies and moths are surprisingly adaptable creatures. Almost every land mass in the world has its own particular range of butterfly and moth species. They inhabit a great number of different places, from the fringes of the hottest deserts to the icy lands of the Arctic. Species are adapted to living in these very different environments. For example, butterflies and moths that live in cold areas tend to be darker than those that live in warm regions. This is because they need to be warm in order to fly, and dark colours absorb sunlight more easily. In mountainous areas, the local species usually fly close to the ground. Flying any higher than this would create a risk of being blown away by the strong winds.

**Orange-tip butterfly**
(*Anthocharis cardamines*)

◀ **MEADOWS AND WAYSIDES**
Farmland is an increasingly hostile habitat for butterflies. Intensive cultivation strips away wild flowers and grasses, while crop-spraying poisons the insects. However, many butterflies still thrive in meadows and hedgerows around the fields. Orange-tips, Meadow Browns, Gatekeepers, Small Coppers, Whites and Blues are still common, as are Noctuid and Geometrid moths.

**Apollo butterfly**
(*Parnassius apollo*)

◀ **MOUNTAINS**
Butterflies that are adapted to life high on the mountains include the Alpine and Mountain Arguses and the Apollo. The Apollo's body is covered with fur to protect it from the extreme cold. Most Apollo eggs that are laid in autumn do not hatch until the following spring because of the low temperatures. Those caterpillars that do hatch hibernate immediately.

◀ **MARSHES AND WETLANDS**
The Marsh Fritillary butterfly flourishes among the grasses and flowers of wetlands in temperate regions (areas that have warm summers and cold winters). Its caterpillar's favourite food plant is devil's bit scabious. Among the other butterflies that thrive in wetlands are the Swallowtail, the White Peacock and the Painted Skipper.

## ▶ DIFFERENT HABITATS

Butterflies and moths inhabit a wide range of regions. Butterfly species such as the Large White live inland, while Spanish Festoons, Greylings and Two-tailed Pashas often live in coastal areas. Deserts are home to Painted Ladies, while White Admiral butterflies flutter around in woodland glades, as do Pine Hawk moths and Lappet moths. Arctic species include the Pale Arctic Clouded Yellow butterfly, and Apollos are examples of Alpine types.

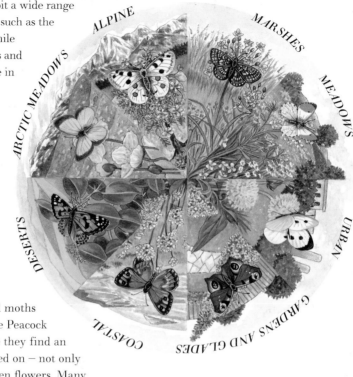

## ▼ GARDENS

All kinds of butterflies and moths visit gardens, including the Peacock butterfly (*Inachis io*). Here they find an abundance of flowers to feed on – not only weeds, but also many garden flowers. Many of these flowers are actually related to wild hedgerow and field flowers such as buddleias, aubretias and Michaelmas daisies.

### The Warrior Symbol

*A statue of a proud warrior stands at the ancient Toltec capital city of Tula in Mexico. An image of a butterfly appears on the warrior's breastplate. The Toltec people knew that butterflies live short but brilliant lives. Consequently, the butterfly became a symbol for Toltec soldiers, who lived brave lives and did not fear death.*

451

# Migration

Some butterflies and moths live and die within a very small area, never moving far from their birthplace. However, a few species are regular migrants. They are able to travel astonishing distances in search of new plant growth or to escape cold or overpopulated areas. Some butterflies are truly worldwide migrants in a similar way to migratory birds. Every now and then, small swarms of North American butterflies turn up in Europe after crossing the Atlantic Ocean. Crimson-speckled moths have been spotted thousands of km/miles out over the southern Atlantic. Nevertheless, butterflies are unlike birds in that most only migrate one way and do not return to their original homes.

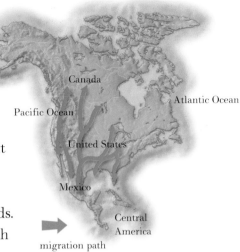

Canada

Atlantic Ocean

Pacific Ocean

United States

Mexico

Central America

migration path

▲ **MONARCH ROUTES**
Monarch butterflies *(Danaus plexippus)* migrate mainly between North and Central America. A few have crossed the Atlantic and settled on islands near Africa and Portugal. Others have flown all the way to Ireland.

▲ **MONARCH MASSES**
Every autumn huge numbers of Monarchs leave eastern and western North America and fly south. They spend the winter in Florida, California and Mexico on the same trees settled by their grandparents the previous year.

▲ **KING OF MIGRANTS**
In March, Monarch butterflies travel over 2,897km/1,800 miles north, lay their eggs and die. When the eggs hatch, the cycle begins again. The month-old butterflies either continue north or return south, depending on the season.

**◄ AN AFRICAN MIGRANT**

This Brown-veined White butterfly has large wings capable of carrying it over long distances. Millions of these butterflies form swarms in many parts of southern Africa. A swarm can cause chaos to people attempting to drive through it. Although this butterfly flies throughout the year, these swarms are seen most often in December and January.

*Did you know?* A large swarm of migrating butterflies can bring farm machines to a standstill by resting on them.

**► HAWK MOTH**

Every spring thousands of Oleander Hawk moths set off from their native Africa and head north. A few of them reach the far north of Europe in late summer. Hawk moths are among the farthest flying of all moths. They are able to travel rapidly over long distances.

Oleander
Hawk moth
(*Daphnis nerii*)

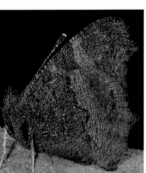

**▲ HIBERNATING PEACOCK**

The adult Peacock butterfly sleeps during the winter. This sleep is called hibernation. The Peacock is protected by chemicals called glycols that stop its body fluids from freezing. Many other butterflies and moths survive the winter in this way instead of migrating.

**► PAINTED LADY**

The Painted Lady butterfly (*Vanessa cardui*) migrates almost all over the world. In summer it is found across Europe, as far north as Iceland. However, it cannot survive the winter frosts, so adults emerging in late summer head south, and a few reach north Africa before the autumn chill starts.

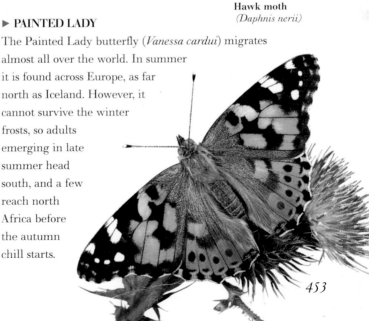

453

# BEETLES AND BUGS

Beetles and bugs are just two groups,
or orders, of the one million different
insects that live on our planet.
Amazingly, one in five animals is a
beetle, and there are at least 55,000 types
of bug, many of which are so small we
don't notice them. These agile beasts
can run, hop, fly and swim, and they
are a crucial part of most food chains.

*Author*: Dr Jen Green
*Consultant*: Mathew Frith

# Nature's Success Story

If you were an alien visiting Earth, which creature would you consider the main life form? We humans like to think we dominate Earth, but insects are far more successful. There are over one million different species (kinds) of insects, compared to just one human species.

Scientists divide insects into groups called orders. The insects in each order share certain features. Beetles and bugs are two major insect orders. The main difference between them is that beetles have biting jaws, and bugs have sucking mouthparts. Beetles are the largest order of all. So far, 350,000 different kinds of beetles and 55,000 different kinds of bugs have been found.

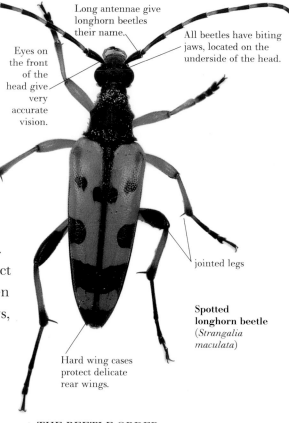

Long antennae give longhorn beetles their name.

Eyes on the front of the head give very accurate vision.

All beetles have biting jaws, located on the underside of the head.

jointed legs

**Spotted longhorn beetle** (*Strangalia maculata*)

Hard wing cases protect delicate rear wings.

## ▲ THE BEETLE ORDER

Beetles belong to the order Coleoptera, which means "sheath wings". Most beetles have two pairs of wings. The tough front wings fold over the delicate rear wings to form a hard, protective sheath, like body armour. Longhorn beetles owe their name to their long antennae (feelers), which look like long horns.

## ◄ LIVING IN WATER

Not all beetles and bugs live on land. Some, like this diving beetle (*Dytiscus marginalis*), live in fresh water. The diving beetle hunts under water, diving down to look for food on the stream bed.

### ◀ FEEDING TOGETHER

A group of aphids feeds on a plant stem, sucking up liquid sap. Most beetles and bugs live alone, but a few species, such as aphids, gather together in large numbers. Although they do not form a community, as ants and bees do, living in a group does give some protection from predators.

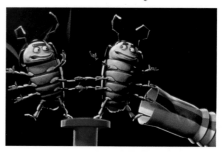

### *What's in a Name?*

*This image comes from the animated feature film* A Bug's Life. *The hero of the cartoon is not actually a bug at all, but an ant. True bugs are a particular group of insects with sucking mouthparts that can slurp up liquid food.*

**Forest shield bug**
(*Pentatoma rufipes*)

Six legs keep the bug stable as it scurries along the ground.

antennae for touching and smelling

thin wing-tip

hard wing base

tube-like mouthparts under the insect's head

eyes on the front of the head

### ◀ THE BUG ORDER

Bugs come in many shapes and sizes. All have long, jointed mouthparts that form a tube through which they suck up liquid food, like a syringe. Their order name is Hemiptera, which means "half wings". The name refers to the front wings of many bugs, such as shield bugs, which are hard at the base and flimsy at the tip. With their wings closed, shield bugs are shaped like a warrior's shield.

*Did you know?*
*Insects are unique in having six legs – three on either side.*

### THE YOUNG ONES ▶

Young beetles, called grubs or larvae, look very different from adult beetles. A young cockchafer (*Melolontha melolontha*) feeds on plant roots in the soil. Almost all young beetles and bugs hatch from eggs. They pass through several stages in their life cycle.

# Body Parts

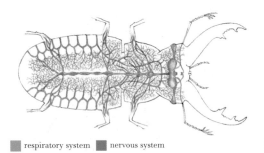

head

thorax

**garden chafer** *(Phyllopertha horticola)*

abdomen

## ▲ THREE SECTIONS

A beetle's main sense organs, the antennae and eyes, are on its head. Its wings and legs are attached to the thorax. The abdomen contains the digestive and reproductive organs. When on the ground, the abdomen is covered by the beetle's wings.

Human bodies are supported by a bony skeleton. Beetles, bugs and other insects have no inner skeleton. Instead, they are protected by a hard outer layer called an exoskeleton. This layer is waterproof and also helps to prevent the insect from drying out in hot weather. The exoskeleton is airtight, but it has special holes called spiracles that allow the insect to breathe.

The word "insect" comes from a Latin word meaning "in sections". Like other insects, beetles' and bugs' bodies are made up of three main parts. All have a head, a thorax (middle section) and an abdomen (rear section). Almost all adult beetles and bugs have six legs, and most have two pairs of wings, which enable them to fly.

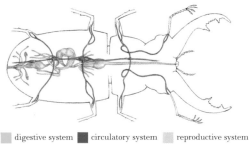

■ respiratory system ■ nervous system

■ digestive system ■ circulatory system ■ reproductive system

## ▲ BREATHING AND NERVOUS SYSTEMS

The respiratory (breathing) system has spiracles (openings) that lead to a network of tubes. The tubes allow air to reach all parts of the insect's body. The nervous system receives messages from the sense organs, and sends signals to the insect's muscles to make it move.

## ▲ OTHER BODY SYSTEMS

The digestive system breaks down and absorbs food. The circulatory system includes a long, thin heart that pumps blood through the body. The abdomen contains the reproductive parts. Males have two testes that produce sperm. Females have two ovaries that produce eggs.

*458*

### ◄ IN COLD BLOOD

Like all insects, beetles and bugs are cold-blooded animals. This means that the temperature of their bodies is similar to their surroundings. Insects control their body temperature by moving about. To warm up, beetles and bugs bask in the sun, as this leaf beetle (Chrysomelidae) is doing. If they need to cool their bodies, they move into the shade.

### SURVIVING THE COLD ►

This tiger beetle egg (*Cicindela*) is buried in the soil. In some parts of the world, winters are too cold for most adult insects to survive. The adult insects die, but their eggs, or young, can survive in the soil because it is warmer. When spring arrives, the young insects emerge, and so the species survives.

### BEETLE CAR

*During the 1940s, the tough, rounded beetle shape inspired the German car manufacturer Volkswagen to produce one of the world's most popular family cars, the VW Beetle. The car's tough outer shell, just like that of a beetle, helped it to achieve a good safety record. The design proved so successful that the Beetle car was recently improved and relaunched.*

rhinoceros beetle
(*Megasoma elephas*)

### ▲ MOVING FORTRESS

The rhinoceros beetle is very well armoured. Its tough exoskeleton covers and protects its whole body. The cuticle (outer skin) on its head forms three long points that look like a rhinoceros's horns. With all that armour, it is fairly safe for this beetle to move about!

# On the Move

Beetles and bugs are expert movers. They can fly, run, leap and even swim. Some species are wingless, but most of those that have wings fly well. All adult beetles and bugs have six flexible, jointed legs, divided into four main sections. Many species have claws on their feet, which help them to cling to smooth surfaces. Others have a flat pad between the claws, with hundreds of tiny hairs. The pads allow the insects to scramble up walls and even walk upside down.

squash bug
(*Coreus marginatus*)

## ▲ JOINTED LEGS
Like all beetles and bugs, squash bugs have four main sections in their legs. The top part is called the coxa, next comes the femur or upper leg, then the tibia or lower leg. The fourth section, the tarsus, is the part that touches the ground. You can also see the bug's feeding tube under its head.

## ▲ SPEEDY RUNNER
Tiger beetles (*Cicindela*) are one of the fastest insects – they can cover up to 0.6m/2ft a second. As it runs, the front and hind legs on one side of the beetle's body touch the ground at the same time as the middle leg on the other side. This steadies the insect, like a three-legged stool.

## ◄ LONG LEAPER
Leafhoppers (Cicadellidae family) are long-jump champions! When preparing to leap, the bug gathers its legs beneath it like a runner on the starting block. Muscles that connect the upper and lower leg contract (shorten) to straighten the leg and fling the bug into the air.

## ◄ SOIL SHIFTER

The burying, or sexton, beetle uses its strong front legs for digging. These ground-dwelling insects bury small animals (such as mice) in the ground to provide food for their young. The beetle's front legs are armed with little prongs that act as shovels, pushing the soil aside as it digs into the earth.

burying
beetle
(*Nicrophorus
humator*)

## ROWING THROUGH WATER ►

Pan-temperate diving beetles (*Dytiscus marginalis*) are strong swimmers. Their flattened hind legs are covered with long-haired fringes, which act like broad paddles. The two back legs push together against the water, helping the insect to "row" itself forward.

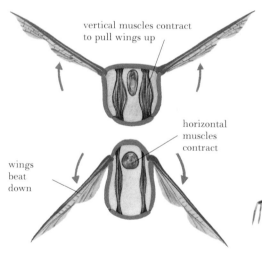

vertical muscles contract
to pull wings up

horizontal
muscles
contract

wings
beat
down

## ◄ FLIGHT MUSCLES

Unlike flies, a beetle uses only its delicate rear wings for flying. Vertical muscles attached to the top and bottom of the thorax contract to flatten it. This makes the wings move up. Horizontal muscles along the body then contract to pull the thorax up, making the beetle's wings flip down. The action of the thorax controls the wings and propels the insect along.

spotted longhorn
(*Strangalia
maculata*)

## GRACEFUL FLIER ►

A spotted longhorn beetle takes to the air. Like other insects, these beetles have two sets of flying muscles in their thorax (mid-body section). The hard front wings are held up to help steady the insect in flight. Most beetles are competent fliers, but they do not specialize in flying like some other insect species.

461

# Focus on

Beetles, bugs and other insects are the only animals without a backbone that are able to fly. They take to the air to escape from their enemies and to move from place to place in search of food. Most beetles and bugs are expert fliers.

Bugs with two pairs of wings use both sets for flying. Their front and rear wings flap up and down together. The hardened front wings of a beetle are called elytra. They are not used for powering flight but to steady the beetle as it flies. The long rear wings sweep up and down to power the beetle through the air.

1 When on the ground, the wing cases of the cockchafer beetle (*Melolontha melolontha*) meet over its body. The delicate rear wings are folded under the elytra and cannot be seen. Cockchafer beetles are also known as May bugs or June bugs, as it is in these months that they are usually seen.

2 A fire-coloured beetle (*Pyrochroa serraticornis*) prepares for take-off by raising its front wings out of the way and flexing its rear flight muscles. This process checks that the wings are in good working order and warms the beetle's muscles for the flight ahead. When the warm-up is finished, the beetle is ready to go.

3 A black-tipped soldier beetle (*Rhagonycha fulva*) positions itself for take-off like a plane taxiing down a runway. It finds a breezy spot by climbing a tall plant stem. Then it balances its body on top. In this exposed place, the wind may carry it away as it raises its wings. If not, the beetle will launch itself by leaping into the air.

# Beetles in Flight

**4** A cockchafer manoeuvres between plant stems. Its wing cases help to provide the lift it needs to remain airborne. Long rear wings provide flapping power to propel the beetle through the air. Cockchafers are clumsy fliers and sometimes stray into houses on dark evenings, drawn by the light. Indoors, the beetle may crash into objects in the unfamiliar setting, but it is so well armoured that it is rarely hurt.

**5** A freeze-frame photograph shows the flapping wing movements of a *Pectocera fortunei* beetle in mid-flight. These small, light beetles find it fairly easy to stay airborne. However, their small size is a disadvantage in windy conditions, when they are sometimes blown off course.

**6** A cockchafer prepares to land on an oak leaf. The beetle's rear wings are angled downwards to help it to lose height. As it comes in to land, the legs will move forward to take the beetle's weight on the leaf. The veins that strengthen the delicate rear wings can be clearly seen in this picture.

◀ **SPINY SENSORS**
Root-borer beetles (*Prionus coriarius*) have long, curving antennae. The antennae are covered with patterns of tiny hairs. Each hair is attached to a nerve that sends signals to the insect's brain when the hair is moved.

▲ **BRANCHING ANTENNAE**
This unusual beetle from Central America has branched antennae that look like the antlers of a stag. The branches are usually held closed, but the insect can also fan them out to pick up distant smells on the wind, such as the scent of a faraway mate. Smells such as these would be far too faint for humans to detect.

# Senses

Beetles and bugs have keen senses, but they do not sense the world in the same way that humans do. Most beetles and bugs have good eyesight and a keen sense of smell, but no sense of hearing. The main sense organs are on the head.

Most beetles and bugs have two large eyes, called compound eyes because they are made up of many tiny lenses. These are particularly good at sensing movement. Some beetles and bugs also have simple, beadlike eyes on top of their heads, which are sensitive to light and dark.

The antennae are the main sense tools for most beetles and bugs. They are used for smelling and feeling, and in some species for hearing and tasting, too. Antennae come in various shapes – some beetles and bugs have special feelers called palps on their mouthparts.

Sensitive hairs all over the insects' bodies pick up tiny currents in the air, which may alert them to enemies nearby.

**SMELL AND TOUCH ▶**
Longhorn beetles (Cerambycidae) are named after their long antennae. An insect's antennae are sometimes called its "feelers".

The term is rather misleading – the antennae *are* used for feeling, but their main function is to pick up scents. Long antennae like the longhorn beetle's are especially sensitive to smell and touch.

464

◄ **ELBOW-SHAPED**

The weevil's antennae are found on its long nose. Many weevils have jointed antennae, which bend in the middle like a human arm at the elbow. Some have special organs at the base of their antennae, which vibrate to sound and act as ears. This brush-snouted weevil (*Rhina tarbirostris*) has a bushy "beard" of long, sensitive hairs on its snout.

**COMPOUND EYES ►**

The huge eyes of the harlequin beetle (*Acrocinus longimanus*) cover its head. Only the area from which its antennae sprout remains uncovered. Each compound eye is made up of hundreds of tiny lenses. Scientists believe that the signals from each lens build up to create one large picture. Even so, scientists are not sure what beetles and bugs see.

◄ **TINY LENSES**

A close-up of a beetle's compound eye shows that it is made up of many tiny facets, each of which points in a slightly different direction. Each facet is made up of a lens at the surface and a second lens inside. The lenses focus light down a central structure inside the eye, called the rhabdome, on to a bundle of nerve fibres, which are behind the eye. The nerve fibres then send messages to the brain. The hundreds of tiny lenses probably do not create the detailed, focused image produced by the human eye. However, they can pick up colours and shapes and are very good at detecting tiny movements.

# Plant-eaters and Pests

Beetles and bugs do not always eat the same food throughout their lives. Larvae often eat very different foods from their parents. Some adult beetles and bugs do not feed at all, and instead put all their energy into finding a mate and reproducing very quickly.

Most bugs and some beetles are herbivores. Different species feed on the leaves, buds, seeds and roots of plants, on tree wood or on fungi. Many plant-eaters become pests when they feed on cultivated plants or crops. Other beetles and bugs are carnivores, or recycle waste by consuming dead plants or animals. Others nibble things that humans would not consider edible, such as clothes, woollen carpets, wooden furniture and even animal dung.

▲ **TUNNEL-EATERS**
This tree has been eaten by bark beetles (Scolytidae). Females lay their eggs under tree bark. When the young hatch, each eats its way through the wood to create a long, narrow tunnel just wide enough to squeeze through.

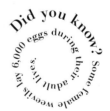

Did you know? Some female weevils lay 6,000 eggs during their adult lives.

squash bug
(*Coreus marginatus*)

◀ **SQUASH-LOVERS**
Squash bugs are named after their favourite food. The squash family includes courgettes (zucchini) and pumpkins. This bug is about to nibble a courgette flower bud. Most squash bugs are green or brown in colour. They feed on the green parts of squash plants, and also on the seeds. This harms future crops. The insects are a pest in the U.S.A.

## ▲ A PLAGUE OF APHIDS

Aphids are small, soft-bodied bugs. They use their sharp, beak-like mouths to pierce the stems and veins of plants and suck out the sap inside. These insects breed very quickly in warm weather.

## ▲ BEETLE ATTACK

Colorado potato beetles (*Leptinotarsa decemlineata*) are high on the list of dangerous insects in many countries. The beetles originally came from the western United States, where they ate the leaves of local plants. When European settlers came and cultivated potatoes, the beetles ate the crop and did great damage. Colorado potato beetles later spread to become a major pest in Europe, but are now controlled by pesticides.

## ▲ SCALY FEEDERS

Most female scale insects (Coccoidae family) have neither legs nor wings, but they can be identified as bugs from the way in which their mouth is formed. Scale insects are usually well camouflaged, but the species shown here can be seen clearly. They are feeding on a juicy melon by piercing the skin and sucking up the sap.

## ▲ THE EVIL WEEVIL

These grains of wheat have been infested by grain weevils (*Sitophilus zeamais*). The adult weevils bore through the grain's hard case with their long snouts to reach the soft kernel inside. Females lay their eggs inside the kernels. Then, when the young hatch, they can feed in safety.

467

# Scavengers and Hunters

**ground beetle**
*(Lorica pilicornis)*

▲ **SPEEDY HUNTER**
A ground beetle feeds on a juicy worm it has caught. Ground beetles are a large family of beetles, with over 20,000 species. Many species cannot fly, hence their name. However, most ground beetles are fast runners. The beetle uses its speed to overtake its fleeing victim. Once trapped, the victim is firmly grabbed in the beetle's powerful jaws.

Many beetles and some bugs are carnivores (meat-eaters). Some hunt and kill live prey, others prefer their meat dead. Called scavengers, they feed on the remains of animals. Some other beetles and bugs are parasites that live on larger animals and eat their flesh, or drink their blood, without killing them.

Most predator beetles and bugs hunt fellow insects or other small creatures such as millipedes. Some tackle larger game, such as fish, tadpoles, frogs, snails and worms. Beetles and bugs use a variety of different tricks and techniques to catch and overpower their prey. Most beetles seize their victims in their jaws, and crush or crunch them up to kill them. Bugs suck their victims' juices from their bodies while they are still alive.

◄ **GONE FISHING**
Pan-temperate diving beetles (*Dytiscus marginalis*) are fierce aquatic hunters. They hunt down fish, tadpoles, newts and other creatures that live in ponds and streams. This beetle has caught a stickleback. It grabs the fish in its jaws, then injects it with digestive juices that dissolve the fish's flesh. When the victim finally stops struggling and dies, the beetle begins to feed.

## Famous Victim

*Charles Darwin (1809–82) was a British naturalist who first developed the theory of evolution – the idea that species develop over time to fit their environment. Darwin's theory was inspired by a trip to South America to study wildlife. On returning to Britain, Darwin fell victim to a mysterious illness, which weakened him for the rest of his life. Some historians believe that he was bitten by a South American assassin bug that carried a dangerous disease.*

### ▲ VAMPIRE BEETLE

Most assassin bugs (Reduviidae) are killers. Many species hunt small creatures and suck their juices dry. Some are parasites. The species above feeds on humans by injecting their skin with a painkiller so that it can feast unnoticed.

### EATEN ALIVE ▶

This shield bug *(Palomena prasina)* has caught a caterpillar. With a victim in its clutches, it uses its curving mouthparts to suck its prey dry. Most types of shield bugs are plant-eaters, but some hunt living creatures. The bugs use their front legs to hold their victims steady while they feast on them.

**Did you know?** Great diving beetles store air under their wings when they dive.

### ◀ NO ESCAPE

A snail-hunter beetle *(Calosoma)* tackles a small snail. To protect itself, the snail retreats into its shell and seals the opening with slime. In response, the beetle squirts a liquid into the shell to dissolve the slime and kill the snail.

# Natural Disguises

Many beetles and bugs have colours and patterns on their bodies that disguise them in the natural world. Such disguises are called camouflage and hide the insects from their predators. Various species imitate natural objects, including sticks, grass, seeds, bark and thorns. Others are disguised as unpleasant objects, such as animal droppings, which predators avoid when looking for food.

Some beetles and bugs have another clever way of surviving – they mimic the colour or shape of insects such as wasps and ants that are poisonous or can sting. Predators recognize and avoid the warning signs of the harmless imitators, mistaking them for the dangerous insects.

**▲ BLADERUNNER**
The top of this grass stem is actually a damsel bug (*Stenodema laengatum*) posing as a blade of grass. This bug's camouflage helps it to hide from its enemies – *and* sneak up on its prey, for the damsel bug is also a fierce predator.

wasp beetle
(*Clytus arietis*)

**▲ STRIPY WARNING**
This beetle's bold black-and-yellow stripes suggest it is a wasp, armed with a painful sting. Although the insect is harmless, the warning colours are enough to put most predators off.

**UNDER COVER ▶**
A group of female scale insects (Coccoidae family) feed on a bay tree, disguised by their camouflage. The bugs also produce a bad-tasting waxy white substance around their bodies. In this way, they can feed without being attacked by their enemies.

## THORNY PROBLEM ▶

The sharp thorns on this twig look like part of the plant. They are, in fact, thorn bugs (*Umbonia crassicornus*). Each bug perfects its disguise by pointing in the same direction as the others on the twig. If they pointed in different directions, the bugs would look less like part of the plant. Even if a predator does spot the bugs, their prickly spines deter any passing enemy.

## ◀ ANT COSTUME

This treehopper (*Cyphonia clavata*) from the West Indies is a master of disguise. Its green body and transparent wings make it almost invisible when feeding on leaves. In addition, it has an amazing black ant disguise on its back, which can be seen clearly by predators. True ants are armed with biting jaws and can also squirt stinging acid at their enemies. Predators will avoid them at all costs, and so the insect's clever disguise allows it to feed without being disturbed.

## EYE SPY ▶

Click beetles have mottled colours that help them to blend in with grass or tree bark. The big-eyed click beetle (*Alaus oculatus*, *right*) has two large eyespots on its thorax. These resemble the eyes of a large predator, such as an owl. These frightening markings will be enough to stop any predatory bird from attacking the beetle.

*471*

# The Life Cycle of Beetles

Beetles and bugs have different life cycles. During their lives, beetles pass through four stages. From eggs, they hatch into larvae (young) called grubs. The grubs do not look like their parents. Some have legs, but many look like long, pale worms. They all live in different places from the adults and eat different food.

Beetle larvae are hungry feeders. They feed, grow and moult their skins several times, but do not change form or grow wings. When the larva is fully grown, it develops a hard case and enters a resting stage, called a pupa. Inside the case, the grub's body is totally dissolved and then rebuilt. It emerges from its pupa as a winged adult. This amazing process is called complete metamorphosis. The word "metamorphosis" means transformation.

### ▲ LAYING EGGS

A female fire-coloured beetle (*Pyrochroa coccinea*) lays its eggs in dead wood. The hard tip of the beetle's abdomen pierces the wood to lay the eggs inside. When the eggs hatch, the log provides the larvae with a hiding place. They feast on the timber until they are fully grown.

### ◄ THE FOUR STAGES

There are four stages in a beetle's life cycle. It begins life as an egg (1), then becomes a larva or grub (2). The full-grown larva then becomes a pupa (3) before it reaches adulthood (4). At each stage, the beetle's appearance is almost totally different from the last stage. In a way, a developing beetle is several animals in one. When the beetle finally emerges from its pupa as an adult, it is ready to breed, and so the life cycle can begin again.

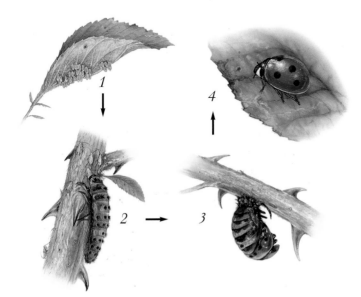

### ◀ BEETLE EGGS

The female ladybird (ladybug) glues her eggs on to leaves so that they stand on end. Beetle eggs are generally rounded or oval. They are usually yellow, green or black for camouflage. Most eggs are laid in spring or summer, and most hatch between one week and one month later. Some eggs are laid in autumn and hatch the following spring. They take longer to hatch because of the cooler conditions.

### LARVA ▶

This cockchafer larva (*Melolontha melolontha*) looks nothing like the adult. Its long, fat body is very different from the adult's rounded shape. However, unlike many beetle grubs, it does have legs. The larva has no compound eyes or long antennae. Nor does it have wings, but moves about by wriggling its way through the soil.

### ◀ PUPA

When a beetle grub is fully grown, it attaches itself to a plant stem or hides underground. Then it develops a hard outer case to become a pupa. Unlike the grub, the pupa doesn't feed or move much. It looks dead, but inside its hard case, an amazing change is taking place. The insect's body breaks down into a kind of soup, and is reshaped into an adult beetle.

### ADULT FORM ▶

An adult seven-spotted ladybird (ladybug) (*Coccinella septempunctata*) struggles out of its pupa case. It emerges complete with long, jointed legs, wings and antennae. Its yellow wing cases will develop spots after just a few hours. Some beetles spend only a week as pupae before emerging as fully grown adults. Others pass the whole winter in the resting stage, waiting to emerge until the following spring.

*473*

# The Life Cycle of Bugs

Bugs develop in a different way from beetles. Most bugs hatch from eggs laid by females after mating. Newly hatched bugs are called nymphs and look like tiny adults, but they are wingless. Nymphs often eat the same food and live in the same places as their parents.

Unlike human skin, an insect's exoskeleton is not stretchy. Nymphs are hungry eaters, and as they feed and grow, their hard skins become too tight and must be shed several times. This process is called moulting. The nymphs then develop new skins, inside which there is space to grow. As they grow, they gradually sprout wings. After a final moult, the bugs emerge as winged adults. This process is called incomplete metamorphosis because, unlike beetles, bugs do not go through the pupa stage and totally rebuild their bodies.

▲ BUG EGGS
Like other young insects, most bugs start out as eggs. These little yellow balls are shield bug eggs (*Eysarcoris fabricii*). They are all at various stages of development. The yellow eggs on the left are more developed than the paler eggs on the right, and will soon hatch into young.

Did you know? In summer, female aphids give birth to up to 50 young in a week.

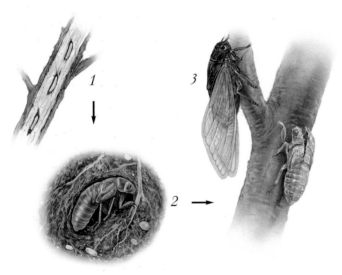

◄ THE THREE STAGES
There are three different stages in a bug's life. The first stage is the egg (1), from which the bug hatches as a nymph (2). The nymph gradually grows and moults a number of times. At each moult it becomes more like an adult. The wing buds appear after several moults, and gradually lengthen as the nymph reaches adulthood (3).

### EASY TARGET ▶

This young shield bug looks like its parents, but it is wingless and cannot fly. After moulting, the nymph has no hard skin to protect it and is extremely vulnerable. At this stage, young bugs are "sitting ducks", and many fall victim to predators such as lizards and birds. After moulting, the new exoskeleton hardens within just a few hours. With luck, this new layer will protect the young bug for long enough for it to reach adulthood.

### ◀ FOAMY HIDEOUT

Some nymphs have special ways of avoiding predators. This froghopper nymph (*Philaemus spumarius*) hides inside the unpleasant-looking foam behind it, known as "spittle". The bug produces the froth itself by giving off a sticky liquid, which it blows into a foam. The spittle makes a good hiding place from predators, and also screens the bug from the sun.

### YOUNG HUNTER ▶

Just a few hours after hatching, a young water strider (*Gerris najas*, right) begins to live and feed on the water's surface, just like its parents. A water strider's feet are covered in dense water-repellent hair, which allows it to walk on the surface of the water. Water striders are expert predators, catching other water creatures and then feeding by sucking out the victims' juices with their long feeding tubes.

### ◀ BREEDING WITHOUT MALES

In autumn, male and female aphids breed and lay eggs in the normal way. In summer, however, female aphids can reproduce without males, and give birth to live offspring without mating or even laying eggs. This aphid (*left*) is giving birth to its fully formed young. This amazing process is called parthenogenesis (meaning virgin birth). The babies grow up quickly, and can themselves breed after just one week.

# Homes and Habitats

Around the world, beetles and bugs are found in all sorts of different habitats. Most live in hot, tropical regions or in mild, temperate areas. Many beetles and bugs are found in places that have moderate or heavy rainfall, but some tough species manage to live in deserts. Others can survive on snow-capped mountains or frozen ice fields, in caves, sewers and even hot springs.

Beetles and bugs that live in very cold or very hot places must be able to cope with extreme temperatures. Many survive the harsh weather as pupae, or as eggs in the soil. In deserts, most species are active at night, when the air is cooler. The toughest species can go for long periods without food or even water. These insects are small enough to shelter from storms or predators in tiny nooks and crannies.

▲ **PARASITES**
Bedbugs (*Cimex lectularius*) are parasites that live and feed on warm-blooded animals. Some species suck human blood. Bedbugs that infest birds and furry mammals live in their nests, or among their feathers or hair. Kept warm by their host animal, some bedbugs can even survive in cold places such as the Arctic.

Did you know? Water boatmen can fly many km/ miles to find a new home.

◄ **UPSIDE-DOWN WORLD**
Back swimmers (*Notonecta maculata*) live upside down in water. The bug hangs just below the water surface, and uses its oarlike legs to move about, similar to rowing. Like many bugs that live in water, the boatman is a hunter. It grabs small creatures that have fallen into the water, and sucks their juices.

### LONG LIMBS ▶

This stilt-legged bug (Berytidae) lives in caves
in the Caribbean. Its long, thin legs and antennae
help it to feel its way in the dark. The legs and
antennae are also covered with hairs that can
detect the slightest air currents, alerting the
bug to the presence of other animals.

### ◀ DESERT SURVIVOR

The fog-basking beetle (*Onymachris unguicularis*)
lives in the Namib Desert, in southern Africa.
This beetle has an ingenious way of drinking.
When fog and mist swirl over the dunes, it does
a handstand and points its abdomen in the air.
Moisture gathers on its body, then trickles down
special grooves on its back into its waiting mouth.

### SURVIVING IN CAVES ▶

This beetle (*Aphaenops*) lives in caves high in
the Pyrenees Mountains, between France and
Spain. Its body is not well camouflaged, but in
the darkness of the caves, disguise is not
important. Scientists believe some cave-
dwelling species developed from beetles that
first lived in the caves during the last Ice Age,
about a million years ago.

### ◀ DUNE DWELLER

The dune beetle (*Onymacris bicolor*) lives in the
deserts of southern Africa. It is one of the few white
beetles. White reflects the rays of the sun and helps
to keep the insect cool. The pale colour also blends
in well with the sand where it lives, which helps it to
hide from predators. The beetle's elytra (wing cases)
are hard and close-fitting, and so help to conserve (keep)
precious body moisture in this dry region. Long legs raise
the beetle's body above the burning desert sand.

477

# SPIDERS

Spiders come in all shapes and sizes, and
are feared and revered across the world.
Although there are over 35,000 different
known species, relatively little is known
about these wonderful weavers. It is
thought that there may actually be as
many as 70,000 different varieties,
of which only 30 are poisonous.

*Author*: Barbara Taylor
*Consultant*: John Michaels

# Introducing Spiders

Spiders are some of the most feared and least
understood creatures in the animal world. These
hairy hunters are famous for spinning silk and
giving a poisonous bite. There are around 35,000
known species (types) of spider, with probably
another 35,000 waiting to be discovered. Only
about 30 species, however, are dangerous to
people. Spiders are very useful to humans,
because they eat insect pests and keep their
numbers down. Spiders live
nearly everywhere, from
forests, deserts and grasslands,
to caves, ships and in our homes.
Some spin webs to catch their prey
while others leap out from a hiding
place or stalk their meals like tigers.
There are even spiders that
fish for their
supper and
one that lives in an
underwater air bubble.

The front part of
a spider is a joined
head and chest called
the cephalothorax.
The body is covered
by a tough skin
called an exoskeleton.
The shieldlike plate
on the top of the
cephalothorax is
called the carapace.

Spiders
use palps
for holding
food and as
feelers.

The chelicerae
(jaws) are used to
bite and crush prey.
Each ends in a fang
that injects poison.

A spider's eight
hollow legs are
joined to the
cephalothorax.

◄ WHAT
IS A SPIDER?
Spiders are often
confused with insects,
but they belong to a
completely different group.
A spider has eight legs, but an
insect has six. Its body has two
parts while an insect's has three.
Insects have antennae and many
have wings, but spiders do not.

The abdomen is the
rear part of a spider.
It is covered by soft,
stretchy skin.

Silk is spun by
organs called
spinnerets at
the back of
the abdomen.

## WEB WEAVERS ▶

About half of all spiders spin webs. They know how to do this by instinct from birth, without being taught. Many spiders build a new web each night. They build webs to catch prey. Spiders have a good sense of touch and can quickly tell if anything is caught in the web.

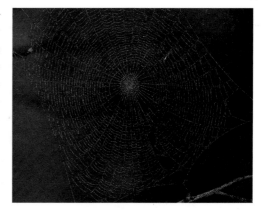

Bright colours help to conceal this spider among flowers.

## ▲ SPIDER SHAPES AND COLOURS

The triangular spider (*Arcys*) is named after its brightly coloured abdomen, which is shaped like a triangle. Its colour and shape help it to hide in wait for prey on leaves and flowers. Other spiders use bright colours to warn their enemies that they taste bad.

*Arachne's Tale*
*A Greek legend tells of Arachne, a girl who was very skilled at weaving. The goddess Athene challenged her to a contest, which Arachne won. The goddess became so angry that Arachne killed herself. Athene was sorry and turned the girl into a spider so she could spin forever. Arachnid is the scientific name for spiders, named after Arachne.*

## ◀ MALES AND FEMALES

Female spiders are usually bigger than the males and not so colourful, though this female *Nephila* spider is boldly marked. The male at the top of the picture is only one-fifth of her size.

Did you know?
All spiders are carnivores (meat-eaters) and many are cannibals.

# Spider Families

To help them study spiders, scientists divide
the 35,000 known species into three groups,
known as suborders. The three groups are:
araneomorphs (true spiders), mygalomorphs
(tarantulas, purse-web spiders and trapdoor
spiders) and the rare liphistiomorphs
(giant trapdoor spiders). Most spiders are
araneomorphs, with jaws that close together
sideways. These groups are further divided
into 105 families. Spiders are put in families
according to such things as the arrangement
of their eyes, their silk-making glands or the
number of claws on their feet. Some of the
larger families, as well as the rarest, are
shown here.

**giant trapdoor spider**
(*Liphistius desultor*)

### ▲ GIANT TRAPDOOR SPIDERS

The Liphistiomorphs are rare
spiders that live in South-east Asia
and Japan. There are about 20
different species. They live in
burrows with trapdoor entrances.
These very primitive spiders have
bands across their abdomens and
may look more like spiders that
lived millions of years ago.

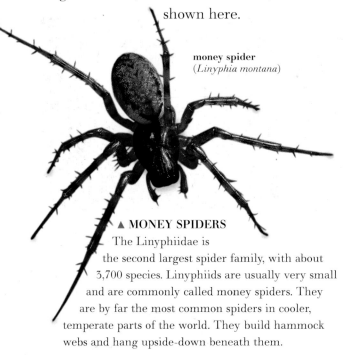

**money spider**
(*Linyphia montana*)

### ▲ MONEY SPIDERS

The Linyphiidae is
the second largest spider family, with about
3,700 species. Linyphiids are usually very small
and are commonly called money spiders. They
are by far the most common spiders in cooler,
temperate parts of the world. They build hammock
webs and hang upside-down beneath them.

### ▲ ORB-WEB SPIDERS

The main family of orb-weavers
is the Araneidae, with about 2,600
species. A typical member is this
Jamaican orb-weaver (*Argiope*).
It has a stout body with a rounded
abdomen and sits in the centre of
its circular web. Garden spiders
belong to this family.

## HUNTSMAN SPIDERS ▶

The Sparassidae (also called Heteropodidae) huntsman spiders are a family of about 1,000 species. Most live in tropical regions where they are sometimes called giant crab spiders. The Australian huntsman is one of its largest members with the body (excluding legs) measuring 3cm/1¼in. Some species of this family have been discovered in crates of bananas.

**Australian Huntsman**
*(Isopeda)*

*Classification Chart*

| Kingdom | **Animalia** (all animals) |
|---|---|
| Phylum | **Arthropoda** (animals with exoskeletons and jointed legs) |
| Class | **Arachnida** (arthropods with eight legs) |
| Order | **Araneae** (spiders) |
| Suborder | **Araneomorphae** (true spiders) |
| Family | **Theridiidae** (comb-footed spiders) |
| Genus | ***Latrodectus*** (widow spiders) |
| Species | ***Mactans*** (black widow spider) |

### ◀ SPIDER NAMES

Scientists classify (group) every spider and give it a Latin name. This chart shows how the black widow spider is classified. Few spiders have common names and these vary from country to country. Their Latin name, however, stays the same all over the world.

*Did you know? The first spiders lived about 400 million years ago.*

**black spotted jumper**
*(Acragus)*

### ◀ JUMPING SPIDERS

The world's largest spider family is the Salticidae, containing more than 4,000 species of jumping spiders. These small, active daylight hunters have large front eyes and an amazing ability to stalk and jump on prey. They mostly live in tropical areas and many are brightly coloured.

### ▲ CRAB SPIDERS

Another very large family is the Thomisidae, with about 3,000 species of crab spiders. Crab spiders are found all over the world. They do not usually build webs and many sit waiting on flowers or leaves to ambush prey. They often rely on good camouflage to blend in with their surroundings and avoid predators.

*483*

# Shapes and Sizes

Can you believe that there are spiders as big as dinner plates? The world's biggest spider, the goliath tarantula of South America, is this big. Yet the smallest spider is only the size of a full stop. Apart from size, spiders also vary a great deal in their appearance. Many are an inconspicuous dull brown or grey, while others are striking yellows, reds and oranges. Some spiders have short, wide bodies, while others are long, thin and skinny. There are round spiders, flat spiders and spiders with spines, warts and horns. A few spiders even look like ants, wasps or bird droppings!

### ▲ FLOWER SPIDERS

Using its shape and colour to hide on a flower, the flower spider (*Misumena vatia*) waits to ambush a visiting insect. This spider is one of a large family of crab spiders, so named because most of them have a shape similar to crabs.

**red-legged widow**
(*Latrodectus bishopi*)

Widow spiders often have bold black and red colouring.

round, shiny abdomen

Bristles on the back legs give the name comb-footed spider.

### ▲ SPINY SPIDERS

Some spiders have flat abdomens with sharp spines sticking out. This kite spider (*Gasteracantha*) has spines that look like horns. No one knows what these strange spines are for, but they may make it difficult for predators to hold or swallow the spider.

### ▲ GRAPE SPIDERS

Several kinds of widow spiders live in areas where grapes are grown. The females tend to have round abdomens, like grapes. Some of the most poisonous spiders belong to this group.

484

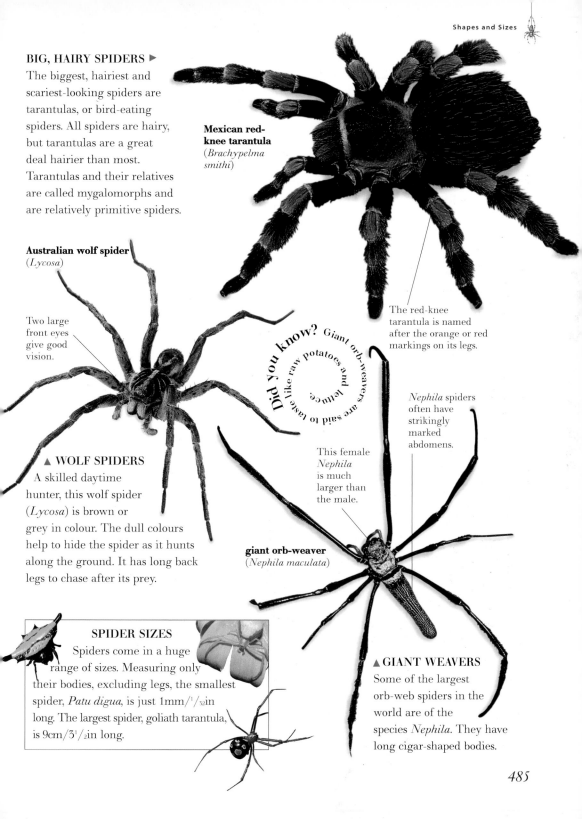

## BIG, HAIRY SPIDERS ▶

The biggest, hairiest and
scariest-looking spiders are
tarantulas, or bird-eating
spiders. All spiders are hairy,
but tarantulas are a great
deal hairier than most.
Tarantulas and their relatives
are called mygalomorphs and
are relatively primitive spiders.

**Mexican red-
knee tarantula**
(*Brachypelma
smithi*)

The red-knee
tarantula is named
after the orange or red
markings on its legs.

**Australian wolf spider**
(*Lycosa*)

Two large
front eyes
give good
vision.

**Did you know?** Giant orb-weavers are said to taste like raw potatoes and lettuce.

## ▲ WOLF SPIDERS

A skilled daytime
hunter, this wolf spider
(*Lycosa*) is brown or
grey in colour. The dull colours
help to hide the spider as it hunts
along the ground. It has long back
legs to chase after its prey.

*Nephila* spiders
often have
strikingly
marked
abdomens.

This female
*Nephila*
is much
larger than
the male.

**giant orb-weaver**
(*Nephila maculata*)

### SPIDER SIZES

Spiders come in a huge
range of sizes. Measuring only
their bodies, excluding legs, the smallest
spider, *Patu digua*, is just 1mm/$^1/_{32}$in
long. The largest spider, goliath tarantula,
is 9cm/3$^1/_2$in long.

## ▲ GIANT WEAVERS

Some of the largest
orb-web spiders in the
world are of the
species *Nephila*. They have
long cigar-shaped bodies.

485

# How Spiders Work

From the outside, a spider's body is very different from ours. It has a hard outer skeleton, called an exoskeleton, and legs that have many joints. It has eyes and a mouth, but no ears, nose or tongue. Instead, it relies on a variety of hairs and bristles to touch, taste and hear things, and it smells things with microscopic pores on its feet. Inside, a spider has many features common to other animals, such as blood, nerves, a brain and a digestive system. It also has special glands for spinning silk and for making and storing poison.

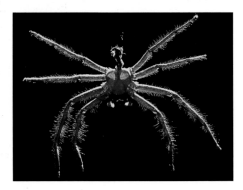

▲ **SPIDER SKIN**

A spider's exoskeleton protects its body like a suit of armour. It is made of a stiff material called chitin. A waxy layer helps to make it waterproof. The exoskeleton cannot stretch as the spider grows so must be shed from time to time. The old skin of a huntsman spider (*Isopeda*) is shown here.

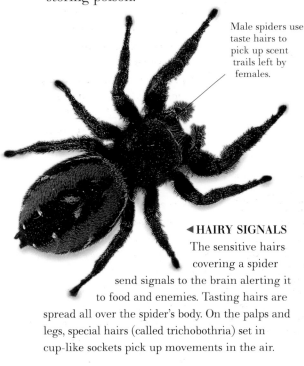

Male spiders use taste hairs to pick up scent trails left by females.

◀ **HAIRY SIGNALS**

The sensitive hairs covering a spider send signals to the brain alerting it to food and enemies. Tasting hairs are spread all over the spider's body. On the palps and legs, special hairs (called trichobothria) set in cup-like sockets pick up movements in the air.

▲ **LEG SENSES**

A green orb-weaver (*Araniella cucurbitina*) pounces on a fly. Spiders use special slits on their bodies to detect when an insect is trapped in their webs. These slits (called lyriform organs) pick up vibrations caused by a struggling insect. Nerve endings in the slits send signals to the spider's brain.

## SPIDER POISON ▶

A spider is a delicate creature compared to the prey it catches. By using poison, a spider can kill its prey before the prey has a chance to harm its attacker. Spiders have two poison sacs, one for each fang. Bands of muscle around the sacs squeeze the poison down tubes in the fangs and out of a small opening in the end.

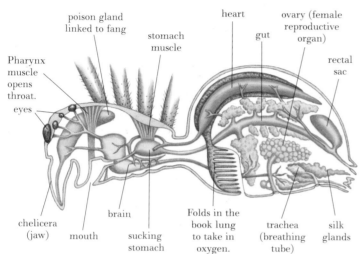

poison gland linked to fang
stomach muscle
heart
gut
ovary (female reproductive organ)
rectal sac
Pharynx muscle opens throat.
eyes
chelicera (jaw)
brain
mouth
sucking stomach
Folds in the book lung to take in oxygen.
trachea (breathing tube)
silk glands

## ◀ INSIDE A SPIDER

The front part of a spider, the cephalothorax, contains the brain, poison glands, stomach and muscles. The abdomen contains the heart, lungs, breathing tubes, gut, waste disposal system, silk glands and reproductive organs. A spider's stomach works like a pump, stretching wide to pull in food that has been mashed to a soupy pulp. The heart pumps blood around the body.

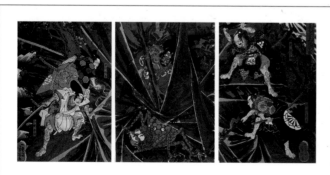

*Raiko and the Earth Spider*
*People have regarded spiders as dangerous, magical animals for thousands of years. This Japanese print from the 1830s shows the legendary warrior Yorimitsu (also known as Raiko) and his followers slaying the fearsome Earth Spider.*

# On the Move

Have you ever seen a spider scuttle swiftly away?
Spiders sometimes move quickly, but they cannot
keep going for long. Their breathing system is not
very efficient so they are soon out of
breath. Spiders can walk, run, jump, climb and
hang upside down. Each spider's leg has seven
sections. The legs are powered by sets of muscles
and blood pressure. At the end of each leg are
two or three sharp claws for gripping
surfaces. Spiders that spin webs have a special
claw to help them hold on to their webs. Hunting
spiders have dense tufts of hair between the claws
for gripping smooth surfaces and for holding prey.

▲ **AERONAUT**
Many young or
small spiders drift
through the air on
strands of silk. Spiders
carried away on warm air
currents use this method
to find new places to live.

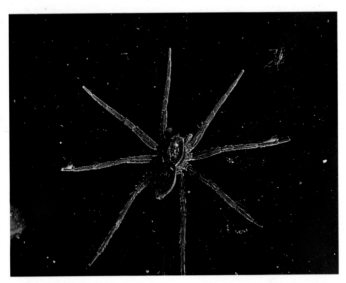

▲ **WATER WALKER**
The fishing spider (*Dolomedes fimbriatus*) is also called the raft
or swamp spider. It floats on the surface skin of water. Its long
legs spread its weight over the surface so it does not sink. Little
dips form in the stretchy skin of the water around each leg tip.

▲ **SAFETY LINE**
This garden spider (*Araneus*)
is climbing up a silk dragline.
Spiders drop down these lines
if they are disturbed. They
pay off the line as they go,
moving very quickly. As they
fall, spiders pull in their legs,
making them harder to see.

## ▲ SPIDER LEGS

Muscles in the legs of this trapdoor spider (*Aname*) bend the joints like we bend our knees. To stretch out the legs, however, the spider has to pump blood into them. If a spider is hurt and bleeds, it cannot escape from enemies.

## ▲ CHAMPION JUMPERS

Jumping spiders are champions of the long jump. They secure themselves with a safety line before they leap. Some species can leap more than 40 times the length of their own bodies.

## ▼ CLAWED FEET

Two toothed claws on the ends of a spider's feet enable it to grip surfaces as it walks. Web-building spiders have a third, middle claw that hooks over the silk lines of the web and holds the silk against barbed hairs. This allows the spider to grip the smooth, dry silk of its web without falling or slipping.

scopulate pad

toothed claw

middle hook

barbed hair

## ▲ HAIRY FEET

Many hunting spiders have dense tufts of short hairs called scopulae between the claws. The end of each hair is split into many tiny hairs a bit like a brush. These hairs pull up some of the moisture coating most surfaces, gluing the spider's leg down. Spiders with these feet can climb up smooth surfaces such as glass.

489

# Spider Eyes

Spiders have poor eyesight and rely mainly on scents and vibrations to give them information about their surroundings. Even spiders with good eyesight, such as the jumping spiders, can see only up to 0.3m/1ft away. Most spiders have eight eyes arranged in two or three rows. The eyes are pearly or dark and are usually protected by several bristles. Spider eyes are called ocelli and are of two types, main and secondary. Main eyes produce a focused image and help in pouncing on prey. Secondary eyes have light-sensitive cells to pick up movement from a distance.

## ▲ NO EYES

This cave spider (*Spelungula cavernicola*) has no need for eyes, because there is no light in the cave to enable the spider to see. Like many animals that live in the dark, it relies on other senses. It uses many sensitive hairs to find its way around, catch its prey, and avoid enemies.

## ◄ BIG EYES

A spider's main eyes are always the middle pair of eyes in the front row. In most spiders the main eyes are small, but this jumping spider has very well-developed main eyes, as this enlarged picture shows. They work like a telephoto lens on a camera. Inside, the large lens focuses light on to four layers of sensitive cells. The main eyes see clearly over a small area a few cm/in away and let the spider stalk and pounce when it gets close to its prey.

Did you know? A jumping spider's two big eyes are bigger than its brain.

Eyes arranged in a compact group.

### ▲ POOR VISION

Spiders that spend much of their time under stones or in burrows usually have small eyes. This trapdoor spider (*Aname*) has eight tiny eyes in a close group. Spiders that catch their prey in webs also have very poor eyesight. These spiders rely much more on their sense of touch than their eyesight. They use their legs to feel objects around them.

### ▲ EYES FOR HUNTING

The spiders with the best eyesight are active daylight hunters, such as this jumping spider. A jumping spider's eight eyes are usually arranged in three rows with four in the front, two in the middle, and two at the back. Lynx spiders and wolf spiders also have good eyesight.

### ▲ HUNTSMAN SPIDER

The giant huntsman (*Holconia immanis*) is an agile, night-time hunter. Most hunting spiders have fairly large front eyes to help them to find and pounce on prey. Secondary eyes help the hunters to see in three dimensions over a wider area. They detect changes in light and dark.

a wolf spider (family Lycosidae)

an orb-web spider (family Araneidae)

a woodlouse spider (family Dysderidae)

a jumping spider (family Salticidae)

### ▲ ALL TYPES OF EYES

The position and arrangement of a spider's eyes can be useful in telling which family it belongs to and how it catches food. Only a small number of spiders have six eyes or fewer. Many male money spiders have eyes on top of little lobes or turrets sticking up from the head.

# Spinning Silk

All spiders make silk. They pull the silk out of spinnerets on their abdomens, usually with their legs. The silk is a syrupy liquid when it first comes out, but pulling makes it harden. The more silk is pulled, the stronger it becomes. Some spider silk is stronger than steel wire of the same thickness. As well as being very strong, silk is incredibly thin, can stretch more than rubber and is stickier than tape. Spiders make up to six different types of silk in different glands in the abdomen. Each type of silk is used for a different purpose, from making webs to wrapping prey. Female spiders produce a special silk to encase eggs.

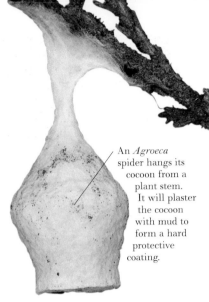

An *Agroeca* spider hangs its cocoon from a plant stem. It will plaster the cocoon with mud to form a hard protective coating.

▲ **EGG CASES**

Female spiders have an extra silk gland for making egg cases called cocoons. These protect the developing eggs.

***The Industrious Spider***
*Spiders have been admired for their tireless spinning for centuries. This picture was painted by the Italian artist Veronese in the 1500s. He wanted to depict the virtues of the great city of Venice, whose wealth was based on trade. To represent hard work and industry he painted this figure of a woman holding up a spider in its web.*

▲ **A SILKEN RETREAT**

Many spiders build silk shelters or nests. The tube-web spider (*Segestria florentina*) occupies a hole in the bark of a tree. Its tube-shaped retreat has a number of trip lines radiating out like the spokes of a wheel. If an insect trips over a line, the spider rushes out to grab its meal.

### ▲ STICKY SILK

Silk oozes out through a spider's spinnerets. Two or more kinds of silk can be spun at the same time. Orb-web spiders produce gummy silk to make their webs sticky.

### SPINNERETS ▶

A spider's spinnerets have many fine tubes on the end. The smaller tubes, or spools, produce finer silk for wrapping prey. Larger tubes, called spigots, produce coarser strands for webs.

Spinnerets vary in size and number.

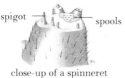

spigot    spools

close-up of a spinneret

### ▲ COMBING OUT SILK

This lace-weaver (*Amaurobius*) is using its back legs to comb out a special silk. It has an extra spinning organ (the cribellum) in front of its spinnerets that produces loops of very fine silk.

### ▲ FOOD PARCEL

A garden spider (*Araneus*) stops a grasshopper from escaping by wrapping it in silk. The prey is also paralysed by the spider's poisonous bite. Most spiders make silk for wrapping prey.

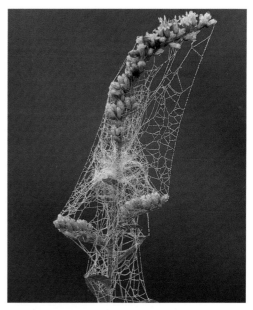

### ▲ VELCRO SILK

The lacy webs made by cribellate spiders contain tiny loops, like velcro, that catch on the hairs and bristles of insect prey. Combined in bands with normal silk, the fluffy cribellate silk stops insect prey from escaping.

493

# Catching Food

Only about half of all spiders spin webs to catch prey. Of the other half, some hide and surprise their victims with a sneak attack — crab spiders do this very well. Others, such as trapdoor spiders, set traps as well as ambushing prey. Many spiders, such as jumping spiders, are agile, fast-moving hunters that stalk their prey. Spiders are not usually very fussy about what they eat. Insects, such as grasshoppers, beetles, ants and bees are their main food, but some eat fish, while bigger spiders may catch mice and birds. Many spiders eat other spiders.

**▲ SILK TRAPS**

Orb webs are designed to catch insects up to about the size of the spiders that made them. This orb-web spider is eating a crane fly. The prey has been bitten and wrapped in silk, then cut free from the web and carried away to be eaten. Some insects, such as moths, manage to escape from webs. Smaller spiders will free large insects from their webs before they do too much damage.

empty shell of a partly eaten fly

Dead flies wrapped in silk are left hanging for eating later.

**◄ DAISY WEB**

In the centre of this oxeye daisy sits a green orb-web spider (*Araniella cucurbitina*). It has built its web over the middle of the daisy. Small flies, attracted to the flower, are trapped in the web. They end up as food for the spider who kills them, then crushes them to a pulp before sucking up a meal.

### WATER HUNTER ▶

This fishing spider (*Dolomedes*) has caught a blue damselfly. It lives in swamps and pools where it sits on the leaves of water plants. It spreads its legs on the water's surface to detect ripples from insects that fall into the water, then rushes out to grab them. Fish swimming in the water below are also caught by this hunting spider. The spider may even dabble its legs in the water to attract small fish towards its waiting fangs.

### ◀ HAIRY HUNTER

Tarantulas are voracious hunters, consuming birds, lizards, frogs, small snakes and even an occasional mouse, as shown in the photograph on the left. However, their diet consists primarily of insects, which they stalk at night by scent or by picking up vibrations with their sensitive hairs, and catch easily, due to their unusual speed. The tarantulas' bite releases an enzyme that "pre-digests" its prey, allowing the spider to suck in the resulting mush with the help of its powerful stomach muscles.

### ATHLETIC HUNTER ▶

Lynx spiders hunt their prey on plants. They sometimes jump from leaf to leaf after their prey, but at other times they sit and wait. The green lynx spider (*Peucetia*) is an athletic hunter with long spiny legs that enable it to leap easily from stem to stem. It often eats other spiders and is even a cannibal, eating members of its own species. This one has caught a termite.

# Moulting

Spiders do not grow gradually, like we do.
Instead they grow in a series of steps. At
each step, the spider grows a new outer
skin, or exoskeleton, under the old one
and moults (sheds) the old one. Lost or
damaged legs and other body parts can
be replaced during a moult. Small spiders
moult in a few hours, but larger spiders
may need several days. A young spider
moults about five to ten times as it grows
into an adult. A few spiders continue to
moult throughout their adult lives.

▲ **COLOUR CHANGE**
Adult spiders that have just moulted
are quite pale for a while and do not
show their true colours for a day or so.
The fangs of this newly moulted
tarantula have no colour as yet.

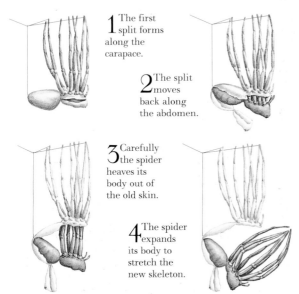

1 The first split forms along the carapace.

2 The split moves back along the abdomen.

3 Carefully the spider heaves its body out of the old skin.

4 The spider expands its body to stretch the new skeleton.

▲ **STAGES IN MOULTING**
The main stages in the moulting process of a spider
are shown above. It is a dangerous process. Legs can get
broken and spiders are vulnerable to enemies as they
moult, since they cannot defend themselves or run away.

▲ **THE OLD SKIN**
This is the old exoskeleton of a fishing
spider (*Dolomedes*). The piece at the top
is the lid of the carapace. The holes are
where the legs fitted inside the skin.

### HOW MANY MOULTS? ▶

This young red and white spider (*Enoplognatha ovata*) is in the middle of moulting. It is hiding under a leaf out of sight of enemies. A larger adult spider seems to have come to investigate. It is not until the final moult that a spider takes on its adult colours. Most spiders stop moulting when they become adults. Smaller species need fewer moults to reach adult size. Males also go through fewer moults than females because they are smaller when fully grown.

### ◀ MOULTING PROCESS

A tarantula pulls itself free of its old skin. Before a spider moults, it stops feeding and rests for a while. During this time, a new wrinkled exoskeleton forms underneath the old one and part of the old skin is absorbed back into the body to be recycled. The spider then pumps blood into the front of its body, making it swell and split the old skin, which is now very thin.

*Did you know? Spiders can grow new palps, fangs, and spinnerets when they moult.*

### A NEW SKIN ▶

This Chilean rose tarantula (*Grammostola cala*) moulted recently. Its new skin is bright and colourful. It looks very hairy because new hairs have replaced those that have been lost or damaged. When a spider first escapes from its old skin, it flexes its legs to make sure the joints stay supple. As the new skeleton dries out, it hardens. The skin on the abdomen stays fairly stretchy, so it can expand as the spider eats, or fills with eggs in females.

497

# Spiders Everywhere

From mountain tops, caves and deserts to forests, marshes and grasslands, there are few places on earth without spiders. Even remote islands are inhabited by spiders, perhaps blown there by the wind or carried on floating logs. Many spiders are quite at home in our houses, and some travel the world on cargo ships. Many spiders live on sewage, where there are plenty of flies for them to feed on. Spiders are not very common in watery places, however, since they cannot breathe underwater. There are also no spiders in Antarctica, although they do manage to live on the edge of the Arctic. To survive the winter in cool places, spiders may stay as eggs, hide away under grass, rocks or bark, or make nests together. Some even have a type of antifreeze to prevent their bodies from freezing.

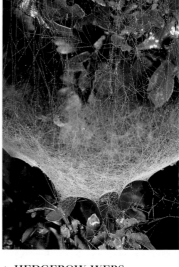

**▲ HEDGEROW WEBS**
One of the most common spiders on bushes and hedges in Europe and Asia is the hammock-web spider (*Linyphia triangularis*). One hedge may contain thousands of webs with their haphazard threads.

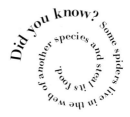

Did you know? Some spiders live in the web of another species and steal its food.

**◄ SPIDER IN THE SINK**
The spiders that people sometimes find in the sink or the bath are usually male house spiders (*Tegenaria*) that have fallen while searching for a mate. They cannot climb back up the smooth sides because they do not have gripping tufts of hair on their feet like hunting spiders.

## ▲ CAVE SPIDER

The cave orb-weaver (*Meta menardi*) almost always builds its web in very dark places, often suspended from the roof. It is found in caves, mines, hollow trees, railway tunnels, sewers, wells and the corners of outbuildings in Europe, Asia and North America.

## ▲ DESERT SPIDER

The main problem for desert spiders such as this white lady (*Leucorhestris arenicola*) is a lack of water. It hides away from the intense heat in a burrow beneath the sand and, in times of drought, may go into suspended animation. Desert spiders live in different places to avoid competition for food.

## ◄ SEASHORE SPIDER

This beach wolf spider (*Arctosa littoralis*) is well camouflaged on the sand. It lives in a very hostile place. Waves pound on the beach and shift the sand, there is little fresh water and the sun quickly dries everything out. It will wait to eat insects as they gather on seaweed, rocks, and plants growing along the edge of the shore.

## RAINFOREST SPIDER ►

The greatest variety of spiders is to be found in the rainforests of the tropics. Here the climate is warm all year round, and plenty of food is always available. This forest huntsman (*Pandercetes plumipes*) is well camouflaged against a tree trunk covered in lichen. To hide, it presses its body close against the tree. It lives in Malaysia where it is found in gardens as well as in the rainforest.

# GLOSSARY

**adaptation**
A change in a living thing to suit a new set of conditions. This change helps the animal (or plant) to survive in its environment.

**aestivation**
A period of rest during heat and drought that is similar to hibernation.

**afterbirth**
Any birth membranes and other tissues discarded or discharged during the third period of labour, after a baby has been born.

**albino**
An animal that has no colour on all or part of its body but belongs to a species that is usually coloured.

**algae**
A group of very simple plants, some of which are only the size of a single cell. Most types of algae live in water, but they also grow on damp soil and tree trunks.

**altitude**
The height of a place given in metres (or feet) above sea level.

**ambush**
When an animal conceals itself and waits for prey to walk past, before pouncing on it in a surprise attack.

**Antarctic**
The region around the South Pole and Southern Ocean, including the continent of Antarctica.

**antivenin**
A substance made from the blood of mammals and/or snake venom that is used to treat a snakebite.

**Arctic**
The region of Earth around the North Pole.

**artery**
A blood vessel that carries oxygenated blood away from the heart.

**bacteria**
A type of micro-organism – a living thing that is so miniscule that it cannot be seen by the living eye.

**baleen**
A tough and flexible material, which forms comb-like plates in the upper jaw of baleen whales in the place of teeth.

**billabong**
An Australian term for a branch of a river or stream that comes to a dead end in a stagnant pool or backwater.

**binocular vision**
The ability to see with both eyes at the same time .

**bioluminescence**
The production of light by living organisms.

**bladder**
Organ where waste is stored as urine in the body before being expelled through the urethra.

**blubber**
The layer of fatty tissue beneath the skin of sea mammals, such as whales, that acts as insulation against cold water.

**breed**
An animal that belongs to one species, but has definitive characteristics, such as colouring, body shape and coat markings.

**breeding season**
The time of year when pairs of animals of different genders come together to mate.

**bull**
The adult male of certain species, such as whales and elephants.

**calf**
The baby of certain species, such as whales and elephants.

**camouflage**
Colours or patterns on skin that allow animals to hide in their surroundings.

**canine**
A sharp, pointed tooth found in all carniverous animals that grips and pierces the skin of prey.

**cannibalism**
Animals eating others of their own kind.

**carcass**
The dead body of an animal.

**carnassial**
A strong, shearing tooth at the back of a carnivore's mouth.

**carnivore**
An animal that feeds partly or mainly on other animals.

**carrion**
The flesh of dead animals.

**cartilage**
The strong but flexible material from which the skeletons of sharks and rays are made, rather than the bone found in most other animals with backbones.

**classification**
Grouping of animals according to their similarities and differences, in order to study them.

**cloaca**
Combined opening of the end of the intestines, the reproductive system and the urinary system in reptiles, amphibians and birds.

**clutch**
The number of eggs laid by a female at one time.

**cold-blooded**
An animal whose temperature varies according to its surroundings.

**conservation**
Protecting living things so that they survive in the future.

**continent**
One of the seven main land masses on Earth. The continents are Europe, North America, South America, Asia, Africa, Australia and Antarctica.

**cow**
The name of an adult female of certain species, including whales and elephants.

**culling**
Legally killing animals when there are too many to survive in one area. The idea is that culling some animals will leave more food and space for the remaining animals and help them to survive.

**dentine**
A hard substance, also called ivory, which makes up the bulk of the teeth of animals with backbones.

**diaphragm**
A sheet of muscle separating the chest cavity from the abdominal cavity, the movement of which helps with breathing.

**diapsid**
A type of skull with two openings on either side, behind the eye socket.

**diet**
The usual types of food eaten by an animal.

**digestion**
The process of absorbing food into the stomach and bowels.

**digestive tract**
The long, winding tube running through an animal's body, in which food is digested and absorbed.

**digit**
Finger or toe at the end of an animal's limb.

**diurnal**
Active by day.

**DNA (deoxyribosenucleic acid)**
The genetic material inside the cells of most living organisms. It controls the characteristics that are passed from parents to their offspring.

**domestication**
The process of bringing an animal under human control.

**dominance**
A system between social animals, such as lions, in which one or a few animals rule the group.

**dominant animal**
An animal that leads others of its own species and to which other members defer.

**dormant**
When an animal lies motionless and inactive, as in sleep.

**drag**
The resistance to movement in water or air.

**drought**
A long period of dry weather when no rain falls.

**ecosystem**
A group of living things in an area that live together and interact with and depend on each other.

**ectotherm**
A cold-blooded animal.

**electrical field**
A zone surrounding an object, such as a muscle or nerve cell, that generates electricity.

**embryo**
The early stage of an animal before birth.

**endorphin**
A chemical produced by the brain that makes animals feel relaxed.

**endotherm**
A warm-blooded animal.

**environment**
The surroundings in which an organism lives. It includes animate (living) things – other animals and plants – and inanimate (non-living) things – such as stones, the air, temperature and light.

**epidermis**
The outer layer of the skin.

**Equator**
An imaginary line running around the centre of the Earth, separating north from south.

**estuary**
The tidal mouth of a large river.

**evolution**
The continual process of gradual development.

**evolve**
When an animal or plant species develops and changes over a long period of time.

**extinction**
When a whole species of animals or plants dies out completely.

**fang**
A long, pointed tooth which may be used to deliver venom.

**fermentation**
A chemical process that breaks down sugars and starches. Fermentation occurs in the stomachs of animals that eat a lot of grass.

**fertilization**
The joining together of a male sperm and a female egg.

**filter-feeder**
Animals that strain water for very small particles of food.

**fledgling**
A young bird that is just beginning to fly.

**fossils**
The preserved remains of living things, found in rocks.

**gait**
The way an animal moves at certain speeds. It refers to the order in which an animal moves its legs.

**gastroliths**
Hard objects, such as stones, swallowed by crocodilians, that stay in the stomach to help to crush food.

**generalist**
An animal that eats all types of food.

**genes**
The material inside the cells of most living organisms. They control the characteristics passed on from parents to their offspring.

**genus (plural: genera)**
A grouping of living things, smaller than a family, but larger than a species. The genus is the first word of the Latin name, e.g. in the King vulture's Latin name – *Sarcoramphus papa* – the genus is *Sarcoramphus*.

**gestation**
The period of time between conception and the birth of an animal.

**gills**
The organ by means of which aquatic animals breathe.

**gizzard**
A muscular chamber in the gut that grinds up lumps of food.

**gland**
An organ in the body that makes chemicals for a particular use.

**habitat**
The particular place where a group of animals usually live.

**herbivore**
An animal that only eats plants.

**herd**
A group of animals of one species that remain together.

**hibernation**
A period of rest for certain animals during the winter, when all body processes slow down.

**incisor**
Front tooth used for biting off chunks and cutting up meat.

**incubate**
To sit on eggs to keep them warm so that baby animals will develop inside the eggs.

**infrasound**
Very low sounds which humans are unable to hear.

**insect**
One of a group of invertebrate animals (without a backbone). An insect has three body parts.

**insulation**
Keeping warm things warm and cool things cool.

**intestine**
Part of an animal's digestive system where food is broken down and absorbed into the body.

**invertebrate**
An animal that does not have a backbone.

**ivory**
The dentine of teeth, usually that of tusks, such as those in elephants, walruses and narwhals.

**jungle**
The dense undergrowth found in a rainforest.

**juvenile**
A young animal, before it grows into an adult.

**keratin**
The protein used to make hair and fingernails and the scales of lizards and snakes.

**kidney**
An organ in the body that filters blood to remove waste products, which are then expelled in urine.

**lift**
The upward force acting on a bird's wings when it moves through the air.

**ligament**
A band of white, fibrous tissue that cannot stretch. It connects bones in a joint and strengthens them.

**liver**
An organ that produces bile, which helps to process food from the digestive system (gut). One of the liver's main tasks is to remove any poisons from the blood.

**lung**
A vital organ of the body that takes in oxygen from the air and removes carbon dioxide from the body.

**mammal**
A warm-blooded animal with fur or hair and a backbone, which can control its own body temperature rather than being reliant on the surrounding temperature. Females feed their young on milk made in mammary glands.

**mangrove**
Trees that grow in muddy swamps near the sea.

**mating**
The pairing up of a male and female to produce young. During mating, fertilization of the female's egg takes place.

**mature**
Developed enough to be capable of reproduction.

**membrane**
A thin film, skin or layer that separates one area from another.

**migration**
The regular, two-way movement of animals to and from feeding and breeding grounds.

**milk teeth**
A young animal's first, or primary, teeth, which are later replaced by permanent teeth.

**mineral**
A type of chemical that is contained in food and which is essential for good health.

**molar**
A chewing and grinding tooth at the side of the jaw.

**moulting**
The process by which animals such as snakes shed their skin and birds shed their old feathers.

**muscle**
An animal tissue made up of bundles of cells that can contract (shorten) to produce the body's movements.

**name**
The same species (kind) of animal often has a different common name in different countries, which is why animals are better identified by their scientific (Latin) name, which never alters.

**nerves**
Fibres that carry electrical impulses to and from the brain.

**niche**
The position a species takes in an ecosystem. It may refer to an animal's diet or the time of day it eats.

**nictitating membrane**
A third eyelid that can be passed over the eye to keep it clean or shield it.

**nipple**
A teat through which young mammals suck milk from the mammary glands of their mothers.

**nocturnal**
Active by night.

**nutrients**
Chemicals in food that, when broken down and digested in the gut, build blood, bone and tissue to maintain growth and strength.

**oesophagus**
Part of the gut in an animal, usually long and tube-shaped. It transports swallowed food from the mouth to the stomach.

**oestrus**
The time during which female mammals are receptive to mating because their eggs are ready for fertilization.

**orbit**
The circular part of an animal's skull that holds the eye.

**order**
A major grouping of animals, larger than a family.

**palate**
The roof of the mouth. An extra or secondary bony palate separates the mouth from the breathing passages.

**parasite**
An organism that lives on or in another living thing (its host), using the host as a source of food and shelter.

**pigment**
Colouring matter.

**placenta**
A round organ that is attached to the lining of the womb during pregnancy. It is through this that the embryo receives oxygen and nutrients.

**plankton**
Tiny aquatic organisms that drift with water movements.

**plumage**
The covering of feathers on a bird's body.

**poaching**
Capturing and/or killing animals illegally and selling them for commercial gain.

**polar region**
The area around the North or South Pole, where it is very cold.

**predator**
An animal that catches and kills other living things (prey) for food.

**pregnant**
When a female mammal has a baby developing in the womb.

**prehensile**
A part of the body that is adapted for grasping and gripping. Many monkeys and other mammals have prehensile tails.

**prehistoric**
Dating from a time long ago, before people kept records.

**prey**
An animal that is hunted and eaten by other animals.

**primitive**
Keeping physical characteristics that may have originated millions of years ago.

**protein**
A type of nutrient used to make muscles and other structures in an animal's body.

**pupil**
The opening, which can be round or slit-like, through which light passes into the eye of an animal.

**quadruped**
An animal that walks on four legs.

**rainforest**
Dense tropical forest where it is hot and wet all year round. Rainforest is found in the regions of the world closest to the Equator.

**range**
The maximum area in which an animal roams.

**receptor**
A cell or part of a cell that is designed to respond to a particular stimulus such as light, heat or smell.

**regurgitate**
Bring up food that has already been swallowed.

**reptile**
A scaly, cold-blooded animal with a backbone, including turtles, snakes, lizards and crocodilians.

**saliva**
A colourless liquid that is produced by glands in the mouth. Saliva helps food to slide from the mouth to the throat. In some animals, saliva also aids digestion by breaking down proteins.

**savanna**
Regions of open grassland found in places such as Africa.

**scavenger**
An animal that lives mainly on the meat of dead animals.

**scutes**
The thick, sometimes bony, scales that cover the bodies of crocodilians and snakes and the shells of chelonians.

**sensory system**
The collection of organs and cells by which an animal is able to receive messages from its surroundings.

**sexual dimorphism**
The difference in size, structure or appearance between male and female animals.

**skeleton**
A framework of bones inside an animal's body.

**social animal**
An animal that lives in a group, usually with others of its own kind. Social animals cooperate with other group members.

**solitary animal**
An animal that lives on its own.

**species**
A group of animals that share similar characteristics and can breed together successfully. When naming animals scientifically, this is the basic unit of classification.

**stalk**
To follow prey quietly and carefully so that the predator is within striking distance.

**stooping**
When a falcon dives on its prey from on high at great speed, with wings nearly closed.

**stranding**
Coming out of the water on to the shore and becoming stuck, or stranded.

**streamline**
The rounded, tapering shape that allows air or water to flow smoothly around an object.

**subspecies**
A species is sometimes divided into even smaller groups called subspecies, which are sufficiently distinct to have their own group.

**succulents**
Plants such as cacti, which store water in their stems and leaves and often live in dry conditions.

**suckle**
To suck milk from the breast of a female mammal.

**swamp**
A waterlogged area of land or forest.

**sweat glands**
Small organs beneath an animal's skin that produce sweat.

**symbiosis**
A partnership between different types of animal which benefits them both.

**taiga**
Forested parts of far northern regions of the world. Taiga lies just south of the tundra.

**taste buds**
Tiny bumps on an animal's tongue, which have nerve endings that pick up taste signals.

**temperate**
Mild regions of the Earth that do not experience extreme climate conditions.

**territory**
An area of land that one or more animals defend against members of the same and other species.

**thermal**
A rising current of warm air, on which vultures and other birds of prey soar.

**thermal corridor**
A layer of water at a particular temperature.

**threat display**
The aggressive behaviour shown by some species when confronted by other members of their own or other species.

**trachea**
The windpipe running frem the nose and mouth which transports air to the lungs.

**Tropics**
The hot regions or countries near the equator and between the Tropic of Cancer and the Tropic of Capricorn.

**tundra**
A treeless region of the Earth with permanently frozen soil just below the surface.

**tusk**
Long pointed tooth sticking out of an animal's mouth when it is closed.

**vein**
A blood vessel that carries deoxygenated blood towards the heart.

**venom**
Poisonous fluid produced in the glands of some snakes and spiders and which is used to kill prey.

**vertical migration**
The daily movement that sharks make downward into the deep sea by day and upward to the surface waters at night.

**vocal cords**
Two folds of skin in the throats of warm-blooded animals that vibrate and produce sound when air passes through them.

**warm-blooded**
An animal that can maintain its body at roughly the same warm temperature all the time.

**warning colours**
Bright colours that show others that an animal is poisonous, or warn predators to keep away.

**windpipe**
In air-breathing animals, the breathing tube that leads from the mouth opening to the lungs.

**wingspan**
The distance across the wings, from one wing-tip to the other.

**womb**
An organ in the body of female mammals in which young grow and are nourished until birth.

**yolk**
Food material rich in protein and fats, which nourishes a developing embryo inside an egg.

# Acknowledgements

The publisher would like to thank the following for the use of their pictures in the book (b=bottom, t=top, c=centre, l=left, r=right). Every effort has been made to acknowledge the pictures properly; however, we apologize if there are any unintentional omissions, which will be corrected in future editions.

**BIG CATS** ABPL: 13tl, 25cbl, 25cbr, 25c; /Nigel Dennis: 12b; /Clem Haagner: 10–11c, 16b, 28t; /Dave Hamman: 27tr; /Roger de la Harpe: 25ctl; /Gerald Hinde: 18b; /Beverly Joubert: 26c; /Peter Lillie: 26b. Anness/Jane Burton: 33t. BBC Natural History Unit/Lynn Stone: 12c; /Tom Vezo: 19tl. Bridgeman Art Library: 26t, 31tr. Bruce Coleman Ltd/Erwin & Peggy Bauer: 28bl, 29b; /Alain Compost: 25t; /Christer Fredriksson: 27b; /Paul van Gaalen: 19tr; /HPH Photography: 15bl; /Leonard Lee Rue: 21t, 29c; /Joe McDonald: 29t, 31br; /Antonio Manzanares: 27tl; /Rita Meyer: 21b; /John Shaw: 11b, 30b, 33b; /Kim Taylor: 21t; /Norman Tomalin: 24t; /Gunter Ziesler: 28br. FLPA/Philip Perry: 20t, 25tr; /Terry Whittaker: 11tl, 17t, 19b, 25b, 25b, 35cr. Grant Museum/A. Lister: 15br. Michael Holford: 16t. Natural History Museum: 32. Natural Science Photos/D. Allen Photography: 12t, 24b; /Ken Cole: 13c, 14b; /Carlo Dani & Ingrid Jeske: 13b; /Lex Hes: 25b, 30–1t; /David Lawson: 30c; /M.W. Powles: 31bl. NHPA/Yves Lanceau: 18t. Papilio Photographic: 10t, 13tr, 21c, 22t, 25ctr, 25tl. Tony Stone: 10b; /Geoff Johnson: 20b. **WOLVES** Bryan & Cherry Alexander Photography: 49tr, 50br, 51tl, 52t. Ardea London/Liz Bomford 50bl; /Jean Paul Ferrero: 44b. BBC Natural History Unit/Christopher Becker: 53tr; /Jeff Foott: 38tr; /Louis Gagnon: 37cr; /Andrew Harrington: 53tl; /Pete Oxford: 39cr, 46bl; 45b; /Françoise Savigny/C. Hamilton James 58b; /Keith Scholes: 41br; /Vadim Sidorovich: 54t; /Richard du Toit: 45tr; /Tom Vezo: 36l; /Bernard Walton 57t. Bruce Coleman Collection/Erwin & Peggy Bauer: 57bl; /Rod Williams: 45tl; /Gunter Ziesler/Hans Reinhard: 57br, 45br. Getty Stone Images/Art Wolf: 51tr; /Rosemary Calvert: 47c. NHPA/K. Ghani: 55t; /Martin Harvey: 39tr; /Gerard Lacz: 45c; /Andy Rouse: 50t. Oxford Scientific Films/Anthony Bannister: 55cr; /Daniel J. Cox: 41cr, 46tl, 49bl, 51b; /Richard Day: 54b; /Lon E. Lauber: 48t, 49cr; /Michael Leach: 55cl; /Victoria McCormick: 46br; /Stan Osolinski: 43tr; /Charles Palek: 41tr; /Krupakar Senani: 55c; /Michael Sewell: 55b; /Steve Turner: 44t; /Peter Weiman: 55b; /Konrad Wothe: 48br. Peter Newark's Pictures: 41bl. Planet Earth Pictures/Ken Lucas: 45tl; Science Photo Library/George Bernard: 57c. Still Pictures/Klein/Hubert: 39cl. Warren Photographic /Jane Burton: 47tl. **WILD HORSES** ABPL/Thomas Dressler: 70tl. Ardea London: 81b. BBC Natural History Unit: 64br; /John Cancalosi: 62tr; /Alistair MacEwen: 69cr; /Colin Preston: 80tr; /Anup Shah: 77cr, 79br. Bruce Coleman Collection: 60br, 72bl; /Christer Fredriksson: 65cl; /Robert Maier: 62bl, 65tl, 71t, 76br; /Dr Eckart Pott: 61tr, 64tl, 68bl. Mary Evans Picture Library: 61br, 67bl. Kit Houghton: 63tl, 65br, 66tr, 69br, 70br, 74t, 76t. Natural History Museum/M. Long: 81cl, 81tr, 81ct. Only Horses: 73br. NHPA: 78bl. Oxford Scientific Films/Martyn Chillmaid: 64bl; /Eastcott/Momatiuk: 63bl; /Carol Geake: 77bl; /Alistair MacEwen: 76bl; /Ben Osborne: 71t; /Kjell Sandved: 78br; /Anup Shah 63tr; /David Tipling: 60–1, 73bl; /Philip Tull: 67cr; /Tom Ulrich: 75br; /Fred Whitehead: 67br. Planet Earth Pictures: 71bl, 72tr, 75cl, 75b; /Richard Coomber: 63br; /Georgette Douwma: 70bl; /Eastcott/Momatiuk: 61cr. Tony Stone/Eastcott/Momatiuk: 71br, 74b, 75t. **BEARS AND PANDAS** B. & C. Alexander: 104br, 105bl. Heather Angel: 85c, 102tr. BBC Natural History Unit/Thomas D. Mangelsen: 97tr; /Klaus Nigge: 93bl; /Lynn M. Stone: 91cr. Bridgeman Art Library/Oxford University Museum of Natural History: 91b. British Museum: 94bl. Bruce Coleman/Erwin & Peggy Bauer: 84bl, 98br; /Stephen J. Krasemann: 105br; /John Shaw: 89br, 86bl. E.T. Archive: 98tr. Mary Evans: 92br. FLPA/Cordier/Sunset: 97tl; /Gerard Lacy: 92bl; /Mark Newman: 88br, 92tr, 95bl, 95tl, 87bl. Image Bank/Joseph Van Os: 90tr, 96bl. LB&W: 84tr. Adrian Lister: 106tr. NHPA/B. Hanumantha Rao: 105br/T. Kitchin & V. Hurst: 88c. Oxford Scientific Films/Michael Austerman: 89bl; /Liz Bomford: 91cl; /John Brown: 102bl; /John Chellman: 86tl; /Daniel J. Cox: 85bl, 95tr, 96tr, 99bl, 100tr, 86br; /David C. Fritts: 93br; /Dan Guravich: 104bl; /Djuro Huber: 101bl; /Frank Huber: 102br; /Zig Leszczynski: 88tl, 95br; /Stephen Mills: 101tl; /Norbert Rosing: 101tr; /Vivek Sinha: 99tr; /Stouffer Productions: 100bl; /Keren Su: 94tr. Papilio Photographic: 87bl. Planet Earth/Brian Kenny: 84br; /K. Lucas: 91tr, 94br; /L. Murray: 85tl; /N. Ovsyanikov: 99tr, 101br; /T. Walker: 89tl, 97br, 99tl. Whittaker's Star Atlas, Plate 6: 104tr.

**MONKEYS** Ardea/F. Gohier: 114c, 133tr, 128br; /C. Haagner: 123cl; /P. Morris: 131br; /B. Osborne: 132bl; /P. Steyn: 111tr, 119tr, 132tl; /M. Watson: 9c. BBC NH Unit/I. Arndt: 129bl; /N. Gordon: 114tr, 124br; /T. Martin: 127bl; /P. Oxford: 115tl, 115cl, 126tl; /A. Shah: 125tl, 124bl, 125tr; /D. Wechsler: 117cl; /S. Widstrand: 126bl; /M. Wilkes: 127tl. BBC Wild/C. Taylor: 130tl. B. Coleman: 121tl; /W. Layer: 119tl; /R. Magnusson: 128tr; /J. & P. Wegner: 120tr. Corbis/Heather Angel: 122bl, 124tr, 125cr/G. Neden: 111bl. Hutchinson Library/H.R. Dorig: 122br. Natural History NZ Ltd: 123tr. NHPA/M. Bowler: 130br, 133br; /N. Garbutt: 110tr; /P. German: 113br; /D. Heuclin: 111c, 121br; /T. Kitchin & V. Hurst: 118tl; /G. Lacz: 119b; /K. Schafer: 117tr, 129tl; /J. Warwick: 133tl. OSF/S. Breeden: 121cl, 131tl; /C. Bromhall: 115tr; /J. Chellman: 125bl; /M. Colbeck: 115tr, 18br; /D. Curl: 120bl; /M. Deeble & V. Stone: 112tl; /D. Haring: 111tr, 117br, 122tr, 123br; /Z. Leszczynski: 114br, 131cl, 131c; /K. Lucas: 122cr; /H. Pooley: 115br; /L.L.T. Rhodes: 118bc; /M.W. Richards: 113c; /K. Wothe: 133bl; /B. Wright: 127cr, 131cr. SPL/T. Davis: 116tr; /T. McHugh: 118cr. **GREAT APES** ABPL/Anup Shah: 138tl. Heather Angel: 145tl. BBC Natural History Unit/Bruce Davidson: 153tr; /Michael W. Richards 155tr; /Anup Shah: 141bl, 145bl, 151cl; /Tom Vezo: 138bl. Bob Campbell: 144tr. Bruce Coleman/R.I.M. Campbell: 137tl; /Gerald S. Cubitt: 155tl; /Mary Plage: 155b; /Jorg & Petra Wegner: 139br; /Rod Williams: 157br; /Gunter Ziesler: 142bl. Mary Evans Picture Library: 157bl. FLPA/Frank W. Lane: 149cr. Georgia State University/Anna Clopet: 147bl, 147tr. The Kobal Collection: 137cr, 139bl, 147br. NHPA/Jeff Goodman: 152tl; /Martin Harvey: 158br, 145br, 153tl; /Michael Leach: 137br; /Christophe Ratier 151br; /Steve Robinson: 151bl. Oxford Scientific Films/Bob Bennett: 143br; /Clive Bromhall: 150br, 153bl, 156tl; /Martyn Colbeck: 139tl; /Jackie Le Fevre: 143bl, 152b; /Michael Leach: 143tr; /Joe McDonald: 151tl; /Stan Osolinski: 150bl; /Andrew Plumptre: 137tr, 155tr, 148tl; /Konrad Wothe: 142tl, 145tr, 149c. Planet Earth/K. & K. Ammann: 147tl, 148b, 149br, 151tr; /Andre Baertschi: 141br; /Brian Kenney: 143tl; /Anup Shah: 136bl, 154t. **ELEPHANTS** ABPL/Daryl Balfour: 179tl, 166bl, 177bl; /Paul Funston: 175cl; /Martin Harvey: 176b; /Gerald Hinde: 179bl; /Beverly Joubert: 162tl; /Philip Kahl: 176tr; /Gavin Thomson: 179br. BBC Natural History Unit/Lockwood & Dattari: 161br; /Keith Scoley: 167tl. Bios /Michel Denis Huot: 162bc. The Bodleian Library: 169tl.

Bridgeman: 167tr. CFCL/ Image Select: 160tr, 175br. Bruce Coleman/Paul Van Gaalen: 163bl. E.T. Archive: 165cl. Mary Evans: 183cr. FLPA/F. Hartmann: 165br; /David Hosking: 166tl; /Terry Whittaker: 168tr; /Martin Withers: 174b. Michael Holford: 160bl. Adrian Lister: 183br, 183bl; Ken Lucas: 164bl. Natural History Museum London: 167br. Natural Science Photo Library/D. Allen Photography: 172tl; /S.G. Neginhal: 177tc; /Pete Oxford: 173tl; /Hugo Van Lawick: 161tr. NHPA/Daryl Balfour: 175tr, 175bl, 174cl; /Anthony Bannister: 172br; /K. Gani: 165tl, 163tr; Philip Ware: 178c. Oxford Scientific Films/Martyn Colbeck: 160c, 178bl, 168bl, 175tr; /Stan Osolinski: 174tr; /Gavin Thurston: 168tl. Papilio: 163br; John R. Jones: 169tr. Ian Redmond: 164br. Ann Ronan: 165tr. **WHALES AND DOLPHINS** Animals Animals: 196tr, 206tc. Bruce Coleman: 186b, 191b, 195tr, 195br, 197tl, 199tl, 207t. Ecoscene: 190cb, 190bl, 191c and 209br. Mary Evans Picture Library: 191tl. FLPA: 189tr, 189bl, 192t, 192bl, 194b, 196t, 199cl, 199cr, 202c. NASA: 201br. Natural History Museum, London: 186-187c, 188c. Natural Science Photos: 198c. Nature Photographers: 193c. NHPA: 194tr, 197b, 202tl, 202b, 205t, 205b, 206bl. Oxford Scientific Films: 187bl, 188b, 190cr, 195bl, 200bl, 200br, 198tl, 203b, 204t, 204b, 205cl, 205cr, 206cr, 207b, 208b, 209t, 209bl. Planet Earth Pictures: 186tr, 195bl, 196b, 198b, 199b, 200t, 203t, 39c, 207t. Spacecharts: 187tl and 201b. Visual Arts Library: 192vc, 197c. Zefa Pictures: 187tr. **SHARKS** BBC Natural History Unit/A. James: 229t; /J. Rotman: 219br, 221tl, 225tl, 225tr, 227tl. British Museum: 213br. Mary Evans Picture Library: 215cr. FLPA/D.P. Wilson: 229br, 233tr. Gallo Images /J. Rotman: 219bl, 220bl. Innerspace Visions/M. Conlin: 215cl; /B. Cranston: 215br; /B. Cranston: 221bl; /B. Cropp: 227cl; /S. Drogin: 226tl; /D. Fleetham: 222tr; /T. Haight: 229bl; /H. Hall: 222cr; /R. Kuiter: 216br; /A. Nachoum: 218bl; /M.S. Nolan: 221tl; /D. Perrine: 222bl, 225bl, 14cl, 224bl, 225cl, 225bl, 231c, 232br, 233bl; /D. Shen: 216tl; /M. Snyderman: 220br, 226br; /J.D. Watt: 212bl, 230tr, 233br. National Geographic/N. Calogianis: 253tl. NHPA: 217cr, 217bl, 228tl, 228bl; /N. Wu: 251bl. OSF/D. Fleetham: 15br, 252cl; /K. Gowlett: 221tr; /H. Hall: 213tr, 233cr; /R. Herrmann: 226bl, 215tl; /G. Soury: 227br, 230bl; /N. Wu: 216bl. Papilio Photographic: 224tl, 215bl. Planet Earth/P. Atkinson: 223tr; /G. Bell: 217l, 220tl; /K. Lucas: 214tl; /M. Snyderman: 213bl, 219tr; /N. Wu: 217tr, 221br. Seitre Bios: 218br. Zefa/M. Jozon: 251tl.

**TURTLES AND TORTOISES** Corbis: 240t, 241t, 241c, 242b, 246t, 249tl, 249br, 250t, 251bl, 254b, 256, 257l. Mary Evans Picture Library: 237tl, 243br. Bill Love: 240b, 241b, 243tr, 245l, 249bl, 249tr, 253t, 255c. Chris Mattison: 257cr, 239b, 242c, 245r, 247c. Natural History Picture Agency: 236t, 238b, 239t, 251tr, 255l. Nature Picture Library: 257tr, 239c, 252, 253b, 254t, 257r. Mark O'Shea: 255br. Oxford Scientific Films: 236b, 237bl, 238t, 246b, 247b, 248, 255tr. Science Photo Library: 242t, 251tl. Tortoise Trust: 237br, 243tl, 243bl, 247t, 250b, 251br. **CROCODILES** ABPL/C. Haagner: 261c, 276b; /S. Adev, 277b; /M. Harvey: 261tl, 272bl. Heather Angel: 273cr. BBC Natural History Unit/M. Barton, 264bl; /J. Rotman: 266bl. Bruce Coleman/L.C. Marigo: 281br; /R. Williams: 262br. C.M. Dixon: 264br. E.T. Archive 278bl. Mary Evans Picture Library: 260bl, 274br, 281bl. FLPA/W. Wisniewski: 16b. M, & P. Fogden: 270t, 275bl. Natural History Museum London: 282b, 285c. Nature Photographers Ltd/S.C. Bisserot; /E.A. James: 266br; /R. Tidman: 265b: 278br. NHPA/M. Harvey: 274bl; /D. Heuchlin: 267c, 277t; /H. & V. Ingen: 263bl; /S. Robinson: 271br; /K. Schafer: 279t; /M. Wendler: 261tr, 260tc; /N. Wu: 279b. Oxford Scientific Films/M. Deeble & V. Stone: 17tl, 275cl, 276tl; /E.R. Degginger: 265cr; /E. Ehrenstrom: 262tr; /M. Fogden: 271tl; /S. Leszczynski: 271cr; /J. Macdonald: 265c; /O. Newman: 281t; /S. Osolinski: 262bl, 268tr; /E. Robinson: 260tr; /J. Robinson: 274tl; /F. Schneidermeyer: 271cl; /M. Sewell: 264t; /W. Shattil: 275t; /F. Whitehead: 280t; /B. Wright: 267tr. Planet Earth/G. Bell: 277c; /M. & C. Denis-Huot: 270cl; /K. Lucas: 260–1, 267bl; /D. Maitland: 280b; /D.A. Ponton: 273bl; /J.A. Provenza: 272tr. Survival Anglia/V. Sinha: 265t. **LIZARDS** Art Archive/Chris Brown: 299tr. Bill Love: 284b. Chris Mattison: 289bl, 295cl, 295b, 304t. Natural History Museum: 283b. NHPA: 285t, 285c, 289t, 290l, 295cr, 294b, 295tl, 295tr, 297t, 297c, 298t, 299b, 300t, 302br, 303tr, 304bl, 305b, 307t. Nature Picture Library: 301tl. Papilio: 284t, 292t. Science Photo Library: 306t. John Sullivan/Ribbit Photography: 306b. Kim Taylor/Warren Photographic: 288t, 296, 298c, 301tr, 306c. **PENGUINS** B. & C. Alexander: 334b, 335t, 335c, 335bl, 336, 337c, 338, 339, 340, 341t, 344t, 345tr, 346cl, 346bl, 349tl, 350l, 351br, 352t, 353, 354, 355t; /P. Drummond: 345tr; /H. Reinhardt: 337t, 344b. Corbis/Bettmann: 345tl; /W. Kaehler: 337b, 355b; /J. McDonald: 345bl. Nature Picture Library/D. Allen: 342t, 350r, 356; /P. Oxford: 341bl, 345tr. NHPA/I. Green 347b; /M. Harvey 335br, 345br, 355cr; /K. Schafer: 347c, 352l; /D. Tomlinson: 343bl. Oxford Scientific Films/D. Allan: 334t, 348t, 349bl; /R. Bush: 346tl, 346br, 346b; /D. Cameron: 349br; /D. Curl: 345tl; /H. Hall: 349tr; /T. Jackson: 351tr; /G. Merlen: 351bl; /B.G. Murray 355cl; /Tui De Roy 347t; /K. Westerskov: 341br; /K. Wothe: 351bl. **BIRDS OF PREY** Heather Angel: 367bl, 377bl, 362br. Ardea/Ake Linday: 581bl. BBC Natural History Unit/Bernard Castelein: 374tl; /Nick Garbutt: 370tr; /David Kjaer: 381bl; /Dietmar Nill: 365tr; /Rico & Ruiz: 578bl; /Richard du toit: 369mr, 370br. Bruce Coleman/Robert P. Carr: 375tr; /Jeff Foot Productions: 375bl; /Jose Luis Gonzalez Grande: 369b. Peter A. Hinchliffe: 367br; /Steve Kaufman: 374br; /Antonio Manzanares: 376tr, 379tr; /Alan G. Potts: 361br; /Hans Reinhard: 379mr; /Rod Williams: 362tl; /Gunter Ziesler: 365tl. Mary Evans Picture Library: 361b, 371tl, 375br, 377tr, 362bl. Gallo Images/Anthony Bannister: 366tr, 369tl; /N. Dennis: 379bl, 363bl; /C. Haagner: 377m, 363tr; /Hein von Horsten/E. Reisinger: 377tl. Images Colour Library: 372–3. NHPA/Stephen Dalton: 371m;

/M. Harvey: 581br. OSF/B. Bennett: 368bl; /C. Farneti-Foster: 371tr; /D. Green: 379br; /Mike Hill: 381tr; /L.E. Lauber: 365m; /M. Leach: 364tr; /T. Levin: 581tr; /R. Nunnington: 570bl; /S. Osolinski: 364bl, 365br; /M. Price: 365tl; /K. Wothe: 361tr, 576bl. Papilio: 568tr. Planet Earth/Frank Blackburn: 378tr; /Darroch Donald: 360bl; /Carol Farneti-Foster: 363m; /Susan & Alan Parker: 364br. Kim Taylor: 561tl, 367tr, 372br, 372tl, 372tl, 373bl, 373tr, 575tl. Warren Photographic/Jane Burton/Kim Taylor: 360–1m, 371br. Thanks to the National Birds of Prey Centre in Newent for their help in creating this part of the book. **TROPICAL BIRDS** Corbis: 392bl, 397bl, 401t; /Theo Allofs: 394tr; /Martin Harvey: 390mr; /Peter Johnson: 387br, 589ml. Ecoscene: 386tl, 387ml, 388tl, 389br, 395br, 397tl, 401tr, 402tr. NHPA/A.N.T.: 398br; /Daryl Balfour: 584tl, 585br; /Bruce Beehler: 403tl; /John Buckingham: 404bl; /Bill Coster: 599mr; /Stephen Dalton: 384tr, 596bl, 596tr; /Nigel J. Dennis: 390tr, 591ml; /Melvin Grey: 589tl; /Martin Harvey: 585tr, 586ml, 588br, 598tl, 599bl; /Brian Hawkes: 392br; /Daniel Heuclin: 598bl; /Ralph & Daphne Keller: 400bl; /Stephen Krasemann: 404tr, 405br; /Mike Lane: 400tl; /David Middleton: 395ml; /Peter Pickford: 591mr; /Andy Rouse: 599tr; /Kevin Schafer: 587tr, 402bl; /John Shaw: 591br; /Morten Strange: 593br; /Martin Wendler: 585ml; /Alan Williams: 405ml; /Norbert Wu: 597mr. **ANTS, BEES, WASPS AND TERMITES** Anness Publishing: 410bl; /Kim Taylor: 410tr. BBC Natural History Unit/Jeff Foot: 422tr; /Pete Oxford: 424tr; /Premaphoto: 427br, 422cl. Bruce Coleman Collection/J. Brackenbury: 409bl; /Jane Burton: 414br; /Christer Fredriksson: 417tr; /Kim Taylor: 415cr; /Gunter Ziesler: 424bl. Corbis: 413br. Ecoscene/Dr John B. Free: 426br, 401cr; /Kjell Sandved: 423cl. Mary Evans Picture Library: 411bl. Nature Picture Library: 427bl. NHPA/Anthony Bannister: 420cl; /G.I. Bernard: 415tr, 417br, 422cr; /N.A. Callow: 420br; /Dan Griggs: 427tl; /Daniel Heuclin: 419cl. OSF/J.A.L. Cooke: 424br; /Kjell Sandved: 423cr; /Barrie Watts: 421bl. Papilio Photographic/Michael Maconachie: 415bl; /Robert Pickett: 427bl. SPL/ Michael Abbey: 419br; /Dr Jeremy Burgess: 418tr; /J. Koivula: 429tl; /J.H. Robinson: 419tl; /D. Scharf: 416bl; /D. Spears: 414tr; /S. Stammers: 428tr; /A. Syred: 412br, 416tr, 425cr. Kim Taylor: 410cr, 415cl, 419tr, 425br, 429tr. Warren Photographic/Jane Burton: 417tl; /Kim Taylor: 408c, 409tl, 409c, 411br, 412tl, 412bl, 415tl, 418cl, 418tl, 426tr, 420tl, 421tl, 425bl. **BUTTERFLIES AND MOTHS** Heather Angel: 445bl, 445r. Bridgeman: 432cr ('The Legend of Cupid and Psyche' by Angelica Kauffman [1741–1807], Museo Civico Rivoltello). Bruce Coleman Collection/I. Arndt: 450c; /J. Brackenbury: 449bl; /G. Dore: 450bl; /P. Evans: 451bl; /M. Fogden: 444bl; /G. McCarthy: 438br; /A. Purcell: 458bl; /J. Shaw: 446tl; /K. Taylor: 459cl, 450tr. Mary Evans Picture Library: 441tr. FLPA/R. Austing: 452br; /B. Borrell: 440bl; /F. Polking 448tr; /I. Rose: 453cr; /L. West: 440cl. Garden/Wildlife Matters/M. Collins: 449bl. NHPA/Daniel Heuclin: 457cl; /Papilio Photographic: 458tr. Planet Earth: W. Harris: 457tr; /S. Hopkin: 445ct; /K. Jayaram: 459tl. Premaphotos Wildlife/Ken Preston-Mafham: 432tr, 444bl, 449cr, 454br; /Kim Taylor: 452bl, 453ct, 456bl, 459cr, 440br, 441cl. Visual Arts Library/ Artephot, Roland: 451br. Warren Photographic/J. Burton: 456br, 444br; /K. Taylor: 455cb, 457cr, 457br, 459br, 440tl, 440tr, 441cb, 446bl, 446r, 447tl, 447cb, 448bl, 448cr, 453tl, 453cl 453br. Thank you to Worldwide Butterflies in Sherborne, Dorset for their help in creating this part of the book.

**BEETLES AND BUGS** Ronald Grant Archive: 457tr. NHPA: 460c, 462t, 462bl, 463b, 464c, 467tr, 467bl, 468t, 469tl, 469br, 471t, 475b, 476t, 477br. Oxford Scientific Films: 457tl, 457cr, 459c, 459br, 463t, 466tl, 466tr, 467br, 469tr, 469bl, 470c, 471cl, 471bl, 473tl, 473br, 475c, 477t. Papilio Photographic: 467t. Kim Taylor: 456tl, 457bl, 458, 460t, 461t, 461b, 462br, 464t, 466l, 470t, 475tr, 476b. Volkswagen: 459bl. Warren Photographic: 456b, 459t, 460b, 461c, 464b, 468b, 470c, 472, 473tr, 473bl, 474, 477bl. **SPIDERS** AKG: 492bl, 32br. BBC Natural History Unit/Doug Wechsler: 488bl. Bridgeman Art Library: 487b. Bruce Coleman Ltd/Jane Burton: 493cr; /Gerald Cubitt: 490t; /A. Dean: 499b; /Jeremy Grayson: 499t; /Janos Jurka: 486br; /George McCarthy: 497t; /Dieter & Mary

Plage: 501tr; /Andrew Purcell: 500b; /John Shaw: 484t; /Alan Stillwell: 489c, 492t, 498t, 499c; /Kim Taylor: 491b, 496b; /John Visser: 493tl; /Rod Williams: 485tr. Mary Evans Picture Library: 481c. FLPA: 493br; /Larry West: 501c. Microscopix Photolibrary: 489b, 490b. Natural Science Photos: 497b, 482t. Nature Photographers Ltd: 488br, 497c. NHPA: 482bl. Papilio Photographic: 487t, 496t, 501tl. Planet Earth Pictures/Brian Kenney: 498br; /D. Maitland: 486t. Ken Preston-Mafham/Premaphotos Wildlife: 484bl, 485b, 491tl, 491tr, 500t, 501b, 483bl, 483br. Dr Rod Preston-Mafham/Premaphotos Wildlife: 484br, 492br, 493bl. Warren Photographic/Jane Burton: 486bl, 495t, 482br; /Jan Taylor: 481tl, 489tl, 483t; /Kim Taylor: 481tr, 481b, 485c, 488t, 489r.

# INDEX

## A

Abominable Snowman 139
acrodont 291
Adélie penguin 337, 340, 344, 350, 353, 354
Aegyptopithecus (Egyptian ape) 156
African dwarf crocodile 264, 266
African egg-eater snake 327
African elephant 160–5, 167, 172, 173, 177, 179, 181, 182
African fish eagle 370
African hunting dog 41, 45, 46
African jacana (lily-trotter) 391
African (Jackass) penguin 347, 348, 351, 355
African slender-snouted crocodile 277
agama 291, 298, 300, 305
albatross 356
albinos 267, 303
alligators 260–4, 267, 268, 269, 271, 273, 274, 280, 282
allopreening 339
ameiva 299
American bald eagle 365, 375
American black bear 84, 88, 96, 98, 99, 100
American crocodile 275
American racer 328
amphipods 200
amphisbaenians 288, 307
ampullae of Loenzini 224
anaconda 280, 281, 315
Anchitherium 81
Andean condor 364, 365
antelope 26, 27, 73
ants 5, 99, 408, 409, 412, 414–24, 426–9, 470
ants, bees, wasps and termites 408–29
  amazing senses 416–17
  body parts 410–11
  habitats 426–7
  how insects eat 418–19
  how insects evolved 428–9
  how social insects communicate 420–1
  insect enemies 424–5
  lively legs 414–15
  on the wing 412–13

the search for food 422–3
what are social insects? 408–9
apes 5, 110, 112, 113, 121
*see also* great apes; lesser apes
Aphaenops 477
aphids 418, 419, 457, 467, 475
Araneidae 482
araneomorph 482
Archelon 256
Archosauria 307
Arctic (tundra) wolf 38, 45
Arctiidae 434
Asian elephant 160, 162–7, 169, 173, 177, 181, 182, 183
Asiatic black bear 84, 87, 88, 103
asp viper 327
ass 60, 61, 64, 72, 76, 78, 79
  wild 63, 64, 73, 74
assassin bug 469
auk 335
Australasian death adder 326
aye-aye 110

## B

baboons 112, 115, 117, 121, 123, 129, 132
back swimmers 476
baguales (Argentinian feral horses) 63
baleen whales 186, 188, 189, 191, 192, 198, 200, 349
barbels 250
barbets 386
bark beetle 466
barking 47, 57
barn owl 367, 379
barn swallow 404, 405
basilisks 294
basilosaurus 186
basking shark 213, 217, 219, 229, 232
Batagurinae 239
beaked whale 188, 189, 201
bears 5, 84–107
  ancient 106–7
  the bear facts 84–5
  bones and teeth 90–1
  family groups 86–7
  finding food 98–9
  finding the way 104–5
  size of a bear 88–9
  strong muscles 92–3
  using brain and senses 96–7
  warm fur 94–5
  where bears are found 102–3
  winter hibernation 100–1

bedbugs 476
bee-killer 425
bees 5, 99, 408, 410, 411, 412, 413, 414, 415, 416, 418, 422, 424, 425, 426, 427, 428, 429
beetles and bugs 456–77
  body parts 458–9
  focus on beetles in flight 462–3
  homes and habitats 476–7
  the life cycle of beetles 472–3
  the life cycle of bugs 474–5
  on the move 460–1
  natural disguises 470–1
  nature's success story 456–7
  plant eaters and pests 466–7
  scavengers and hunters 468–9
  senses 464–5
beluga (white whale) 188, 198, 201, 205
big cats 5, 10–35
  big bite 10
  big cat relatives 32–3
  bones and teeth 14–15
  communication 24–5
  domestic 33
  ears 11
  hunting prey 26–7
  killing prey 28–9
  living together 30–1
  long tail 10
  muscles and claws 16–17
  names 33
  night sight 11
  purring 12
  sight and sound 18–19
  spots and stripes 22–3
  touching, tasting and smelling 20–1
  what is a big cat? 10–11
Bigfoot 139
birds of paradise 385
birds of prey 360–81, 400
  bill and talons 374–5
  building nests and laying eggs 378–9
  how the body works 366–7
  the hunted 376–7
  on the move 380–1
  orders and families 362–3
  the senses 368–9
  shapes and sizes 364–5
  what is a bird of prey? 360–1
  wings and flight 370–1
Black Forest heavy horse 62
black-lored babbler 393
black spotted jumper 483
black-tipped soldier beetle 462

blacktip reef shark 225, 227, 231, 233
blind snake 312, 315
blue shark 212, 214, 216, 226
blue whale 186, 189
bluntnose sixgill shark 225
boa constrictor 311, 312
boas 311, 312, 313, 315, 319, 331
bobcat 33
Bombycidae 435
Bombycoidea 434
Bonelli's eagle 378
bonnethead shark 216
bonobo 136, 138, 139, 140, 144, 146–9, 154
Bosc monitor lizard 293
bottlenose dolphin 187, 193, 195, 197, 203, 205
bowhead whale 188
box turtle 251
Brazilian rainbow boa 331
broadnose sevengill shark 215
brown bear 84, 85, 86, 88–91, 93, 95, 97–103, 105
brumbies 78
buffalo 26, 28, 57
bugs *see* beetles and bugs
bull shark 214, 215, 216, 232
bullhead shark 214
bumble-bee 410, 413, 427
burying (sexton) beetle 461
bush baby 110, 111, 128
bush elephant 178, 179
buteo 365
butterflies and moths 432–53
  around the world 450–1
  focus on flight 442–3
  focus on metamorphosis 446–7
  how butterflies look 436–7
  how moths look 438–9
  migration 452–3
  nectar and food 448–9
  scaly wings 440–1
  senses 444–5
  superfamilies 434–5
  winged beauties 432–3
buzzards 365, 368, 374, 380

## C

caching food 55
caiman 260, 261, 263, 264, 265, 279, 281
Camargue horses 65
camouflage 4, 5, 22–3, 44, 153, 217, 261, 281, 300,